The Archaeology of French and Indian War Frontier Forts

UNIVERSITY PRESS OF FLORIDA

Florida A&M University, Tallahassee
Florida Atlantic University, Boca Raton
Florida Gulf Coast University, Ft. Myers
Florida International University, Miami
Florida State University, Tallahassee
New College of Florida, Sarasota
University of Central Florida, Orlando
University of Florida, Gainesville
University of North Florida, Jacksonville
University of South Florida, Tampa
University of West Florida, Pensacola

THE ARCHAEOLOGY OF
French and Indian War Frontier Forts

Edited by Lawrence E. Babits
and Stephanie Gandulla

University Press of Florida
Gainesville · Tallahassee · Tampa · Boca Raton
Pensacola · Orlando · Miami · Jacksonville · Ft. Myers · Sarasota

Copyright 2013 by Lawrence E. Babits and Stephanie Gandulla
All rights reserved

Printed in the United States of America on acid-free paper

This book may be available in an electronic edition.

First cloth printing, 2013
First paperback printing, 2015

Library of Congress Cataloging-in-Publication Data

The archaeology of French and Indian War frontier forts / edited by Lawrence E. Babits and Stephanie Gandulla.
p. cm.
Includes bibliographical references and index.
ISBN 978-0-8130-4906-9 (cloth: alk. paper)
ISBN 978-0-8130-6179-5 (pbk.)
1. United States—History—French and Indian War, 1754–1763. 2. Fortification—United States—History. 3. Excavations (Archaeology)—United States. 4. Historic sites—United States. I. Babits, Lawrence Edward. II. Gandulla, Stephanie.
E199.A73 2013
973.2'6—dc23
2013024206

The University Press of Florida is the scholarly publishing agency for the State University System of Florida, comprising Florida A&M University, Florida Atlantic University, Florida Gulf Coast University, Florida International University, Florida State University, New College of Florida, University of Central Florida, University of Florida, University of North Florida, University of South Florida, and University of West Florida.

University Press of Florida
15 Northwest 15th Street
Gainesville, FL 32611-2079
http://www.upf.com

This book is dedicated to J. C. Harrington, Jacob Grimm,
Gilbert Hagerty, and Charles Fisher

Contents

List of Figures ix
List of Tables xiii
Preface xv
French and Indian War Chronology, 1750–1765 xvii

Introduction 1
Lawrence E. Babits

1. Clash of Empires 9
R. Scott Stephenson

2. Forts on the Frontier: Adapting European Military Engineering to North America 17
James L. Hart

3. Fort Prince George, South Carolina 52
Marshall W. Williams

4. Fort Loudoun, Tennessee : Defensive Features and Artifactual Remains 69
Carl Kuttruff

5. Fort Dobbs, North Carolina: How Documents and Artifacts Led to Rebuilding the Fort 84
Lawrence E. Babits

6. Fort Loudoun, Virginia: A French and Indian War Period Fortification Constructed by George Washington 102
Robert L. Jolley

7. The Second Fort Vause: A Crucial French and Indian War Fort in the Roanoke Valley of Virginia 122
Kim A. McBride

8. "To Preserve the Forts, and the Families Gathered into Them": Archaeology of Edwards's Fort, Capon Bridge, West Virginia   139
   W. Stephen McBride

9. Fort Loudoun: A Provincial Fort on the Mid-Eighteenth-Century Pennsylvania Frontier   158
   Stephen G. Warfel

10. Style Wars in the Wilderness: The Colonial Forts at Crown Point   174
    Charles L. Fisher and Paul R. Huey

11. Fort Frontenac, Kingston, Ontario, Canada   191
    Susan M. Bazely

12. Michilimackinac, a Civilian Fort   216
    Lynn L. M. Evans

13. War and the Colonial Frontier: Fort de Chartres in the Illinois Country   229
    David J. Keene

    Conclusion   241
    Lawrence E. Babits

    Glossary   255
    References Cited   261
    List of Contributors   287
    Index   291

Figures

2.1. Representation of "antiquated fortifications" 23

2.2. Le Blond's illustration of the weakness of medieval square and round towers 24

2.3. Plate employed by Le Blond to illustrate "the first system of M. de Vauban" 26

2.4. Table employed by Le Blond to provide the appropriate dimensions of various parts of a fortification 27

2.5. Close-up of the front of fortification *BC* 29

2.6. Plan of an irregular fortification 30

2.7a and b. Two tables provided by Le Blond to allow the designer to approximate the results of a regular fortification in the ground plan of an irregular fortification 31

2.8. Two illustrations of defense in depth 39

2.9. Franquet's plan of Fort St. Frédéric 42

2.10. Franquet's plan of Fort Chambly 44

2.11. Franquet's schematic plan of the fortifications at Montréal 46

3.1a and b. Location of Fort Prince George in Pickens County, South Carolina 53

3.2. Configuration of the gun platform in the northwest bastion 60

3.3. Composite map of the excavations at Fort Prince George 62

3.4. Hand-drawn conception of Fort Prince George based on excavation data 64

4.1. Plan of excavation, Fort Loudoun, Tennessee 71

4.2. Artifact distribution maps 75

4.3. FAP Kitchen Group percentages 77

5.1a–d. Ditch profile drawings and photos 89

5.2a and b. Fort Dobbs ditch excavations and abatis 90

5.3. Aerial photograph of 1969 Fort Dobbs excavations 94

5.4. Conjectural rendering of Fort Dobbs, 2006 100

6.1. Washington's design plan for Fort Loudoun 103

6.2. Map of Winchester, 1777, depicting Fort Loudoun 109

6.3. Location of archaeological excavations and conjectural location of Fort Loudoun 110

6.4. Test Trench 1, north profile 111

6.5. Test Trench 2, plan view after excavation 112

7.1. Typical fort plan by George Washington 124

7.2. Map of present excavations 131

7.3. Map of topography, showing bastions 132

7.4. Unit 3 profiles 134

7.5. Unit 4, east profile 135

7.6. Unit 5, east profile 135

7.7. Fort Vause inventory 137

8.1. Site map showing features 146

8.2. Fort Allen, Pennsylvania 151

8.3a and b. Profiles of Feature 60 and Feature 73 153

8.4. Grid iron 154

9.1. Location of Fort Loudoun with respect to Pittsburgh and Philadelphia 159

9.2. Archaeological plan of Fort Loudoun 164

9.3. Post pattern in partially excavated east palisade trench, facing north 165

9.4. Exterior view of reconstructed northeast bastion, facing east 166

9.5. Interior view of reconstructed northeast bastion, facing northeast 167

9.6. Hand-blown case bottle with inscribed name 169

9.7. Oak bucket recovered from the well 170

10.1. Location of Lake Champlain and Crown Point 175

10.2. Detail from 1759 plan of the fort and fortress at Crown Point 176

10.3. Tour de Camaret near Brest, France, built by Vauban from 1693 to 1696   178

10.4. Digital reconstruction of the redoubt or citadel at Crown Point, built in 1734   179

10.5. Plan of the new fort and redoubt at Machecoulis, drawn in 1736   180

10.6. Drawing from a model of Fort St. Frédéric   181

10.7. Detail from a map of Lake Champlain since the building of Fort Chambly to that of St. Frédéric, 1740   182

10.8. Spy map of Crown Point, drawn by Robert Rogers in 1755   184

10.9. View of Fort St. Frédéric from the south   188

11.1. Location of Fort Frontenac surrounded by landfill and covered by roads and buildings in present-day downtown Kingston, Ontario   192

11.2. Plan of 1685, depicting the transition from the second Fort Frontenac of 1675 to the third by 1687   195

11.3. Foundations uncovered during archaeological research at Fort Frontenac between 1983 and 1985   197

11.4. Plan of Fort Frontenac, 1738, depicting the elevation of the fort   204

11.5. Trade and domestic items recovered during archaeological investigations at Fort Frontenac between 1983 and 2006   207

11.6. Excavations along the west curtain of Fort Frontenac demonstrating later nineteenth- and twentieth-century impacts   212

12.1. The upper Great Lakes   217

12.2. Lotbinière map of 1749   221

12.3. Michilimackinac Archaeological Master Map, 1959–97   223

12.4. Magra map of 1765   224

13.1. The relative frequency of artifacts by category for each site   233

13.2. Fort de Chartres and surroundings   234

13.3. Profile of a typical wall at Fort de Chartres   236

13.4. View of the reconstructed wall and ditch   238

G.1. Outline of a four-bastion fortification   255

G.2. Cross-sectional view of an entrenched fortification   257

Tables

4.1. Areas of selected forts   73

4.2. Frontier artifact pattern calculations for selected forts   80–81

6.1. South's artifact pattern percentages for French and Indian War sites   118

7.1. Profile types as seen in the shovel test pits   133

8.1. Artifacts from Edwards's Fort stockade features   149

8.2. Artifacts from other Edwards's Fort eighteenth-century features and units   150

8.3. Identified faunal elements from Edwards's Fort   155

C.1. The Carolina artifact pattern   251

C.2. South's adjusted frontier pattern mean and range, with standard deviation and predicted range for the next site   251

C.3. FAP comparison with contemporary forts   252

Preface

Some of the chapters in this book were presented in 2007 as papers at the Society for Historical Archaeology in Williamsburg, Virginia. This session was designed to bring to light the newer work on French and Indian War fortifications, especially lesser-known sites away from the main war theaters. Despite their distant locations, many sites exhibited similar attributes, and the overviews tied them together. A decision was made to incorporate the expanded papers into a book that could be useful for teaching and research purposes, in part because the various papers' bibliographies would lead to additional information about forts.

Over the ensuing three years, the papers were received and reworked to present a more coherent view of the forts built during the mid-eighteenth century. While each site had different research questions, all provided some basic information that showed there were patterns at the forts that could be researched at still other posts. Even though most forts were at the very end of very long logistical trails, most exhibited traits typically found in the home countries.

We are indebted to the authors who worked with us to produce this text. The chief archaeologists were diligent in keeping excavation notes and providing interpretive information about what they found. Old field notes allowed new interpretations long after the fact, something that is seen in these chapters. More important, we must thank all those people who researched and dug on the forts presented here. We could probably never identify them all at even one site because the list is so long. Without their enthusiastic and diligent work, much information would be lost.

The text is dedicated to four archaeologists who worked on French and Indian War forts. The first is J. C. Harrington, who really started historical archaeology with his detailed examination of documents, maps, and the archaeological record at Fort Necessity, Pennsylvania. The second is Jacob Grimm, whose detailed report on Fort Ligonier set a standard for reporting and also served as the equipment book for two generations of reenactors and their suppliers. The third is Gilbert Hagerty, the researcher who not only clarified a multi-fort location but also trekked the route followed by the French who destroyed Fort Bull. The fourth archaeologist is Chuck Fisher, who was slated to give one of the Williamsburg papers but became terminally ill. Regrettably, he has since passed away, and his chapter was reworked by Paul Huey. These four archaeologists represent what the French and Indian War forts have always needed: good research, careful excavation, detailed recording, and a clear eye for interpretation.

We owe them all a debt of gratitude and a great deal of thanks. If they hadn't done good work, we couldn't have produced this study. Any errors are our own.

French and Indian War Chronology, 1750–1765

1673

13 July: Construction starts on Fort Frontenac

1726

Construction starts on third fort at Niagara

1734–42

Construction of Fort St. Frédéric at Crown Point, N.Y.

1753

Summer: Construction starts on Fort Presque Isle, Erie, Pa.
31 October: Washington departs Williamsburg for Ohio Country
11 December: Washington at Fort Le Boeuf, Pa.

1754

16 January: Washington returns to Williamsburg
17 February: Virginians sent to Forks of the Ohio to build Fort Prince George
18 April: French arrive at Forks of the Ohio; Virginia garrison surrenders
28 May: Washington surprises French under Jumonville, Pa.
14 June: Anglo-Iroquois conference at Albany, N.Y.
19 June–11 July: Albany Congress
3 July: Washington surrenders Fort Necessity, Pa.

1755

February: Braddock arrives in Virginia
17 June: British capture Fort Beausejour, seize Acadia (Nova Scotia)
9 July: Braddock defeated in Battle of the Monongahela, Pa.
17 August: British forces arrive at Oswego
4 September: William Eyre lays out Fort William Henry on Lake George
8 September: Battle of Lake George
September: Fort Carillon construction starts; completed spring 1758
Winter: Fort Niagara strengthened and enlarged

1756

1 March: Montcalm named French commander in chief in North America
17 March: Earl of Loudoun appointed commander in chief of British forces
27 March: De Léry expedition destroys Fort Bull, Oneida Carry, N.Y.
7 April: Virginia Regiment troops ordered to Edwards's Fort, Va.
18 April: Edwards's Fort garrison ambushed and defeated by Indians outside fort
18 May: Britain declares war on France
19 May: France declares war on Britain
25 June: French and Indians raid, burn first Fort Vause, Va.
10 July: Council of War at Fort Cumberland decides to build chain of forts to defend Virginia's frontier
25 July: Indians raid Draper's Meadow, Va.
14 August: French capture British Forts Ontario, Pepperell, and George at Oswego, N.Y.
5 October: Construction starts on Fort Loudoun, Tenn.
19 November: Work commences on Fort Loudoun, Pa.

1757

19 March: French attack, fail to take Fort William Henry, N.Y.
20 June: British fleet leaves New York to attack Louisbourg, Nova Scotia
23 July: French attack Fort Edwards, N.Y.
26 July: French destroy New Jersey Regiment at Sabbath Day Point, Lake George, N.Y.
30 July: Fort Loudoun, Tenn., major construction completed
3 August: French begin siege of Fort William Henry, N.Y.
August: British abandon attempt on Louisbourg
9 August: Montcalm takes Fort William Henry, N.Y.
10 August: British retreating from Fort William Henry attacked by Indians
11–12 August: Fort William Henry destroyed by French
December: British decide on three (Louisbourg, the Hudson River/Lake Champlain Corridor, and Fort Duquesne) main efforts against the French North American possessions

1758

4 March: Forbes named general to lead Fort Duquesne campaign
11 March: "Battle on Snowshoes"
24 May: Henry Bouquet arrives in Carlisle, Pa., to serve as Forbes's deputy commander
28 May: British move against Louisbourg, Pa.
2 June: Work starts on Forbes Road at Fort Loudoun
14 June: Bouquet meets Cherokee and Catawba warriors at Fort Loudoun, Pa.

24 June: Bouquet and advance force start building base camp (Fort Bedford) at Rayston, Pa.
4 July: Forbes arrives in Carlisle, Pa.
8 July: Abercromby defeated at Fort Carillon, N.Y.
8 July: Rogers's Rangers and the French fight "Battle of Fort Anne"
23 July: Surveying starts on road to Loyalhanna, Pa.
26 July: Amherst takes Louisbourg
July: Amherst camps at Fort William Henry site, starts Fort George, N.Y.
2 August: Forbes orders Bouquet to open road through Alleghenies to Loyalhanna, Pa.
27 August: Fort Frontenac surrenders to Bradstreet
3 September: Pa. Col. John Burd arrives at Loyalhanna, starts building Fort Ligonier, Pa.
14 September: Battle outside Fort Duquesne, Pa., Grant defeated
6 October: Rogers's Rangers raid Abnaki village (Odanak/St. Francis)
12 October: French attack Fort Ligonier, Pa., and are repulsed
24/25 November: French evacuate/destroy Fort Duquesne, Pa.; British begin building Fort Pitt on site

1759

6 July: Siege of Fort Niagara, N.Y., begins
20 or 24 July: Fort Niagara, N.Y., relief force defeated at "La Belle Famille"
25 or 26 July: Fort Niagara, N.Y., taken by Sir William Johnson and Vice General John Prideaux
26/27 July: French abandon Fort Carillon, N.Y., after siege by Amherst
31 July: French abandon Fort St. Frédéric at Crown Point, N.Y.
31 July: British attack Montmorency Falls, three miles east of Quebec
1 August: Construction begins on Fort Pitt (Pittsburgh), Pa.
13 September: Battle of Quebec, Wolfe and Montcalm mortally wounded
17 September: Quebec surrenders
6 October: Rogers's Rangers attack and burn Indian village at St. Francis
26 December: South Carolina treaty with Cherokee

1760

16 February: Cherokee ambush Fort Prince George garrison outside fort
27 February: Cherokee attack Fort Dobbs, N.C.
28 April: British routed while attacking French outside Quebec, second battle of Plains of Abraham or Sainte Foy
3 May: Amherst starts moving against Montreal
11–16 May: French siege of Quebec fails
22 June: Battle of the Restigouche, Quebec, begins
8 July: Battle of the Restigouche ends

9 August: British evacuate Fort Loudoun, Tenn., after Indian siege
8 September: Vaudreuil capitulates at Montreal, surrendering Canada to British
29 November: British occupy Detroit, Mich.

1761

1762

4 January: Spain enters war on French side
13 August: British defeat Spanish at Havana, Cuba
18 September: French fail to retake Newfoundland

1763

10 February: Treaty of Paris ends Seven Years' War (French and Indian War)
15 February: Treaty of Hubertusburg (Prussia, Austria, Saxony) marks end of Seven Years' War
27 April: Pontiac holds Grand Council at Detroit, Mich.
9 May: Indian siege of Fort Detroit begins
2 June: Fort Michilimackinac falls to Indians
22 June: Siege of Fort Pitt, Pa., begins
31 July: Battle of Bloody Run (or Bloody Bridge), Mich.
5–6 August: Battle of Bushy Run, Pa.
10 August: Fort Pitt relieved by Bouquet
7 October: Proclamation of 1763 issued
30 October: Pontiac ends siege of Detroit, Mich.

1764

28 November: Hostage repatriation between British and Indians completed

1765

28 August: Preliminary peace treaty signed by Indians at Detroit, Mich.

Introduction

LAWRENCE E. BABITS

The French and Indian War was a defining moment in American history. For the first time the various colonies organized and acted in concert. While this ultimately failed, they nonetheless worked together to defeat the French. The war marked the first time there was large-scale theater-level military activity in North America. The impact of over 40,000 British soldiers, their equipment, ideas, and money was dramatic and played a role in developing what turned into the American Revolution a few short years later. These changes can be seen in the popular introduction of a new architectural style and its accompanying furnishings and the rise of national figures, particularly George Washington and Benjamin Franklin.

The period marks the British army's introduction to the "American Way of War" and American perceptions about the vulnerability of the British army. In the long term, British logistical efforts during 1755–63 heavily influenced the notion that local North American resources could support British military forces. This misperception caused a disaster during the Revolution when two British armies, cut off from seaborne reinforcement and supplies, were forced to surrender. The British had forgotten that local support during the French and Indian War from an Anglo-American effort against a common enemy was much different than the situation throughout the Revolution.

The war also generated a national debt that caused Parliament to seek ways of paying for the war and for postwar North American garrisons. In turn, new tax laws and the attempted enforcement of older navigation acts led to colonial resentment, smuggling, and resistance.

Military construction activity on the Anglo-American frontier included settlers, colonies, and the British army working to create a defensive barrier against the French and their Indian allies. This study focuses on the frontier:

a cutting-edge stress area where traditional styles and expertise, new technology, tactics, and attitudes were exposed to trial and error against an experienced foe who did not fight "by the rules." Some Old World aspects worked, others did not. As the war went on, colonists, the French, and the British refined how they waged war. In terms of fortifications, various approaches can be seen in the documents, images, and the archaeological record. Each of these resources provides evidence and contributes to understanding the forts and the fortification system as a whole.

The documentary evidence about fortifications includes initial, verbalized plans and directions to subordinates, inspection reports, and ultimately the sale or destruction of the posts. If the post was attacked, reports often contain supplemental details overlooked by the original planners. These documents are somewhat cryptic, often using image-laden, highly technical military and architectural terminology. They generally hold only snippets of information that must be tested against eighteenth-century language and extant examples of fortifications for more precise interpretation.

The images include maps, plans for various sites and cross sections, and artistic views of fortifications. Two starting points are Mary Ann Rocque's 1763 and 1765 publications of her deceased husband's drawings (Rocque 1765 is used here) and holdings in numerous repositories. Many of these sites are referenced in the following chapters. While the images are exceptionally helpful, they are only thin sections in a fort's chronology and may not accurately reflect earlier and later construction episodes.

While the archaeological record is often the most incomplete, it can also be the most accurate. When features and artifacts are found on a site, they must be explained. In the search for meaning, specific questions are asked of documents and images that may not have been thought of before. In that sense, the presence of archaeological material might lead to new information. At the same time, if archaeologists do not ask the right questions of their artifacts, documents, and imagery, the answers are irrelevant (Pynchon 1987:251).

As a total package then, the documents, images, and artifacts can provide a composite, interpretive impression of a fort site that allows the current generation, now celebrating the 250th anniversary of the war, access to the past. When interpretation is further augmented by a reconstruction, the learning process continues as even more detailed questions arise through the course of construction.

This study focuses on a range of sites, extending from the southern frontier zones to the Great Lakes. It is not meant to be complete but representative. In conjunction with other studies, most notably Charles Stotz's *Outposts of the War for Empire* (1985), which examined Pennsylvania, and Michael D. Coe's *Line of Forts* (2006), which dealt with northwestern Massachusetts, this current work provides a wider view of French and Indian War material culture and fortifications. Two other important studies should also be mentioned. J. C. Harrington's analysis of 1754 Fort Necessity (1970) is justifiably regarded as one starting point for historical archaeology (Schuyler 1978:xi). In similar fashion, Jacob Grimm's wonderful 1970 study of Fort Ligonier represents a key episode in material culture and military history studies, not only for the mid-eighteenth century but for archaeology in general.

Modern historical research on the French and Indian War began with Francis Parkman (1885, 1892, 1995), continued with Stanley Pargellis (1966), Lawrence Gipson (1949, 1954), Howard Peckham (1947), Edward Hamilton (1959, 1962), and James and Stotz (1958) and continues today with Anderson (1984), Leach (1973, 1986), Schwartz (1994), Stotz (1985), Todish (2002), Waddell (1995).

Readily available, French and Indian War historical archaeology research really began in the 1950s when J. C. Harrington was tasked with learning about George Washington's Fort Necessity. His research into that post set a standard for historical research, archaeological test excavations, and interpretation that is used as a model today. Since then, well over three dozen French and Indian War fortifications have been examined archaeologically. Many site reports ended in the realm of gray literature that few students or historians ever have the chance to read. Others were never published, including work on some major fortifications.

In this book, no attempt was made to examine some well-known major sites that have been subjected to research and excavation for years. These sites include Fort William Henry (Starbuck 2002), Fort Michilimackinac (Stone 1974), Fort Ligonier (Grimm 1970; Stotz 1974), Louisbourg, Nova Scotia (Fry 1984), Québec (Charbonneau et al. 1982), Fort Chambly, Québec (Gélinas 1983), Niagara (Dunnigan 1996, 1989; Dunnigan and Scott 1991), Fort Stanwix (Hanson and Hsu 1970), Fort Ticonderoga (Hamilton 1970, 1995; Pell 1978), and Fort Toulouse in Wetumpka, Alabama (Heldman 1973). Other sites have been examined and published, including Fort Gage (Feister and Huey 1985) and Fort Bull (Hagerty 1971). Overviews with details of individual forts have been published for the northwestern Massachusetts frontier (Coe 2006), Pennsylvania (Stotz 1974; Kummerow et al. 2008; Waddell and Bomberger 1996), and the Lake Champlain corridor

(Bellico 1992). The upper Potomac River valley has a short study of its forts (Ansel 1984). Many frontier sites from the southern frontier and what was then the Far West have not been generally published. That oversight is partially rectified here.

Of particular interest is the mix of fortification types as they range from civilian/militia fortified farmsteads to provincial colonial fortifications and finally British and French works designed to show imperial power at the border of their respective realms. Many also served as trading posts, acting as an interface locus between European and Native American cultures for their mutual exploitation of resources. However, not all fortifications fit into this model of frontier military, diplomatic, and trading post. These latter fortifications were largely self-funded sites erected by the local citizenry for a particular emergency situation and then, in many cases, abandoned or returned to the landscape.

The forts were erected in accordance with tactical considerations modified by local terrain, expenses, and time. As will be seen, several forts incorporated preexisting structures to save time and effort. Others had irregular traces (enceinte) because the terrain dictated coverage of approach lines and dead space. Hart's essay presents something of these issues, but as he points out, engineers and fort builders were quick to adapt military principles to the local setting.

Some sites have been heavily collected by relic hunters, few of whom maintained any record of what they found and where. This is unfortunate, but happily the situation is evolving as archaeologists recognize that metal detectorists are both knowledgeable and dedicated to researching the past. Many professionals are now reaching out to the metal detecting community for advice and assistance, creating a more effective research effort at these very delicate sites. Some of that effort is reported in these chapters.

The book begins with two chapters on the war and fortifications. In "Clash of Empires," Scott Stephenson presents an overview of the war, making several points about supplies and the importance of waterways in the wilderness. In some ways, especially in the northern theater and Pennsylvania, the war became a war of posts used as stepping-stones to threaten the next enemy fort. Stephenson is followed by James Hart's "Forts on the Frontier," an essay on academic fortification as applied in North America. Hart's study of fortification principles concentrates on French Fort St. Frédéric at the Lake Champlain choke point, a short distance north of Fort Ticonderoga. One of his main points is that adaptation to frontier conditions was fairly quick, but within the framework of accepted Vauban-style fortification principles. This controlled adaptation will be seen in the other authors' analyses of their respective forts.

The sequence of chapters then shifts to South Carolina's two frontier forts. The first is by Marshall Williams, who covers the history and archaeological work conducted at the site of Fort Prince George in 1966–68. This key fortification was excavated but not reported until Williams, drawing from his personal field notes and the archaeological drawings, set down his recollection of the project. The site is now underwater.

Next, Carl Kuttruff presents a summary of work conducted at Fort Loudoun, a post located west of the Appalachians in present-day eastern Tennessee. It was constructed to solidify Overhill Cherokee alliances with the British and to prevent French encroachments into the area from Fort Toulouse. As planned, the Fort Loudoun defenses were perhaps the largest of frontier forts of this period. The fort is described and compared with other French and Indian War frontier forts, especially Fort Prince George, its sister fort on the eastern side of the Appalachians. Artifacts recovered from hand excavations of approximately 90 percent of the fort interior and large portions of the surrounding ditch are summarized. Distributions of several artifact categories are presented to illustrate refuse disposal patterns within and outside the fort. The overall artifact assemblage is compared to the current Carolina and Frontier Patterns, and suggestions are made for developing a separate Frontier Fort Pattern.

Moving north, Lawrence Babits details the history of 1756–63 Fort Dobbs, North Carolina, and discusses how 40 years of archaeological and historic research produced enough information to re-create the fort. This led to new interpretations about the main structure and outworks. Fieldwork and research involved numerous people, many of whom developed ideas of what the fort once resembled. This latest endeavor, essentially a historical architectural study of a building no longer extant, utilizes documentary research, archaeological findings, and comparisons with slightly earlier British frontier fortifications in the Scottish Highlands to explain terminology used by those who designed and inspected the fort.

Moving into Virginia, three forts (two civilian and one provincial) are interpreted from the documents and the archaeology. The civilian forts Edwards and Vause were researched and excavated by the McBrides, who confirmed site locations and learned that the forts were built on property owned by local elites. Through Fort Edwards, Stephen McBride examines Virginia's response to Braddock's defeat in July 1755. The Virginia Regiment under Colonel George Washington began constructing forts along

Virginia's western frontier to defend settlers against anticipated French and Indian attacks. In 1756, this defensive line was greatly expanded by new forts and by incorporating existing private forts. Among the forts added to the Virginia frontier defensive chain was privately built Fort Edwards, in present Hampshire County, West Virginia. The investigations were directed toward assessing the nature of archaeological deposits across the site and successfully located evidence of the French and Indian War fort and its occupation.

Kim McBride conducted the research at Fort Vause, Virginia—a post that was built and occupied from fall of 1756 to fall of 1757 by soldiers from the Virginia Regiment under the command of Peter Hogg. The construction was the local response to the June 1756 destruction of the first Fort Vause by a party of Shawnee and French. Period accounts suggest that the first Fort Vause, located at the home of Ephram Vause, was a wooden stockade, but little was known of the second fort, except that it was not to Washington's liking. Preliminary archaeological investigations were conducted at this second fort under the direction of Ned Heite in 1968, and the site was listed as a Virginia Historic Landmark. Recently, excavations were expanded and a more comprehensive survey of the site was conducted, providing better knowledge of the boundaries of deposits and the physical construction of the fort.

Fort Loudoun at Winchester is one of the few frontier forts associated with a town. Unlike the civilian forts, this post was constructed of earth-filled cribs to create bastions connected by palisade walls. Robert Jolley found that even though it was a major depot, Fort Loudoun was still plagued by the same construction and supply issues typical of virtually all the forts in this study.

In Pennsylvania, Stephen Warfel conducted excavations at a third Fort Loudoun. This post was one of the chain of forts built to support the Forbes expedition against Fort Duquesne. The excavations were designed to learn more about the specifics of this fort's chronology and structural features in conjunction with earlier research on other Forbes forts.

Charles Fisher and Paul Huey address the basics of the two sequential posts on Lake Champlain. British Crown Point was erected adjacent to the earlier French Fort St. Frédéric, a site theoretically discussed by Hart. This location was an ideal point to project imperial power, attract allies, and hold the Lake Champlain Narrows. By 1742, Fort St. Frédéric was the most powerful fortress in terms of cannon, second only to Québec (Bellico

1992:20). The 1979 excavations uncovered remains of the trench built in 1755 off the southwest corner of the French Fort St. Frédéric. The French fort was built in 1734 as a material symbol of French presence and served to attract Indian allies. When the French evacuated, the British immediately built their own stone bastioned fort on the site.

Traveling north, Susan Bazely presents the results of historical research and archaeology conducted at French Fort Frontenac, a site that was subsequently taken over by the British. The remnants of the Fort Frontenacs are located in present-day Kingston, Ontario. The posts were initially situated on the north shore of the eastern end of Lake Ontario to control the fur trade but became militarily significant as the imperial struggle between France and England spread into the Great Lakes country. Today, the fort exists only in the archaeological record, although extensive investigations from 1982 to 1985 led to a partial reconstruction of the northwest bastion and the west and north curtain walls. Subsequent utility installation, road widening, and safety upgrades to existing buildings allowed further archaeological examination. Here Bazely compares archaeological findings with commanders' statements and inspectors' reports to explain existing structural remnants.

Lynn Evans summarizes the results of excavations at Fort Michilimackinac, a trading post and mission erected on the south shore of the Straits of Mackinac around 1715. This fort was one of a series of defensive works built to control this strategic location during the colonial period. Although military at times, it was much more a fortified trading post in actual practice. Archaeological excavations have taken place at Michilimackinac every summer since 1959, and approximately two-thirds of the fort has been excavated. This post saw sequential occupations by French and British forces until the late eighteenth century.

The final fort in this presentation is French Fort de Chartres, located well west of the other sites. David J. Keene reports his findings about the third Fort de Chartres. The project was begun to recover artifacts and expose construction elements of what was thought to be a fur trade outpost in the far-reaching network of the French colonial North American empire. The early excavations did not reveal an artifactual assemblage similar to other fur trading posts. The new archaeological data, in conjunction with a reassessment of the documents, demonstrates how historical archaeology can change the understanding of a region's history. Each of these chapters offers insight into the widespread projection of imperial power and exploitation in the seventeenth and eighteenth centuries. These vignettes of diverse yet contemporary fortification sites can be assembled to enlighten our modern-day perceptions of the French and Indian War in terms of similar material culture, elite patronage and social organization, and academic knowledge applied to the frontier setting at the end of a long supply line.

1

Clash of Empires

R. SCOTT STEPHENSON

> It would require a greater philosopher and historian than I am to explain the causes of the famous Seven Years' War in which Europe was engaged; and, indeed, its origin has always appeared to me to be so complicated, and the books written about it so amazingly hard to understand, that I have seldom been much wiser at the end of a chapter than at the beginning, and so shall not trouble my reader with any personal disquisitions concerning the matter.
>
> William Makepeace Thackeray, *The Memoirs of Barry Lyndon, Esq., Written by Himself*, 1844

It has been more than a century and a half since Thackeray's roguish character, the Irish upstart Redmond Barry, reflected on the seemingly impenetrable complexity of the Seven Years' War. The far-flung clash of arms that spread from North America to Europe, West Africa, Asia, the Caribbean basin, and the seas between would later inspire British statesman and historian Winston Churchill to dub it the first "world war," but unlike the world wars of 1914–18 and 1939–45, a universally accepted title remains elusive. In India, the fighting is known as the Third Carnatic War, while the campaigns in central Europe are often designated the Third Silesian War. In North America, where hostilities erupted in 1754, two years before formal declarations of war by Britain and France, and major fighting ended three years before the peace treaty of 1763, the conflict is known among Francophone Canadians, whose cultural and political memory of it remains vivid, as La Guerre de la Conquête (War of the Conquest). In the United States, the American campaigns of the Seven Years' War have come to be known as the French and Indian War (Churchill 1956:148; Bandyopādhyāẏa 2004:49; Snyder and Brown 1968:124; Desbarats and Greer 2007:146).

Inspired in part by recent 250th anniversary commemorations, there has been renewed public and scholarly interest in the conflict that historian

Fred Anderson has called "the most important event to occur in eighteenth-century North America" (Anderson 2000:xv). Long overshadowed by the American Revolution, the French and Indian War and the global conflict it sparked and that influenced its course and outcome are now widely understood to have altered profoundly the balance of power on both sides of the Atlantic. Creating conditions without which it is difficult to imagine the revolutionary forces that arose to sweep British North America in the 1770s and France in the 1790s, the wide-ranging conflicts of 1754–63 have also drawn the interest of historical archaeologists.

The North American campaigns of the Seven Years' War are traditionally viewed as falling into several distinct phases. From the outbreak of armed conflict in 1754 through the end of 1757, French and allied Indian forces inflicted a series of defeats on their more numerous Anglo-American enemies. William Pitt's rise to leadership in 1758 marked a shift in British strategy and a stunning reversal in France's position. Dramatically increasing Britain's overseas military and naval forces and the nation's indebtedness, Pitt oversaw a string of successes so remarkable after the dismal failures of recent years that 1759 could with justice be celebrated in Britain and its American colonies as the *annus mirabilis* (year of miracles). Canada fell to British forces in September 1760, and with the exception of a failed French attempt to seize the British outpost of St. Johns on Newfoundland, major military operations shifted to the Caribbean, Europe, and finally the Philippine archipelago. Another way to view the French and Indian War, one that may serve historical archaeology as well as a purely chronological treatment, is to consider regional variation in the experience of war.

The Ohio Valley

Even though the roots of the Seven Years' War are strikingly complex, as Thackeray's hero mused, there is little debate over the spark that set the world on fire. By the late 1740s, British, French, and Iroquois leaders had become increasingly alarmed at the prospect that some power other than themselves would control the upper Ohio River valley, a region widely recognized to be a strategic key to North America's Middle West. This three-way rivalry centered on the Forks of the Ohio River (modern-day Pittsburgh) and was complicated by the presence of several thousand Native inhabitants—often referred to collectively as the "Ohio Indians"—who stubbornly defended their independence from all three powers. Late in 1752, French officials decided to take action, dispatching a military expedition the following summer to build a series of forts along the upper Ohio (or Allegheny) River in the disputed territory. The British response, spearheaded by Virginia's ardent expansionist governor Robert Dinwiddie, included a formal warning delivered by then unknown militia officer George Washington and a military expedition led by Washington the following summer (1754) that finally sparked armed conflict (Anderson 2005, chap. 4).

Over the next four years (1754–58), the French Fort Duquesne at the Forks of the Ohio served as a base from which French soldiers, Canadian militia, and a diverse and shifting alliance of warriors from nations in the Great Lakes, St. Lawrence Valley, and Ohio Country conducted a devastating campaign against the backcountry settlements and fortifications in Pennsylvania, Maryland, and Virginia. Although greatly outnumbered by the population of the neighboring British provinces, these forces took advantage of the dispersed colonial settlement pattern and (in the beginning) poorly organized military forces. The vast network of inland waterways that linked French garrisons and settlements in Canada, the Great Lakes, and the Illinois Country aided Fort Duquesne's defenders, while trade goods, arms, and munitions from France cemented native alliances that played a crucial part in defending New France.

Following George Washington's defeat at the Great Meadows (Fort Necessity) on 3–4 July 1754, British and American provincial forces mounted two additional overland campaigns across the Allegheny Mountains. Unlike their opponents, the British, provincial, and allied Cherokee and Catawba forces were forced to rely on long overland routes to reach the Ohio valley. In 1755, the newly arrived British commander in chief, Maj. Gen. Edward Braddock, led a force against Fort Duquesne consisting of two British regiments from the Irish establishment, several companies of British soldiers previously stationed in New York and South Carolina, and colonial troops from Virginia, Maryland, and North Carolina. Setting out from a base at Wills Creek (modern-day Cumberland, Maryland) on the upper Potomac River, Braddock's force, which included a formidable train of siege artillery and supply wagons, marched northwest across the mountains. On 9 July 1755, an advanced detachment under Braddock's direct command suffered a humiliating defeat at the hands of a smaller French and Indian force on the banks of the Monongahela River, several miles east of Fort

Duquesne. The resulting panic and disorder led Braddock's successor to order the remaining forces to retreat to Wills Creek and beyond (Kopperman 1977, esp. chap. 4).

A new British commander, Brig. Gen. John Forbes, organized a third expedition to seize Fort Duquesne in 1758. With Britain and France now officially at war, and with British naval control of the Atlantic strengthening, Forbes commanded a larger army than Braddock and benefited from weakening French alliances with Native nations who were dissatisfied with serious shortages of essential trade goods and military support. Drawing on lessons learned in the disastrous Braddock expedition, Forbes chose to base his expedition in southeastern Pennsylvania, where the horses, wagons, and foodstuffs essential for the long expedition across forested mountains were more numerous. Forbes also pursued a strategy of "protected advance," constructing a series of fortified camps and supply depots along his route to ensure that in the event of a check like that which sent Braddock's army into headlong retreat, his army would have a secure base to fall back on (Skaggs and Nelson 2001:57). The Forbes expedition ultimately succeeded. Abandoned by local Native allies who had been drawn into neutrality by British and colonial diplomatic overtures, the French garrison destroyed Fort Duquesne and abandoned the site on 24 November 1758. The following summer, the British siege of Fort Niagara forced the remaining French garrisons to leave the upper Ohio valley, and the British garrison at newly christened Pittsburgh began constructing the massive earth and brick Fort Pitt, dwarfing the ruins of nearby Fort Duquesne (Anderson 2005:233).

The Appalachian Borderlands

Following the outbreak of armed conflict in 1754, French and Indian attacks on the permeable British settlements created an armed borderland stretching nearly 1,000 miles from Maine's Kennebec River to the Carolina backcountry. There was considerable variation in the patterns of conflict from region to region along the inland arc of the Appalachians, but the common experience of civilian populations forting up and local military organizations taking a leading role in organizing defensive measures distinguishes this type of experience from military campaigns and expeditions.

Perhaps the heaviest fighting and greatest impact on the civilian population of any of the non-Native participant societies fell on the Pennsylvania and Virginia backcountry, stretching roughly from the Delaware Water

Gap to the headwaters of the Roanoke River. Unlike other parts of British North America, this region was woefully unprepared for attacks that began to fall in rapid succession following Braddock's July 1755 defeat at the Battle of the Monongahela. Founded and controlled politically by pacifist Quakers, Pennsylvania had no standing militia organization, frontier fortifications, or stocks of public arms and ammunition at the start of the conflict. "Virginia is a country young in war," a youthful Col. George Washington likewise observed after a frustrating year trying to organize the Old Dominion's defenses against attacks originating from Fort Duquesne (Stephenson 1995:196–98). Between the winter of 1755–56 and the end of 1758, when Forbes's army captured Fort Duquesne, thousands of refugees flocked eastward, and several thousand more were killed, wounded, or captured (Ward 2003:61–65). Many of those who remained in the backcountry gathered together to fortify homesteads or build forts in which they could take refuge from attacks. Those sites that have been investigated archaeologically have revealed a tremendous variety of local responses to the challenge of defending scattered settlements from attack by highly mobile raiders.

The French and Indian War impacted noncombatants in Native towns and settlements on both sides of the Appalachian divide as well. Although poorly documented (and thus excellent candidates for archaeological study), a number of American Indian communities took steps to fortify their homes against attacks by European and native enemies. Catawbas living on the western fringes of South Carolina, Delawares settled at Kittanning on the Allegheny River north of Fort Duquesne, and Abenakis at Odenak on the borderland between Canada and New England all erected defensive structures and suffered attacks even as they fielded armed forces engaged in the complicated struggles of the 1750s (Merrell 1989:162–64; Myers 1999:410–12; MacLeod 1996:147–49).

Military action during the Seven Years' War eventually extended down the length of Appalachian backcountry to the Carolinas, a region that has begun to receive much needed attention. Sporadic attacks on backcountry settlements by French-allied Indians, coupled with fears that the conflict in Pennsylvania and Virginia would spread south, promoted local communities and provincial officials to build forts, raise military forces, and call for an increased British military presence. Having been largely spared fighting that devastated large swaths of frontier Virginia in 1754–58, widespread violence came to the Carolina backcountry and neighboring Cherokee territory during the 1759–61 Anglo-Cherokee War (Maass 2002; Oliphant 2001; Hatley 1993, esp. 92–115).

Northern Campaigns

At the start of the Seven Years' War, British colonists in New York and New England had a much longer experience with frontier war than their neighbors to the south. Having engaged in wars with Canada and neighboring Native nations with great regularity since the mid-seventeenth century, New England's military culture was particularly vibrant (Anderson 1984; Selesky 1990). The most recent Anglo-French conflict, known as King George's War (1744–48), had left a string of forts that provided some protection for settlements in New Hampshire, western Massachusetts, and northern New York (Coe 2006). British and Iroquois (particularly Mohawk) settlements in the Mohawk valley west of Albany remained vulnerable to attack throughout much of the war, producing a variety of local defensive structures and organizations (Leach 1973:381–83; Anderson 2000:150–57). As British and provincial forces pushed the seat of war north to the Lake George–Lake Champlain corridor, New England's frontier population experienced less direct military action, but continued to feel the effects through recruiting and logistical support for the northern campaigns against Canada.

Some of the largest and best-known campaigns of the French and Indian War took place along northeastern North America's great inland waterways: the Mohawk River–Lake Ontario corridor that runs east–west through central New York, and the Hudson River–Lake Champlain–Richelieu River route that runs north–south from New York to Montreal. The proximity of French and British colonies, with the Iroquois heartland in the center, ensured that this strategic quarter would receive a lion's share of military manpower and resources from all three powers (Anderson 2005:74–87, 106–40). The campaigns in this region drew the largest concentration of combatants in continental North America and included forces drawn from a broad swath of territory ranging from the Algonquian peoples of the Mississippi valley and the western Great Lakes to the German and Swiss officers and men who served in the British Royal American Regiment. The seasonal ebb and flow of forces differed from other regions. Tens of thousands of troops and support personnel gathered in densely populated camps and garrisons each summer for a short campaign season that frequently left commanders (particularly British) only a few precious weeks to act before their ponderous armies began to unravel from disease, desertion, and the looming expiration of enlistment periods for provincial soldiers (Steele 1990:78–83; Anderson 2000:135–49, Brumwell 2002:74–75). To a far greater extent than the southern theater of the war, the northern campaigns brought colonial and regular forces—whether Canadian and French or British and American—into closer and more sustained contact as the war dragged on.

Braddock's 1755 campaign planning included attacks on the French posts at Niagara on Lake Ontario and at Crown Point on Lake Champlain, which like Forts Duquesne and Beauséjour were considered to be an encroachment on British territory that might be reduced without sparking a European war. Braddock entrusted command of the Crown Point expedition to Irish immigrant William Johnson, a wealthy trader and land speculator based in the Mohawk valley whose ties to the Iroquois Confederacy led to his appointment as British superintendent of Indian affairs. Johnson led the largely New England army, supplemented by New York troops and several hundred Mohawk warriors, northward from Albany to the southern shore of Lake George. His force was still preparing to move north toward Crown Point when a large force of French regulars, Canadian militia, and allied Indians attacked Johnson's camp. The 8 September 1755 Battle of Lake George left the provincial army in possession of the field but forestalled the campaign against Crown Point. Both sides dug in at opposite ends of the lake. The French built Fort Carillon (later Ticonderoga) at the northern end, and the provincials laid out Fort William Henry on the Lake George battleground under the direction of a British military engineer (Fowler 2005:55–57; Steele 1990:28–56).

For the next four years, French, British, and Indian forces struck at each other up and down the Lake George corridor. The 1756 arrival of the new British commander in chief, John Campbell, Earl of Loudoun, brought the first large influx of British troops to New York, although the provincial forces remained predominant on the northern front until after the August 1757 fall of Fort William Henry to Gen. Louis-Joseph de Montcalm's army (Brumwell 2002:19–21). Loudoun's successor, Maj. Gen. James Abercromby, personally led a massive British and American expedition of more than 17,000 men against Fort Carillon in 1758, but suffered what would remain one of the bloodiest defeats in American history before the Civil War when his men assaulted a strong defensive wall with bayonets on 8 July 1758 (Anderson 2005:133–40). Gen. Jeffrey Amherst finally succeeded in capturing Ticonderoga and Crown Point in 1759, forcing the outnumbered and poorly supplied French garrisons to retreat and destroy their posts as he cautiously advanced up Lakes George and Champlain (Anderson 2005:189–90). As they had at Fort Duquesne, the British constructed a massive earthen fort alongside the ruins of the destroyed French post. Crown Point served as a base for one of the three British expeditions that converged on Montreal from the west, south, and east in the final campaign against Canada in 1760 (Anderson 2005:214–17).

British, French, and Indian forces also skirmished back and forth along the Mohawk River–Lake Ontario front from 1755 until 1760. Oswego, Britain's sole post on Lake Ontario, fell to a French and Indian siege in 1756, and henceforth British and provincial forces struggled to hold a series of posts and fortified settlements along the Mohawk River corridor until Fort Frontenac fell to Anglo-American troops in September 1758. Unlike the Ohio valley campaigns to the south, British and provincial forces enjoyed relatively easy water transport for supplies, munitions, and troops when they launched a raid deep into French territory to capture Fort Frontenac in August 1758 (Anderson 2005:146–51; Fowler 2005:87–98). The following summer, British troops reoccupied Oswego and used it to launch a successful expedition against Fort Niagara (Dunnigan 1996). The siege and capitulation of Fort Niagara effectively ended fighting in the west until a pan-Indian uprising known as Pontiac's Rebellion challenged British occupation of the former French posts in the Great Lakes and Ohio Country (Anderson 2005:231–40).

The essays in this volume reflect the remarkable diversity of local conditions and experiences suggested by this brief sketch of the Seven Years' War in North America. Together, the sites and investigations described herein illustrate the rich potential for archaeology to both enrich historical understanding and to ask different questions of the past than those typically posed by traditional historians. Indeed, the once vast divide separating historical archaeology from the historical field in general has narrowed and blurred considerably over the past few decades and is reflected in the excellent interdisciplinary studies in this volume.

2

Forts on the Frontier

Adapting European Military Engineering to North America

JAMES L. HART

In 1879, Francis Parkman discovered a remarkable document during the course of archival research in French Canada (Wade 1947:577, 676). This "copious journal, full of curious observation" (Parkman 1995:314) was the record of a French military engineer's tour of Canada in 1752 and 1753. Louis Franquet had been sent by the French court to inspect the defenses of New France in anticipation of another war with Great Britain and the British American colonies. The journal records Franquet's tour from Québec to Trois Rivières, Montréal, and the forts along Lake Champlain and the Richelieu River. It also includes descriptions of the Native American mission settlements at Sault St. Louis (Kahnawake), the Lake of the Two Mountains, St. François, Bécancour, and Lorette.

Franquet's interests were too broad to confine his journal entries narrowly to his military assignment. Indeed, Parkman and other historians since his time have found Franquet's observations and comments on non-military matters too interesting to pay much attention to Franquet the military engineer. Parkman himself drew on Franquet's journal for its "bright glimpses" of "Canadian society in the upper or official class" (Parkman 1995:314). More recently, John Demos relied on Franquet for significant details of life at the Iroquois Christian mission settlement of Sault St. Louis, where Eunice Williams spent eighty years after her capture at Deerfield in 1704 (Demos 1994:144–49). However, Franquet's formal reports provide a remarkably comprehensive account of the defenses of French Canada on the eve of its final military struggle. They also offer a working example of how a professional military engineer applied and adapted the standard principles of eighteenth-century military engineering and fortification design to conditions very different from the European context in which those principles had been developed.

Louis Franquet was born at Condé, France, in 1697, the son of an engineer. He was commissioned in the army at the age of 12 and served in infantry regiments from 1709 to 1720. In 1720, he was admitted to the engineering corps, and he served as a military engineer in Europe for the next 30 years. During that time, he participated in campaigns in Italy, Germany, and the Netherlands. He was awarded the Cross of Saint-Louis in 1741 and was promoted to lieutenant colonel in 1747. While serving as chief engineer at Saint-Omer, he was asked to go to Isle Royale (Cape Breton Island) to inspect the defenses of the colony and to develop plans to put the fortresses at Louisbourg and other places in a state of readiness (Thorpe 1974:228–32).

After arriving at Louisbourg in August 1750, Franquet examined its buildings and fortifications and conducted tests to determine the causes of structural deterioration. He developed voluminous maps, plans, and sections detailing the existing structures and recommendations for repairs and improvements. In 1751 he toured the remainder of Isle Royale as well as Isle Saint-Jean (Prince Edward Island), Baie Verte, and Fort Beauséjour (in present-day New Brunswick). The next year, his assignment was expanded to include inspection of fortifications in the St. Lawrence and Richelieu valleys (Thorpe 1974:229, 231; Franquet 1924).

French military engineering enjoyed great prestige during the eighteenth century, due in large part to the achievements of Marshal Sébastien le Prestre de Vauban (1633-1707). Building on innovations in Italy, the Netherlands, and France during the preceding centuries in response to the development of effective artillery, Vauban achieved an impressive record both in the conduct of sieges and in the design and defense of fortifications. He conducted many of the major sieges during the wars of Louis XIV and built a chain of fortresses to guard the frontiers of the kingdom (Rothrock 1968:v–xi, 1–16; Charbonneau 1982:85–109; Fry 1984:1:37–45; Cowley and Parker 1996:486–87).

Vauban was much more a practitioner than a theorist. He insisted that defensive works must suit local conditions. With few exceptions, he avoided any discussion of his "system" of fortification. He also insisted that there was no such thing as an impregnable fortification, and he devoted his published works to siegecraft and the attack of fortifications (Rothrock 1968:viii, 178; Fry 1984:1:41–42). In fact, his greatest innovations may have been in siegecraft rather than in the design and construction of fortifications (Duffy 1985:78ff.).

Other prominent figures included the Frenchman Blaise-François, comte de Pagan, and the Dutchman Menno van Coehoorn (Langins 2004:45–47; Duffy 1985:63–71). Both the siege methods and the fortification designs of these and other recognized authorities were intensively studied and extensively copied. In particular, Vauban's fortifications were so impressive that his contemporaries endeavored to discern the system behind his designs. From this study, they distinguished several systems of great conceptual clarity and methodological power, which formed the basis for a number of manuals and treatises in wide circulation during the eighteenth century. Franquet's own library contained a representative collection of these manuals. The estate inventory of Franquet's sister, to whom the engineer had bequeathed his estate, lists among other relevant volumes (Bibliothèque et Archives nationales du Québec 1780–81):

(1) *Introduction de la Fortification avec les Cartes et plans*
(2) *Architecture hydrolique par Monsieur Bélidor en deux tomes*
(3) *La Science des Ingénieurs dans la Conduite des travaux par Bélidor*
(4) *Element de fortification*

The entry for *Introduction de la Fortification* probably refers to a volume with an almost identical title (*Introduction à la Fortification*) published by Nicolas de Fer in 1693. Fer (1646–1720) was a prominent cartographer, engraver, and publisher who served as official geographer to the kings of both France and Spain. He produced several hundred maps of regions on the European continent. His maps of walled cities and towns apparently stimulated his interest in fortification, and he incorporated nine large plates (accompanied by six pages of explanatory notes) illustrating fortification methods and design into his widely cited volume.

Two of the volumes listed represent the landmark work of Bernard Forest de Bélidor (1698–1761). Bélidor served in the French army at a young age. He then developed an interest in science and engineering and became professor of artillery at the school of Fère-en-Tardenois in Aisne. He published works of great importance on a wide range of subjects, including hydraulics, mathematics, and civil and military engineering. His most important work was probably *L'architecture hydraulique* (published in four volumes from 1737 to 1753), which employed integral calculus for the first time in solving technical problems. *Le Bombardier Francoise ou nouvelle methode de jeter les bombes avec precision* was based on empirical experiments in ballistics and became an established early work on that subject. His *Dictionnaire portatif de l'ingénieur* was a useful field manual on engineering and truly was portable. (My copy was apparently used by an officer in the Danish artillery corps as late as 1829; I have carried it in my coat pocket in order to keep it available for reference.) Bélidor's use of applied mathematics and his empirical approach to subjects such as strength of materials, soil mechanics, and ballistics are also evident in his *La Science des Ingénieurs dans la Conduite des travaux de fortification et d'architecture civile*, which remained a standard reference work well into the nineteenth century (Langins 2004:223–24).

The inventory does not identify the author of the volume entitled *Element de fortification*, but it is quite likely that this entry refers to *Élémens de fortification* (Principles of Fortification) by Guillaume Le Blond (1704–81). Le Blond was a professor of mathematics who published a number of works on mathematics and military engineering. His *L'arithmétique et la Géométrie de l'officier* was one of the first works to offer a comprehensive treatment of applied mathematics for military officers. He first published *Élémens de fortification* in 1739, and several expanded editions were published through 1762. Le Blond was also the author of 720 articles dealing with fortification, military engineering, and applied mathematics in Diderot's *Encyclopédie*, including the summary article entitled "Fortification" (Le Blond 1757:191–203). That article was, in fact, largely an abridged version of *Élémens de fortification*, and many of the plates illustrating the volume on the "Arts Militaires" in the *Encyclopédie* were identical to plates in Le Blond's book.

Despite Vauban's resistance to discussion of general principles and his emphasis on adaptation to local conditions, the manuals offered extensive accounts of maxims or principles of fortification. For example, an early section of Le Blond's *Élémens* was entitled "Maximes ou Principes de la Fortification" (Le Blond 1756:39–48). As we shall see, the principles and methods described in these volumes provided the standards against which Franquet evaluated the fortifications in French Canada. It is therefore worthwhile to review these principles in some detail. However, it is important to note that the manuals did not view these maxims as inflexible rules to be applied by rote in every situation. Rather, such discussions frequently acknowledged that the principles were subject to adaptation according to circumstances. Abbé Deidier, a prominent commentator on the "system" of Vauban, noted:

> It is difficult, in practice, to observe with rigor each of these maxims in particular: . . . the secret consists in knowing how to discern what is suitable in the circumstances, and to arrange things in such a man-

ner that the fortification does not considerably transgress against the principal maxims. (Deidier 1734:19)

The acknowledgment that general principles must be adapted to local conditions was often related to a distinction between regular fortification, which represented the application of ideal principles at the draftsman's table, and irregular fortification, which adapted the ideal principles to real terrain, abandoning the perfect symmetry of theory. Le Blond defined *fortification régulière* as "that in which all its similar parts are equal," while in *fortification irrégulière* there is "unevenness in the sides or angles of the similar parts" (Le Blond 1756:61, 404; Bélidor 1755:135). He also acknowledged that irregular fortification was "almost the only one in use," because there were scarcely any circumstances in which the "terrain of the place was uniform or regular." Therefore, this part of the art was "the most necessary and generally useful [part] of the art of fortification." However, Le Blond, like other manual writers, also insisted that the study of fortification must begin with *fortification régulière*. Despite its infrequency, "regular fortification is preferable to irregular" because in regular fortifications the "defense is equally distributed," while in irregular fortification, "the nature of the terrain of the place . . . often causes essential differences in the strength of the sides." Under such circumstances, the enemy will seek "to determine the weakest [sides]" in order to direct his attack there, and when "he has succeeded in doing so, the better fortified sides will produce no particular advantage to the defense." Even in irregular fortifications, therefore, it was necessary to apply the principles of regular fortification as precisely as possible, in order to minimize differences in strength between the various parts of the fortification. Indeed, the principles of regular fortification also serve as "the principles for irregular fortifications, which are all the more perfect, as these [principles] are more exactly observed" (Le Blond 1756:309–11).

The manuals therefore almost always began with regular fortification and with a discussion of those "principles or maxims" that could be most perfectly realized in that form of fortification. The most frequently cited principles might be termed the principle of commanding heights, the principle of flanking defense, and the principle of defense in depth. Vauban was not the first to observe that "high positions command lower positions" (Vauban 1968:157). The manuals emphasized that the "rampart ought to command the countryside all around the place as far as the range of a cannon" (Le Blond 1756:43). The military engineer had to be familiar with the features of the land on which he would actually construct his fortifications and the surrounding territory from which an enemy might conduct siege operations. In particular, the engineer should avoid situations in which higher ground commanded any part of his fortification. Otherwise, as Le Blond observed, "the enemy will not be exposed to the cannon of the town all around the extent of the area within range." Of course, commanding ground also exposed the defenders to greater danger. Engineering manuals distinguished situations in which the commanding ground overlooked a fortification from the front, the side, and the rear (*de front, d'enfilade*, and *de revers*). The most dangerous of these was *commandement de revers*, in which the commanding heights expose "those who are on the ramparts from the rear," forcing defenders into the impossible situation of dealing with deadly fire from behind while simultaneously returning fire from the front (Le Blond 1756:44). If such a situation could not be avoided because, for example, of the situation of a town that was the focus of the fortification, the engineer should take measures to deny the advantages of the commanding ground to a besieger, either by enclosing that ground within the fortification or by constructing external works there.

The principle of flanking defense dictated the basic layout of fortifications. Bélidor stated the principle in this way:

> It is necessary that all the parts of a perfectly fortified place flank each other reciprocally; any work which has only a defense along its front is defective." (1755:130)

Le Blond elaborated on the principle:

> It is necessary that there is no part of a circuit wall [*enceinte*] of a fortified place which is not seen and defended from some other part of this circuit wall, that is to say, that they ought to flank each other reciprocally: the parts that flank, such as the flanks [of the bastions], ought to be as large as it is possible to make them, without being detrimental to the other parts. (1756:39–40)

This principle of flanking defense dictated an emphasis on applied geometry to develop designs in which the parts "flank each other reciprocally." For example, the most widely known English-language work, John Muller's 1746 *Treatise Containing the Elementary Part of Fortification, Regular and Irregular*, begins with a section entitled "Of Practical Geometry." The practical application of this principle in the eighteenth century was the use of

Figure 2.1. Representation of "antiquated fortifications," featuring towers and extremely high, simple walls furnished with loopholes (*crenaux*). (Nicolas de Fer, *Introduction à la Fortification*, plate 6.)

bastions along the main defensive wall, at intervals dictated by the range of the musket, as strong points from which all segments of the wall could be defended (Le Blond 1756:40–42, 325). So prominent were bastions in the defensive structures of this period that the methods taught and practiced by military professionals of that era are often referred to as "bastioned systems" (Fry 1984:1:23).

Strictly speaking, fortifications in the ancient and medieval periods had employed flanking defense. For example, the medieval castle featured square or round projecting towers for this purpose. Figure 2.1 shows the representation, from Nicolas de Fer's *Introduction à la Fortification*, of the flanking towers in "antiquated fortifications." The manuals frequently discussed medieval fortification and contrasted it with their forms of "modern fortification," especially with regard to flanking defense and defense in depth. In particular, the manuals emphasized that the towers of the medieval castle, whether square or round, had a glaring weakness. As Le Blond observed, "The circuit wall of a [castle] presented parts . . . arranged in such a manner that if the enemy wanted to employ scaling ladders or to bring their siege engines against different parts of the wall, they would be exposed [to the defenders] from the front, the side, and almost from the rear, so that they were as much as enveloped by the batteries of the place that they were attacking" (Le Blond 1756:32). However, because towers were either round or square, and the walls and towers of a castle were typically quite high (which, as we shall see, presented another contrast between "antiquated"

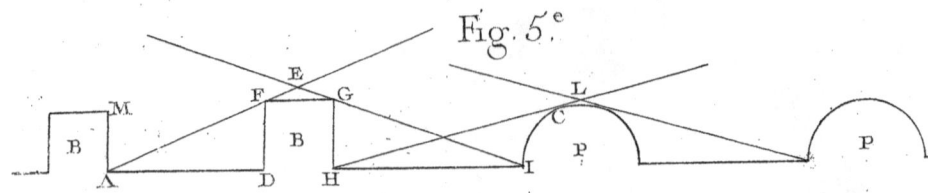

Figure 2.2. Guillaume Le Blond's illustration of the weakness of medieval square and round towers in providing flanking defense for a fortification. The area *FEG* in front of the square tower *B* and the smaller area just inside of point *L* outside the round tower *P* were undefended from any other part of the fortification in the absence of a *machicoulis*. The *machicoulis*, however, itself became impractical and indefensible with the advent of artillery. (Le Blond, *Élémens de fortification*, plate 2, figure 5.)

and "modern" fortifications), there could be a "dead space" in front of a castle tower that could not be defended from the neighboring towers or any other part of the circuit wall. Le Blond demonstrated the problem with the illustration reproduced in figure 2.2, which shows this potential dead space in front of square towers (the area *FEG* in front of the square tower *B*) and round towers (the smaller area just inside of point *L* outside the round tower *P*).

Castles often employed a structure called a machicoulis to provide a defense for this otherwise undefended space. The machicoulis consisted of a narrow gallery hanging out from the height of the castle wall over the ditch at the base of the wall. Openings in the floor between the supports that held up the structure allowed defenders to strike any besiegers who reached the foot of the wall with arrows, stones, melted lead, or boiling oil (Le Blond 1756:31–32). Le Blond believed that the existence of this dead space and the obsolescence of the machicoulis by the introduction of artillery explained in large part the origin for the use of bastions in place of towers for purposes of providing adequate flanking defense. As he observed, the castle form of fortification, with tall towers and machicoulis, "persisted until the invention of the gunpowder cannon," that "formidable machine for battering and ruining fortified places." With the advent of gunpowder artillery, it became "necessary to abandon the machicoulis, which was immediately ruined by [cannon], and to increase the thickness of the parapet, in order to put it in the condition to resist the force of cannon" (Le Blond 1756:34–35). With the loss of the machicoulis as the means of defending this otherwise dead space, this "inconvenience gave rise to the thought of enclosing within the towers the space that they otherwise left without a defense" (Le Blond 1757:192). Specifically, the triangular area *FEG* in Le Blond's illustration (figure 2.2) was now incorporated into the fortification, forming a new structure with an angle pointed toward the countryside, and straight sides (soon to be called flanks) linking the faces forming this angle with the wall connecting to the neighboring structures. "The towers revamped in this way were first called *boulevards* and then *bastions*. Their use appears to have been established only around the year 1500 or 1550" (Le Blond 1756:37).

Whether or not Le Blond's account is historically correct, it certainly represents the logic behind substituting bastions for the flanking towers of the castle. A major challenge of fortification design was then to draw the outline, or trace, of bastions and connecting walls so that they provided adequate flanking without the dead space that (among other problems) doomed the medieval castle. There were numerous ways of doing so in the era, each one of which was commonly referred to as a "system" of fortification. Le Blond's *Encyclopédie* article surveyed about a dozen of these design methods (Le Blond 1757:191–203). In his manual, he gave pride of place to one, which he called "the first system of M. de Vauban" (Le Blond 1756:274). Like many commentators, Le Blond claimed to discern three successive systems of fortification in the practice of Vauban. This assertion was widespread but controversial and is in any case a consequence of the attempt by others to describe the system that Vauban himself refused to lay down. Whatever its relation to the actual practices of Vauban, this method clearly illustrates the essential features of flanking design.

The design (illustrated by Le Blond in the plan reproduced as figure 2.3) began with a circle with the length of its radius dependent upon the number of intended sides. For that purpose (and others), reference was made to a table (reproduced here as figure 2.4). According to the table, the radius should be 180 toises for a hexagon, shorter for squares and pentagons, and progressively longer for fortifications with more sides. (The toise was a common unit of measurement in France before the Revolution, equivalent to 1.949 meters.) Le Blond nowhere stated explicitly why this should be the case, but it is reasonable to infer from the table that the number of sides increased with the overall size of the fortification in order to ensure that each side remained at the proper range for the weapons that would provide covering fire. Elsewhere, he discussed the importance of ensuring that the "parts of the circuit wall that are flanked by other parts ought to be within the range of the arms with which they are supposed to be defended." He also discussed whether this "flanking fire range" ought to be determined by the range of the cannon or the musket, settling on musket range as more appropriate because "defense with the musket does not exclude defense with the cannon, but not the other way around." He concluded on this basis that the "lines of defense" in a fortification, which ran from the point where the side (flank) of one bastion met the curtain wall to the external point (salient) of the neighboring bastion, ought to be between 120 and 150 toises. In Le Blond's example of Vauban's first system, a front of 180 toises would

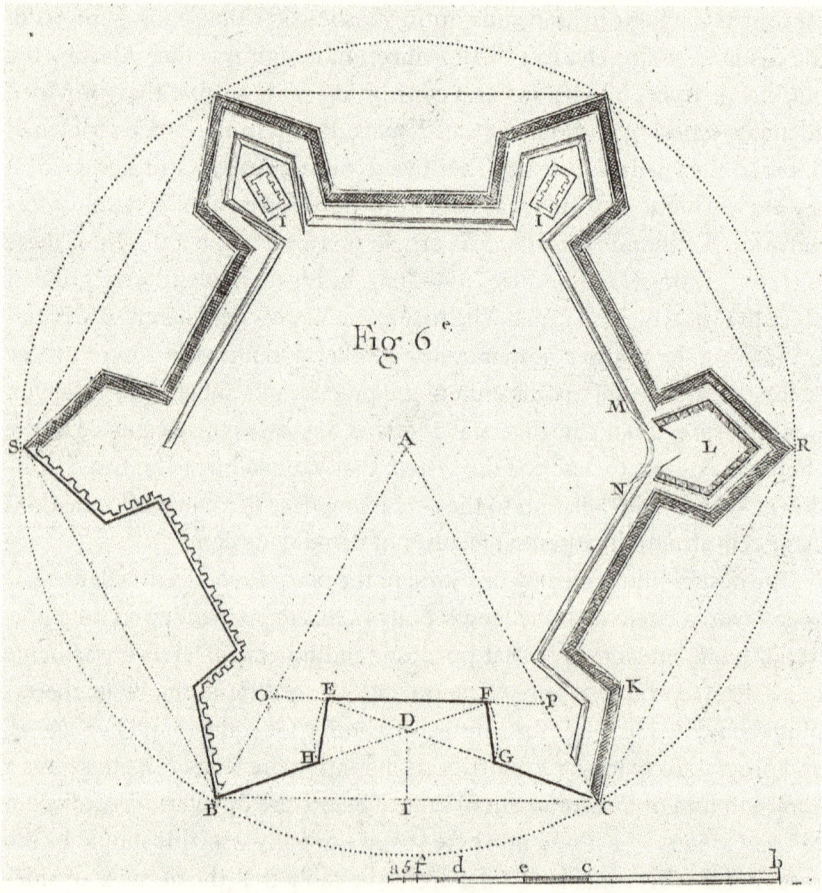

Figure 2.3. Plate employed by Le Blond to illustrate "the first system of M. de Vauban." Le Blond's *Encyclopédie* entry on fortification employs an almost exact duplicate of this plate. (Le Blond, *Élémens de fortification*, plate 3.)

DE FORTIFICATION.

TABLE des différentes lignes qui servent à former le principal trait de la fortification de M. le Maréchal de Vauban.

		du Quarré.	du Pentag.	de l'Exag.
Côté extérieur.		180. T.	180. T.	180. T.
Perpendiculaire.		22. T.	25. T.	30. T.
Face.		50. T.	50. T.	50. T.
Rayon.		127. T	153. T.	180. T.
Rayons.	de l'Eptagone.			206. T. 3 p.
	de l'Octogone.			234. T. 3 p.
	de l'Ennéagone.			262. T. 2 p.
	du Décagone.			291. T.
	de l'Endécagone.			314. T.
	du Dodécagone.			346. T. 4 p.

F ij

Figure 2.4. The table employed by Le Blond to provide the appropriate dimensions of various parts of a fortification, with reference to "the first system of M. de Vauban." (Le Blond, *Élémens de fortification*, 67.)

imply a line of defense of 135 toises, in the middle of the prescribed range for flanking fire (Le Blond 1756:40, 42, 325).

Once the proper length for the radius had been established, the hexagon itself was inscribed (referring again to the plan in figure 2.3) within the circle by "carrying the radius *AB* six times around the circumference (as has been observed in geometry), that is, from *B* to *C*, from *C* to *R*, etc., and then drawing the lines *BC*, *CR*, etc." (Le Blond 1756:62). The end of each radius became the salient point of a bastion (e.g., points *B* and *C*). Each front of the fortification was then designed along the lines between these points (e.g., *BC*). The key to providing appropriate flanking was establishing the proper relationship between

- the length of the front (in this example, 180 toises),
- the faces of the bastions (meaning the two sides of the bastion facing the countryside) at each end of the front, and
- an imaginary perpendicular drawn to align the faces of the bastion at the correct angles.

Here again, reference was made to the table reproduced in figure 2.4: for a hexagon, the perpendicular must be 30 toises and the faces of each bastion 50 toises. From this point, the ground plan of a front with proper flanking could be designed in about eight steps, using only ruler and compass. (For purposes of following these steps, a close-up of the front of fortification *BC* in figure 2.3 is reproduced in figure 2.5.)

(1) Draw line *BC* to represent the 180-toise front between the points of the bastion at each end.
(2) At *I*, the center of *BC*, erect a perpendicular of 30 toises (as indicated in the table): *ID*.
(3) Connect points *C* and *D*, *B* and *D*: this determines the alignment of the faces of the bastions.
(4) Fix the length of these faces at *G* and *H*, 50 toises from the points of the bastions (as indicated in the table).
(5) Determine the points where the flanks of the bastions meet the curtain walls by fixing a compass at point *H* and drawing an arc through *G*, then fixing a compass at *G* and drawing an arc through *H*. (These arcs are shown as hashed lines in figure 2.5.)
(6) Establish points *E* and *F* where these arcs meet the extensions of the lines *BD* and *CD* (drawn in step 3 to determine the alignment of the faces of the bastions).
(7) Establish the flanks of each bastion between points *H* and *E* and points *G* and *F*.
(8) Establish the curtain wall between points *E* and *F*. (Le Blond 1756:62–66; Duffy 1975:33–34)

While the perpendicular (*ID*) was an imaginary line, a draftsman's device, it was in many ways the key to the design. As the steps above indicate, the perpendicular determined the orientation of the bastion faces, the lengths of the bastion flanks, and the length of the curtain wall between the bastions. A front of defense, designed according to the specifications in the

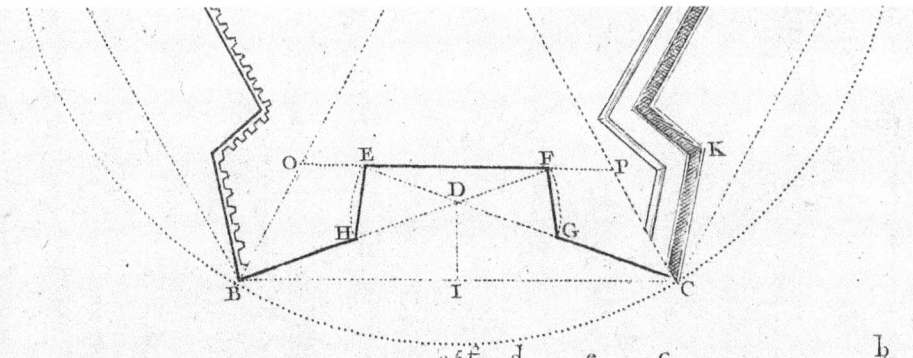

Figure 2.5. Close-up of the front of fortification *BC*. The close-up shows the imaginary perpendicular, *ID*, employed to align the bastions faces, *BH* and *CG*, for proper flanking. *HE* and *GF* are the flanks of the bastions, and *EF* is the curtain wall running between the bastions. (Le Blond, *Élémens de fortification*, plate 3.)

table (figure 2.4) with a properly defined perpendicular, provided flanking fire for every spot along the entire length of the front. The design of this front would, in Le Blond's example, be reproduced in the other five sides of the hexagon, resulting in the ground plan of a complete fortress shown in figure 2.3.

Of course, the goal of studying regular fortification was to master the general principles that should be applied in the more frequent circumstances where irregular fortification was necessary. As Le Blond declared, "The rules that one follows in that case [regular fortification], serve as well as the principles for irregular fortification" (1756:310). Indeed, the goal of irregular fortification was to "arrange all the parts of the circuit wall of an irregular place in accordance with the maxims taught in regular fortification, which ought to be observed in all kinds of fortifications" (Le Blond 1756:316). The point was to apply these principles as precisely as possible, although the application of these ideal principles had to proceed more indirectly than in those rare cases where regular fortification was possible. And although irregular fortification was the "most necessary and generally useful part of the art of fortifying" (Le Blond 1756:309), the treatment of this topic was always much more restricted in the manuals than the treatment of regular fortification. One manual author, John Muller, even asserted that "all the authors who have wrote on fortification, that I have seen, are so deficient in regard to this, that not the least knowledge can be gathered from their writings, they do not even mention anything about it" (Muller

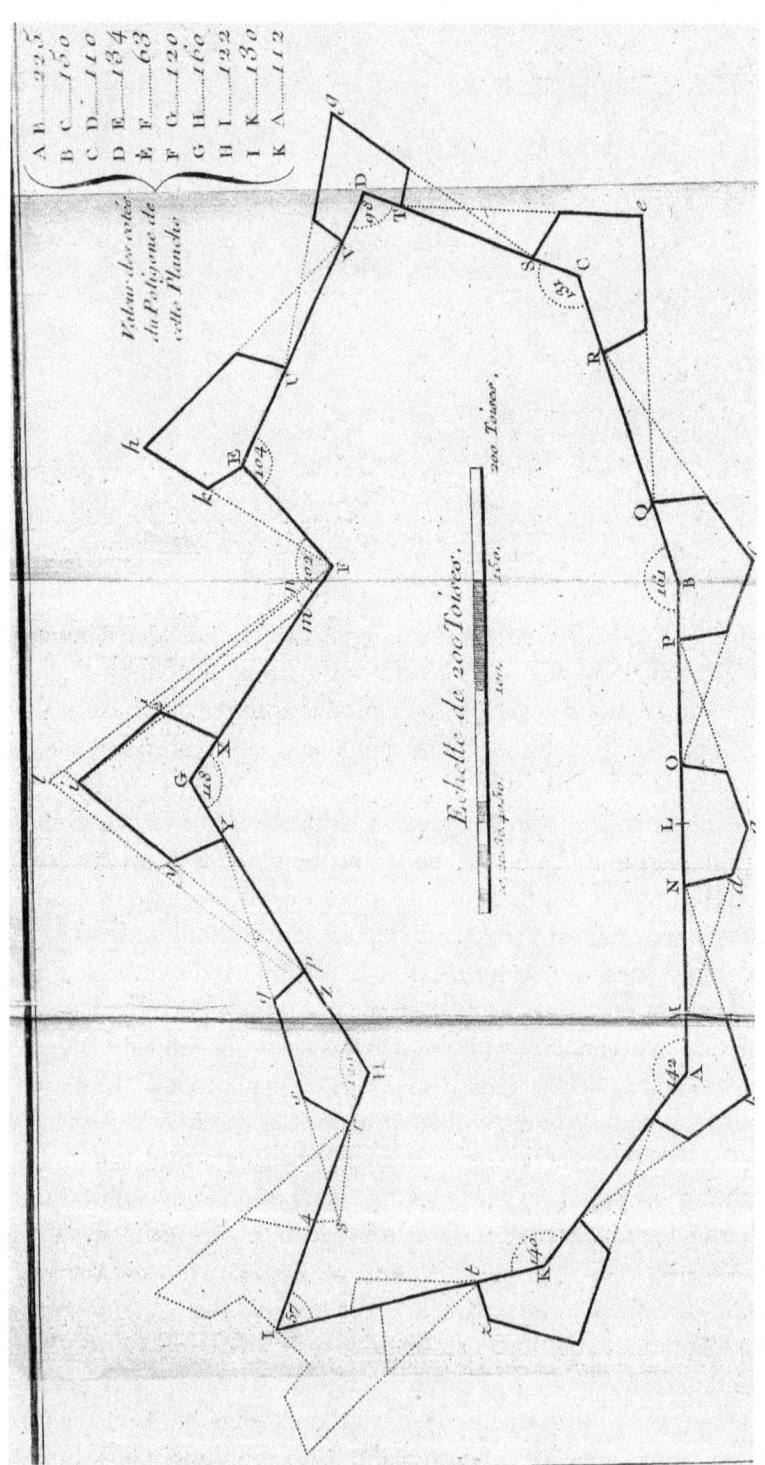

Figure 2.6. Plan of an irregular fortification. In this example, Le Blond assumes an existing "old circuit wall" around a town and proceeds to show how to add modern bastions with proper flanking by approximating the application of the maxims for regular fortification. (Le Blond, *Élémens de fortification*, plate 19.)

148. TABLE des côtés intérieurs des Polygones réguliers, depuis le quarré jusqu'au Dodécagone, avec les demi-gorges des Bastions construits sur ces côtés.

		Quarré.	Pentagone.	Exagone.	Eptagone.	Octogone.	Ennéagone.	Décagone.	Endécagone
		Toises.	Toises.	Toises.	Toises.	Toises.	Toises.	Toises.	Toises.
Pour une ligne de défense de 120 toises.	Côtés intérieurs,	105	115	120	122	128	131	135	138
	Demi-gorges.	17	23	26	27	30	32	34	35
Pour une ligne de défense de 135 toises.	Côtés intérieurs,	119	127	135	138	144	148	152	156
	Demi-gorges.	20	25	29	31	34	36	38	40
Pour une ligne de défense de 150 toises.	Côtés intérieurs,	146	139	150	153	160	164	168	173
	Demi-gorges.	24	26	33	34	37	40	42	44

A

TABLE des angles flanquans intérieurs & des angles de la circonférence des polygones réguliers, depuis le quarré jusqu'au dodécagone & la ligne droite.

	Quarré.	Pentagone.	Exagone.	Eptagone.	Octogone.	Ennéagone.	Décagone.	Endécagone.	Dodécagone.	Ligne droite.
Angles flanquans intérieurs.	Deg. min. 13. 44.	Deg. min. 15. 30.	Deg. min. 18. 26.	Deg. min. 18. 26.	Deg. min. 18. 26.	Deg. min. 18. 26.	Deg. min. 18. 26.	Deg. min. 18. 26.	Deg. min. 18. 26.	Degrés. 20.
Angles de la circonférence.	90.	108.	120.	128.	135.	140.	144.	147.	150.	180.

B

Figures 2.7a and 2.7b. The two tables that Le Blond provides to allow the designer to approximate the results of regular fortification in the ground plan of an irregular fortification (as illustrated in figure 2.6). (Le Blond, Élémens de fortification, 330, 341.)

1746:139). Le Blond admitted in his *Élémens de fortification* that it was not his intention "to enter into an examination of everything which could be involved in the fortification of irregular places, relative to their different irregularities, which could be varied in an infinite manner; one seeks only to present some general principles on the most common [irregularities]" (Le Blond 1756:316). However, Le Blond's *Élémens* provided one of the lengthiest and most detailed treatments of irregular fortification, including a special plate illustrating the ground plan of an irregular fortification (reproduced as figure 2.6), and two tables (reproduced together in figure 2.7) that allowed the designer to proceed by constructing lengths, angles, and other features of his irregular design in ways that approximate the results for similar features in regular design. The information provided by these tables was all the more important, since irregular fortification usually required engineers to proceed in designing these fortifications in the opposite direction from the design of regular ground plans.

Most systems for the design of regular fortifications, as in the case of "the first system of M. de Vauban" illustrated by Le Blond, employed a polygon drawn outside the locations intended for the bastions and curtain walls and designed the main outline of these bastions and walls by proceeding inward from this polygon. This manner of fortifying was said to employ an exterior polygon and to proceed in drafting the ground plan from the outside in, or inward (*en dedans*), so that this method was sometimes called interior fortification (Le Blond 1756:101–2(a), 318). (In figure 2.3, the exterior polygon is the one inscribed inside the circle, defined by points S, B, C, R, etc.) Some methods for regular fortification proceeded in the opposite direction. Two of the methods illustrated by Le Blond in his *Encyclopédie* article on fortification employed this other method (Le Blond 1757: plate 2, figures 4, 6). In these cases, a polygon was drawn along the lines where the curtain walls would run, from midpoint to midpoint of the bastions along each side. (In figures 2.3 and 2.5, one side of the interior polygon is shown: line OP.) Drafting of the ground plan then proceeded from this interior polygon inside out, or outward (*en dehors*). This method was also sometimes called exterior fortification (Le Blond 1756:101–2(a), 321–24). Exterior fortification was used more often than interior fortification to design irregular fortifications. Indeed, the very same reasons that made regular fortification impossible in certain cases also rendered interior fortification more difficult. According to Le Blond, "If the place that one wants to fortify is irregular, and the position and size of the interior sides are givens [*donnés*], or if the town has an old circuit wall that has to be put to use as the curtain walls, it is very difficult to succeed by way of fortification with the exterior polygon in employing the sides given by the [existing] circuit wall as the interior sides [of the new fortification]" (Le Blond 1756:321). A special illustration showed that the ground plan dictated by regular fortification *en dedans* would almost certainly fail to accommodate the contingencies imposed by irregular terrain or an existing circuit wall (Le Blond 1756: plate 18, figure 2.6).

In the example discussed by Le Blond, irregular fortification proceeded from the inside out, with reference to the tables reproduced in figure 2.7. In order to understand the use of these tables, it is necessary to define some terms. Beginning with the terms in the top table, the line of defense (*ligne de defense*), as we have seen, ran from the point where the side (flank) of one bastion met the curtain wall to the external point (salient) of the neighboring bastion. (In figures 2.3 and 2.5, the lines of defense are *BF* and *CE*.) The line of defense was employed as shorthand for the range of flanking fire that was necessary along a front of fortification. (Le Blond 1756:11, 407) The interior sides (*côtés intérieurs*) were the sides of the interior polygon. (In figures 2.3 and 2.5, line *OP* is one side of the interior polygon.) The term *gorge* referred to the entrance into a bastion from the interior of a fortification. A demi-gorge was half of this entrance, usually measured by prolonging the line of the curtain wall from the point where it met the flank of the bastion to the point where it met the radius of the circle in which the exterior polygon was inscribed (Le Blond 1756:10, 401). (In figures 2.3 and 2.5, the demi-gorges are lines *OE* and *FP*.) The length of the demi-gorge was often employed as an indication of the size of the bastion (and hence the capacity of the bastion to accommodate defensive forces). The top table therefore captured the measures of the interior sides and demi-gorges of several regular polygons (square, pentagon, hexagon, etc.) for different lengths of the lines of defense (120, 135, and 150 toises, all within the appropriate range of flanking fire for a front of fortification) (Le Blond 1756:40, 46, 325).

In the bottom table, the term *interior flanking angle* referred to the angle formed by the line of defense and the curtain wall (Le Blond 1756:12, 393). (In figures 2.3 and 2.5, the interior flanking angles are *BFE* and *CEF*.) In this kind of fortification, the value of this angle captured the relationship between the orientation of face of the bastion and the curtain wall running between the bastions. Finally, the term *angle of the circumference* referred to the angles formed by two sides of the polygon used in the design of the fortification (Le Blond 1756:11). In cases where the design proceeded *en dedans*, these angles were formed by sides of the exterior polygon. In Le Blond's example of irregular fortification *en dehors*, these were the angles formed by sides of the interior polygon. (In figures 2.3 and 2.5, the interior angles of the circumference are not shown, but they would be equal to twice the value of angles *AOP* and *APO*. The exterior angles of the circumference are *SBC* and *RCB*.) The bottom table in figure 2.7 thus captures the measures of the interior flanking angles and the angles of the circumference for several regular polygons (square, pentagon, hexagon, etc.), including the measures related to a bastion erected along the straight line (*ligne droite*) of a curtain wall rather than at one of the angles of a polygon.

With this information at hand, Le Blond's example showed how the irregular interior polygon could be fortified with modern bastions and proper flanking. In figure 2.6, Le Blond assumed a "town has an old circuit wall," forming an "irregular polygon *ABCDE*, etc.," that "has to be fortified. It is supposed that . . . it is a matter of establishing the curtain walls on top of parts of this circuit wall" (1756:341, plate 19). (Although Le Blond supposed an existing circuit wall, the methods that he describes would apply equally well in cases where the features of the terrain or an open town required developing the fortification around a similar irregular polygon.) The plan reproduced in figure 2.6 also showed the measurements of each side (in the upper right corner: side *AB*, for example, measures 225 toises) and each angle (indicated within the oval hash marks at each angle, e.g., 142 degrees for angle *A*). Le Blond provided a complete account of how to design the flanking bastions shown on the plan, working around each side of the polygon while using the values in the tables as guides to approximating application of the general "maxim or principles of fortification" used in regular fortification.

Le Blond began by observing that, with a length of 225 toises, side *AB* exceeds the range of musket fire and is thus "too long for bastions placed at the ends *A* and *B* to be able to provide reciprocal defense." Therefore, he concluded that it would be necessary to construct a flat bastion (*bastion plat*) in the middle of this side" (Le Blond 1756:344). In regular fortifications, bastions were always located at the corners of the regular polygons. This was because, in regular fortifications, no side would exceed the range of covering fire. However, in irregular fortifications the length of a front often exceeded the range of flanking fire. In these cases, flat bastions, defined as "those which are constructed on a straight line," were added to provide adequate covering fire along the entire length of a front. The term derived from the fact that the gorge of such a bastion was defined by a straight line, rather than by the corner angle of the interior polygon. Depending upon the length of the front, the location of a flat bastion was determined by "dividing [the wall] into two equal parts" and placing the bastion "in the middle of this line" (Le Blond 1756:327, 339–40, 395). (As we shall later see in the case of one North American fortification, it was sometimes necessary to erect more than one flat bastion along a front of irregular fortification in order to ensure that the distance from one bastion to the next did not exceed the range of covering fire.) To this end, then, the side *AB* is cut "into two equal parts at *L*," yielding the side "*AL* and *BL*, each of 112 toises" (Le Blond 1756:344).

The next task was to design bastions to be located at points *A* and *B*, the extremities of this section of the wall, and at point *L*, the midpoint. Specifically, the design of these bastions required determining their width (using the measurement of the gorge or demi-gorge), the length and orientation of their flanks, and the orientation of their faces. All these tasks were accomplished by reference to the tables. The length "*AL* is 112 toises, and the angle *A* is 142 degrees, which corresponds approximately to that of the enneagon." Therefore, "one will take 27 or 28 toises for the length of the demi-gorge, that is to say, approximately a quarter of *AL*" (Le Blond 1756:344). Thus Le Blond established the width of the demi-gorge (*AM*) for the bastion at point *A* by referring to the bottom table in figure 2.7 to determine that the angle of *A* is close to the angle of regular enneagon (142 degrees compared to 140 degrees for a regular enneagon). Referring then to the top table, it is evident that the demi-gorges of bastions erected on regular enneagons are about one-quarter of the length of the interior side (e.g., 32/131 = .244, or about 1/4). A quarter of 112 toises, the length *AL*, yields a demi-gorge at *AM* of 27 or 28 toises. Similar reasoning established a demi-gorge of 28 toises at *LN* for the flat bastion. At points *M* and *N*, the ends of these demi-gorges, the flanks of the bastions could then be erected at 100 degree angles to the curtain walls, following another standard result of regular fortification design (Le Blond 1756:392–93).

Next, it was necessary to determine the orientation of the bastion faces. Referring again to the bottom table in figure 2.7, "the interior flanking angle for a straight line," on which a flat bastion is erected, is "20 degrees." Therefore, "at point *M* we will make with *ML* an angle of 20 degrees" and "draw the line of defense *Ma*." In this way, the face (the line *da*) of the flat bastion erected around point *L* will have the correct orientation to the curtain wall. Similarly, by reference to the value of the interior flanking angles for a regular enneagon (18 degrees, 26 minutes, as shown in the bottom table), "at point *N* we will make with *MN* the angle *MNb* of about 18 and a half degrees," yielding the line of defense *Nb* that gives to the face (the line *bc*) of the bastion at *A* the correct orientation to the curtain wall. The ends of the bastion flanks were then established where the lines of defense *Ma* and *Nb* meet those flanks at points *d* and *c* (Le Blond 1756:344).

Finally, the defense of AB was completed by "likewise establishing *BP* and *LO* [demi-gorges for the bastions at points *B* and *L*, respectively] at 28 toises and completing the fortification of *LB* as we have done with *AL*. Thus we will have fortified the long side *AB* with two half-bastions at its extremities, *A* and *B*, and a complete flat bastion *L* constructed in the middle." During this step, the line of defense *Pa* was established, as in the case of the line of defense *Ma*, by making with *OP* the angle *OPa* of about 20 degrees, the interior flanking angle for a straight line. Together, *Ma* and *Pa* determined the salient angle of the flat bastion at point *a*. The salient points of the bastions at points *A* and *B* would be established at points *b* and *f* in the course of fortifying sides *KA* and *BC*, which would determine the lines of defense (e.g., *Rf*) for the other faces of those two bastions (Le Blond 1756:345).

For the most part, the design proceeded in much the same way around the remaining sides of the irregular polygon *ABCDEFGHIK*. However, three of the remaining angles (at *F*, *H*, and *I*) posed problems for the design that merit a few additional observations. At each of the points *F* and *H*, the old curtain wall in Le Blond's example formed a reentrant or entering angle (*angle rentrant*), defined as an angle "whose summit or point is turned toward the place," in contrast to a salient angle (in this case, all the other angles around the polygon), "whose point is turned in the direction of the countryside" (Le Blond 1756:393). Because each curtain wall adjacent to a reentrant angle was within the line of sight of the other, it was sometimes unnecessary to erect a bastion at such an angle. Specifically, in the case of the reentrant angle *EFG*, "the side FE . . . is only 63 toises, and it can flank the bastion constructed at *G*." Furthermore, "the two sides of the reentrant angle F can flank each other mutually." Therefore, "we will be able to dispense with constructing this bastion at angle *F*." Le Blond provided only for constructing lines of defense (*Fh* and *Fi*) from that angle to define the faces of the neighboring bastions at *E* and *G*. Note as well that the entire gorge (*EU*) of the bastion at *E* is located on the line *ED*. This was because "the adjacent side FE is too small at 63 toises to form a front of fortification" (Le Blond 1756:347–48).

However, the reentrant angle at *H* posed a different situation. "The two sides of the reentrant angle *IHG* cannot flank each other like those of the preceding angle, *F*, because the angle is wider, and they [the fronts] are longer." Therefore, Le Blond constructed a demi-gorge at *Hp* that is wide enough to provide a line of defense (*pi*) within the range of covering fire required to defend the bastion at point *G* (Le Blond 1756:349). (The hashed lines, such as *Zl*, represent initial approximations and illustrate that a process of trial and error was often necessary in irregular fortification.) The other sides of the unusually shaped bastion at *H* were defined to provide an adequate defense for the salient angle at *I*. That angle was only 57 degrees, too narrow "to construct a bastion across this angle, as we have done on the other angles of the proposed circuit wall; but there are several ways to fortify it" (Le Blond 1756:351). Briefly, one method was to restructure the curtain walls on either side of *I*, in order to create a bastion with proper faces and flanks (e.g., the flank shown by the hashed line *34*, meeting the restructured curtain wall *r3*). Another method was to construct "on this angle a kind of hornwork (*ouvrage à corne*), or front of fortification, such as the one shown by the hashed line in the plan." (Hornworks, such as the one shown in hashed lines at the upper left corner of the plan in figure 2.6, were usually constructed outside the main curtain walls to add defense in depth, and consisted of a curtain wall and two half-bastions.) However, while a hornwork would provide better defense than other measures, it would also be "a greater expense" (Le Blond 1756:351–52). In irregular fortification, the need to approximate the application of the general principles so easily employed in regular fortifications often allowed for more than one way to proceed. The engineer's art in the sphere of irregular fortification thus included an irreducible, and ultimately indefinable, element of judgment.

In addition to bastion-based flanking defense, the introduction of artillery also accounted for another of the basic "maxims or principles of fortification," defense in depth. Le Blond expressed the principle in this way: "The works that one constructs in order to shelter oneself from the effect of the arms with which the enemy attacks places ought to be secure against those arms; thus if the enemy attacks towns with cannon, the parapets ought to be cannon-proof" (Le Blond 1756:42–43). During the medieval period prior to the development of powerful artillery, it was the height of walls and towers that rendered fortifications strong and secure. By the early modern period, however, high towers and walls became vulnerable to breaching by concentrated bombardment, even with the inaccurate artillery of the era. Thus fortifications of the seventeenth and eighteenth centuries "continued to use many of the elements of medieval defenses but covered against artillery fire by dropping the entire complex into a hole in the ground." The *depth* rather than the *height* of defensive structures became the basis for strength and security against the kind of attack that besiegers could mount with artillery. Low, thick structures provided defensive strength by reducing and even hiding the potential targets of a besieger's artillery. The structures which did remain visible were designed to be thick enough to absorb artillery fire (Rothrock 1968:4).

Defense in depth actually had two dimensions. The first dimension was to ensure that each work had the appropriate depth to resist artillery fire. Thus bastions were designed with angles sufficiently wide to allow great quantities of earth to be heaped up inside the walls to form deep ramparts. Curtain walls running between bastions consisted of low ramparts with deep ditches in front. Le Blond summarized the conventional assessment about the required thickness: "Experience indicates that earthen parapets must be 18 feet thick . . . [and] masonry parapets ought to be 8 or 9 feet thick in order to resist cannon" (Le Blond 1756:43). With his characteristic thoroughness and scientific rigor, Bélidor devoted two entire books of his *Science des Ingénieurs* to an empirical treatment of the strength of materials, the formulas to be used in determining resistance to the force of weapons, and tables to guide engineers in designing works with sufficient strength to resist artillery. The ditches running around the ramparts posed a great obstacle to attacking infantry, who had to cross them under fire from the walls and bastions towering above the level of the ditch. To protect the wall from artillery fire, the earth from the excavation of the ditch was piled on its outer side, and the pile was then tapered down to the surrounding countryside. This embankment, called the glacis, not only restricted the targets available to artillery fire, but also required besiegers to approach by trenching and mining in order to avoid marching straight up into the defenders' line of fire. In addition to thickening each individual work, outer works, such as tenailles, lunettes, and ravelins, were often employed outside the central circuit of wall and bastions, nesting the fortified place within layers of defensive structure. These external works were employed to assist in concealing the inner works from artillery fire and to serve as additional obstacles which attacking infantry had to overcome in order to reach the main body of the place (Le Blond 1756:149–87). Figure 2.8 illustrates both dimensions of defense in depth. The plan at the top, from Le Blond's *Élémens*, shows the profile of a simple fortification, with a deep curtain wall, a wide ditch, and glacis. The bottom plan, from Bélidor's *Science des Ingénieurs*, shows a more complex fortification, which increases the defense in depth by adding new layers of thick earthen walls and wide ditches.

Fortifications designed to these standards in Europe were supposed to be able to withstand a siege of several weeks to several months by numerically superior forces furnished with heavy artillery and siege equipment. Along these lines, Vauban's work on siegecraft provided an example of a siege against a well-conducted defense, in which he estimated the duration of the siege at 43 days for a fortress designed with the basic works of bastions, demilunes, ditches, and glacis. He also estimated that the amount of time necessary for besiegers to take a fortress could be increased to 65 to 70 days with the addition of redoubts and other outworks (Vauban 1968:140–41). Eighteenth-century military engineers generally did not speak of designing and constructing impregnable fortifications, except, on rare occasions, relative to the offensive weapons that could be brought against them. With sufficient time and resources, besiegers could take almost any

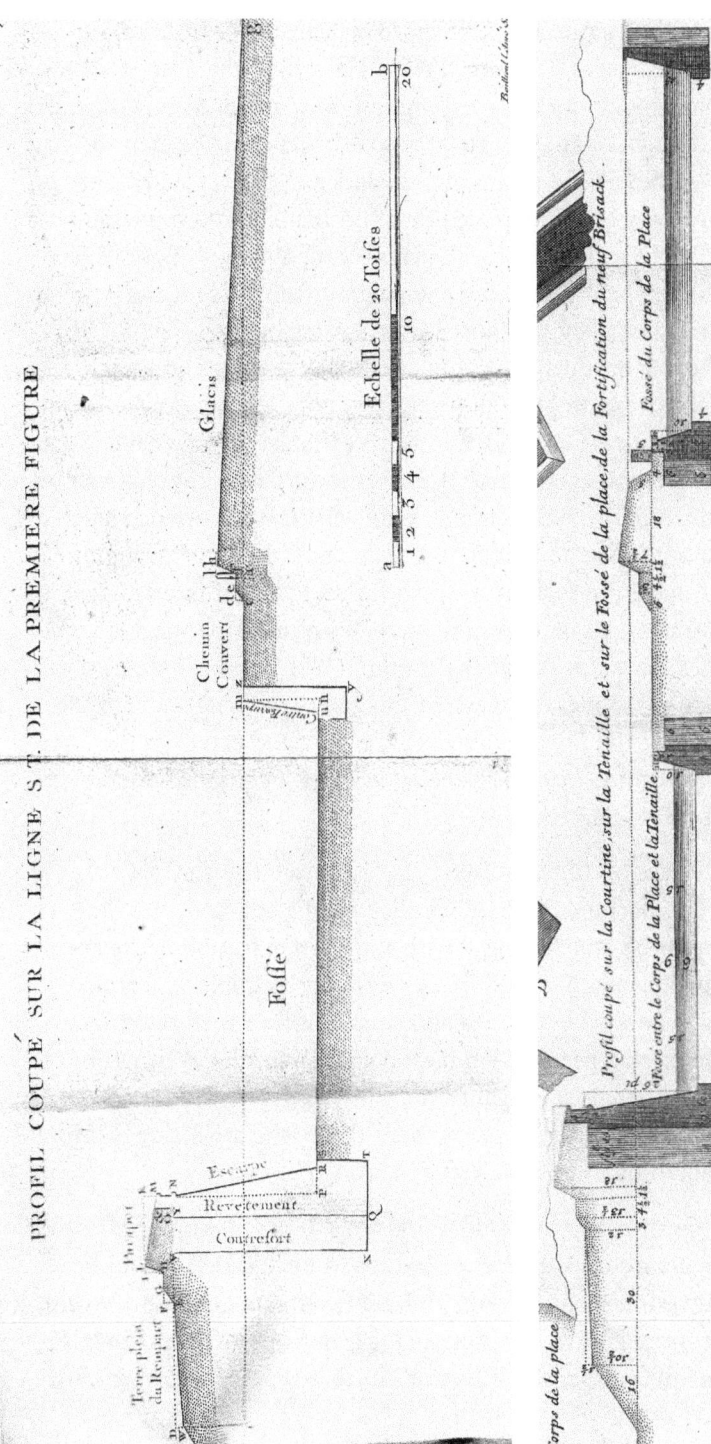

Figure 2.8. Two illustrations of defense in depth. *Top*: Profile of a simple fortification, with a thick curtain wall of parapet and terreplain, a ditch, glacis, and covered way (*chemin couvert*) from which garrison troops could defend the approach up the glacis to the ditch. (Le Blond, *Elémens de fortification*, plate 7.) *Bottom*: Complex fortification, which increases defense in depth by adding new layers of thick earthen walls and ditches, in this case a tenaille with its ramparts and ditch. Each layer of defense provided further cover against artillery fire and added to the time and strategic complexity required of besiegers to break into a fortification. (Bélidor, *Science des Ingénieurs*, plate 53, figure 5.)

fortress. Rather, the engineers spoke more realistically of fortifications as tools to hinder and delay an enemy, perhaps to raise the cost of a siege beyond what an enemy would be willing to bear, perhaps to buy time for relief forces to organize and come to the rescue, and perhaps merely to hold out long enough before the inevitable surrender to preserve the honor of the country's sovereign and its armed forces. A memorandum on the state of defenses at Fort Carillon (known later after rebuilding as Fort Ticonderoga), written just before the final campaign of the Seven Years' War in the Lake Champlain valley, contains a striking statement of the prevailing mentality regarding the duty of a commander to conduct an honorable defense. "In order to deserve general esteem, it is not even necessary that the commandant have an excellent fortification entrusted to him; it is enough that its defects are known and that the defense surpass what ought to be expected of an ordinary man" (Casgrain 1889–95:4:113). Le Blond expressed this understanding when he defined fortification as "the art of arranging all the parts of a place . . . so that the men who are contained there can defend themselves and resist for a long time a greater number of attackers who want to seize the place or to drive them from it" (Le Blond 1756:1–2).

The manuals sometimes emphasized that the capacity of a fortification "to resist for a long time" was relative to the type and extent of the force that could be brought to bear in besieging it. In his *Encyclopédie* article on fortification, Le Blond noted:

> Fortifications are of different types, that is to say that they are relative . . . to the machines with which they can be attacked. . . . Thus, if places are to be attacked only with the musket, simple walls are sufficient fortification to resist. . . . A castle, for example, is fortified when it is surrounded by ditches and simple walls, which put it in a condition to resist a party which has no cannon at all; but this same castle becomes defenseless against an army equipped with artillery, because it can then be destroyed without those who are inside being able to do anything to prevent it. (Le Blond 1757:191)

In a world without artillery, a castle would suffice, and by implication, the elaborate design and deep features of bastioned fortification would be an unnecessary investment. In the very different context of the New World, Louis Franquet would find adaptations of the general principles of fortification that sometimes dispensed with features that were necessary to resist artillery effectively.

In the course of his 1752 inspection tour, Franquet conducted formal inspections of the French fortifications defending the Lake Champlain and St. Lawrence valleys, including Fort St. Frédéric, Fort Chambly, and the walled town of Montréal (Franquet 1889:1). At that time, Fort St. Frédéric and Fort Chambly were the major strongholds in a chain of posts protecting the approach to French Canada from British New York and New England by way of Lake Champlain and the Richelieu River. This valley was a major trade corridor (including the contraband trade in furs with the Iroquois and the Dutch traders at Albany), and its waterways offered a promising invasion route. Fort St. Frédéric, then the southernmost post of the chain, was constructed between 1734 and 1737, overlooking a narrows of Lake Champlain (Furness and Titus 1985:8–9; Fisher 1991:2–3; Roy 1946:20–40). The purpose of this post was to control the flow of traffic going up and down the lake through this narrows. Fort Chambly was built in 1711 at the Chambly Rapids on the Richelieu River to protect navigation further up the valley (Gélinas 1983). Montréal, of course, was one of the major towns in French Canada and the seat of one of its three regional governments (Trudel 1968:155–56). It was French Canada's commercial center, the staging area for the annual fur trading expeditions to the West, and a center for trade and diplomacy with the Native American tribes. For these reasons, a large proportion of the troops stationed in French Canada were garrisoned at Montréal, and the town had been fortified at an early date. At the time of Franquet's visit, it was a walled town, surrounded by stone ramparts built between 1717 and 1738 (Franquet 1889:118, 129; Lambert 1992:19–65; Robert 1994:38–41, 46–71).

Franquet submitted formal reports on the state of defenses at each of these fortifications, along with detailed plans of the existing structures and, in one case, a proposed extension. These plans are reproduced in figures 2.9, 2.10, and 2.11. Figure 2.9 shows the existing fortifications at Fort St. Frédéric, along with Franquet's proposed plan for an extension to the fort. The larger scale plan to the left in figure 2.9 shows the existing fortification, including the circuit walls and a massive redoubt. The redoubt is nestled into the irregular section of the walls at the bottom of the plan along the lakefront (Vachon 1985:144). To the right is Franquet's plan to expand the fort, stretching out from the existing circuit walls to a ravelin that would secure the commanding heights nearby (upper right part of the extension). Along the top, Franquet shows a cross-section of the proposed extension, including barracks within the area to be enclosed.

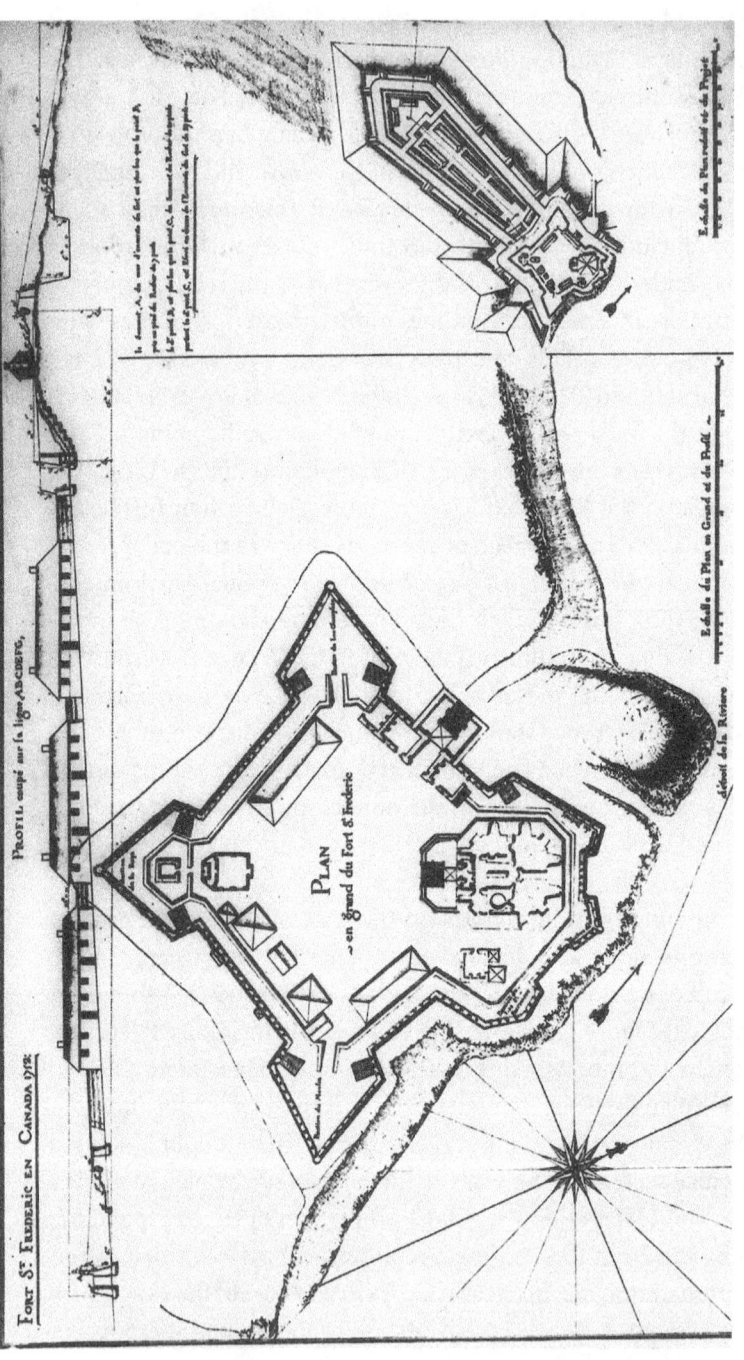

Figure 2.9. Franquet's plan of Fort St. Frédéric. *Left*: Existing fortification including the circuit walls and the redoubt. *Right*: Franquet's ground plan for extending the fort from the existing circuit walls to a ravelin that would secure the commanding heights nearby (upper right part of the extension). *Top*: Cross-section of the proposed extension including barracks within the area to be enclosed. (Louis Franquet, Plan du Fort Saint-Frédéric en Canada. Reproduction provided by the Library and Archives Canada, NMC 001950I; original held at the Bibliothèque National, Ministère de la Défense, Paris [fol. 210º]; used with permission of the Service Historique de la Défense, Ministère de la Défense, République Française.)

Figure 2.10 reproduces Franquet's plan of Fort Chambly. The plan shows the square fort, with its four corner bastions, at the top with the rapids of the "Rivière de Chambly" (more commonly referred to as the Chambly Rapids of the Richelieu River) to the left. Below the plan of the fort are explanatory notes about parts of the structure and Franquet's summary statement of the fort's defensive strength.

Finally, figure 2.11 reproduces Franquet's schematic plan of the fortifications at Montréal. The irregular wall, with thirteen bastions (including nine flat bastions), is shown in the plan at the top. The St. Lawrence River runs along the lengthy front at the bottom of the plan. Profiles of three sections of the wall are below the ground plan of the circuit wall. Franquet's plans and reports demonstrate that he discovered several departures from standard European practices in these fortifications. These departures included some features that were surprisingly reminiscent of medieval fortifications, an egregious violation of the structures about commanding heights, and even some instances in which careless design produced deficiencies in flanking defense. Franquet also found that none of these fortifications provided defense in depth sufficient to withstand artillery.

For the most part, Franquet found that the existing flanking defenses at these fortifications were adequate. At Fort St. Frédéric, the "circuit wall is composed of six bastions, flanked in all its parts" (Franquet 1889:164). Fort Chambly was "a perfect square with 4 bastions, of 28 *toises* on the exterior side. The curtain walls are 17 *toises*, the flanks 9 feet, and the faces [of the bastions] 5 *toises*, 3 feet." Franquet did not specifically state that the flanking defense at Chambly was adequate, but his report also calls it "the best [fort] that we have in Canada," a highly unlikely designation if he had identified any significant flanking issues there (Franquet 1889:169–70). As a point of comparison, the relative dimensions of the curtain walls, demi-gorges, and interior flanking angles at Fort Chambly compare fairly well with the proportions suggested by Le Blond's tables. Specifically, the scale on the plan suggests that a side of the interior polygon was about 20 toises, with demi-gorges of about 3 toises. This suggests a ratio of demi-gorge to interior side of about 1/7, fairly close to the 1/6 ratio for squares in le Blond's table (top table in figure 2.9). The interior flanking angles are harder to measure on the plan, but they seem to be somewhat more acute than the 13 degrees, 44 minutes suggested in Le Blond's table. Nevertheless, they were not so acute to prevent effective flanking of each bastion face from the flanks and faces of the neighboring bastions.

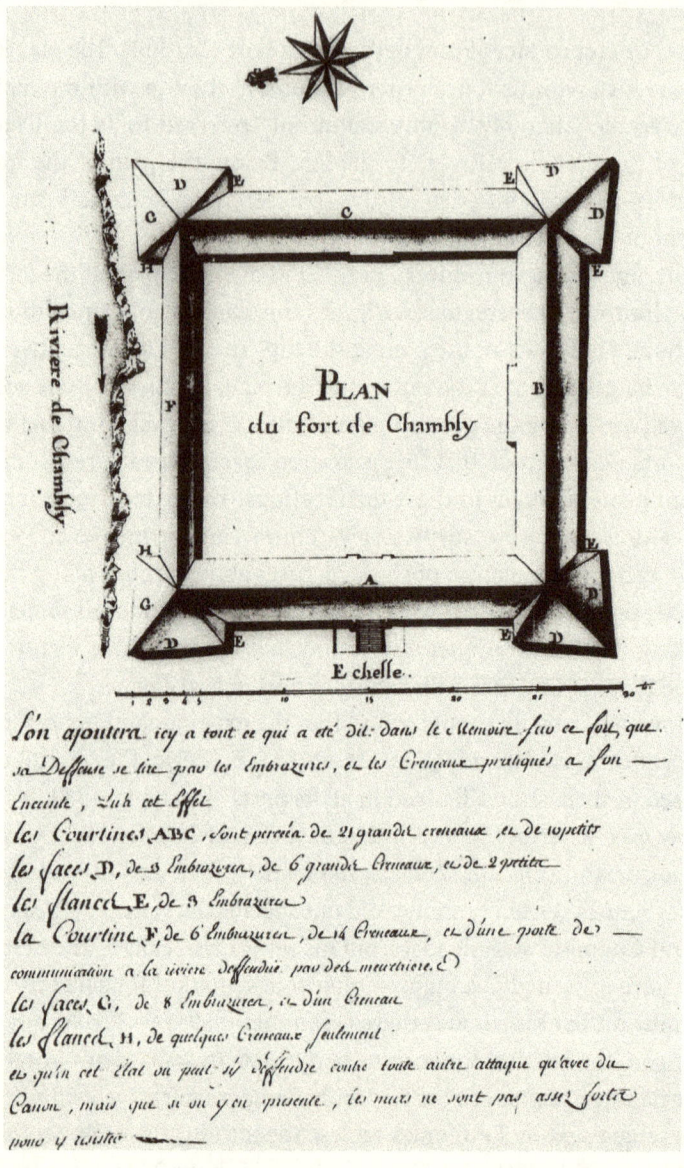

Figure 2.10. Franquet's plan of Fort Chambly. The plan shows the square fort, with its four corner bastions at the top with the rapids of the Rivière de Chambly to the left. Below the plan are explanatory notes about parts of the structure (e.g., "the curtain walls *ABC* are pierced with 21 large loopholes") and Franquet's summary statement of the fort's defensive strength (bottom three lines): "In this condition, it can be defended against any kind of attack other than with cannon, but if they produce some there, the walls are not strong enough to resist." (Louis Franquet, Plan du Fort de Chambly. Reproduction provided by the Library and Archives Canada, NMC 0002052; original held at the Bibliothéque National, Section Technique du Génie, Paris [fol. 210ᵉ]; used with permission of the Service Historique de l'Armée de Terre, Ministère de la Défense, République Française.)

At Montréal, however, Franquet identified some weaknesses in the flanking defense. As the plans indicate, Montréal was a more irregular fortification than Fort Chambly or Fort St. Frédéric. Chambly was a regular, almost perfect square. At Fort St. Frédéric, three fronts were fairly regular, while the fourth side was irregular to incorporate the redoubt within the walls and to accommodate the contours of the lakeshore. Montréal's irregularities were due in part to its position along the riverfront, which accounts for the elongated outline of the town and hence the wall erected around it. As was often the case with irregular fortifications, flat bastions were necessary in order to provide adequate flanking fire. In fact, Montréal's situation was a classic case in which flat bastions were necessary to provide adequate flanking. As Le Blond observed: "If the town is found to be located on the bank of a river, or its position compels giving a great length to one of its sides, such as 300 or 400 toises, a distance great enough so that the bastions locations at its ends cannot defend each other reciprocally, one divides it into two equal parts, and fortifies each part like the other sides of the circuit wall. The bastions placed in the middle of this line . . . are called *flat bastions*" (Le Blond 1756:339–40). As a result, 9 of Montréal's 13 bastions were flat bastions, and these flat bastions were located along three of its four fronts. The greatest need for flat bastions was, of course, along the two lengthier sides of the wall, the side along the riverfront and the parallel side facing the countryside.

While the use of flat bastions at Montréal was only to be expected, these bastions were not properly designed: "inspection of the plan reveals that its flanks are too small, the flanked angles too open, and that the section between the gate Y of the fort and the flanked angle of bastion 6 is not seen from any part." The wide angles and short flanks rendered the flanking defense generally weak at Montréal, but the problem was especially acute in one section along the riverfront, which could not be seen, and therefore could not be flanked, from any other part. The section to which Franquet referred can be located in figure 2.11. It begins on the right face of the second bastion from the right (the very wide bastion) along the riverfront, and runs to the point of the next bastion to the right. The angles formed by the faces of these bastions (flanked angles) were so wide that it was difficult to see the flanks and faces of the neighboring bastions or the stretch of curtain wall running between these bastions. It was therefore also difficult to deliver flanking fire on other sections of the wall from the faces of the bastions or to bring flanking fire to bear on those faces from other locations.

Franquet also noted that there were at Montréal some features of the

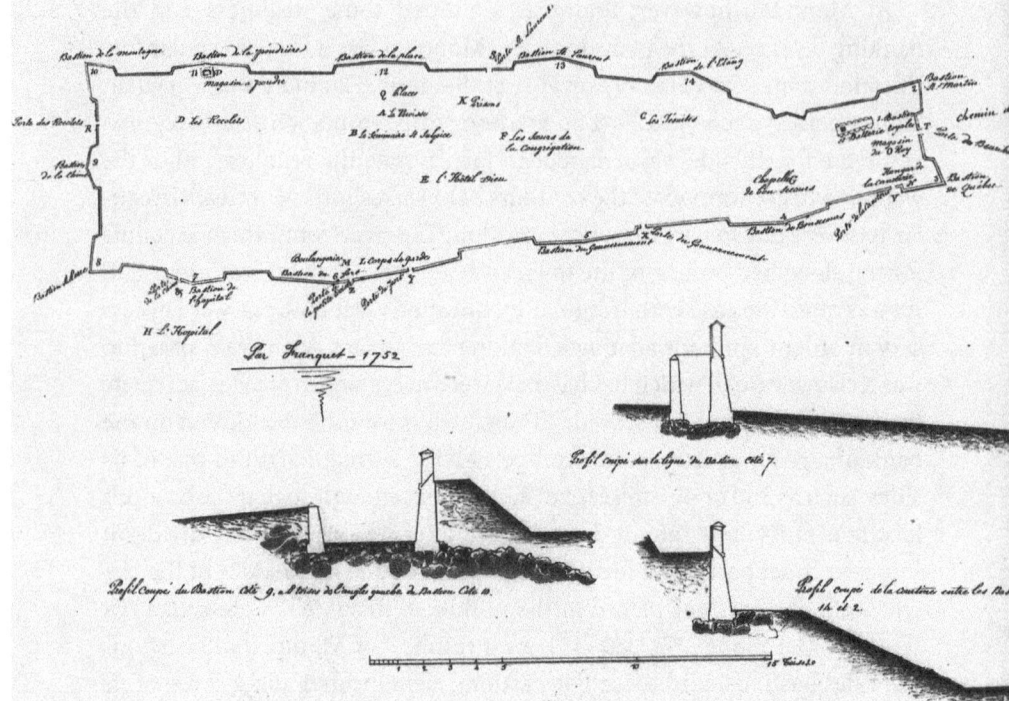

Figure 2.11. Franquet's schematic plan of the fortifications at Montréal. The irregular wall with 13 bastions (including 9 flat bastions) is shown in the plan at the top. The St. Lawrence River runs along the lengthy front at the bottom of the plan. Profiles of three sections of the wall are below: the riverfront (upper right of the three profiles); the stretch along the upper right (northwestern side) of the plan with the reentrant angles (lower right of the three profiles); and the short front on the left (southwestern side) of the plan (left of the three profiles). (Louis Franquet, Plan de l'enceinte de la ville de Montréal. Reproduction provided by the Library and Archives Canada, NMC 1490; original held at the Bibliothéque National, Section Technique du Génie, Paris [fol. 210ᵉ]; used with permission of the Service Historique de l'Armée de Terre, Ministère de la Défense, République Française.)

"the terrain to which it seems the fortification has been adapted," causing "alteration to some of its fronts." While these sections had adequate flanking, the section with the "break in its alignment could stand some improvement with regard to [its] angles" (Franquet 1889:117–18). The section to which Franquet referred is located at the upper right of the plan, where the terrain forced the curtain wall to bend inward. Two reentrant angles were constructed there to provide for flanking, along the lines suggested by Le Blond when he observed that reentrant angles can provide adequate flanking without resort to bastions along short fronts. However, Franquet determined in this case that alteration of the angles could have provided more effective flanking.

At Fort St. Frédéric, Franquet identified the redoubt as "the primary work of this fort." The redoubt had four stories and towered over the curtain walls. It housed a storehouse, armory, powder magazine, guard room, and the commandant's quarters. Its walls were "thick enough to withstand cannon," although in case of a siege cannon, shots penetrating the windows could eventually bring down the arches. The redoubt was also defended by moat and drawbridge. Towers were unusual in bastion fortifications, although Vauban had included bastion towers in a few of his fortresses (a feature not often copied by his many disciples). The Fort St. Frédéric redoubt also had a feature more commonly employed in medieval fortification: a machicoulis to defend against an enemy gaining access to the foot of the redoubt's walls (Franquet 1889:163, 168). Bélidor's widely used engineering dictionary contains the definition of a structure called a *redoute à machicoulis,* which matches the descriptions and plans that depict Fort St. Frédéric's primary work: "These are masonry redoubts, which have several stories, and whose upper story projects out from the wall of the redoubt for about a foot. In this projecting part, openings are used to expose the foot of the redoubt, which facilitates its defense" (Bélidor 1755:267). While use of a machicoulis was not absolutely unknown in the eighteenth century, it was certainly unusual. As Le Blond indicated, this structure was widely recognized to be obsolete in the era of artillery. A prominent English-language military dictionary nicely captured the archaic character of the term: "Machicoulis is an old word, sometimes applied to projections in old castles, and over gates of towns, left open above, to throw down stones, &c. on the approaching enemy" (Smith 1779:151). By the seventeenth and eighteenth centuries, use of the machicoulis was generally confined to "special circumstances such as coastal defense-towers where lightly armed attacks only were to be expected" (Fry 1984, 1:204). The inclusion of a machicoulis therefore suggests that, despite providing for walls in the redoubt thick enough to withstand some artillery, the engineers who designed Fort St. Frédéric were not deeply concerned about facing an artillery siege at that remote site.

Other aspects of Franquet's reports do in fact confirm that these fortifications were not designed to withstand sieges. At each of these fortifications, Franquet found that there was insufficient defensive depth to resist artillery. His comments read like a refrain:

- At Fort St. Frédéric, circuit wall was "too feeble for artillery and stronger than necessary against musketry; nevertheless, in this location it offers a defense that . . . requires some artillery to take it." (Franquet 1889:164)
- At Fort Chambly, "the height and . . . thickness [of the walls] are more than sufficient to resist any attack other than with cannon." In "this condition, it is attackable only with some cannon, and considering the difficulties which present themselves to the English in bringing some cannon there, it ought to be regarded as unassailable." (86, 169–70)
- At Montréal, "it is easy to see that this circuit wall . . . is feebly constructed, and that it is only able to resist against an attack undertaken by surprise or by escalade, and not at all against any attack with some cannon." (117)

Fort Chambly, Fort St. Frédéric, and even Montréal were considered too remote to be likely targets of European-style sieges. Defense against artillery was therefore dispensable, and relatively thin walls with few external works were an acceptable adaptation of the general principles to existing conditions.

The most egregious departure from the standard principles was at Fort St. Frédéric. Franquet's report took note of a commanding "height which is 27 feet higher at a distance of 99 *toises*," that exposed the fortification from the rear (*de revers*) within musket range of the fort. Franquet proposed to correct this "essential defect" with an advanced work, specifically a "redoubt or lunette to be placed there" in order to prevent an enemy from exploiting those heights. The lunette would be connected to the existing fort by a wall and communications trench. This extension would thus provide room for an expanded garrison, and greater capacity to shelter local settlers in case of emergency (Franquet 1889:164, 167). Franquet's plan, reproduced in figure 2.9, shows the ground plan of this proposed extension, as well as a cross-section. To the right is the ground plan, with the extension stretching out from the existing circuit walls to a ravelin that would secure the commanding heights nearby (upper right part of the extension). The cross-section, along the top of the plan, clearly shows how the existing wall (extreme left of the cross-section) was dominated by the nearby heights (right, including cross-section of the wall and ditch of the proposed ravelin). It also shows the new barracks that Franquet proposed in order to take advantage of the new area to be incorporated into the fortifications.

Franquet admitted that there was a major flaw in this proposal: "one can see, from inspection of the plan, that all the parts of the project flank each other," except that *"the two faces of the lunette have only a direct defense"* (emphasis added). However, he also noted that this was a "defect that would be reproached in any other terrain than here, where the utterly rocky quality of the ground takes away all the usual means of advancing." In other words, the soil was too rocky for the normal trenching operations of a siege to be conducted. Furthermore, "the people that the English could employ in a siege of this nature, being not at all accustomed to an attack of such works, would be confounded there" (Franquet 1889:167). Essentially Franquet had proposed to remedy an "essential defect," a blatant departure from one of the basic "maxims or principles of fortification," by deviating from another of these basic principles. And the justification turned on the assessment that the fort was unlikely to be subjected to the conduct of a European-style siege—or at least not an effectively conducted siege. Franquet did not state specifically why deviating from one of the basic principles of fortification was preferable to deviating from the other, but the reason was probably that even in the absence of artillery, musket fire from the heights could have wreaked havoc on the parts of the fort that were exposed from the rear by those heights.

Franquet's remarks, and the nature of his proposed solution to an "essential defect," provide a remarkable statement both of the extent to which the general principles of fortification were adapted to the North American context and the degree to which even a professional European engineer regarded some of these adaptations as acceptable. The clear assumption was that war was not conducted in Canada as it was done in Europe and that the defenses of the St. Lawrence and Richelieu valleys therefore needed only to be able to resist colonial militia, frontiersmen, and Native Americans. His assessments of the other fortifications that he inspected during the tour were similar. Even at Québec, Canada's "chief place," Franquet could only affirm that "the circuit wall around the Upper Town . . . is sufficient . . . due to its height and the thickness of its walls, against the kind of attack that could be conducted there." As with the other fortifications in Canada, Franquet apparently did not contemplate an artillery siege at the colony's "principal establishment . . . whose taking would bring about the loss of the entire country" (Franquet 1889:61, 119, 122–23, 201).

During the final campaigns of the Seven Years' War in 1759 and 1760, just a few years after Franquet's inspections, Fort St. Frédéric, Fort Chambly, and Montréal did face European armies. In 1759, an army under Jeffrey

Amherst advanced up Lake Champlain. Meanwhile, the British navy navigated down the St. Lawrence to bring James Wolfe's army to Québec. The goal was to overwhelm the defenses of French Canada by squeezing them between these two forces. Louis-Antoine Bougainville, aide-de-camp to the commanding French general, Montcalm, noted the change in the way that war was now conducted in North America:

> They never made war in Canada before 1755. To leave Montreal with a party, to go through the woods, to take a few scalps, to return at full speed once the blow was struck, that is what they called war, a campaign, success, victory. . . . Now war is conducted here on the European basis. Projects for the campaign, for armies, for artillery, for sieges, for battles. It no longer is a matter of making a raid, but of conquering or being conquered. (Bougainville 1964:252)

During the winter of 1758–59 Montcalm had dispatched Bougainville to report to the French court about conditions in New France. His reports included comments on the fortifications, including many of those inspected by Franquet. Bougainville's evaluations of the forts were entirely consistent with Franquet's, although the much harsher terms that he employed may reflect the new situation in which European-style sieges were an imminent prospect. He reported to the court that only Fort Niagara, guarding the portage between Lakes Erie and Ontario, "could hold out more than three weeks" against a good attack. "All these other dumps [*bicoques*] that are called forts are scarcely secure against a surprise attack." Fort St. Frédéric "is only a bad stone wall with an interior keep [*donjon*], commanded within musket range and in no condition to withstand two discharges of cannon." Fort Chambly "could not stop an enemy marching with only four pieces of cannon." Montréal and Québec were "no exceptions." Montréal was basically an "unfortified place," and Québec was "not a strong place." Québec could not withstand a siege: "if an enemy appears once at the foot of its walls, it will be necessary to capitulate" (Bougainville 1924:9–10, 15, 27, 31).

The results of the last campaigns were predictable. In the face of Amherst's advance, Fort St. Frédéric was abandoned after its imposing redoubt was blown up. At Québec, Montcalm arranged his defenses to keep the British army at a distance from the city, forcing Wolfe to spend weeks probing these defenses for an approach. When Wolfe surprised him by appearing on the Plains of Abraham outside the city's poorly fortified wall, Montcalm gave battle immediately. The town surrendered a few days after the defeat outside the walls. According to the standard modern account, the surrender was immediately motivated by a shortage of food, but the surviving French officers were also acutely aware of the inadequacy of the land defenses (Stacey 1959:28–33, 158). The next summer, Fort Chambly was abandoned without a fight, and Montréal quickly surrendered as three British armies converged outside the walls of the town. In no case did the French put their fortifications to the test for which they had not been designed (Lambert 1992:38–40).

Franquet's own role in the war had already come to an unhappy conclusion. After a trip to report to the French court in 1753, he returned to Louisbourg where he took up the position of director of fortifications, with the responsibility for preparing the fortress for the next war. His tenure at Louisbourg was controversial. There was a dispute with the governor over defensive strategy. The governor favored establishing a system of coastal redoubts in order to resist and repel an English landing. Franquet had proposed elaborate plans of outer works around the fortress's main walls in order to increase its strength against a regular siege (Fry 1984, 2:77–85). Urgent repairs to the existing structures were never carried out. Some contemporary observers accused him of lethargy in making the necessary preparations, which may have been due to a debilitating illness (McLennan 1918:197–98). A fellow officer at Louisbourg wrote that "the chief engineer was a man of war, loving good (all his actions were directed to that end), a gentleman and a good citizen; but unfortunately an illness which undermined his health had so weakened the body that the spirit of the man was lost, he had only moments" (Thorpe 1974:232).

In 1758, a British army under Jeffery Amherst executed a difficult amphibious landing and invested the fortress. The British artillery quickly inflicted severe damage on the dilapidated walls and bastions of the fort. Franquet was one of the last officers to hold out against the inevitable surrender as the British guns threatened to breach the walls. After the surrender he was paroled to France, where he was forced to defend his conduct at Louisbourg against criticism that he had failed to make adequate preparations and to respond effectively to the British siege. He retired to his family's estate in Condé, where he died in 1768 (Thorpe 1974:230–31).

3

Fort Prince George, South Carolina

MARSHALL W. WILLIAMS

Fort Prince George was a British frontier fort situated on the Keowee River in what is now Pickens County, South Carolina. It was located in the Keowee's flood plain, which became prime bottomland. The fort site was a few hundred yards above (north) Crow Creek's mouth. Downstream on the west side of the river was the Cherokee town of Keowee. Other Cherokee towns lay within fifteen miles. In the mid-eighteenth century, the valley and surrounding country were subjected to great turmoil as settlers, traders, and Indians vied for control of the valley's resources. The fort was built in 1753 and garrisoned by British regulars and American provincials until 1768, when the garrison was withdrawn and sent to New York and Boston. The fort then became a trading post until the land was purchased by William Tate for a plantation.

During its 15-year existence, Fort Prince George continually changed its appearance from the first construction until abandonment in 1768. There are periods during which there is virtually no documentary information; at other times descriptive material is almost overwhelming. The archaeological findings present a composite picture of the fort's occupation. Temporal construction interpretation is almost totally dependent on participant accounts. This report's focus is to present information concerning the archaeological findings as they relate to structures. The artifact catalogue and the faunal material have disappeared. The artifacts are curated at the South Carolina Institute of Archaeology and Anthropology, University of South Carolina, in Columbia.

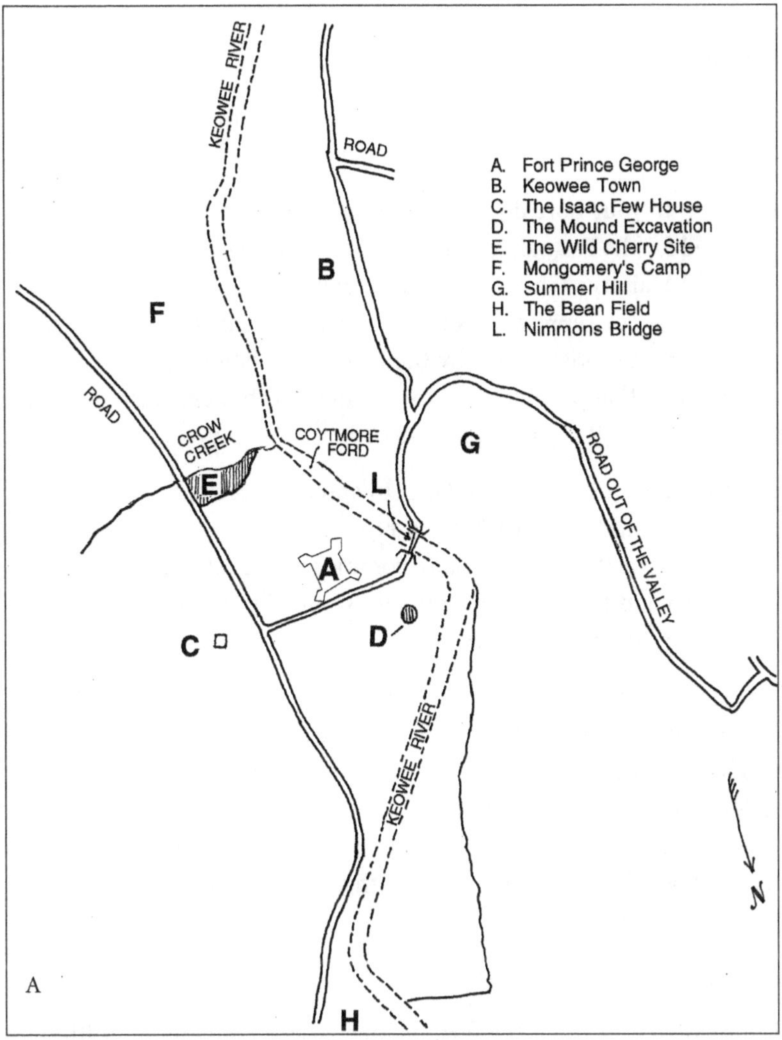

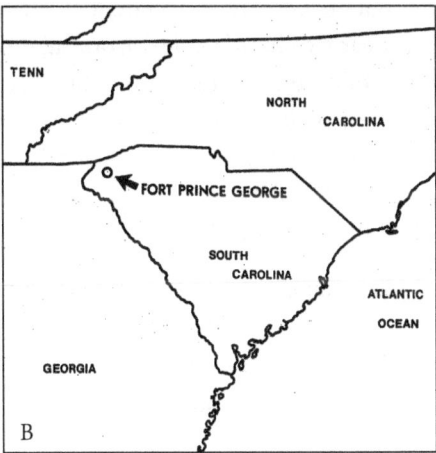

Figures 3.1a and 3.1b. Location of Fort Prince George in Pickens County, South Carolina. (South Carolina Institute of Archaeology and Anthropology.)

Fort History

The British government's decision to build a fort among the Cherokee Indians was first noted in a 9 June 1748 letter:

> Pursuant to your Lordship's Order of the 20th of last Month, we have prepared for the Draught of an Additional Instruction for James Glen, Esq., His Majesty's Governor of the Province of South Carolina, conformable to our representation to His Majesty dated 13th of August, 1747 upon a proposal made by the Cherokee Nation of Indians bordering upon that province that a Fort might be built & Garrisoned in their Country. (Privy Council 1748)

The letter went on to authorize Glen to enter into a treaty with the Cherokee for securing land on which to build the fort. Several years elapsed between authorization and actually commencing construction. In a letter from James Glen to the Privy Council, written "in the woods above two hundred miles from Charles town,"

> I propose to build a small Fort that I have been solicited to do for seven years past by the Indians. . . . Before the Council advised me to take this step they examined all the traders and they all agreed that unless it were built this Fall it would never be in the power of the Government to do it again for that all the Lower Town Indians declared that they would never plant more on this side of the Mountains unless it were built. (Glen 1754)

Governor Glen wrote the next year:

> I immediately laid out the fort, having carried instruments with me for that purpose. It is a square with regular bastions and four ravelins. It is near two hundred feet from salient angle to salient angle, and is made of earth taken from the ditch, secured with fascines and well-rammed, with a banquet on the inside for the men to stand on when they fire over the ravelins made with posts of Lightwood, which is very durable; they are ten feet in length, sharp points, three foot and a half in the ground. (Glen 1754)

Raymond Demere wrote to Governor Lyttelton, adding that "Fort Prince George was first erected by digging a Ditch two Feet wide at the Top, and five wide at the Bottom [sic], and five Feet deep, and a Parapet or Breast Work raised five Feet high, ten Feet wide at the Bottom, and five Feet at Top, and a Banquet, or Foot Bank on the outside [sic] of the Parapet" (Demere 1756). Aside from the transposition of top and bottom, outside and inside, Demere's account is relatively straight forward as seen by a soldier's comment that the "ramparts are daily falling with the least rain and has already rendered the ditch capable of being leaped over by Indian children who with ease also climb the ramparts at any part" (Soldier 1756:312).

The "ramparts" were apparently the parapet created by throwing dirt from the ditch excavation inside the fort's trace. Glen's stockade posts were put into the top of the "well-rammed" 5 ft. high parapet to a depth of 3 ft. In other words, the stockade was set into loose earth, and each time it rained, the walls would collapse as the soil washed back into the ditch. Demere described attempts to repair and strengthen the parapet, noting that "as additional strength to the Gateway, the Bridge being fallen down, there is one built with rails along the same, and the inside of the fort is repairing with Pickets and Fascines, and four Swivels being mounted one in each Bastion" (Demere 1756).

In 1757, a major reconstruction took place at the instigation of then commander Lachlan Shaw. Shaw's 19 October 1757 letter provides a good description of the fort:

> The large stockades have been planted above ten days, and the Lynings will be finished in two days. I have a very strong gate framed ready to put up tomorrow, and think it intirely unnecessary to have a Draw Bridge as I will make the gate the strongest part of the fort besides I had not people proper to make a Draw Bridge. However, if yr. Excalencie thinks it absolutely necessary it may be done yet when the Carpenters and proper materials arive here. I have been very hardly put to it for Rum for without Rum there could be no worke I was obliged at last to give them what I had for my own use for ther is nothing arrived of what the Commissary sent from Charles Town, either Rum, tools, or materials.

The following is a description of the fort when finished:

> The whole works stocaded with large puncheons 16 foot long four foot in the ground and 8 foot above the parapet which covers the inside of the fort intirely from the Neighboring Hills the crevices between the stocades covered with smaller pieces of wood made fitting for them and nail'd to the stocades with large Iron Spickes, the loop holes in the Courtains [curtains] and faces of the Bastions in every Sise [six]

feet and in the Shoulders of the Bastions in every three foot.... Four Swivels mounted on four large oak trees [posts] in the middle of the four Bastions, the Swivels raised two foot above the top of the Stokades so that they can bear upon anything that is without the fort and within ther Reach even to the bottom of the ditches along the Courtains. Scafolds 12 feet square erected on four strong suporters round the Swivel Stockes for the men that works the Swivel and a Centurie [sentry] to stand upon. Two Swivels on Iron Carriages placed oposite to the Gates.... The Gates will be made very strong with two inch plank doubled and Strong oak Stands and Stiles, with a stage inside for a Centurie. (Shaw 1757)

Nearly a year later, the fort had a new commander, Lachlan Mackintosh. He also reported to Governor Lyttelton concerning the status of Fort Prince George. On 21 August 1758, he wrote:

We are at a great loss for Barracks to house the men for the old command had no other than little Hutts they had build for themselves. I have given [them] [some newly arrived troops] . . . of these little houses and two tents I had here, and crowded our own people with the rest.... I intend with your Excellency's consent to build a long Barrack on Each side of the fort that may contain the command, but these houses cannot be Build but slightly by Reason we have Neither Horses nor Waggons to carry us Home Timmer [timber] and therefore we must build them of Clapboards and in the light manner as the men must carry home the wood. (Mackintosh 1758a)

Less than a month later, on 18 September, Mackintosh wrote Lyttelton again:

I have . . . build two long Houses, one on Each side of the fort Each House divided into three rooms and Every rooms holds well ten men so that both Houses Holds sixty Men and a House at each End of the Fort Holds Twenty Men Each I have been obliged to buy from the Traders here a great Quantity of Nails for the Houses I have sunk the well 12 feet deeper than it was and now have good water. What we want now Most of all is a Magazine and that we cannot build without a Waggon to carry us home Stone. (Mackintosh 1758b)

On 16 October, Mackintosh informed Lyttelton that "at last I have got a good Strong Magazine build the length of it is 15 feet the Breadth 6 1/2 feet the walls 18 inches thick and cover't all over with Large Sclat [slate] with a Double Doors and two locks" (Mackintosh 1758c).

On 9 April 1759, a new commander, Lt. Richard Coytmore, arrived. Coytmore reported that he "found this fort in good repair and Barracks within it lately built by Ens. Mackintosh sufficient for the command; a good magazine, a well, and centry [sentry] boxes, also the Provisions, Ammunition, and [assorted] Presents & I gave Ens. Mackintosh Receipt for them" (Coytmore 1759a). Among the items Coytmore receipted were six swivel guns with two iron carriages, twelve brick layer's trowels, a whipsaw, handsaws, crosscut saws, broad axes, adz, four chains for a drawbridge, two bags of nails, and eighty spikes. This list of South Carolina property provides an indication of the tools moved to the frontier for fort construction. Later in the summer Coytmore decided to lower the swivel gun positions, and on 3 August wrote that "as the swivel guns are mounted so high above the stockades as to be of very little service if required, I am going to put them on carriages and make a small platform in every Bastion" (Coytmore 1759b).

Feelings between the British and Cherokee were heating up, and it was affecting the fort and the garrison. On 21 November 1759, Coytmore wrote Lyttelton that he intended "to pull down all the houses without the fort, and everyone to lie within, which though attended with many inconveniences I am obliged to guard against the worst" (Coytmore 1759c). In January 1760, Coytmore issued an order to pull down any remaining houses outside the fort and use them for firewood. On 28 January, he ordered spikes driven into the tops of the stockade pickets. Bad weather brought heavy rains and by the end of January the well collapsed, causing a water crisis.

On 16 February, Cherokee warriors ambushed Coytmore and two men; Coytmore was mortally wounded. Cherokee hostages were then put to death, and one soldier was killed in the ensuing fray. The garrison was now under siege and ventured out at their peril. On 21 February, the two remaining officers, Miln and Bell, wrote Lyttelton that they might have to pull down the barracks for firewood. On 22 February, the Indians started firing from the hills, putting holes in the barrack roofs. On 25 February, Coytmore died of his chest wound. The post's new commander, Ens. Alexander Miln, wrote Lyttelton on 28 February that he had "taken all the loose boards I could find about the fort and made blinds to shelter the sentries and men as they walk the curtain lines . . . not having a port hole [through which to fire the cannons at Keowee Town] I took a proper observation on every bastion and found at the corner of one it would answer" (Miln 1760).

Over the summer of 1760, the siege continued sporadically. In September, a desperate soldier stationed at the fort sent a letter to Charles Town that was published in the *South Carolina Gazette:*

> Indians are come down to the Lower Towns, having actually blockaded and pent us up ling a parcel of cattle for the slaughter. . . . I may bid you and my friends an Eternal Adieu. . . . As I came hither to serve my king and Country, . . . I shall only regret that I can serve them no longer. . . . For God's sake! What are they about? . . . Mr. Milne, our commanding officer, seems resolved to defend [the post] to the last extremity or perish with it.

A relief force under James Montgomery came and went, leaving the situation no better than before. In the spring of 1761, an army under Col. James Grant came into the Cherokee country. Grant's soldiers brought a great many wagons full of supplies and provisions, determined that the Cherokee would be punished severely. He left 150 wagons at Fort Prince George because they could not be taken into the mountains. To secure them, he built a "corral" on the north side of the fort. Maj. Alexander Moneypenny left an account of this "wagon cover" in his 1761 journal.

Grant virtually rebuilt Fort Prince George during his stay. John Laurens, a soldier at the time, recorded that "New barracks, new Store Houses, and a New Well, Magazine" were built (Laurens 1763). At the end of the Cherokee War, there is another gap in specific evidence about the fort. The garrison was withdrawn in 1768. During a 1776 visit, William Bartram mentioned a trading post at the site, but it bore no resemblance to a fort. After the Revolution, the site went under cultivation, which continued until the mid-1960s.

The Archaeological Excavations

Excavation at Fort Prince George began late in 1966. Based on a local tradition that placed the fort on the bottomlands near Nimmons Bridge, John Combes put down his first test trenches. At least one was sited directly on the fort ditch adjoining the northeast bastion. Just beside the ditch was a second ditch that turned out to be the palisade trench. The mottled soil contrasted with surrounding fill, making it a simple matter to follow the palisade trench and obtain a complete outline of the fort in minimal time. The palisade trench was not excavated but simply exposed to outline the fort's trace. Work was terminated with the onset of winter.

In the spring of 1967, after a grader was used to remove the topmost six or seven inches of soil, the outer ditch was sectioned in two places and the well was investigated to a depth of 8 ft. In August, the plow zone was removed from the westernmost 10 ft. of the fort, working inward from the inner palisade ditch with 10 ft. sq. excavation units. The lower plow zone was removed by hand, and then the features were examined. The plow zone was not screened, but feature fill was passed through a half-inch screen.

The first features appeared as post molds with postholes for the west barracks. Each post had been set into the ground by first digging a larger hole, then placing the post in the hole against one edge and raising it. Soil was then packed around the post.

Work continued, moving eastward from the southwestern corner (but not including the southwest bastion). By October, the plow zone was removed from half the fort. It was then, just east of the gate, that a large area of rock was noted. After soil removal, the rock assumed the shape of a nearly square house. A wall of neatly laid rock was on the periphery; within the wall was a jumble of stone.

Exposing, drawing, and photographing this rock feature consumed a great deal of time. It seemed evident that it was a stone-lined cellar, one that had been filled up with rock. This was interpreted as having been filled by some early civilian occupant of the fort site who cleared the area by filling the cellar with stone. One stone removed from the northwest corner had the date 1761 inscribed on it. Below the 1761 date were the initials "H S" and the date 1770. No other inscriptions were found.

Remnants of charred planks were present on the floor at the bottom of the cellar, suggesting that the house had burned. These were very fragile, and they crumbled at the slightest touch. The stains ran north-south and were mixed with many nails, musket parts, and other iron concretions. A sledgehammer, later stolen by raiding vandals and pothunters, was uncovered along with other artifacts in the cellar including an iron hatchet, greenstone Indian pipe, and aboriginal ceramic sherds.

After excavating the cellar, more plow zone was removed by shovel schnitting. Post molds were showing up regularly, but there was no discernible pattern. After the molds had "aged," it became apparent that there were two buildings: the west barracks and the small building to the left of the gate. Shoveling also revealed nails, ceramics, musket balls (in both trade and Brown Bess bore sizes), buttons, and kaolin pipe fragments.

Around the well there was a search for any superstructure, but nothing was identified. It was established that a rock lining had been constructed

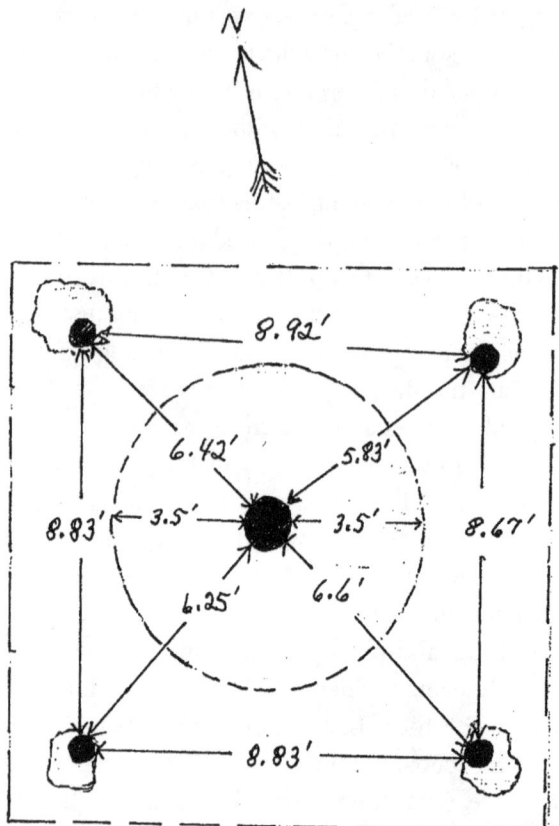

Figure 3.2. Configuration of the gun platform in the northwest bastion. Distances are from center to center of post molds. The central post was 12 inches in diameter, and the gun was mounted on this. The dotted circular line represents the post excavation. The outer dotted line is an estimate of the size of the gun platform, which was 12 ft. square. Scale: 1 in. = 3 ft. (South Carolina Institute of Archaeology and Anthropology.)

inside the well hole and then backfilled. South of the well, there was an iron bar grating. After more excavation, a square wooden pipe was discovered that ran from the fort ditch to this grating. It appears that the pipe was used to dispose of excess water from the well or as a drain for the central part of the fort. The pipe was 10 in. sq. and made of 2 in. thick planks. The pipe had filled with sand, and there were some indications than an earlier pipe had been replaced by this larger one.

The shape of the bastions was surprising. The actual forms differed rather dramatically from historical accounts. Some nineteenth-century historians called the bastions square when in reality they were diamond shaped. Excavation drawings for the northwest bastion corresponded well with the 1758 description (Mackintosh 1758b), even to the depth of the 12-inch diameter swivel gun post, placed 4 ft. into the ground. There was also a 12 ft. sq. platform mounted on four support posts, positioned high enough when first built to allow firing over the stockade pickets.

The southwestern bastion was unique in another respect—a human burial was found at its entrance. It was thought at the time that this was the grave of Lt. Richard Coytmore, the fort commander who was mortally wounded in a riverside ambush on 16 February 1760. There were no grave goods and no evidence of a coffin, but the body was laid out very neatly with the hands folded across the lower abdomen. The man was tall; the grave measured 6.5 ft. in length and the corpse was still forced into the grave. The incisors were not shovel-shaped, lessening the probability that it was an American Indian.

A second burial was found just to the right of the gate, between the rock cellar and south curtain. The skeletons were incomplete, but it was obvious that there were three individuals in the same pit, all seemingly tossed in with little care. It is possible that these were three hostages killed by Coytmore's soldiers after Coytmore was wounded.

The southwestern bastion was unique in another way: there were several grave-sized rectangular holes. Before excavation they resembled burials, but there was nothing in them. The sides of the holes were vertical, the corners square. It is possible they were dug as graves but never used.

The area between the northern end of the western barracks and the gorge of the northwestern bastion was free of features. It is possible the powder magazine was here because the rest of the fort interior was so cluttered with structures there was no room for the magazine.

A building against the north curtain wall posed interpretive problems about its use. The eastern end had a large stone chimney with its base still in situ. During excavation, a great deal of bone and many kitchen-related artifacts were found. Three post molds were found in front of this building. One was aligned opposite each end of the building, and one was centered between the other two. These may have been flagpoles, and if so, this building may have been the officers' quarters.

The gate to the fort was centered in the south curtain wall. In the 1758 rebuilding, it was described as "the strongest part of the fort," with "strong stands and stiles." The gate itself was made of "two inch plank, doubled." The gate was about 9 ft. wide, much too wide for a single gate, therefore, there were possibly two 4.5 ft. gate segments; references to "the gates" imply

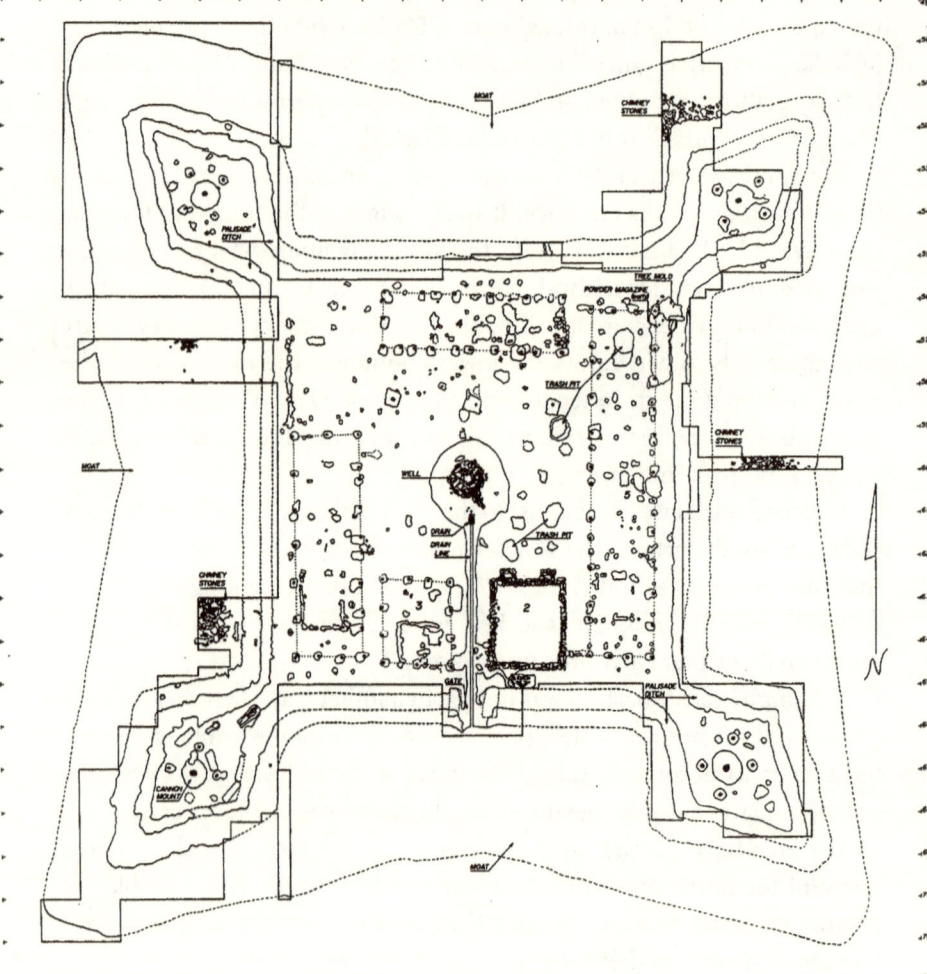

Figure 3.3. Composite map of the excavations at Fort Prince George. (Institute of Archaeology and Anthropology, University of South Carolina.)

that it was a double gate. An associated burned area represented a fire where wood with nails may have been burned.

The last building excavated was the east barracks, and it was the most perplexing. Post molds kept appearing. The building stretched 80 ft., almost the entire east side of the fort. It was difficult to believe a building this long was erected, but yet it was there. In the Moneypenny account, there is a description of such a building, built by Grant on the northern side of the fort during 1761.

There was a large, irregular feature in the east barracks that predated the building. It was partially excavated, and some squarish black features were noted at the north end's bottom. A sample of this material was found to be composed of nitrogen, oxygen, sulfur, and carbon. This suggests that the black material was gunpowder and that the irregular feature was a subterranean powder magazine.

Several large trash pits were found in the fort. Their contents were largely food bone. They were carefully excavated but apparently not analyzed.

An effort was made to deepen the well excavation using a winch and bucket. This operation was terminated when water entered the well faster than it could be taken out. The well had been filled with rock, and the walls were well laid rock. Grant had dug this well in the 1761 rebuilding. In January 1760, the old well collapsed, apparently because it did not have rock-shored walls.

All artifacts were located by 10 ft. grid square references. Artifacts from features were recorded by reference to feature number. An artifact catalogue was maintained that was left at SCIAA when the principal investigator, John Combes, departed.

The Buildings

Archaeological evidence of five buildings was found inside the fort. These were built by inserting posts into the ground and using them to support a framework. Based on the 1758 Mackintosh letter, four structures were erected: "two long Houses one in each side of the fort Each House divided into three rooms and Every room holds well ten men so that both Houses holds sixty men and a House at each End of the Fort Holds twenty Men" (Mackintosh 1758b). In 1761, Grant built new barracks (Laurens 1761).

Building Number 1 (West Barracks)

Whether the post molds for the buildings were from the 1758 or 1761 construction phases cannot be stated with certainty. The spacing of posts in the west barracks certainly matches a building divided into three rooms as described by Mackintosh (1758b). The other buildings similarly used 3 ft. spacing for probable doors as well. There were no false post molds to confuse the issue, so the posts seemingly represent a single building. The side of the West Barracks facing east (toward the parade) shows three narrower gaps (two of 3.58 ft., one of 3.16 ft.). These are in the centers of wider spaced

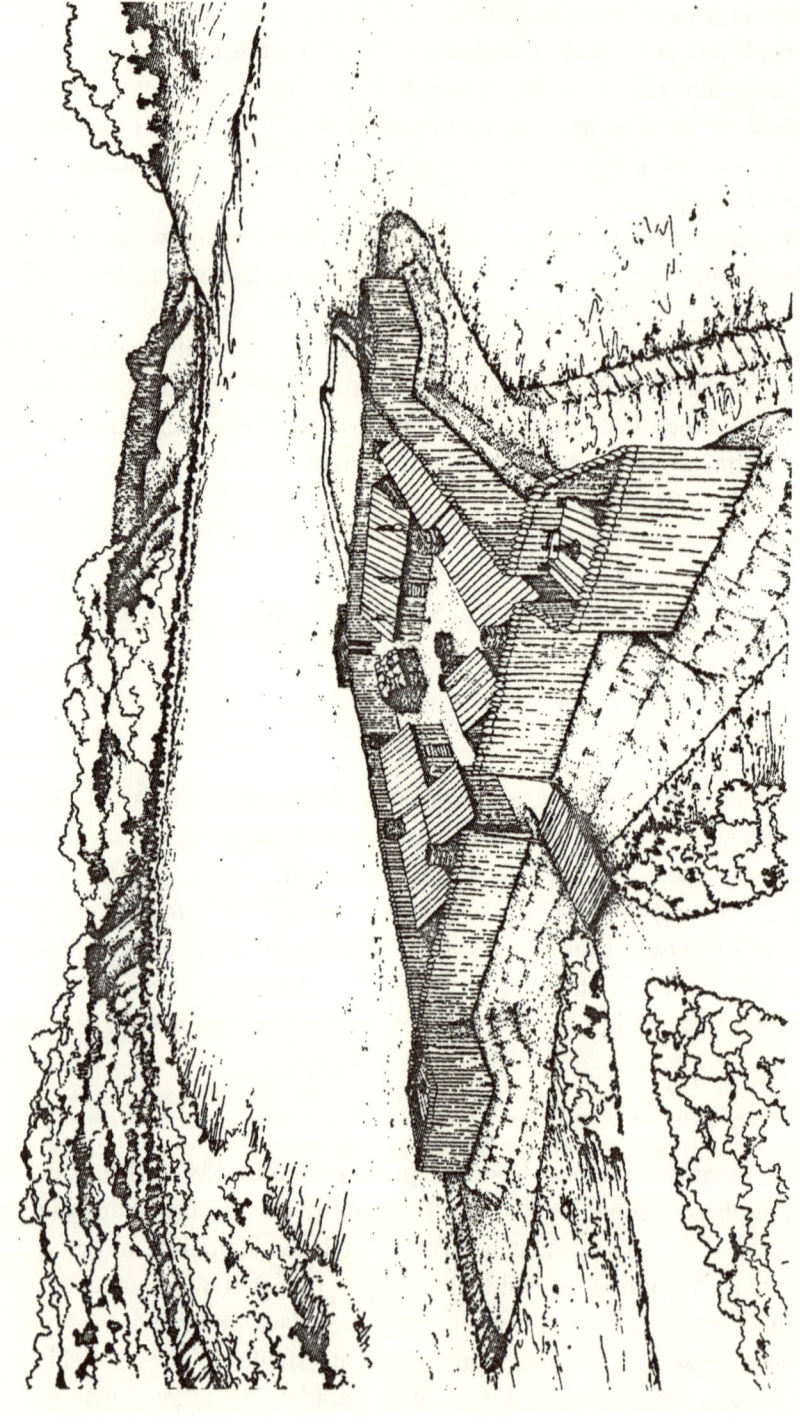

Figure 3.4. A student-drawn conception of Fort Prince George based on excavation data. (Institute of Archaeology and Anthropology, University of South Carolina.)

posts and almost certainly represent door openings. Thus, in this building, partitions placed at the fourth and seventh posts from the south end would provide three rooms approximately 16 ft. deep and 17 ft. wide. If the dividing walls were fairly thick, each room would be 16 ft. sq.

Building Number 2 (1761?)

This building was thought to have been erected by Grant in 1761. It is difficult to tell whether or not the house was stone or the stone represented the foundation. Two offsets on the parade side of the building have been interpreted as chimney bases. In the bottom of the western chimney base, an iron trade axe, a greenstone American Indian–style pipe, and the remains of a pewter vessel were found. The stone dated 1761 was found in the northwest corner of the cellar adjacent to the western offset. A large American Indian ceramic vessel was found in the southeastern corner. The cellar measured 3.8 ft. deep with a dirt floor. A cache of rocks at the southeastern corner hinted that there might have been a stairway into the cellar at this point.

In 1761, Col. James Grant built new barracks in the fort and almost certainly built the rock cellar house. The other structures were built on posts in the ground. While Grant may have built them, they seem to fit the Mackintosh period (1758b) better. The post molds found had not been pulled from the ground, and in some cases wood powder and bark were still present. Every building had some posts in perfect position for building, and there appeared to be no rebuilding. If the posts represent Mackintosh's structures, then Grant may have used stone pillars as footings for his house.

Building Number 3 (South Building)

Mackintosh indicated that he sited a house for twenty men at the south end of the fort, but no structure was found. Instead, there was a small structure designated Building 3. A path from the gate ran between Building 3 and Building 2. It is possible that Building 3 is the western end of an earlier structure and that Building 2 occupied what was the east end of the house. Building 4, the north building, was 45 ft. long. The 19.25 ft. of the cellar house, the 9 ft. pathway between buildings 2 and 3, and the 16.9 ft. Building 3 total 45 ft. There was also a pair of post molds on the side of Building 3, which, if they represented a door, opened onto the fort's parade.

Building Number 4 (North Building)

The "house at each end of the fort" in Mackintosh's letter (1758b) refers to buildings at the north and south sides. Building Number 4, the northern building, may have served as an officers' quarters and as post headquarters, since what are probably flagpoles were mounted in front of the building. These three post molds were smaller than the typical building posts and were mounted about 12 ft. in front of the building with regular spacing. A good number of kitchen artifacts were found during excavation, which caused it to be dubbed the "mess hall." This could have been true, as sometimes the building's use changed. At the east end of the house was a large chimney base, offset from the center. It was conjectured that it was offset so that a door could be set next to the fireplace, a common feature in early nineteenth-century houses.

Building Number 5 (East Barracks)

This structure initially caused a problem in interpretation because, as excavation proceeded, no posts to close off the north end were found. From the southern end, the posts seemed to indicate that it was similar to the West Barracks (Building 1). When no interior posts were found to end the building at the 52 ft. mark, excavation continued northward until an exterior wall was found 29 ft. farther along. This distance represents a structure some 80 ft. long and left only 10 to 12 ft. between the ends of the building and the curtain walls.

Fort Defenses

The Stockade

Here the terms *stockade* and *palisade* have been used interchangeably, as they are often used in contemporary documents in a similar fashion. Both denote a fence around the fort made of vertical logs, the purpose of which was to keep out intruders. The formal military distinction is that a palisade has gaps between the upright timbers whereas stockade timbers abut each other (Simes 1768; Robinson 1977:204–205). A curtain is the connecting link between two bastions. The first stockade was built in 1753 by Governor Glen, who apparently erected pine posts in back dirt from the moat ditch (Glen 1754). This wall fell down due to rain. The parapet washed back into the ditch, and the posts fell over. In 1757, Lachlan Shaw built a more substantial stockade, using 16 ft. long "puncheons." He planted each post 4 ft. into the ground (Shaw 1757). Since the stockade showed evidence of banquette supporting posts, one was present. Whether it was built in 1757 or added by Mackintosh (1758b) or Coytmore (1759c) is difficult to state. Shaw says the stockade was "8 foot above the parapet" (Shaw 1757). If the parapet used earth from the stockade trench (2.5 to 3 ft. wide, 4 ft. deep), the parapet would have been 4 ft. high inside the wall with the banquette (firing step) placed on the parapet.

Shaw cut out smaller timbers to cover spaces between the stockade posts and nailed them to the posts with large spikes. He cut loopholes at 6 ft. intervals in the curtains and bastion faces and at 3 ft. intervals in the bastion shoulders. These additional refinements would not be seen in the archeological record.

The Gate

The only real, nonarchaeological data on the gate is from the 1757 Shaw letter. He described the "gates" as being very strong, with two-inch planks doubled to make it a bulletproof 4 in. thick. He also described making strong oak "stands and stiles" as the supports and braces for the gates (Shaw 1757). The archaeological data suggest that the gates may have been about 9.5 ft. wide, so there would have been two doors, each 4.25 ft. wide. If pine was used, then each gate would have weighed about 675 pounds. There was no other evidence for a gate elsewhere.

The Swivel Guns and Mounts

Shaw is also the authority for the guns mounted in each bastion. He is explicit about how he mounted the swivels on four large oaks in the middle of each bastion. The gun support posts extended 2 ft. above the stockade "so they can bear upon anything that is without the fort and with Reach even to the bottoms of the ditches along the courtains [sic]" (Shaw 1757). The firing platforms were 12 ft. sq. around the swivel gun post. Mackintosh wanted iron bands to fasten around the gun posts to keep them from splitting. In 1759, Coytmore noted that the swivels were mounted too high and that he was going to mount them on carriages set on small platforms in each bastion. This probably resulted in cutting embrasures for the guns to fire along the curtain walls, as Alexander Miln (1760) stated that he cut a "Porthole" in the corner of a bastion so they could fire at Keowee Town.

The Powder Magazine

There was no archeological evidence for the powder magazine built in August and September 1758 (Mackintosh 1758c). This was described as 15 ft. long, 6.5 ft. deep with walls 18 in. thick and covered with "slate," the locally abundant schist, which has a fairly good horizontal cleavage. Since the fort was so full of other buildings, there was only one place it could have been put: the north end of Building 1. This location placed the magazine between Building 1 and the entrance to the northwest bastion. No post molds or any other features were found in this area.

The Well

A well is mentioned a few times in contemporary documents. Mackintosh mentioned in his 18 September 1758 letter that he had sunk the well 12 ft. deeper (Mackintosh 1758b). Coytmore noted that the well fell in during January 1760 (Coytmore 1760). Grant dug the well out as part of his rebuilding effort and installed the rock lining. During the archaeological project, the well was dug out to 14 ft., but the inrush of water was too great to continue.

Archaeological excavation at Fort Prince George ended in early 1968. The work had exposed much of the fort, allowing suggestions about use, changes over time, and linking structures with specific construction episodes mentioned in the documentary sources. Archaeology expanded information about the post to the point that a fairly accurate model could be built. Once the site was flooded, this model served as a three-dimensional image of what the post looked like for those who would later study the site and its garrison. The Keowee River covered the site on 12 May 1968.

Note

This chapter is an edited summary version of "A Memoir of the Archaeological Excavation of Fort Prince George, Pickens County, South Carolina," by Marshall W. Williams, published by the South Carolina Institute of Archaeology and Anthropology as Research Manuscript Series #226. A digitized version of the original is available from the South Carolina Institute of Archaeology and Anthropology. The author and editors gratefully acknowledge the generosity of the South Carolina Institute of Archaeology and Anthropology in allowing this abstracted report to be published here.

4

Fort Loudoun, Tennessee

Defensive Features and Artifactual Remains

CARL KUTTRUFF

Fort Loudoun, Tennessee, was one of many French and Indian War fortifications constructed and occupied in the mid-eighteenth century. It was the westernmost of a series of southern British forts, including Fort Ninety-Six and Fort Prince George, extending from Charleston, South Carolina, to the Overhill Cherokee homeland west of the Appalachian Mountains. Fort Loudoun is located on what was the Little Tennessee River (now Fort Loudoun Lake), near present-day Vonore, Tennessee. This chapter provides a brief history of the installation, abstracted from Kuttruff (2007) and Kelley (1961a, 1961b), an archaeological summary, and a description of the defensive works. The refuse disposal patterns at Fort Loudoun and the Fort Loudoun artifact assemblage are considered in terms of Stanley South's Frontier/Architecture Pattern (South 1977). Suggestions are made for possible modifications of that pattern, especially when applied to fortifications.

History

After years of discussion between the government of South Carolina, the Cherokee Indians, and the Board of Trade in England, construction finally began on 5 October 1756 and was essentially completed by 30 July 1757. The British needed a fort west of the Appalachians to deter French encroachment from Fort Toulouse, at modern-day Wetumpka, Alabama (Thomas 1929, 1959, 1960a, 1960b; Heldman 1973; Waselkov 1984; Waselkov, Wood, and Herbert 1982), and from Fort Massac on the Ohio River in what is now southern Illinois (Bailey 1966:2; Fortier 1969; Babson 1968:28–31; Rackerby 1971). A permanent British installation would also solidify the sometimes tenuous alliance with the Overhill Cherokee (that portion of the Cherokee

Nation located in the Little Tennessee River valley) and serve as a place for recruiting them to fight against the French. In turn, the Overhill Cherokee wanted the fort built as a refuge for their women and children while warriors were away fighting with British expeditions against the French and as a center for obtaining trade goods.

Two companies of South Carolina provincial militia and one company of British regulars, commanded by Capt. Raymond Demere, were sent to build the fort. John William Gerard DeBrahm, an engineer in South Carolina's service, placed the fort on a narrow ridge adjacent to the Little Tennessee River and supervised initial construction (De Vorsey 1971). Provincial militiamen erected the fort, while regular troops provided garrison duty. DeBrahm's fort was planned with an outer work consisting of a ditch and earthen parapet. Inside this perimeter was to have been a square log palisade with four bastions (figure 4.1).

After DeBrahm departed at the end of 1756, Captain Demere quickly abandoned DeBrahm's initial concept. The palisade was taken down and placed against the inside of the earthen parapet. The original plans had called for a hornwork on the river side of the fort, and although this was begun in the autumn of 1756, work halted in January 1757 (Hamer 1925; Kelley 1961a; McDowell 1970). Other structures within the fort, known from contemporary documentation and archaeology, included gun platforms in all four bastions, houses and barracks for officers and men, storehouses, a blacksmith's shop, powder magazine and guardhouse, and Officer of the Day's quarters (Kuttruff 2007).

In August 1757, Capt. Paul Demere replaced his brother as commander, and the two companies of provincial militia were disbanded. Thereafter one company of British regulars manned the fort, with occasional reinforcements. Relations with the Cherokee remained relatively friendly and mutually beneficial until the autumn of 1759. Subsequently they deteriorated, and the Cherokee began harassing the garrisons at Fort Loudoun and Fort Prince George. Throughout the spring and summer of 1760, the siege of Fort Loudoun was tightened to the point where the garrison faced starvation.

Demere surrendered to the Cherokee in early August 1760. The garrison abandoned the fort the morning of August 9. The following morning, the troops were ambushed by the Cherokee about 15 miles from the fort. Paul Demere and all officers except John Stuart were killed, along with 20 to 30 men. A few of the men escaped, but the rest were captured and taken to various Cherokee towns. In November 1760, about 10 captives were ransomed

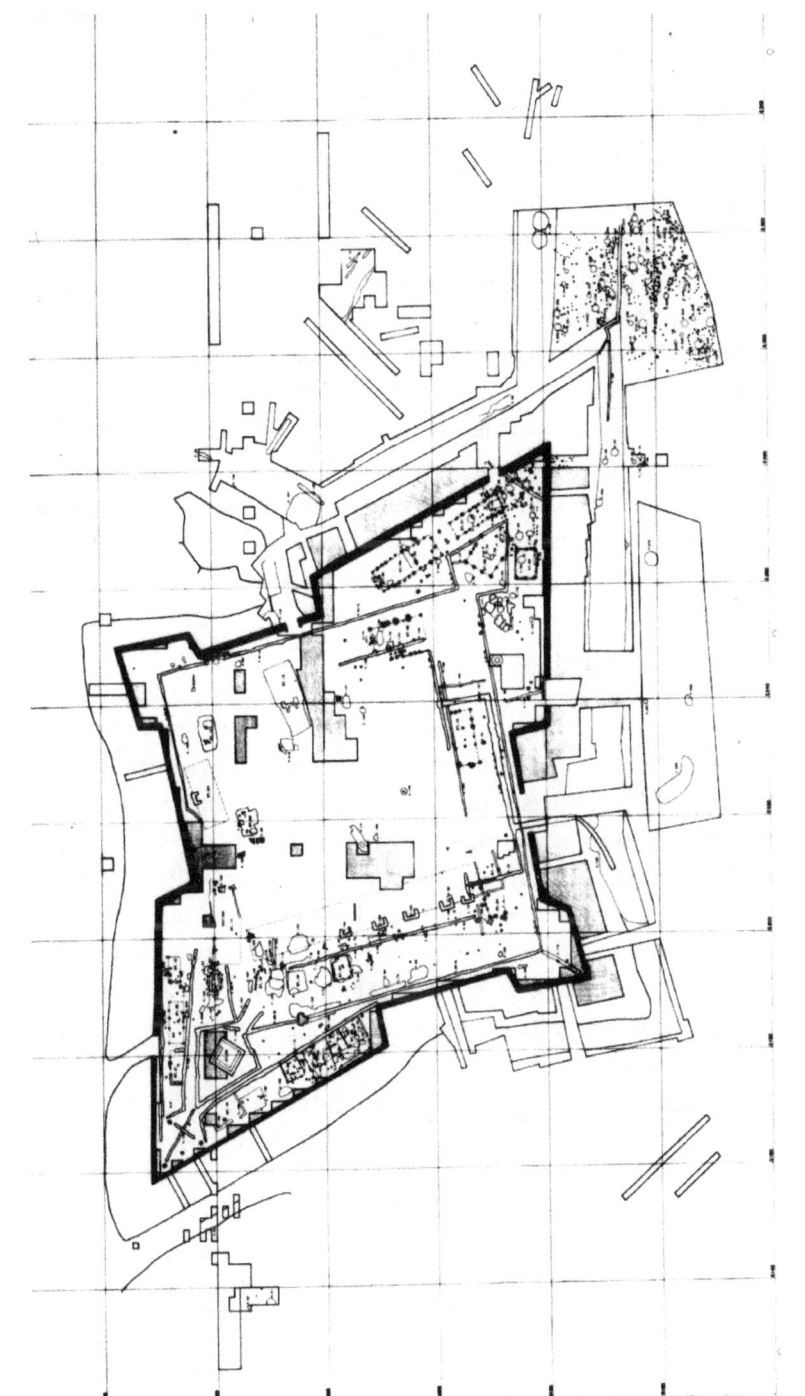

Figure 4.1. Plan of excavation, Fort Loudoun, Tennessee. (Drawing by author.)

in Virginia. Thereafter, others continued returning over a period of about nine months, most of them being delivered to Fort Prince George in South Carolina (Alden 1944; Brown 1965; Hamer 1925; Kelley 1961a; Kuttruff 2007; McDowell 1970).

The state of the fort after the British surrender is not well documented. Nothing has been located that describes its condition when abandoned or during the period immediately following the Cherokee takeover. Apparently the Indians occupied it briefly, while all remaining supplies and portable items were removed to nearby Cherokee towns (Kuttruff 2007). In 1762 Lt. Henry Timberlake visited the fort (Williams 1948). In his map he showed the fort's location in relation to the Little Tennessee valley Cherokee towns, but he did not provide any description other than that it was in ruins. In 1794, Tellico Blockhouse was constructed on the opposite side of the river (Polhemus 1979), and descriptions by visitors to that fort indicate Fort Loudoun was decayed and overgrown (Louis-Philippe 1977). Despite this, the Fort Loudoun site was always a known regional landmark.

Uniqueness of Fort Loudoun

As a French and Indian War period fort, Fort Loudoun was unusual in several ways. First, it was perhaps the most isolated of any, separated from Fort Prince George, the westernmost installation in South Carolina, by 120 miles and the Appalachian Mountains. All men, equipment, and supplies including most foodstuffs required by the garrison had to be walked or moved by pack horses over difficult and sometimes impassable trails. While this was always a matter of concern, it became a critical factor when the fort was placed under siege in 1760. Supplies were cut off completely, communications were severely limited, and a relief expedition could not reach the fort in a timely manner.

Fort Loudoun was one of the largest of the French and Indian War forts, particularly for those located on the frontier. The sizes of several selected forts are shown in table 4.1. With an area of about 5,800 m^2 within the palisade and a total of nearly 11,000 m^2 including the parapet and surrounding ditch, it was nearly the size of Fort Stanwix, New York. It was considerably larger than more typical frontier forts such as Fort Prince George, Fort Loudoun, Pennsylvania, Fort Ligonier, and Fort Dobbs, with interior areas in the 1,000 to 2,000 m^2 range.

The placement of Fort Loudoun was also unusual. Part of the fort was located on a narrow ridge adjacent to the river, about 6 m (20 ft.) higher than

Table 4.1. Areas of selected forts

Fort		Sq. m[1]	Sq. ft.
Fort Michilimackinac, Mich.	Interior[2]	9,425	101,325
Fort Loudoun, Tenn.	Interior[3]	5,822	62,586
	Total[3]	10,989	118,131
Fort Stanwix, N.Y.	Interior[4]	4,358	46,848
	Total[4]	14,372	154,496
Fort Toulouse, Ala.	Interior[5]	4,176	44,893
	Totals[5]	8,178	87,920
Fort Ligonier, Pa.	Interior[6]	2,018	21,701
	Total[7]	13,613	146,348
Fort Loudoun, Pa.	Interior[8]	1,518	16,318
Fort Prince George, S.C.	Interior[9]	1,124	12,083
	Total[10]	3,443	37,018

1. One sq. m = 10.75 sq. ft. or 1.19 sq. yds.
2. Scaled from Fort Michilimackinac Master Map by John Shimnin. Map provided by Donald P. Heldman, Mackinac Island State Park Commission.
3. Scaled from Fort Loudoun Archaeological Plan. Exterior areas include the west, south, and east moats and parapets, the parapet on the north side of the fort, and ravelins Lyttelton. It also does not include the southeast moat extension or Fort Glen.
4. Scaled from Hanson and Hsu 1975, figure 10. Interior scaled along the interior rampart. Exterior scaled along line between covered way and parapet and includes redoubt and ravelin.
5. Scaled from Heldman 1973, map 4.
6. Scaled from Grimm 1970, plate 2.
7. Scaled from Stotz 1974, figure 12. Scaled along retrenchment line and includes east and west batteries, but not the detached batteries to the east of the retrenchment.
8. Scaled from the Archaeological Plan of Fort Loudoun, Pennsylvania, by Mark H. Denton. Map provided by Steven G. Warfel, Pennsylvania Historical and Museums Commission.
9, 10. Scaled from the Archaeological Plan of Fort Prince George, S.C., around interior of palisade. Exterior scaled around the outside edge of the ditch. Map provided by Robert L. Stevenson, Institute of Archaeology and Anthropology, University of South Carolina. See also Williams 1998, figure 11.

the surrounding land, while the remainder of the fort was on level ground. The reason for this was an unfounded concern that the French might attack the fort with gunboats. The ridge where the northern part of the fort was sited provided an excellent command of two bends in the river. As events happened, this location left the upper part of the fort somewhat vulnerable to hostile Cherokee gunfire from the south.

Fort Loudoun was originally star-shaped with the outer works consisting of two large and two small bastions, with short connecting curtain walls. The outer works were to consist of an earthen parapet, with a ditch surrounding three sides, and two ravelins and a hornwork on the river side.

The parapet on top of the ridge used the steep slope along that side in place of a ditch. Within the interior was a log-palisade enclosure with two diamond-shaped bastions. A powder magazine, blacksmith shop, and four large buildings were planned. This palisade enclosure was comparable in size and configuration to several period forts including Fort Prince George. The fort was largely constructed according to this plan, but the palisade line was soon taken down and moved inside the parapet. Only one large barracks building was constructed.

Archaeological Investigations

The first archaeology carried out at Fort Loudoun was by the Works Progress Administration (WPA) in 1936. Those investigations identified the palisade line and several interior structures. In the mid-1950s and the early 1960s, small-scale excavating was done, and the palisade line was reconstructed. This chapter is based on final excavations that began in May 1975 and concluded at the end of August 1976. Excavation was required because of the proposed impoundment of the Little Tennessee River by the Tennessee Valley Authority. There were essentially two phases: first, that directly related to Fort Loudoun, and second, the prehistoric and later historic Cherokee occupations immediately south of the fort. In the fort area, all or parts of some 1,506 2 m units within or adjacent to the fort were excavated. The work allowed definition of 24 structures and the barracks building, 149 historic features, and 600 post molds. Approximately 240 m of the ditch surrounding three sides of the fort were cleared by machine and hand excavations. South of the fort, working behind heavy equipment, about 10,000 m^2 were examined, identifying three Cherokee structures and 19 pit features from the historic occupation, and nine prehistoric structures and 162 features. Over 200,000 artifacts were recovered from all excavations (figure 4.2).

Defensive Works

Based on historical documentation and archaeological excavations, the finalized Fort Loudoun defensive works consisted of a star-shaped fort with four bastions formed by an outer ditch, an earthen parapet, and a palisade line placed against the interior slope of the parapet. The original palisade formed a square 64 m (209 ft.) east–west and 57 m (187 ft.) north–south. Bastions were located at the northwest and southeast corners. The parade

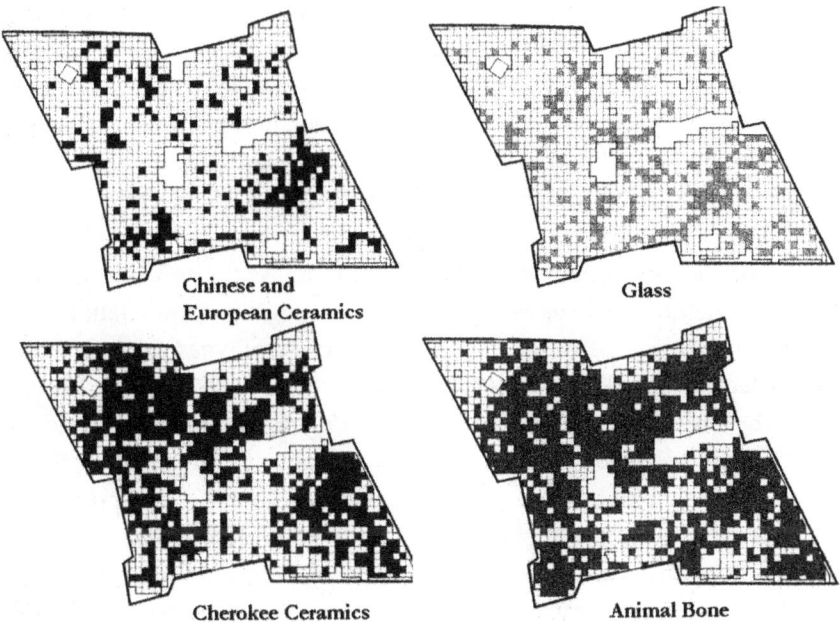

Figure 4.2. Artifact distribution maps. (Diagrams by author.)

inside the earthen parapet encompassed a square of 68 m (223 ft.) east–west and 60 m (197 ft.) north–south. Two large bastions were at the northwest and southeast corners, and smaller ones were on the other two corners. The powder magazine and blacksmith shop were located in the two bastions with the magazine in the northwest bastion. The faces of the larger bastions were 48 m (157 ft.) in length and the flanks were 6 m (23 ft.). The smaller bastions had faces 13 m (43 ft.) long and flanks of 4 m (13 ft.) length. Curtains between the bastions were 28 m (92 ft.) on the north and south and 23 m (75 ft.) on the east and west.

The earthen parapet was erected completely around the fort, averaging about 8 m (26 ft.) in width with an estimated maximum height of about 1.2 m (4 ft.). The ditch was present on the west, south, and east sides of the fort. On the east, the ditch was present only along the southern two-thirds; a steep rocky bluff was present on the northern end. Similarly, the ditch was not present on the north side, due to the steep ridge serving as an obstacle. The ditch was generally about 6 m (20 ft.) in width and less than 60 cm (2 ft.) deep. Gates were constructed in the south and east curtains. Two ravelins were adjacent to the steep bluff just northeast of the east gate. There was considerable evidence for the hornwork's initial construction on the fort's east side, but it had clearly been abandoned well before completion. The final modification to the fort defenses was moving the palisades from inside the parapet and placing them against the parapet interior, sloping outward at an estimated 15 degrees. Twelve cannon brought to the fort with great difficulty were mounted on platforms in the four bastions.

Within the fort, archaeology revealed evidence for 24 structures and a large barracks building along the western side of the parade area. Structures consisted of temporary buildings built to house the garrison during early construction stages as well as more permanent structures intended to last the duration of the occupation. Several structural types were present, dominated, though, by post-in-ground timber-framed structures. Others included semi-subterranean huts and other dugouts built on terraces cut into the hill slope. The powder magazine was made of stone masonry. The large barracks building was a timber-framed structure that was probably set on piers required by the slope where it was sited. Stone chimneys were present along the rear of the barracks building. There was one post-in-trench structure, similar to French construction. Other features included a drain system in the southern part of the fort, a large midden outside both the east and south gates, and numerous pit features of various sorts.

Artifact Assemblage

The 19,139 Fort Loudoun historic artifacts were fairly typical of the period. There were an additional 15,991 Cherokee ceramics and 81,196 animal bones. A complete listing of artifact types and their groups with detailed descriptions and illustrations is in Kuttruff 2007. Analysis of faunal material was presented in Breitburg (1983).

Refuse Disposal Pattern at Fort Loudoun

At Fort Loudoun we were fortunate to excavate 93 percent of the fort's interior by hand, allowing an overall view of artifact classes' spatial distributions. Excavation of most of the surrounding ditch provided a relatively good idea of the distribution of artifacts in that feature. While the collection was not as complete as it would have been had all units and levels been screened, a practical compromise had to be made due to the salvage nature of the project's time frame. Still, all material from historic features, such as pits, drains, palisade lines, and the like were screened, providing a comprehensive sample of the range of artifacts present and against which

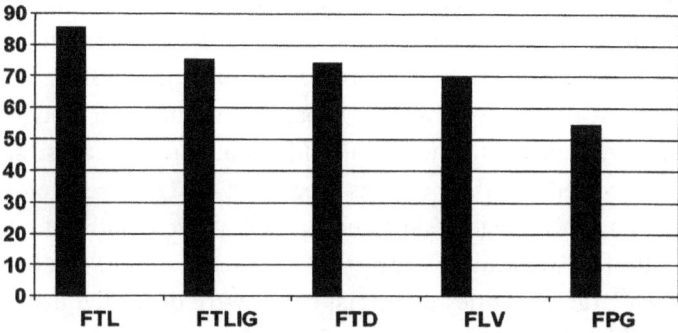

Figure 4.3. FAP Kitchen Group percentages. (Graph by author.)

hand-excavated materials could be evaluated. Based on historic documents, the number of cows and pigs brought into or raised born at the fort during its occupation numbered 327 and 226, respectively. Faunal analysis produced a minimum number of 94 cows and 64 pigs, or archaeological evidence for 29 percent of the known cows and 54 percent of the pigs. This provided a bit of confidence in the artifact recovery rate or at least a possible estimate of rate of survival and recovery. Unfortunately, the documentation did not provide known counts of other artifact classes that might be compared with the excavated materials.

The artifact disposal pattern at Fort Loudoun was relatively straightforward. As expected, and similar to many other sites, a large historic midden was present in the ditch outside each gate. Other refuse was deliberately placed along the counterscarp, along with prehistoric midden material to provide a rich soil in which to plant a defensive hedge of locust trees as a living abatis. While the pattern of deposits outside and near the exits clearly fits South's Brunswick Pattern of refuse disposal (South 1977:47–50), only about 7,885 or 7 percent of the historic artifacts (including bone and Cherokee ceramics) were recovered from ditch deposits and other exterior proveniences.

The remaining bulk of the artifacts and other refuse, some 108,441 specimens, was from features and deposits inside the fort as illustrated by figure 4.3, which shows distributions of European and Chinese ceramics, glass, Cherokee ceramics, and animal bones. While these figures show only gross distribution and not counts, the actual counts show that the densest deposits were clearly on the ridge slope in the northern part of the fort. At the least, they illustrate that the fort's interior was a primary disposal area for refuse.

The third probable place for refuse disposal was the river located about 50 m east of the fort. A single comment in the documents that a shipment of spoiled hams was thrown into the river is the only evidence for such use. This comment might also suggest that the primary type of material thought necessary to remove from the fort was offal, which would rot and cause an odor. It may be expected that the river was used for at least some disposal. The river would have been inaccessible during the last five months of occupation when the fort was under siege by the Cherokee. It may be that this period was when large quantities of animal bones were deposited inside the fort. This might be tested by comparing the known number of animals present at the beginning of the siege with the minimum numbers derived from the recovered animal bones noted above.

Patterning and the Frontier Artifact Pattern

I would now like to make some comments regarding South's (1974) Frontier Artifact Pattern (FAP) as it relates to Fort Loudoun and possibly other forts. South published his Carolina and Frontier Artifact Patterns in 1977, the year after the Fort Loudoun excavation ended. I read the work carefully during the Fort Loudoun artifact processing and analysis, but was never completely convinced that some artifact types included in the artifact groups were completely appropriate for the Loudoun materials or for some other sites. The same was true for some artifact groups themselves. I especially had problems with groups excluded from patterning calculations. Since then, others have either questioned or modified some artifact groups and have puzzled about the often wide divergences of their samples from the original FAP. While these patterns have been widely adapted for historic site artifact presentation and interpretation, I have not done so until now. For this chapter, to determine how Fort Loudoun compared with other period frontier fortifications and how closely it and other forts might match the expected FAP, I opted to use South's groups.

The resulting calculations for Fort Loudoun are shown in table 4.2 along with those for Fort Prince George, Fort Dobbs, Fort Loudoun, Virginia, and Fort Ligonier. Table 4.2 includes the counts of Cherokee ceramics from Fort Loudoun and Fort Prince George and the animal bone counts from all forts. These were not used in the earlier FAP calculations. Some of these forts predated Fort Loudoun, Tennessee, by a few years, but all overlapped the 1756–60 Fort Loudoun occupation, and none lasted more than a few years. This provides a relatively comparable sample of frontier fort sites built and occupied for a limited period of time, all of which were contemporary for part of their occupation. Fort Loudoun, Pennsylvania, could be another, but the artifact tabulations were not readily available. Only one artifact group, the Personal Group, falls within the FAP range. Five, however, fall within the FAP predicted range.

Two artifact groups are particularly bothersome for this study. Both have to do with the Kitchen Group or what might be better called a Kitchen and/or Kitchen Refuse Group. The first, with particular reference to Fort Loudoun, Tennessee, and Fort Prince George, South Carolina, is that indigenous ceramics were present and included in the Activities Group. While indigenous ceramics are not a matter of concern at most fortifications, these ceramics made up (omitting bone) 45 percent of the Fort Loudoun collection and 26 percent at Fort Prince George, both substantial percentages.

I want to make a case for the use of indigenous ceramics by the Fort Loudoun and Fort Prince George garrisons. This means including them in patterning calculations. This is important, since Cherokee ceramics were removed as a "known deviant sample" from the artifact assemblage at Fort Prince George, which was one of four sites used for the original formulation of South's Frontier Artifact Pattern or FAP. The Cherokee ceramics apparently were removed primarily to ensure that the Fort Prince George assemblage (with a ceramic ratio of .50 with the Cherokee ceramics included) remained within the FAP (ceramic ratio range .11 to .25) rather than the Carolina Artifact Pattern (ceramic ratio range .44 to .79) (South 1977:172–75). South, however, did anticipate the possible necessity of considering Colono-Indian or indigenous ceramics for Fort Prince George, a statement also applicable to the Fort Loudoun ceramic assemblage.

Using the ceramic ratio and including Cherokee pottery as the only criterion results in classifying Fort Prince George as a Carolina Pattern Site, not a FAP site. In other words, the shortage of European ceramics at Fort Prince George on the Carolina Frontier appears to have been compensated for by using Cherokee pottery (South 1977:173–74). South further noted, "It is possible that if such forts as these [Fort Ligonier and Fort Prince George] are totally excavated, the resulting relationships [Kitchen to Architecture] will appear more like the Carolina Pattern than is now the case, since we may have a skewed picture from the forts used to define the Frontier Pattern." He added, "We must be prepared, therefore, for the possible revealing of different percentage relationships for artifact groups from totally excavated frontier forts than for the Frontier Pattern relationships seen here" (South 1977:152).

Table 4.2. Frontier artifact pattern calculations for selected forts

South's artifact classification (1)	South's means and ranges (1)			Fort Loudoun, Tennessee (2)			Fort Prince George		
	FAP mean %	FAP pattern range	FAP pred. range	Count	FAP %	Revised %	Count	FAP %	Revi %
Kitchen	26	22.7–34.5	10.2–45.00	1991	5.67	85.26	1679	16.8	54
Architecture	52	40.3–57.5	27.9–74.3	8589	24.45	7.38	4252	42.6	33
Furniture	0.2	0.1–0.3	0.0–0.5	14	0.04	0.01	6	0.1	0.
Arms	5.4	1.4–8.4	0.0–1.56	481	1.37	0.41	471	4.7	3.
Clothing	1.7	0.3–3.8	0.0–6.9	1071	3.05	0.92	70	0.7	0.
Personal	0.2	0.1–0.4	0.0–0.7	263	0.75	0.23	9	0.1	0.
Tobacco pipe	9.1	1.9–14.0	0.0–27.1	652	1.86	0.56	851	8.5	6.
Activities	3.7	0.7–6.4	0.0–11.8	22069	62.82	5.22	2633	26.4	20
Unclassified									
Total FAP artifact counts				35130			9971		
Animal bones				81196			2644		
Cherokee ceramics				15991			2583		
Total artifacts				116326			12615		

Sources for artifact counts: (1) South 1977:160–61; (2) Kuttruff 2007; (3) Babits and Pecoraro 2008; (4) Jolley 2005.

At Fort Prince George, there were 767 European ceramics and 2,583 Cherokee ceramics, or 23 and 66 percent, respectively. At Fort Loudoun, there were only 819 European and Chinese ceramics compared with 15,991 Cherokee, or 5 and 95 percent, respectively. Several factors lead me to believe that at Fort Loudoun, the locally available Cherokee vessels were, indeed, adopted by the garrison to compensate for the difficulty in transporting sufficient numbers of large cooking vessels and other tableware to the fort. In addition to the supply difficulties that would make this a reasonable proposition, other factors were considered.

First, there is no historical or archaeological evidence that there was a Cherokee occupation at the site prior to building Fort Loudoun. Second, some 7,663 Cherokee sherds, about 48 percent, were recovered from numerous, unequivocal fort period contexts, including the two semi-subterranean structures, which were used during the early occupation for habitation, then as refuse deposits, and finally capped during the occupation. The

Fort Dobbs (3)			Fort Loudoun, Virginia (4)			Fort Ligonier (1)		
Count	FAP %	Revised %	Count	FAP %	Revised %	Count	FAP %	Revised %
1905	60.2	74.3	354	39.8	69.0	5566	25.6	75.5
283	8.9	5.8	347	39	19.5	12112	55.6	18.3
0	0.0	0.0	0	0	0.0	44	0.2	0.1
605	19.1	12.3	25	2.8	1.4	1820	8.4	2.7
74	2.3	1.5	23	2.6	1.3	833	3.8	1.3
2	0.1	0.0	4	0.4	0.2	99	0.5	0.1
131	4.1	2.7	54	6.1	3.0	411	1.9	0.6
166	5.2	3.4	66	9.3	3.7	893	4.1	1.3
			17	1.9	1.0			
3166			890			21778		
1754			891			44547		
0			0			0		
4920			1781			66325		

remainder was from units and levels inside the fort. There were also several examples of Cherokee ceramics from Fort Loudoun that were clearly modeled after Anglo forms, suggesting special orders from the garrison to Cherokee potters. Lastly, if there is any credibility to artifact distributions for attributing use and disposal of artifacts, then the distribution of Cherokee ceramics within the fort emphasizes that point. Unless Fort Prince George was built on a previous Cherokee site, it is probable that a similar but less intense use of Cherokee ceramics was also made there.

The second artifact group is animal bone, which often makes up a large percentage of most assemblages, such as those ranging from 26 percent at Fort Prince George to 85 percent at Fort Loudoun. The issue of including animal bone in a Kitchen or Kitchen and/or Kitchen Refuse Group is another problematic area. Omitting them from any model is, in effect, simply ignoring what the Kitchen Group is all about. Admittedly, it is much more difficult to factor in the plant food portion of the diet, most of which was brought in as grain, sacks of meal and flour, and the like, which leave little archaeological trace that can be quantified as bone. Here documents will probably serve better than the archaeological record. From reading documents relating to Fort Loudoun, one of the most important considerations by correspondents was the ability to adequately supply the garrison with foodstuffs. In fact, the eventual lack of food resulted in the garrison's surrender.

Many finer ceramics that are often recovered from forts, such as the porcelains, can reasonably be attributed mostly to officers and are not entirely reflective of the garrison as a whole. One might also make the case that knives, forks, spoons, and the like may have been individual items instead of comprising a mess. One of the distinguishing features of fortified sites such as these frontier forts, in contrast to domestic and other sites, would be the often large numbers of personnel quartered in a relatively small area. During Fort Loudoun's first year, there were approximately 300 men in the garrison. During the rest of the occupation, there were minimally 100 individuals quartered there. Given this, it seems reasonable to expect that if Cherokee ceramics and the animal bones are included in the pattern calculations, we get what might be a more accurate representation of the importance of the Kitchen/Subsistence/Kitchen Refuse Group for such an installation.

Recalculating the percentages for the Kitchen Group/Kitchen Refuse Group for the same several forts, including animal bones and indigenous ceramics in the Kitchen Group, gave results shown in table 4.2. Now the percentages for Kitchen Group dominate all assemblages, ranging from 55 to 86 percent. This provides a more accurate archaeological profile resulting from feeding often large numbers of personnel quartered in a relatively small place.

To provide an accurate interpretation of the given occupations of these forts, the entire assemblage available from a site should be considered. Whether this leads to determining regular patterning common to all installations is not necessarily important. What is important is that the resulting calculations of artifact assemblages direct us not only to explaining any regularities there may be but also to differences that could be based on any number of factors, some often unique to specific installations. Other factors needing consideration are, as previously noted, the proportion of the site that was excavated and the specific areas excavated at forts from which only samples are available. Additionally, the collection strategy should be considered in evaluating applicability of a given assemblage. Some additional factors would include the remoteness of a fort, a location near a town, and ease or difficulty of provisioning and supply.

For additional and more detailed information about Fort Loudoun, see Kuttruff (1990), Distretti and Kuttruff (2004), and Kuttruff (2007).

5

Fort Dobbs, North Carolina

How Documents and Artifacts Led to Rebuilding the Fort

LAWRENCE E. BABITS

This chapter reports on the forty years of historical, archaeological, and interpretive investigations conducted for the Fort Dobbs State Historic Site, Iredell County, North Carolina. The focus is on using documentary and archaeological information, in conjunction with surviving examples of frontier fortified barracks to re-create the fort as a heritage tourism destination. Detailed artifact analysis is not offered except as to how the artifacts provided suggestions for interpreting site structures. A brief historical narrative placing the fort in its French and Indian War context is followed by information about the site's archaeological excavations. Taken together, the history and archaeology suggested interpretations that led to slightly earlier British fortified barracks as suggestions for re-creating the main fort building.

Historical Documents

No contemporary plans or drawings of Fort Dobbs have been located; the few documentary references provide clues about the fort's history and appearance. The lack of extant imagery or full descriptions proved a major stumbling block for restoring the fort as a state historic site. Nevertheless, there were references, some of which could only be understood after considerable research.

The frontier post was part of Governor Arthur Dobbs's plan to defend the frontier and came after Dobbs completed a personal survey of the colony. Dobbs planned on "a Company of 50 men under one Captain one Lieutenant & Ensign for the Defence of this frontier" (Dobbs 1755a:313).

Dobbs wrote later in August 1755 that he wanted the fort on Third Creek, in what was then Rowan County (Dobbs 1755b:357). The actual site, however, is on Fourth Creek. Evidence is lacking as to whether Dobbs's original site was rejected, whether he had confused the two creeks that join about 10 miles to the east before joining the South Yadkin River, or if the builder put it near his own property.

About the same time, Dobbs ordered Capt. Hugh Waddell to scout the frontier and erect a barracks "to winter over" (Dobbs 1755b:357). The lower house voted an allocation of £1,000 for Waddell's Company to build a "small fort or strong barrack" (Assembly 1754b:515; Dobbs 1755c497-98). The terms *barracks* and *strong barrack* are especially important in light of English frontier fortifications in the Scottish Highlands, as will be seen later. The frontier fortified building would provide shelter for the garrison and potential refugees, while still having the strength to hold out until relieved.

The key point is that a barracks was the first planned building, but interpretations changed when historians learned that Dobbs later wrote: "The first thing to be done is to make log houses for the soldiers and then to trase out and clear the Ground about the fort, and then throw up some of the Fosse to form the Glacis and fix the Pallisades; and then after making a proper barrack for the officers, to fall about the raising of the fort" (Dobbs 1755d: 476). The shift from fortified barracks to glacis, ditch, and palisades came despite knowing that Dobbs intended this more traditional fort to be located on North Carolina's coast. Considerable confusion resulted as archaeologists and historians tried to transplant the coastal information to the interior piedmont.

The fort was probably not finished by March 1756, because Dobbs ordered the post "stockaded" and noted that it was temporary and that "only Swivel Guns will be necessary" (Dobbs 1756a:572). Dobbs may have meant that the barracks had been erected but not fortified, because Waddell's men certainly required shelter over the winter of 1755–56. When Dobbs wrote in May 1756 that no construction had taken place (1756b:672), it is likely that he was referring to planned outer fortifications, because a Moravian account dated 1 June 1756 noted that Waddell was "Captain of the Fort" along Fourth Creek (Fries 1922, 1:167).

The barracks' satisfactoriness for wintering over was described by two colonial Assemblymen, Richard Caswell and Francis Brown, who reported that they had likewise viewed the State of Fort Dobbs and found it to be a good and Substantial Building of the Dimentions following (that is to say) The Oblong Square fifty three feet by forty, the opposite Angles Twenty four feet and Twenty-Two In height Twenty four and a half feet as by the Plan annexed Appears, The Thickness of the Walls which are made of Oak Logs regularly Diminished from sixteen Inches to Six, it contains three floors and there may be discharged from each floor at one and the same time about one hundred Muskets. (Caswell and Brown 1756)

This statement forms the basis for understanding and re-creating Fort Dobbs. There are five key elements mentioned. The length (53 ft.) and width (40 ft.) are spelled out, but the length is a very odd dimension. Traditionally, it should have been an even number and probably one divisible by four or eight. The building's other measurements certainly suggest that even measurement units were used, so it may be that the stated length was an error caused by working around the flanking opposite angles that broke up the long run of the building.

Flankers are the "opposite Angles" that served as protective extensions, or protrusions, from the main building. They are on opposite corners, or as some would say, "catty cornered" (Babits 1981:165–73). They serve the same function as bastions on a formal stone, brick, or earthen fort's walls. The term *opposite angles* caused interpretive problems but can be explained by recourse to other fortifications (Babits and Pecoraro 2008:185–86, 189–90). The different lengths mentioned might indicate one flanker was 22 ft. square and the other 24 ft. or may refer to the lengths of the flanker walls. If the latter is the case, then the 24 ft. long walls should parallel the building's long side while the 22 ft. walls paralleled the shorter side according to notions of symmetry addressed by James Deetz (1973:18, 1977:43) and Henry Glassie (1976) in their explanation of the "Georgian Mindset" (Babits and Pecoraro 2008:189–90).

The building's height is stated as 24.5 ft. with three floors. Each floor should thus be 8 ft. high. This dimension, as with others in the report, indicates use of standardized measurements still seen on carpenter's rulers and tapes today. In this case, they also relate to the wall's log sizes, as will be shown. If the flooring is 2 in. thick, then the extra half foot is made up as two-inch thick flooring (Babits and Pecoraro 2008:181).

The walls are described as 16 in. oak logs. The comment indicates they are squared, the usual British practice (Young 1979:12–13). This is an important assumption because 16 in. allows the number of logs per floor to be derived. In Anglo-American construction, 16 in. is a repetitive measurement. It is still in use today as indicated on tape measures where 16 in. increments are highlighted. Six logs, 16 × 16 in., would be required for the ground floor. "Regularly diminished" probably means that the second floor logs were 12 in. thick, the third floor 6 in. Such an arrangement would reduce the number of trees to be cut as well as the weight that had to be lifted to install the second and third floor wall logs. Caswell and Brown could have easily seen that the logs were thinner by looking at the building's corners and observing how log widths, but not height, changed between floors.

Other commentators suggested that "regularly diminished" applied to the depth of notching (Pilling 1976), a believable notion but one that would have been hard for Caswell and Brown to detect and would not alleviate the physical problem of raising 16 in. square timbers to the second and third floors. Reducing wall thickness reduced weight but would not make the wall any less resistant to musket fire, which was all most frontier forts had to deal with (See Hart, Fischer, and Huey, this volume).

After December 1756, there are scattered references to Fort Dobbs that provide information on supplies and occupation, but little on the fort itself. In April 1757, Waddell received 51 stand of arms from the Wilmington armory (Dupre 1756). Two months later, Alexander Osborne, one of five justices of the peace appointed for Rowan County in 1749, was issued 52 stand of arms for Capt. Andrew Bailey's Company (Ramsey 1964:50; Kars 2002:247). Osborne transported the weaponry first to his house and then to Fort Dobbs (Osborne 1759). Given the number of arms, these references probably refer to the same weapons. A stand of arms is "a complete set of arms for one soldier" (Duane 1810:14; Gale 2007:2), indicating that each soldier was issued a musket, bayonet, cartridge pouch, and their slings or belts. Finials for bayonet scabbards have been found at the site (Gale 2007:12; Babits and Pecoraro 2008:101).

Archaeological Evidence

Ditch Interior and "Palisade Line"

In 1968, South uncovered a linear soil stain centrally located in the west fosse. South initially thought this linear soil stain was a palisade line while the ditch was an excavation for its posts. Stone's later photos and profiles do show that there was something in the ditch as the linear stain, profile breaks, and linear artifact distributions confirm.

Influenced by South Carolina's Fort Prince George, South later changed his mind about a palisade in the ditch because he felt the palisade should be on a rampart. "Initially South thought that the midden that showed up along the counterscarp of the parapet ditch was the top of a palisade [*sic*] ditch, but he corrected himself as soon as he sectioned the ditch" (Stone 1974). South's decision influenced Stone, who did not consider a palisade in the fosse either, but South, Stone, and Israel did not explain the linear soil stain, the linear arrangement of artifacts, or soil anomalies in the fosse profiles. They discounted archaeological evidence they recorded to create something that is not mentioned in the documents or supported by the archaeological excavations. South was adamant about this: "No palisade was ever located in the ditch at Fort Dobbs, as clearly revealed by both my archaeology and that of Garry Stone. . . . There was never a palisade in the ditch at Fort Dobbs" (South 1976). Despite not believing in a counterscarp palisade, their excellent technical data recovery revealed evidence allowing our present interpretations. South was correct but left the door open for another possibility that will be discussed later.

Stone noted that artifacts recovered from the ditch fill were usually above the ditch floor, indicating that some silting occurred before cultural material was discarded. They were also in a linear distribution as if something were blocking a more random distribution in the ditch. Artifact distributions can be seen fairly well in profile photos taken in 1969. While profile drawings show only a single thin section, the photographs show a distinct distribution of artifacts to either side of a midline that coincides with a soil break in both photo and profile drawing (figure 5.1). While the photos and profile drawings look virtually the same, the photo shows the west ditch's northern end while the drawing shows the north ditch's western end. That nearly identical profiles were recorded for each ditch suggests that they saw similar filling and artifact deposition as part of the site formation process.

If the ditch filled just by silting, then it is likely that soil eroding into the ditch came from three separate episodes, possibly with clearance projects at different times. The first occurred immediately after construction of the fort building when there was heavy traffic on the parade and the ground cover was likely destroyed, thus abetting soil loss. A second episode likely occurred during 1758 and 1759 while the garrison was in Pennsylvania. Although foot traffic on the parade was much less, there would have been few people to remove any erosional fill. Presumably this was cleared out when

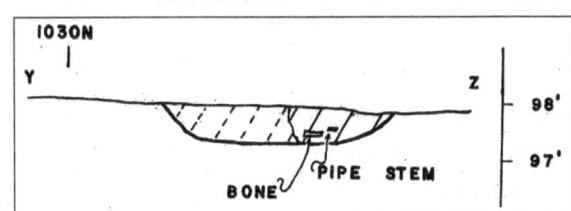
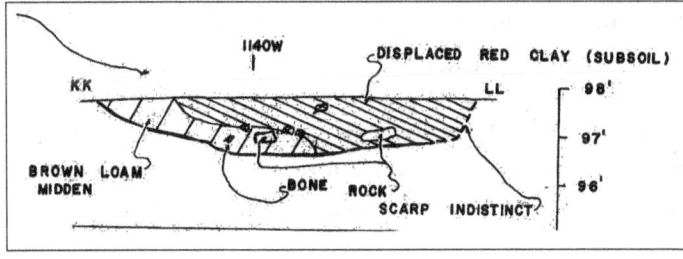

Figures 5.1a–d. Ditch profile photos and drawings. (Courtesy of the North Carolina Office of State Archaeology. In Babits and Pecoraro 2008:213, 214, 215.)

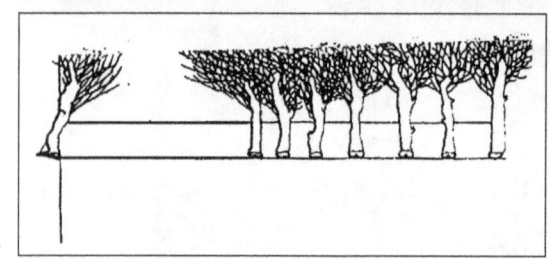

Figures 5.2a and 5.2b. *Above*: Fort Dobbs ditch excavation. *Left*: Abatis drawings after Lochee 1783. (Photo courtesy of North Carolina Office of State Archaeology, Fort Dobbs Ditch Excavations. In Babits and Pecoraro 2008:221, 216.)

the fort was prepared for defense during the 1759–60 winter. The third episode probably occurred after 1760 when the fort saw very little use. Since the fort was put into a state of readiness late in 1759, the most likely last soil depositional episode was as, or after, the fort's main use ceased. Once the fort was abandoned, recycling of the fort building and then agricultural plowing filled in the ditch.

An alternative explanation is that the ditch was not a fosse or fort ditch in the traditional sense but rather the footing for abatis, an obstruction made from tree limbs placed with their butt ends on, or in the ground facing the fort and their branching ends sharpened and facing out, away from the fort. This interpretation is matched by a drawing in a military manual showing abatis anchored in a shallow ditch (Lochee 1783) (figure 5.2). Given the shallow depth with a fairly wide ditch that clearly had something in it to divide the artifacts, the presence of abatis has the best fit with the archaeological evidence. South was vindicated about his interpretation that there was no palisade in the ditch.

The fosse artifacts could have been discarded after the Cherokee crisis in 1759–60. The bones seem to represent single animals being butchered, which might reflect a smaller garrison than the 50 provincials assigned to the post. The presence of high-status ceramic wares in the ditch may be evidence of the officers' exposure to the latest British styles and customs during the Forbes expedition. Exposed to British officers who considered themselves gentlemen, the provincial officers copied their rituals, including the tea ceremony, and acquired the equipment for them (Roth 1961; Babits 1981:176–77).

Scarp

The inside ditch wall (scarp) was little different from the outer wall (counterscarp), with one notable exception. Aligned with the parade "palisade," there was an apparent step cut into the northwestern scarp. Presumably this was to make it easier to cross the ditch at a postulated sally port. If this was a step, then it indicates that the sally port was not very wide and not intended for anything but foot traffic. In the sense of what is now known, sally port is probably a misnomer because there was no wall, only a gap in the abatis, possibly closed by some more portable obstruction.

Associated with the scarp in the minds of South, Stone, and Israel was a parapet with a palisade inserted into it. South made his 1976 statements denying a palisade in the counterscarp based on three 1968 test trenches and incomplete documentary research. He also relied on Stone's statement that there was no palisade in the ditch. However, Stone based his excavation strategy on South's belief that there was no palisade in the ditch. Consequently, Stone excavated key ditch segments in the incredibly hard subsoil with a pick. Fortunately, Stone's data recording was very good, especially considering the difficulty of discerning soil differences in the Lloyd Loam series on the site. His aerial photographs and ground level views of the ditch excavations indicate the presence of an obstruction now interpreted as abatis in the ditch. This present interpretation conflicts with a palisade as advocated by Babits until additional excavations conducted by Robinson and Terrell specifically to test Babits's idea of a palisade in the ditch refuted the notion once and for all (Robinson and Terrell 2006:16).

The idea of a rampart parapet with palisade was also rejected as erroneous. Based on South's interpretation of what was found at Fort Prince George, it would not have been an effective protection as Fort Prince George's collapsing palisade posts and rampart demonstrated in 1756 (Williams, this volume). The rejection is based on documentary evidence to the contrary, tactical evidence from other sites, hydrological observations, plus the archaeological and photographic evidence recorded by Stone. There is no documentary evidence supporting a rampart with a palisade at Fort Dobbs. In fact, a palisade in a ditch with a glacis was only planned for a coastal fort. Tactically, a blockhouse fort would be defended from the building itself, not the palisade line. A parapet less than 15 ft. from the building would provide cover for any attacker who took refuge in the ditch. Without a parapet, the abatis can be swept with gunfire from the building's upper stories. Finally, if a parapet were present, rainwater would have no way to drain from the fort, and the cellar would undoubtedly take in water, a situation that occurs today after any heavy rain.

Like the palisade, no direct evidence of any glacis was recovered. However, some circumstantial evidence was recorded by Stone. Coincident with the step cut into the scarp, on the counterscarp excavators noted there was a "stump mold" because the soil was heavily churned up. It is now thought that this "stump mold" was a passage through the counterscarp associated with the sally port and the "step" in the scarp. No other anomaly of this sort was noted on the counterscarp, so it is not likely it was for placing the butt ends of abates. No other "step" was cut into the scarp indicating it was for a specific purpose. It is suggested there was a passage across the ditch at this point, but no glacis as suggested for coastal Fort Dobbs (1754b:133). The current interpretation links the "palisade" line, scarp step, counterscarp "stump" (or disturbed soil), and artifacts suggesting a sally port or gap existed in the northern west ditch.

The "Palisade Line"

The parade "palisade line" is so called because Stone believed this feature represented footings for a palisade predicted by South. The linear feature appeared "to be the bottom of a palisade ditch (as South conjectured)." The feature was "disturbed subsoil surrounding brown loam (palisade molds) with mottling down center (subsoil that tumbled down molds???)" (Stone, field notes, 16 June 1969). The feature cut across two excavation units approximately on grid line 1114W. The outer edges of the feature, the builder's trench in which vertical logs were placed, were 9.5 ft. long and varied in width from 1 ft. to 9 in. The line of post molds, vestigial remnants of the posts themselves, was circa 0.6–.8 ft. wide and 8.5 ft. long. The posts were represented by distinct clumps of mottled soil that was clearly different from the mottled posthole soil. The depth was irregular but circa 0.5 ft. below the surface. If some .6 ft. of soil eroded from the site, then the posts were originally set slightly over 1 ft. deep. A flattened musket ball was recovered from the southern half of this feature.

Stone's notes refer to this feature as a "bastion ditch," a "stratigraphic enigma, with humus and colorful patches of carbon and yellow material (complete with flattened musket ball) in the center of a shallow ditch. It was probably too deep (although only .45 ft. survived after erosion), too narrow, and too irregular for a sill trench, but the "palisade bastion" interpretation is based largely on architectural geometry" (Stone 1974). The architectural geometry comment mentioned by Stone was because he envisioned this palisade as forming the wall on one of the fort building's flankers.

While this feature seems to be a defensive wall, it was probably never connected to the building. Instead, based on its orientation, it is related to the fort ditch. It apparently served as an internal defensive structure providing interior cover for the gap through the ditch and abatis.

The Cellar

The cellar was a 24 ft. square, 3 to 3.5 ft. deep, after removal of the plow zone. Before excavation, it was visible as a slight depression. After removal of a brown loam plow zone that contained only scattered artifacts, the outline of the 24 ft. square was obvious. This slightly darker loam was 2 to 2.5 ft. thick.

A generalized cellar stratigraphy was adopted from the original field notes. The stratigraphy shows a hard-packed yellow/red clay (subsoil) floor. A lens ranging from olive brown to brown loam occurred as an olive-colored clay loam fill in the center of the cellar. Since there was neither charcoal nor ash, this was not explained. From the profiles, it seems that this lens represents a mix of topsoil and other debris deposited shortly after the cellar was no longer in use. Above the mixed brown loam, there was a darker plow zone.

The cellar walls inclined outward at an angle of less than 70 degrees.

Figure 5.3. Aerial photograph of 1969 Fort Dobbs excavations. Postulated hearth and chimney base to right of C. (Courtesy of North Carolina Office of State Archaeology. In Babits and Pecoraro 2008:194.)

Along the cellar edges, there were two depositional lenses, especially along the west wall. The upper layer was thicker and contained charcoal and ash and extended toward the center as much as 5 ft. in some places. The charcoal-flecked upper layer was thickest at the cellar's edge, especially along the north, west, and south walls. Nearer the southwest corner, there appeared to be more charcoal mixed with the soil. Artifacts were comparable to those in the cellar's "post occupational fill," presumably the brown loam (Israel 1971a:14). The profiles suggest that the cellar floor was hard packed with flecks of charcoal.

An aerial photograph shows a soil anomaly immediately outside the cellar's damaged west wall. A close examination revealed that this was rectangular and that the mottled soil was bordered with a darker edge (figure 5.3). The soil stain's north edge is vertical. In the cellar lensing, there is a large quantity of charcoal, ash, and burnt clay. Given the collapsed cellar wall and the evidence of burning and the few brick fragments, it is likely that the lens was created when the chimney was salvaged.

In the approximate middle of the cellar, there was an excavation from the ground surface to the cellar floor. This was almost 5 ft. wide at the bottom. The sides are sloping, so it is unlikely an archaeologist did this. It is more probable that this represents recycling or looting sometime after the cellar filled. The mix of artifacts tends to confirm excavation and subsequent backfilling.

Cellar Post Mold

For reconstruction and structural purposes, the most important feature within the cellar may be a 2 × 2 ft. post mold with a 4 × 4 ft. soil anomaly around the post mold that was excavated into the floor. It was described as "an extension of excavation into the subsoil, roughly 2 ft. × 2 ft. with extension north & artifacts" (Stone, field notes, unit 104A). Neither Stone nor Israel made much mention of this feature. The cellar post mold was a square, 2 × 2 ft. by ca. 1 ft. deep depression. On the north and northeast sides, there was a sloping depression extending higher up and out from the post mold that represents either a prepared slope or damage incurred when the post was erected. Since the field map plan mentions "const. pick scars" for the lower level, the sloping side was seemingly prepared for mounting the timber. The post that once sat in this location would not necessarily have to be deeply embedded because it was supported by joists and beams as the building was raised.

This structural element almost certainly is the location of a main support post for the building. The support would allow joists and beams to span the cellar hole. Given its size and location, the vertical timber probably stood as high as the ridgepole and thus likely defines the break where the hipped roof slanted eastwards. If so, then this post was probably matched by another timber west of the cellar in a similar position.

Chimney and Hearth

Archaeological evidence of the chimney and its salvage appears as a soil anomaly with approximate dimensions of ca. 10 × 10 ft. The anomaly's eastern portion is damaged and the upper cellar wall here is collapsed, but the chimney base would not have extended east beyond the cellar's west wall. This damage suggests the chimney was robbed for its stone and brick. The adjacent west wall profile drawing shows a thick charcoal and burned clay lens coming from the southwest. Given the damaged hearth base and cellar wall, the most likely source for the burned clay and ash is residue from the chimney footing outside the cellar.

The chimney almost certainly fulfilled structural needs as well as taking smoke from the fire. It is very likely that a major east–west beam was mortised into it so as to reduce the gap across the building in the second and third stories. In the same fashion, the east and west chimney shoulders, separated by approximately 8 ft., probably supported north–south beams that framed the stairwell leading to the next floor. To serve these structural functions, the chimney would have been about 8 ft. square.

Little artifactual evidence of the hearth or chimney was found. It is a significant clue that all six brick fragments found during the 1969 cellar excavations were recovered from the post-occupational fill in the cellar's southwest corner. If the building was torn down and the hearth and chimney were salvaged, these brick fragments provide a clue to the chimney and its firebox. The small number of brick fragments indicates that the chimney itself was not brick, although it may have had a brick hearth and possibly a firebox.

It should be noted that a contemporary house, located some 60 yards from the project fort building's west wall, also had a stone chimney. By extension, it is likely that the blockhouse did, too. Therefore, the brick fragments indicate the hearth and possibly the firebox were lined with brick that was later recycled.

Post Molds 1 and 2

During the 1969 excavations, only two other possible post molds were found, aside from the 8 ft. long "palisade" line and the cellar post mold. The Lloyd Loam series is exceptionally difficult to discern, especially after it has been exposed and dried, so some confusion about soil colors, disturbance, and interpretation is expected. The two post molds found between the ditch and the suggested building trace provide intriguing suggestions about the fort's main building. Post mold 1 was 1.25 × 1.3 ft. and extended to a depth of .75 ft. below datum and was originally interpreted as a rodent burrow. The profile drawing indicates it was a post mold, and it was so identified on the 1971 excavation map (Israel 1971b). Post mold 1 was located at a point 20 ft. from the eastern ditch's midpoint and 22 ft. from the cellar's eastern wall. It is 4 ft. north of an east–west line drawn through the center of the cellar post mold.

Post mold 2 has a similar location west of the cellar. It is 20 ft. from the midpoint of the western ditch and 4 ft. south of the east–west line through the cellar post mold. Its dimensions were 1 × 1.25 ft. It extended to a depth of ca .75 ft. below datum. Post mold 2 is 50 ft. from the cellar's western wall.

The nearly identical positioning of these post molds, in terms of the building's postulated alignment, suggests they have architectural significance. Since they are outside the building, it is likely they were the posts for cressets, a pole with a fire basket or fire plate designed to provide light. Their positions suggest that they were designed to light up the short sides of the building without lighting up the entrance doors.

The Well

The well was visible as a circular depression 5 ft. deep beyond the cellar's southwestern corner. The initial depression was more than 20 ft. wide at the surface. At 8 ft. below surface, the shaft was 8 ft. wide. At 16 ft., it was 6 ft. wide. During excavation, water seepage was encountered at a depth of 37.2 ft. At the bottom, 40.25 ft. below surface, the shaft was 4 ft. in diameter. At this point, the lowest 6 in. were described as "muck."

The bottom 3 ft. included portions of a possible windlass used to excavate the well during the 1840s. This determination was made on the basis of a cut nail found in wood preserved at the shaft bottom. A scattering of eighteenth-century artifacts were encountered throughout the excavation, including ceramics, musket balls, and pig teeth.

It is possible that the well was really dug as a cistern or converted into one. If so, then there may have been some way to divert water from the building's roof. The site is on high ground without a visible water source or any nearby evidence of an old spring. The water level was encountered at 40 ft. below surface. Even with the moderate permeability of the subsoil, the depth where water began to seep in at 40 ft. was below bedrock. Soil Conservation Service surveyors noted, "Most wells of the county are put down in hills" (Cawthorn and Jenkins 1964:38, 88). This comment suggests that the Fort Dobbs well was a feasible source of water, especially in the eighteenth century. There was at least one nearby spring utilized during the fort occupation (Waddell 1760) that could indicate the original water level. However, the precise location of that spring is unknown. The possibility that the rainwater runoff collected in the fosse and then percolated into the well has not been adequately discussed as a replenishment source for the well.

Comparison with Similar Sites

After completing the final archaeological study for Fort Dobbs, specific interpretive questions relating to reconstruction were raised about various fort elements. Since it was believed there was a relationship between the 1720s British fortified Ruthven Barracks at Kingussie and Fort Dobbs, a site visit was arranged. This inspection explored several constructional aspects about Ruthen Barracks including gun ports (loopholes), joist size, internal partitioning, chimney flues, and flanker aspects. The on-site inspection revealed other unexpected connections between the sites including basement depth and building dimensions. Ruthven Barracks were erected during the 1720s to help suppress Jacobite insurrections in the Scottish Highlands (Stell 1973). They were capable of housing some 300 men in a defensive structure that was unlikely to face artillery. The South Barracks was measured and found to be 54 ft. long by 20 ft. wide with a very shallow basement. If the two Ruthven barracks facing each other across a narrow parade were combined into one building, they would be the equivalent of the Fort Dobbs main building (53 × 40), which could also hold 300 men. The stone walls were generally about 2 ft. thick. The barracks length is intriguing when compared with Fort Dobbs with its very odd length of 53 ft. Windows facing the parade ground were 3 ft. wide and 5.33 ft. high. There was no evidence for shutters, but there were indications of window framing.

Gunports or loopholes pierced the exterior walls. These were roughly 4 ft. above the interior flooring, but their exterior height was over 6 ft. above the ground surface. If attackers could reach the wall, their weaponry could only shoot at the ceiling of the casemates and barracks. This configuration also compares favorably with the notion that Fort Dobbs had loop holes 4.5 ft. above the interior floor but 6 ft. above the ground surface. At Fort Dobbs the additional height would be obtained by a sill log, 16 × 16 in. square.

The 12 × 9 in. joist mortises were placed into the wall on 16 in. centers. The depth of the cellar below the ground floor was 4.5 ft. The gable ends of the buildings held chimneys that ran from the ground floor up. Each floor had its own flue running up inside the chimney.

The Ruthven flankers were two stories in height with gable roofs. The flankers' second floors were not loop holed for musketry but did have a window allowing fire down on the terreplein behind the curtain wall's parapet or onto approaches to the gate. The window was large enough to mount a swivel gun.

Artifacts

The artifacts discussed here are primarily those relating to reconstructing the fort, with a brief mention of military artifacts. The relatively few nails (N=139) found anywhere on site, but especially in the cellar, tend to confirm local oral traditions that the building was taken down and recycled (Eliason 1976:33; Keever 1976:59). The low nail number also tends to confirm that the building was largely of hewn log construction. As just one example, if shingles are calculated for only the main building, the square footage without considering flankers, pitch, and eave overhang is still 2,120 ft. square. Covering 1 sq. ft. with shingles would require a minimum of three nails, meaning that some 6,360 5d nails would be required, a probable underestimation by well over 50 percent. Obviously most of the nails were recycled after the fort was abandoned.

Two, plain-faced pewter buttons with a "PN" back mark found in features associated with the western house are of particular significance. "PN" buttons are an archaeological signature of a British presence during the French and Indian War (Babits 1982). The back mark is important in two ways. First, it identifies buttons in terms of others with the identical back mark. Second, back marked buttons are quite rare for the 1750s (Albert 1976:464–65). Both are 0.9 in. in diameter, 0.06 in. thick, with a cast eye. They came from the western house area, an exterior structure dating to the fort occupation period that may have been occupied by an officer. This type button has been found at many French and Indian War posts including Fort Ligonier, Fort Stanwix, and Fort Loudoun, Tennessee, as well as Fort Dobbs.

Five bayonet scabbard finials and one scabbard latchet (Gale 2007:12) indicate that numerous bayonets were on site and may have been stored there, certainly not the case in a typical frontier house where bayonets would have been unlikely. The presence of bayonets was expected because "stands of arms" were sent to Fort Dobbs (Dupre 1756; Ramsey 1964:50; Kars 2002:247; Osborne 1759; Duane 1810:14).

A total of 584 lead balls, shot, and sprue were found at Fort Dobbs. Some 350 lead items came from the cellar. Most of the cellar lead recoveries are small pieces of sprue that represent bullet or shot manufacture at the hearth. Shot size distribution percentages compare well with shot sizes from Fort Ligonier and Fort Loudoun, Tenn. (Babits and Pecoraro 2008:107–109).

Conclusion

Taken together, the archaeological information, documentary sources, and comparative resources suggest a fortified barracks designed to provide housing and a base of operations for frontier troops who were not likely to encounter an enemy armed with artillery. After at least a dozen possibilities were discussed (Babits and Pecoraro 2008:160–71, 176–79, 183–93),

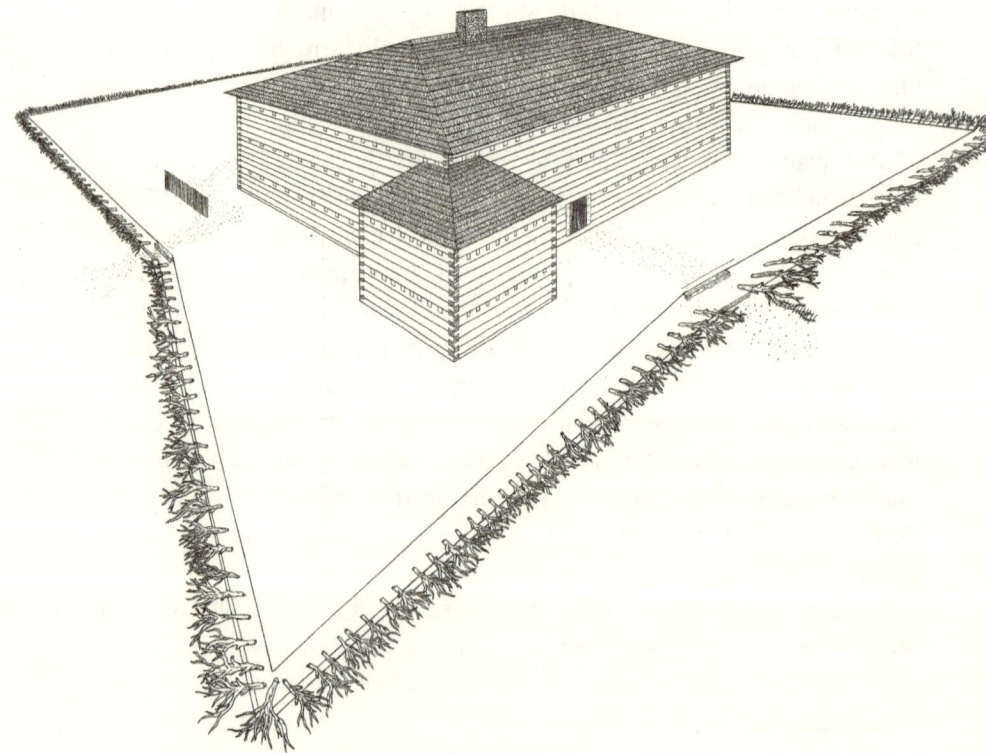

Figure 5.4. Conjectural rendering of Fort Dobbs, 2006. (Drawing by Matthew De Felice. In Babits and Pecoraro 2008:191.)

the following interpretation has the best fit with the information available (figure 5.4).

The fortified strong barracks would be oriented with its long axis east–west with the northeastern quadrant of the building over the cellar. The full hipped roof ridge would be supported by vertical timbers at their ends and the chimney in the middle. It would be covered with clapboards, although they may have later used shingles.

The flankers would be on the northeast and southwest corners of the main building. Their 24 ft. long axes would parallel the long sides of the central building. The walls would be composed of 16 in. high timbers varying in thickness. The first floor walls would be 16 in. thick, the second, 12, and the third, 6. The walls would be penetrated with a regular combination of loopholes and small windows with their bottoms 4.5 ft. above the flooring (Young 1980:16; Babits and Pecoraro 2008:177–79).

Outside the building, there would be two cressets to provide light on the short sides. The star-shaped abatis anchored in the shallow ditch would surround the post with its long axes paralleling the building's long sides. There should be a passage through the abatis on the south side and midway on the northwestern side. Inside the abatis, a defensive palisade wall would be midway between the abatis ditch and the northwestern side of the main building.

Taken as the total sum of all its parts, the Fort Dobbs fortified barracks was an incredibly sophisticated defensive structure designed to be defended from inside the building. The outer works, the ditch-anchored abatis, would impede any attackers without providing cover. If defenders were caught near the northwestern gates, the 8 ft. long inner palisade would provide a point from which to fire, or it would cover their retreat to the building's north door. At night, cressets on the east and west sides would provide light in an emergency while leaving the doorways in shadow.

There are numerous other intriguing postulations about the fort. Loophole floors angled down to shed water as well as allowing gunfire directed at different parts of the fort outside the building. The flankers provided covering fire along all walls with most of their exterior also covered by protective fire from the main building. The doors probably opened so as not to provide cover to anyone attempting to force an entrance, that is, they swung away from the flanker shoulder, exposing attackers to fire. These are covered in much detail in the final report by Babits and Pecoraro (2008).

6

Fort Loudoun, Virginia

A French and Indian War Period Fortification Constructed by George Washington

ROBERT L. JOLLEY

Fort Loudoun, Winchester, Virginia, is one of three French and Indian War period forts named after John Campbell, Lord Loudoun, commander of British troops in North America. The fort was designed and constructed by Col. George Washington in 1756–58 and served as the command center and supply depot for Virginia troops during the war. The fort was never attacked, but men who garrisoned the fort participated in General Forbes's 1758 Fort Duquesne expedition and in an unsuccessful 1760 expedition to relieve the Cherokee siege of Fort Loudoun, Tennessee. Washington commanded the fort from 1756 to 1758 and William Byrd III commanded the fort after Washington resigned his commission.

Historical research and limited archaeological investigations were conducted to address research questions and to raise community awareness of this largely forgotten but important historical site. The investigations were conducted by the Winchester Regional Preservation Office of the Department of Historic Resources with the support of the Northern Shenandoah Valley chapter of the Archeological Society of Virginia. Figures were drafted by Marcus Lemasters of the Frederick County Department of Geographic Information Systems.

Historical Background

In March 1756, the Virginia House of Burgesses authorized construction of a fort "for the protection of the adjacent inhabitants against the barbarities daily committed by the French and Indian allies" (Hening 1819:33). The

Fort Loudoun, Virginia: A French and Indian War Fort Built by George Washington · 103

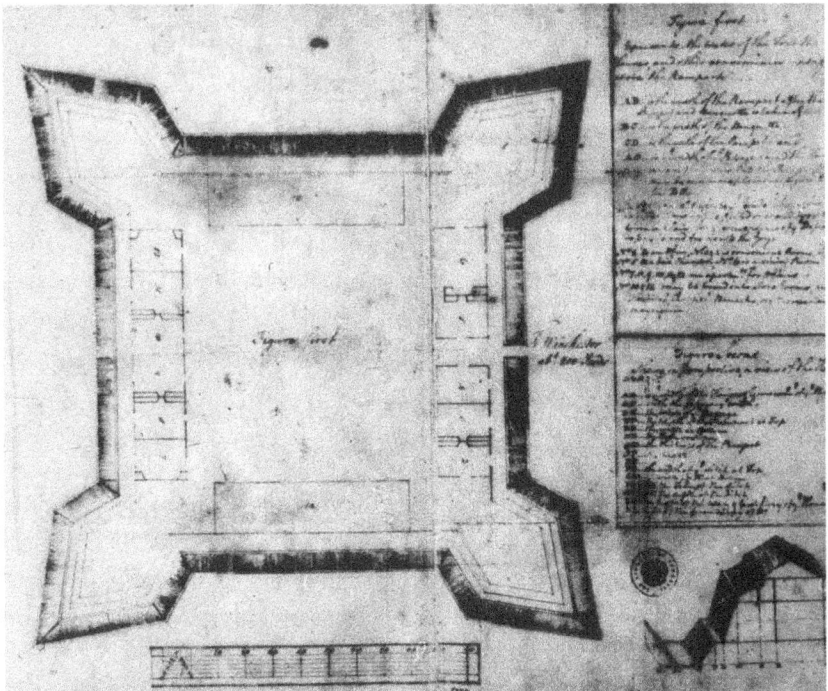

Figure 6.1. Washington's design plan for Fort Loudoun. (Library of Congress.)

location chosen for the fort was the immediate high ground north of Winchester. Colonel Washington justified this location based on its proximity to the closest French fort (Fort Duquesne), and convenience to its commander who was stationed at Winchester (Abbot 1984a:60).

Fort Loudoun was the first formal fort designed by Washington, and there are two sets of plans. Both depict a four-bastion square fort with structures located along each curtain and a gate facing the town. One plan incorporates concerns raised by William Fairfax (Abbot 1984a:247) and is likely the one used for construction. In this plan, the buildings are shown for the officers' guard room, the soldiers' guard room, the prison kitchen, the powder magazine, magazines for provisions, a two-tiered soldiers barracks with large fireplaces for cooking, the well, a sally port, and two large houses to be converted into barracks or store houses "as occasion shall require" (figure 6.1).

Colonel Washington was an inexperienced officer with no formal military training, yet the fort plans indicate that he designed the fort himself. He may have used information contained in military manuals. The fort design is similar to Fort LeBoeuf, which he visited in 1753 and described in his diary (Fitzpatrick 1925:59). He selected a practical plan similar to Pennsylvania frontier forts (Waddell and Bomberger 1996). Washington sent plans of the fort for William Fairfax to review, apparently seeking advice from others more experienced in military matters.

Completing the fort took more than two years (spring 1756–fall 1758) and was a constant concern of Washington's. He complained about the slow progress of construction on several occasions. On 24 September 1757, after construction had proceeded for over a year, Washington informed Robert Dinwiddie that illness and the need to dispatch troops for other duties prohibited completing principal parts of the fort before winter (Abbot 1984b:420).

Even after two years, the fort was not finished, and questions arose as to whether it would be completed. On 28 May 1758, Washington asked John St. Clair, "Are the works at Ft. Loudoun to go on?" (Abbot 1988a:201). In June 1758, the Council of Colonial Virginia postponed construction due to a lack of funds (Hillman 1966:98). That the fort remained unfinished on 12 December 1758 was indicated in a letter by Robert Stewart informing Washington that there was no material to finish the barracks (Abbot 1988b:167).

Problems with construction mentioned in the correspondence provide information on the sequence of building, the structures that were erected, and the materials used. The most informative account is in a letter written by Charles Smith to Washington on 23 February 1758:

> The third barrack is intirely covered in, and the last one now aframing in order to raise, the parapet on the last curtains up, the last Bastin is lay'd over with logs and two of the ambuziers [embrasures] done and now is about the other four, we have done all the joyner's work in the second barrack, we are in great want of a barrel of double tens for the last barrack, we not having one, our stone masons has been sick ever since you have been away and our stone work is much behind hand. The well has been almost full of water but is now cleared and they are at work in it again and there is near 90 foot deep. (Abbot 1988a:97)

This letter indicates that four barracks were constructed and that stone was used in the fort's construction. Although Smith mentions logs for bastion construction, later correspondence indicates that stone was used in the southeast bastion. On 7 September 1758, Smith informed Washington that stone work on the southeast bastion is "intirely dropping out" (Abbot 1988b:3), and he later reported employing two masons for ten days to conduct repairs (Abbot 1988b:75).

Other repairs had to be made while the fort was being constructed. Smith wrote Washington in July 1758 that the powder magazine needed repair (Abbot 1988a). The powder magazine was located in the southeast bastion where other repairs were noted. This area has a sloping topography, which may have accounted for some construction problems.

The presence of limestone bedrock also created construction problems. Washington's account books contain numerous entries between April 1757 and April 1758 for payments to John Christian Heintz for digging the well through limestone and for "blowing rock" in the "barracks yard" (Quarles 1974:37).

The fort may have deviated from Washington's design plans. The inexperience of the supervising officers, Washington's frequent absences, and construction problems may have been contributing factors. On 12 January 1757, Washington wrote from Fort Cumberland that Captain Mercer "informs me, that they are at a great loss in respect to the manner of making the Ambrozores thro' the parapet, altho' I gave directions in person before I came away on this head, they propose a method that will spoil the whole work" (Abbot 1984b:94).

A spring 1760 description of the fort by English clergyman Andrew Burnaby provided details on the final fort:

> It is a regular square fortification, with four bastions, mounting twenty-four cannon; the length of each curtain, if I am not mistaken, is about eighty yards. Within, there are barracks for 450 men. The materials of which it is constructed, are logs filled up with earth: the soldiers attempted to surround it with a dry ditch; but the rock was so extremely hard and impenetrable, that they were obliged to desist. It is still unfinished; and, I fear, going to ruin. (Burnaby n.d.:41)

Burnaby's account described how the fort walls were constructed and indicated that the dry ditch was not completed. His account also shows that the 24 guns Washington wanted were finally obtained. On 27 June 1757, Washington wrote Dinwiddie that the fort needed 24 guns and that he currently had 4 twelve-pounder and 10 four-pounder cannon, adding that six more cannon were needed (Abbot 1984b:266). William Fairfax wrote Washington on 17 July 1757 that he would be furnished with two mortars (Abbot 1984b:309), but Washington persisted in requesting more cannon. On 24

September 1757, he wrote Dinwiddie that he had round and grape shot for six pounders, but no cannon to use them, and suggested "a few pieces of that size" (Abbot 1984b:420).

Washington originally proposed a 100-man garrison (Abbot 1984b:10), a number consistent with orders given Washington by Dinwiddie in a letter dated 17 May 1757 (Brock 1883:622). The number garrisoned at Fort Loudoun fluctuated greatly. There were 141 present on 1 January 1757 (Abbot 1984b:76–77), 100 fit for duty were present on 16 June 1757 (Abbot 1984b:221), and of 54 present on 27 October 1758, only 24 were fit for duty (Abbot 1988b:135). A total of 268 men were listed at Winchester in 28 May 1760 when the fort was under William Byrd III (Byrd 1760). Troops garrisoned at the fort were the First and Second Virginia Regiments. On occasion "rangers" and "Carolina" troops are also listed.

Throughout its short life as a military garrison, Fort Loudoun served a number of purposes, including that of a supply magazine for other forts. When Washington wrote Dinwiddie on 27 April 1756, outlining the need for a Winchester fort, he stated the necessity of a large magazine to supply the different forts (Abbot 1984a:61). In early June 1757, Dinwiddie mentioned the transfer from Fort Loudoun of 100 barrels of gunpowder, three tons of lead, 100 six-pound shot, and 1,200 gunflints to Colonel Stanwix (Abbot 1984b:184). Thirty barrels of powder and 150 boxes of bullets were sent on from the fort to Pennsylvania in June 1758 (Stevens et al. 1951:83).

The fort also served as a hospital. On 24 June 1758, Washington ordered a hospital located at a private residence to be vacated, and he converted a room in one barracks into a hospital (Abbot 1988a:238). Soldiers left at the fort during the 1758 Forbes's expedition against Fort Duquesne were chiefly those who were ill. On 28 July 1758, Charles Smith informed Washington that 28 Second Virginia Regiment men left at the fort were "very sick," and on 5 August 1758, he paid a doctor for tending to the sick (Abbot 1988a: 253, 373).

Although the fort served as a depot for Virginia troops and others in the region, there were problems with supplying troops with basic items, including clothing. The soldiers wore a variety of clothing styles in various states of repair. Washington reported to Dinwiddie on 10 December 1756 that the men are "naked" (Abbot 1984b:49). In the spring of 1758, Washington ordered his troops to mend their own clothes if they could not get tailors to do it (Abbot 1988a:191). In the summer of 1758, Washington informed Colonel Bouquet that his men were "bare of cloaths" and suggested that everyone adopt "Indian dress," including the officers (Stevens et al. 1951:159).

When Colonel Byrd arrived in Winchester to take command of the Second Virginia Regiment, he informed General Forbes, "If you have no objection, I propose to dress my soldiers after the Indian fashion" (Forbes 1758:287).

A wide variety of arms, many of which were obsolete and in poor condition, were used at Fort Loudoun. In July 1757, Washington informed Dinwiddie of a shortage of arms and that he was repairing old ones (Abbot 1988b:292). Byrd informed Dinwiddie in June 1758 that none of the 320 guns received from Williamsburg were fit for service "for they had been in the magazine since the reign of King William" (Forbes 1758:327). A 30 July 1758 report on Fort Loudoun's arms indicated that military equipment was under repair. Although 160 muskets and 290 bayonets had been repaired, 440 muskets, 170 musket barrels, and 250 bayonets had not (Abbot 1988a:352).

Unlike other French and Indian War period forts located in the backcountry, Fort Loudoun was adjacent to a town. The proximity of Winchester allowed interaction between the garrison and townspeople. As early as November 1756, Washington complained about the soldiers visiting "tippling-houses" (Abbot 1984b:16). In October 1757, Washington continued complaining about "tipling-house keepers in Winchester" giving soldiers too much credit and that he suspected they were receiving and concealing property belonging to the Virginia Regiment (Abbot 1988a:10–11). Regiment property had been reported as recovered from local houses the previous month, including military equipment, clothing, and other provisions (Abbot 1984b:424–26).

Indian allies such as the Cherokee, Catawba, Tuscarora, Nottaway, and Saponi operated out of Fort Loudoun. Cherokees and Catawbas were at Fort Loudoun as early as December 1756 (Abbot 1984b:50). In July 1757, Dinwiddie indicated there were around 200 Cherokee at Fort Loudoun and that 14 scalps and two French prisoners had been brought in by them (Brock 1883:663). Large numbers of Indian allies recruited to serve in Forbes's Fort Duquesne expedition were at Fort Loudoun in 1758. By May 1758, as many as 700 Cherokee had passed through the fort (Anderson 2000:268), and some Indians may have stayed. Byrd wrote Forbes in June 1758, "My room, according to custom, is crowded with savages" (Forbes 1758:287).

Indian allies expected goods in return for their support, but providing them with equipment proved to be as difficult as supplying soldiers. Washington informed Dinwiddie in December 1756 that the Catawbas expected to receive clothing, wampum, pipes, tomahawks, and silver trinkets and that he purchased wampum and tomahawks for them (Abbot 1984b:35). In

March 1758, Thomas Bullit indicated that 300 Cherokee at Fort Loudoun were equipped and "sent out against the enemy" but that "light firearms" and match coats are needed for another 100 Indians (Forbes 1758:99).

Rations are mentioned in a letter dated June 1758 written by Henry Bouquet to Washington. The allowance per week consisted of seven pounds of flour, seven pounds beef (or four pounds of pork), three pints of peas, half an ounce of butter, half a pint of rice or one pound flour and one pound of pork (Abbot 1988a:209). In the same letter Bouquet stated that the allowance for Fort Cumberland was 8 pounds of flour, eight pounds of beef or five pounds of pork per week until further notice, indicating flexibility in the rations.

After the British occupied Fort Duquesne in November 1758, there was no need to finish Fort Loudoun. Washington returned to Winchester after leaving some men at Fort Duquesne (Quarles 1974:42). He resigned his commission as colonel of the First Virginia Regiment before the end of the year (Anderson 2000:289). Francis Fauquier, who replaced Robert Dinwiddie as lieutenant governor of Virginia in 1758 (Reese 1980:14), offered Washington's command to William Byrd III in January 1759 (Byrd 1735:72).

Little information about Fort Loudoun, Virginia, is contained in the correspondence of British and American military leaders after the capture of Fort Duquesne. The correspondence of the Virginia Regiment's two commanders after Washington resigned, William Byrd III (Byrd 1760; Byrd 1735–72; Tinling 1977) and later Adam Stephen (Stephen 1749–1849; Keesecker and Keesecker 1972–82), make only occasional reference to the post(s) at Winchester. The records and correspondence reference Winchester rather than Fort Loudoun, possibly to avoid confusion with the two other Fort Loudouns in Pennsylvania and the Overhill Cherokee country in present-day Tennessee.

One historian suggests that a token force was kept at the fort during the later part of the French and Indian War (Ward 1989:67). This suggestion is supported by documents indicating large numbers of Virginia troops were located in western Pennsylvania and southwest Virginia. Conversely, the only Virginia Regiment muster roll found for this period, dated May 1760 (Byrd 1760), lists 268 men at Winchester, a number that exceeds the total during Washington's command.

Winchester continued to supply cattle, sheep, horses, forage, pork, salt, Indian corn, and flour to western Pennsylvania garrisons (Kent et al. 1976:594; Waddell et al. 1978). In November 1759, Stanwix sent the Virginia

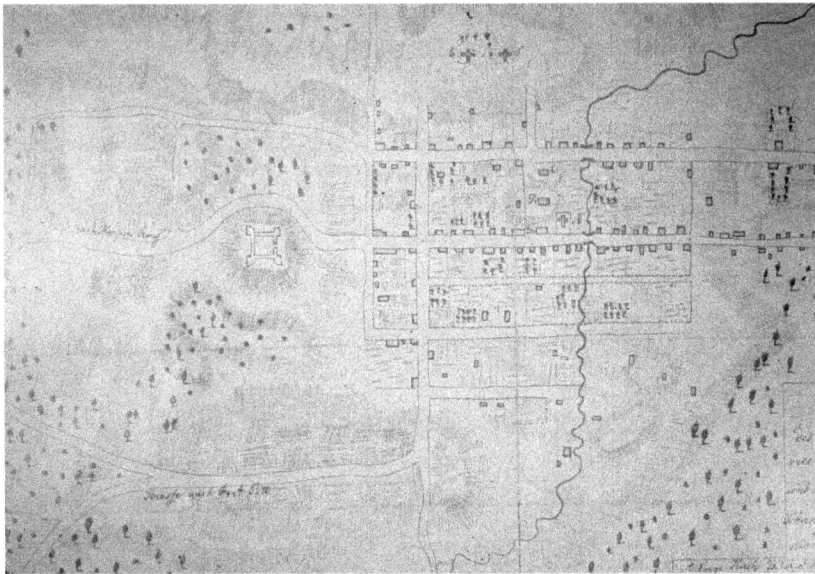

Figure 6.2. Map of Winchester, depicting Fort Loudoun. (Andreas Weiderhold, 1777.)

Regiment to Winchester and informed Fauquier that they were not needed until spring 1760 (Waddell et al. 1978:353).

Fort Loudoun remained garrisoned by Virginia troops during the spring of 1761 (Byrd 1735–72). In February 1761, Fauquier ordered Virginia troops who returned from Fort Pitt and "the other posts at Winchester" to march southward (Reese 1981:476). In early 1762, Fauquier disbanded the Virginia Regiment (Reese 1981:667, 671), but after news of Britain declaring war on Spain, the decision was reversed and the Virginia Regiment was retained until it finally disbanded in December 1762 (Ward 1989:76, 79).

Virginia militia units may have briefly garrisoned at Fort Loudoun during Pontiac's War. In 1763 Fauquier gave Adam Stephen 500 men to defend the backcountry. Stephen was based at Fort Cumberland but wrote several letters from Winchester (Reese 1981:1005; Keesecker and Keesecker 1972–82). In April 1764, Fauquier mentioned that Stephen had 250 men posted in Frederick and Hampshire Counties (Reese 1983:1095). Since Fort Loudoun is located in Frederick County, it may have been one of those posts.

A 1777 map of Winchester drawn by Andreas Weiderhold depicts Fort Loudoun as an intact rectangular fort with four bastions (figure 6.2). There are conflicting accounts as to whether the fort was used to quarter British prisoners during the Revolutionary War (Anburey 1791; Miles 1988:33). The fort had fallen into disrepair by the early nineteenth century as evidenced by an 1809 map, which depicts a road bisecting it.

Today, the site of Fort Loudoun is a residential neighborhood consisting of structures dating from the mid-nineteenth through the twentieth century. The site has been extensively compromised, and it is estimated that no more than 20 percent of the fort survives on individual house lots. Extant remains include the well and the northwest bastion earthwork.

Field Investigations

The fieldwork was limited in scope but designed to address research questions relating to (1) the construction of the fort wall/ditch, (2) the construction/function of two structures within the fort, (3) the material culture of French and Indian War soldiers living on the Virginia frontier, (4) social stratification (officers versus enlisted men), (5) refuse disposal patterns, (6) subsistence, (7) interaction/trade with Native Americans, and (8) interaction with local townspeople.

The historic Darlington Hardy lot located over the fort's northwest corner was chosen for investigation as it encompasses the fort well. The field

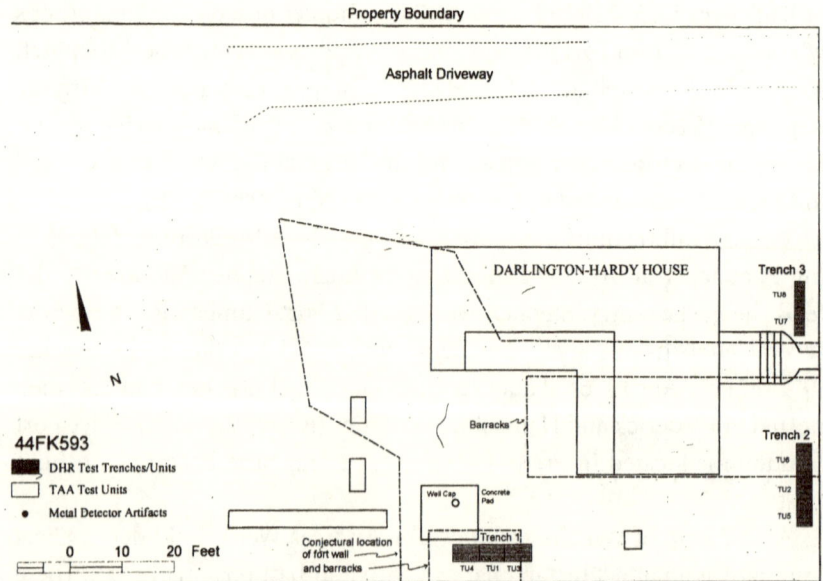

Figure 6.3. Location of archaeological excavations and conjectural location of Fort Loudoun. (Used by permission of the Virginia Department of Historic Resources.)

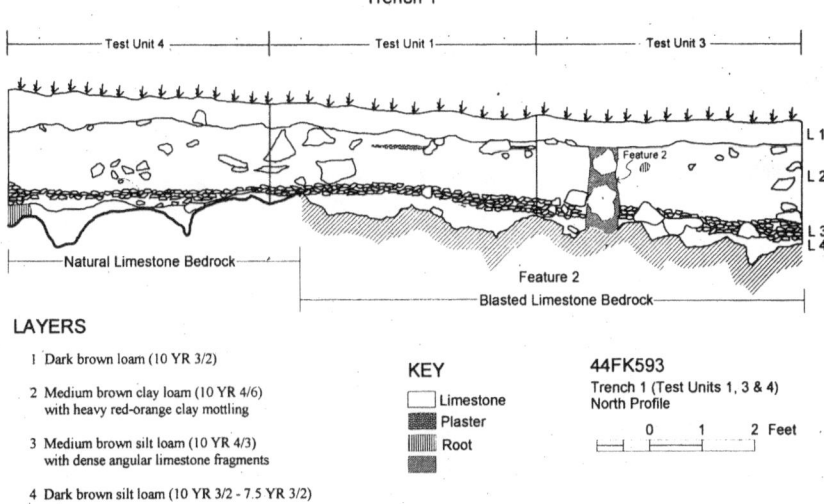

Figure 6.4. Test Trench 1, north profile. (Used by permission of the Virginia Department of Historic Resources.)

strategy was established after considering (1) existing site conditions, (2) previous archaeological work, (3) Washington's design plans, (4) anticipated locations of nineteenth- and twentieth-century disturbances, and (5) the research questions. Washington's plan depicting the well's location was used to site test units to intersect other fort structures and features. Three fort structures or features were targeted: (1) the west barracks, (2) the north barracks, and (3) the fort wall and ditch.

Three exploratory trenches encompassing 110 sq. ft. were excavated (figure 6.3). All test units were excavated according to natural stratigraphy. Intact Fort Loudoun period deposits were found in two test trenches. One structure, four features, and one posthole dating to the Fort Loudoun period were identified.

Test Trench 1 was excavated to intersect the west barracks depicted on Washington's plans. Two of the four layers contained fort period deposits. Layer 3 consisted of extensive limestone blasting debris mixed with soil. The layer of blasted limestone appeared uniformly spread to form a level surface, possibly a living floor. Layer 4 is a fort period midden deposit under Layer 3. Beneath Layer 4 is natural and blasted limestone bedrock (figure 6.4).

Test Trench 2 was excavated to intersect the north barracks. At the base of Layer 3, one structure, three features, and one posthole dating to the Fort

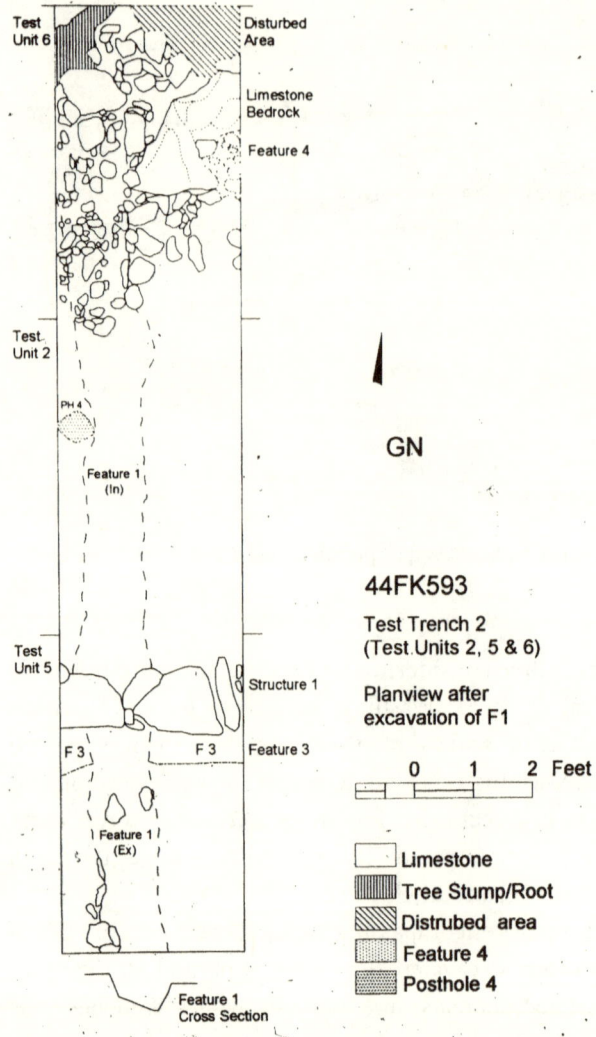

Figure 6.5. Test Trench 2; plan view after excavation. (Used by permission of the Virginia Department of Historic Resources.)

Loudoun period were encountered. A limestone wall, likely the south wall of the north barracks, was found. A trench lined with limestone provided drainage to keep the barracks dry. The intrusion of this feature into the barracks foundation suggests that additional drainage was needed. Feature 4, a concentration of fort period artifacts found in a crevice of bedrock, may be where artifacts were deposited when fort grounds were policed (figure 6.5).

Test Trench 3 was excavated to locate the fort wall and ditch. Few artifacts were found, and no intact period deposits were present. Layer 4 consisted of sterile gray clay with natural limestone bedrock present at the base. The paucity of fort period artifacts and absence of period features and deposits suggests that this trench is possibly located in the area of a planned ditch. The presence of natural limestone bedrock here is consistent with a 1760 account indicating a ditch was attempted but aborted because "the rock was so extremely hard and impenetrable" (Burnaby n.d.:41).

Artifact Assemblage

Fort period artifacts were screened through ¼" hardware cloth (N=890), and selected samples were screened through 1/16" hardware cloth (N=154). South's (1977: 90–102) classificatory scheme for historic artifacts was used. Modifications to South's scheme include consolidating his bottle classes into one glass container category. An unclassified category was established to accommodate artifacts that could not be identified or did not comfortably fit into South's categories.

Kitchen Group

Ceramic Containers

Ceramics recovered from Fort Loudoun are similar to those recovered from other contemporary French and Indian War sites such as Fort Michilimackinac, Fort Stanwix, Fort Ligonier, and Fort Frederick (Stone 1974; Hanson and Hsu 1975; Grimm 1970; Boyd 2001). They are also similar to colonial domestic sites dating to this time period (Miller and Stone 1970:94).

Ceramics, in order of greatest number, are coarse earthenware (56.3%), white salt-glazed stoneware (17.3%), tin-glazed earthenware (16.8%), Rhenish stoneware (4.1%), Chinese porcelain (3.2%), English porcelain (1.8%), and Whieldon (.5%). The majority (56.3%) consists of coarse earthenware used for utilitarian purposes. Vessel forms for finer ceramics include teacups and saucers (Chinese porcelain, English porcelain, and white salt-glazed stoneware), mugs or tankards (Rhenish stoneware), jars, and a large tin-glazed earthenware bowl.

South's (1977:210–12) date ranges for 87 ceramics (Chinese porcelain, English porcelain, white salt-glazed stoneware, Rhenish stoneware, tin-glazed earthenware, and Whieldon ware) were used to calculate a mean ceramic date. The date derived is 1747.96, approximately 10 years earlier than the mean date of Fort Loudoun. The mean ceramic date formula may reflect time lag between when the ceramics were manufactured and when they were deposited in the ground (Adams and Gaw 1977:228).

Glass Containers

Glass recovered from Fort Loudoun (N=134) was analyzed according to color and type of container. The majority of glass (84%) is olive-green. This color was used primarily for alcoholic beverage containers, specifically wine and case bottles (Jones and Smith 1985). Five fragments of stemmed ware were recovered. The social use and cost of stemmed wares suggest that it was owned by an officer (Brown 1971:107). Other glass includes four blue-green fragments, which may be of French origin (Brown 1971:105; Hanson and Hsu 1975:130). This color glass has been previously found on British military sites dating from the 1750s to the 1760s (Jones and Smith 1985:63).

Architectural Group

The Architectural Group (N= 347) consists of nails (98.8%) and window glass (1.2%). Most complete nails are greater than 8d in size. A variety of nail sizes (2d, 4d, 6d, 8d, flooring brads, and spikes) were stored at Fort Loudoun during construction (Washington 1741–99:827). Windowpanes were used in the fort: Washington ordered 200 panes of window glass measuring 8 × 10 in. in a 1757 letter (Abbot 1984b:165).

Arms Group

This group consists of musket balls (N=14), gunflints (N=4), and gun parts (N=2). Most musket balls (75%) fall within the caliber range (.69–.74) of English military muskets. One ball falls within the caliber range for a French musket or British officer's fusil (Hamilton 1976:33; Hanson and Hsu 1975:80), and two are smaller balls. Six buck and swan shot were also recovered (Hamilton 1976:35). Three musket balls have uneven seam marks, suggesting they were cast in the field rather than manufactured in a production mold (Hamilton 1980:28). Such casting methods reflect frontier conditions where lead from imported pigs or local mines was used for musket ball manufacture (Hamilton 1980:28).

Four gunflints were recovered. Two gunflints made on spalls of dark gray-black flint are likely of English manufacture. The other two gunflints were made on blades of grayish, honey-colored flint and are likely of French origin. Gunflints were used and stored at Fort Loudoun and, on one occasion, 1,200 gunflints were shipped from Fort Loudoun to Colonel Stanwix (Abbot 1984b:184).

Two gun parts, a cock and a sear, were found. Guns were repaired at Fort Loudoun. A 1758 report on arms at Fort Loudoun indicates that 160 muskets had been repaired (Abbot 1988a:352).

Clothing Group

This group consists of buttons, buckles, and hook and eye fasteners. Fifteen buttons, five buckles, and three parts of hook and eye fasteners were recovered.

Few generalizations can be made about the sample of buttons recovered from Fort Loudoun. A diversity of types (N=6) is represented consistent with the assemblages recovered from other contemporaneous forts. The greatest number of buttons (N=5) conform to South's Type 7. Stone's (1974:53) analysis of buttons recovered from Fort Michilimackinac suggests that these buttons date from 1750 to 1780 and were used by civilians. If Stone's assessment of these buttons is correct, this suggests that the prevalent button type at Fort Loudoun reflects soldiers wearing civilian attire.

Eighteenth-century buckles served several functions (Hanson and Hsu 1975:91). Three buckles fall within the size range for shoe buckles, one falls within the size range for a knee buckle (Grimm 1970:56, 59), and one may be a belt buckle used for military purposes (Noel Hume 1969:84). Two buckles are iron. Iron shoe buckles were inexpensive and reflect the low socioeconomic status of the enlisted men garrisoned at Fort Loudoun.

Personal Group

Three items of jewelry and one lead pencil were recovered.

Jewelry items include a brass cuff link with a black glass inset and two cut triangular sheets of silver. The silver items may have been ornaments traded to Native Americans.

Tobacco Pipe Group

White clay pipes were found (N=54). The stems measure 4/64 in. and 5/64 in. Sample size is too small to apply different dating methods for pipe diameters proposed by archaeologists (Binford 1972; Heighton and Deagan

1972). Previous applications of these formulas produced date ranges that vary from the known historic dates of the sites.

Activities Group

Military

Sixty iron balls representing either canister or grapeshot were recovered from the excavations. Whether these artifacts were used as canister or grapeshot depended on how they were loaded into the cannon and the size of the gun (Hanson and Hsu 1975:76). The size of the iron shot (20–28 mm) is consistent with shot recovered from two other French and Indian War period forts: Fort Ligonier (Grimm 1970:76) and Fort Stanwix (Hanson and Hsu 1975:78). This type of shot was mainly used for defense at ranges up to 300 yards (Rogers 1975:72).

The amount of iron shot recovered from limited testing at Fort Loudoun is high when compared with iron shot recovered by extensive excavations at Fort Ligonier (N=17) and Fort Stanwix (N=609), but Fort Loudoun had a large number of cannon. In 1760, Burnaby (n.d.:41) indicated 24 cannon were present. Washington reported he had grapeshot for six-pounder cannon but no six-pounder guns to use it (Abbot 1984b:420). The six-pounder grapeshot may have been expendable, since there were no cannon to use them in.

The distribution of iron shot at Fort Loudoun indicates that most (78.3%) were deposited in the barracks (Test Trench 2). The greatest concentration of iron shot at Fort Stanwix was also located in one of the barracks (Hanson and Hsu 1975:76). Concentration of this artifact in the barracks suggests two possibilities: iron shot may have been used for other purposes, or the barracks were used to store munitions.

Two mortar shell fragments were recovered. A 1757 letter to Washington from William Fairfax indicated that "two good mortars" will be sent to Fort Loudoun (Abbot 1984b:309). No round solid shot was recovered from the excavations, although it constituted the greatest percentage of artillery ammunition used by the British in the eighteenth century (Rogers 1975:72). The large size of this ammunition minimized its incidental loss, but it has been recovered at other French and Indian War period military sites (Grimm 1970:76; Hanson and Hsu 1975:76).

One bent bayonet blade was found. A 1758 report on the arms at Fort

Loudoun indicates that there were 540 bayonets on hand, 290 of which had been repaired (Abbot 1988a:352).

Recreation

One limestone marble was recovered. Stone marbles have previously been found at other eighteenth-century military fort sites (Stone 1974:154; Smith and Nance 2000:260). South (1977:182) suggests that their presence may reflect the youth of soldiers.

Stable and Barn

One decorative brass ornament for horse tack was found.

Artifacts Recovered from 1/16 in. Water Screening

Artifacts recovered from 1/16 in. water screening include six straight pins, six small shot, and one glass bead. The large number of window glass fragments (N=73) stands in contrast to the small number (N=4) recovered from the ¼ in. recovery process. Arms related artifacts include birdshot (.10–.18 caliber) and gunflint use/resharpening flakes.

Faunal Remains

The sample of faunal remains (N=891) suggests that cattle and pig were the most important sources of protein in the soldiers' diet (Clark 2003). Other supplemental sources of protein included sheep and goat, turkey, chicken, deer, turtle, and fish. The presence of wild game and fish indicate that hunting and fishing were practiced. The absence of burned bone indicates that meat portions were boiled rather than roasted.

The butchering patterns for cow and pig indicate extensive hacking with heavy-duty tools such as axes or cleavers to produce portions for communal soups or stews. The butchering pattern is similar to that found at Fort Ligonier, another French and Indian War period military site, where axes were used for butchering (Guilday 1970).

Artifact Patterns

The Fort Loudoun artifact pattern and previously compiled artifact patterns from other French and Indian War period military sites (South

Table 6.1. South's artifact pattern percentages for French and Indian War sites

Artifact group	Fort Loudoun, Virginia	Fort Ligonier	Fort Prince George	Fort Loudoun, Tennessee	Fort Frederick
Kitchen	39.8	25.6	22.7	10.3	28.5
Architecture	39.0	55.6	57.5	45.2	53.4
Furniture	0	.2	.1	0.1	.1
Arms	2.8	8.4	6.4	2.5	.7
Clothing	2.6	3.8	1.0	5.6	1.4
Personal	.4	.4	.1	1.4	.1
Tobacco pipes	6.1	1.9	11.5	3.0	1.6
Activities	9.3	4.1	.7	31.9	14.2
Unclassified	1.9	—	—	—	—

1977:111; Boyd 2001:50; Kuttruff, this volume) are presented in table 6.1. Several variables (sample size, differential recovery methods) affect the reliability of making comparisons between sites. Investigators have also modified South's scheme in different ways. Nonetheless, the Fort Loudoun assemblage fits into the predicted range of the Frontier Artifact Pattern (FAP) established by South (1977:145). Fort Loudoun, Virginia, has the highest percentage of Kitchen Group artifacts, which may be the result of interaction with local Winchester townspeople.

The presence of two distinct Fort Loudoun period deposits, Layers 3 and 4 from Test Trench 1, is of interest since the fort was occupied for only six years. The artifact patterns for the two layers recovered from ¼ in. hardware cloth suggest similar artifact composition, with Layer 3 having a greater percentage of personal, clothing, and military artifacts. The artifacts recovered from 1/16 in. hardware cloth suggest Layer 3 was a living area, and Layer 4 may represent midden deposited in the blasted bedrock crevices during fort construction.

Interpretations and Conclusions

Fort Loudoun is the best-documented fort under Washington's command. There are two design plans for the fort, extensive correspondence relating to construction, and a 1760 description by a civilian. The archaeological deposits dating to the fort are buried beneath nineteenth- and twentieth-century fill, possess a high degree of integrity, and have not been disturbed by agricultural practices or relic hunters.

The excavations provide insight into how the fort was constructed. Since

Washington produced two different plans for the fort and correspondence indicates construction problems, the final fort may have deviated from the original design. Construction problems with bedrock are evidenced by the presence of dense quantities of blasted limestone, some of which display auger holes. Problems with drainage at the fort are reflected in historic documents (Abbot 1988a:307) and are supported by a drainage ditch cutting across a dry-laid foundation.

A description of the fort after it was constructed indicates that a dry moat was attempted but discontinued due to impenetrable rock (Burnaby n.d.:41). This account appears confirmed by Test Trench 3. Since the fort ditch was not finished, it is possible that abatis may have been constructed as suggested for Fort Dobbs (Babits 2007). Abatis would have been easy to emplace and may have presented a more defensive obstacle than a ditch.

Washington's design indicates that he intended the interior of Fort Loudoun to measure ca. 21,000 sq. ft. or approximately one-half acre. The fort is comparable in size and construction to Fort Ligonier, a western Pennsylvania fort (Grimm 1970). Comparative data on fort size recently compiled by Kuttruff (this volume) indicates considerable variability in the interior size of French and Indian War forts(ranging from 12,083 to 101,325 sq. ft.).

Archaeological investigations conducted at other frontier French and Indian War forts indicate that most had upright log palisades. Since earth was used in the construction of Fort Loudoun, the fort wall was most likely built with two rows of horizontal logs filled with earth. Horizontal logs filled with earth were used to construct part of the fort wall at Fort Ligonier (Waddell and Bomberger 1996:90). Historic documentation also indicates that stone was used in the southeast bastion (Abbot 1988b:3). Such construction may have taken longer to complete and may account for some of the problems associated with Fort Loudoun.

The archaeological investigations also provided some insights into social stratification between officers and enlisted men. Previous archaeological studies found status differences in the artifacts and types of materials for living quarters (Feister 1984; Fisher 1995). Officers should have a more diverse diet and consume better cuts of meat than enlisted men. At Fort Loudoun, some artifacts, such as the inexpensive iron shoe buckles, reflect the low status of enlisted men. Other artifacts, especially fine ceramics and glassware, were the individual property of officers or the officers' mess. Most of the ceramics associated with high status (porcelain, tea wares, and stemmed glassware) were recovered from the west barracks living floor. The location next to the fort's water supply and away from the main gate strengthens the status association, but this suggestion is not supported when the faunal remains are considered.

The presence of tea wares indicates that officers of the Virginia regiments participated in the tea ceremony (Roth 1961). Similar findings have been made at other contemporaneous French and Indian War period military sites (Grimm 1970; Hanson and Hsu 1975; Miller and Stone 1970).

The investigations provided information on refuse disposal patterns. Kitchen refuse (ceramics, glass containers, and faunal remains) was found in Test Trench 1, the location of one barracks. Some refuse may have been deposited along the barracks walls, a pattern previously documented at eighteenth-century colonial sites (South 1977:47). Feature 4 may represent a discrete concentration of artifacts policed from the site and deposited at one location. The extensive excavations at Fort Ligonier indicate that refuse was deposited along fort walls, on the perimeter of the fort, and in an adjacent streambed (Grimm 1970). Similar patterns of refuse may be expected at Fort Loudoun.

Historic documentation indicates interaction with Native American allies at the fort, but little archaeological evidence of this interaction was found. Native Americans were present at Winchester (Forbes 1758:99, 287). Trade goods purchased for Native American allies include wampum and possibly silver trinkets (Abbot 1984b:35). No Native American artifacts were recovered, but three artifacts (one bead and two silver artifacts) may be trade goods. Interaction with Native Americans at Fort Loudoun, Virginia, was ephemeral and unlike that at Fort Loudoun, Tennessee, where Cherokee pottery was used by the garrison (Kuttruff, this volume).

Additional comparison between Fort Loudoun, Virginia, and Fort Loudoun, Tennessee, is instructive as one fort was a remote outpost and the other was located next to a town. The low percentage of Kitchen Group artifacts at Fort Loudoun, Tennessee (Kuttruff, this volume), reflects the outpost's remoteness. The high percentage of kitchen artifacts at Fort Loudoun, Virginia, reflects exchange between soldiers and local townspeople. The different ceramic assemblages at the two forts (European versus Cherokee) are also due to interaction with different cultural groups (Cherokee versus colonial townspeople).

Future study and comparison of sites garrisoned by the French, the British, and provincials may yield information reflecting differences in artifact classes or patterns. Recent comparative analysis of French and Indian War period military sites in New York suggests variation in the material culture (lead shot and ceramics) between those sites occupied by British regulars and provincial soldiers (Farry 2005). These variations may be the result of differences in standardization and consumption patterns (Farry 2005:30). Differences in refuse disposal practices may indicate British Regulars' encampments having well regulated police calls (Farry 2005:23).

Given the rarity, importance, and fragility of French and Indian War military sites, additional archaeological work conducted at Fort Loudoun or other period military sites should address research questions designed to obtain specific types of comparative data. As evidenced by Farry's 2005 study, there is much data that can be extracted from those forts that have already been excavated.

7

The Second Fort Vause

A Crucial French and Indian War Fort in the Roanoke Valley of Virginia

KIM A. MCBRIDE

This chapter presents a summary of recent archaeological investigations at the second Fort Vause (44My59). Fort Vause was constructed on the Whiteside branch of the south branch of the Roanoke River, in southwestern Virginia in 1756, within modern-day Shawsville, Virginia (figure 7.1). It is a significant site, owned today by Jack and Laree Hinshelwood. Fort Vause is used as the designation because it appears in contemporary literature, although in historical documentation Vause's Fort, often abbreviated to Vause's (with several spellings), was more common.

As an earthen fortification, Fort Vause is unusual and the only one of its kind known in George Washington's chain of French and Indian War forts. Archaeological investigations were directed by the author and W. Stephen McBride, McBride Preservation Services, in September 2005 and May 2006. The research was funded by private grants raised by Gregory Adamson and administered by the Pendleton County Historical Society and the Kentucky Archaeological Survey, a joint undertaking of the University of Kentucky's Department of Anthropology and the Kentucky Heritage Council. This work builds on previous excavations conducted at the site by Ed Heite, whose work led to the site's inclusion on the National Register of Historic Places and its designation as a Virginia Historic Landmark in 1969 (Virginia Landmark file 60-17).

Fort Vause's history is well documented, but the fact that there were two forts with this name has led to much confusion regarding their locations. Adding to the confusion was possible transposing of directions on their locations in relation to nearby Christiansburg, Virginia. The first and second sites are about 10 miles east of Christiansburg, but Koontz's 1925 book put them 10 miles west of Christiansburg. There were attempts early on to straighten out this confusion and to suggest that the two forts were in different, though nearby, locales. One of the most important early attempts to clarify the situation was that of F. B. Kegley in 1938, followed by the efforts of Pendleton (n.d.), Sammons (1966), and Goode (2006). The Fort Vause file at the Virginia Department of Historic Resources contains several letters to officials as high ranking as the governor, documenting the chain of errors about the fort locations or asking that an inaccurate highway marker be corrected. These pleas, however, have largely been ignored. In many written accounts, from early classic texts such as Hale's Trans-Allegheny Pioneers (1886), to the Virginia Landmarks Register (Loth 2000) and the highway marker that stands at the site, the locations for the two forts are conflated and the second fort is assumed to have been built on the ruins of the first. We join the many researchers who have suggested that the two forts were in different locales and that site 44My59 is the remains of only the second fort. The historical and archaeological data presented below support this interpretation.

Though an exact location for the first Vause's Fort has not been verified, many sources suggest it was at or near present-day Walnut Grove, less than a mile east of the second fort site (Goode 2006; Kegley 1938; Sammons 1966); more research and fieldwork will be required to document the exact location of the first fort.

Fort History

Ephraim Vause was a prominent early settler in southwestern Virginia who served in various civic capacities and was designated a Captain of the Horse in 1753. He came to the general area by 1746, settling first on Goose Creek (Roanoke River) within present-day Roanoke and then buying land and moving west to the modern-day Shawsville vicinity circa 1749 (Goode 2006) with his wife, Theodosia, and two daughters. He established a plantation with a house and cabins for slaves (Goode 2006, Sammons 1966; Wells n.d.).

It is not known when Ephraim Vause began to fortify his house, but 1755 is likely. This was when conditions were more dangerous and raids such as the 25 July attack on nearby Draper's Meadow became more frequent. Vause probably didn't choose the location for his home primarily for defense purposes, but such might have entered into his calculations. There is

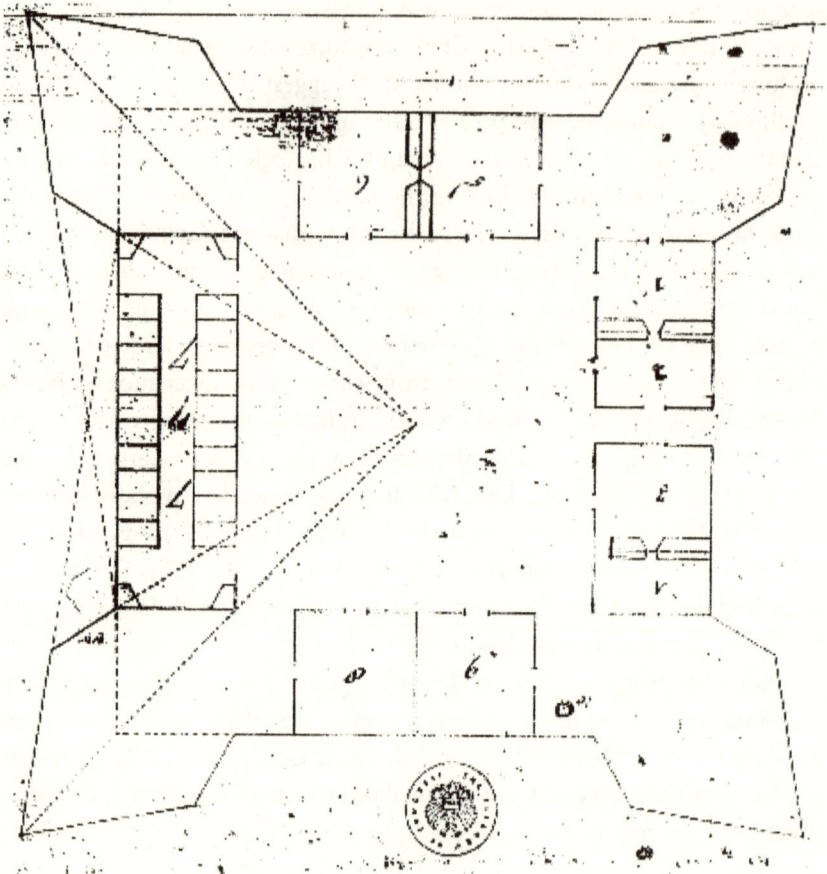

Figure 7.1. Typical fort plan by George Washington. (Library of Congress, Manuscript Division.)

no documentation on the structure of the first fort, and most assume it was composed of vertical stockading around most major structures, perhaps incorporating the outer walls of some structures. Although the original fort was not built as an official state or militia fort, Virginia Regiment troops under Capt. John Smith were garrisoned there, and it may have been a gathering place for local rangers (Sammons 1966: 25–26).

On 25 June 1756, a large and varied force of over 100 Indians, including many from as far away as the Great Lakes, and about 25 French Canadians under Francois-Marie Picot de Belestre burned the plantation and fort, with 25 persons killed or taken captive. Ephraim Vause was not at home and thus escaped. His wife and two daughters, however, along with a slave and two servants, Richard Hadley and William McDaniel, were killed or taken captive. His daughter Levice survived and was later returned (Abbot 1984a:361; Goode 2006; Sammons 1966).

The attack on the first Vause's Fort was a contributing factor to the Virginia government's resolve to strengthen defensive efforts along the entire Virginia frontier. The size of the attacking force provided added incentive to make the second fort much stronger. In a Council of War held at Fort Cumberland on 10 July 1756, a chain of forts for better local defense was proposed. Weeks later, on 27 July 1756, another Council of War held at Augusta Courthouse laid out specifics, including the following comment: "a fort is to be Built at Capt. Vause's where a Large Body of men is to be kept as it is a Very important pass" (Abbot 1984a:243–44).

In November 1756, when presenting an updated proposal on the chain of forts, Washington gave more details on the strategic location of Fort Vause, noting that "the fort at Vass's (which Capt. Hogg is now building) is in a much exposed gap, subject to the inroads of the southern Indians, and in a manner covers the greatest part of Bedford and Hallifax" (Proposal for Frontier Forts, Abbot 1984b:11). Fort Vause's importance is also demonstrated by the number of men it required, 70, while 30 to 60 men were estimated for the other forts. The Augusta Council of War minutes further specified that

> It is agreed that the Commanding officers give Order that Fort Vaus be made at least one hundred feet Square in the Clear and that the Stockades be 14 feet Long that all the other forts be made (60) feet Square with Two Bastions in Each fort provided The Same be agreeable to Capt. Peter Hog who is supposed to have his honr the Governor orders to oversee the Construction of the said Chain of forts. (Abbot 1984a:321–22)

By this time Washington seems to have developed very clear ideas about the structure of forts, and several communications to the potential builders such as Peter Hogg and Thomas Waggener mention enclosed plans. While no specific communication exists regarding deviations for the structure of Fort Vause, the plans detailed (figure 7.1) were likely the general model on hand and have been described in the published Washington Papers as such (Abbot 1984a:279).

The first of the two plans for the frontier forts is a plat of the fort and the plat is keyed to a table giving the various dimensions of the fort.

GW stipulates that the lines of the exterior square of the fort should be 132' and those of the interior square 100'. The curtains were to be 60' long, and the wall was to be 15' high. The bastions at the corners were to have 19¼' flanks, 30' faces, and be 20½' wide at the mouth. "If due attention is given to his plan," GW wrote, "it will be impossible to err. tho. you otherwise may be unacquainted with the Rules of Fortifications." (Abbot 1984a:279)

This information, coupled with the order from the 27 July Council of War that Fort Vause be "100' in the Clear" is the extent of contemporary documentation on possible guidelines for the second Fort Vause.

Primary records suggest that Capt. Peter Hogg had difficulty in keeping order and motivating his men at Vause's. One obstacle may have been procuring tools. Washington's 21 July 1756 orders to Hogg on the construction of forts included these words of advice:

> As the Difficulty of getting Tools in these parts is not easily to be conceived, I would advise you to pursue the same Methods in Augusta, that I have done here vizt to get of the Inhabitants, giving receipts of the Quantity and Sorts of each, and paying for the use, also the Damage & Loss, if any is sustain'd—but to buy would be best if this you can do, take particular care of the whole you receive. (Abbot 1984a:275)

Pay was also a documented obstacle. When Washington visited the fort in October 1756 he noted this problem in a letter to Dinwiddie:

> We got safe to Vass's where Captain Hogg, with only 18 of his company, were building a fort which must employ him 'till Christmas, without more assistance. One Captain Hunt from Lunenburg, was there with 30 men; but none of them wou'd strike a stroke, unless I would engage to see them paid 40 lbs's Tobacco per day, which is provided by act of Assembly for militia Carpenters. This I certainly could not do; as your Honor (who I thought had ordered them purposely out for this Duty) had given no directions in the affair. Whatever expectations your Honor may have had from the militia assistance; I am told they never lent a hand, save a few, that first came out with Capt Hog; who he has paid after the same rates with our men, at 6d per diem. Vass's place is a pass of very great importance, being a very great inroad of the enemy, and secure, if it was strongly garrisoned. (Abbot 1984a:432)

On 21 July 1756, Washington had given orders to Thomas Waggener regarding a fort building on the South Branch, in which he had indicated that men working on the forts would be allowed double pay (Abbott 1984a:279). In a 22 July 1756 letter to Robert Stewart, he directed that tools

> must be put into the hands of the best tradesmen, and most laborious workmen; who will receive six-pence extraordinary pay, for every day they work. . . . The men that remain after the Workers are draughted, must act as covering parties to prevent surprises; against which you must carefully guard. (Abbot 1984a:282)

Ordinary pay for militiamen at the time was 1 s. per day and for artificers, 3 s., and for soldiers in the regiment, 8 d. per day (Abbot 1984a:275). There is no indication that Ephraim Vause had any involvement in building the second fort. He left Augusta County in 1757, disheartened by the failed attempt to send out a retaliatory expedition for the attack on the first Fort Vause (Goode 2006; Sammons 1966).

The men building the forts were exposed to dangers from attack by the French and Indians, hence the mention of covering parties. Shortly after George Washington left Fort Vause in October 1756, on his way south to inspect other forts, John Robinson and John Walker were killed along the same road he had traveled, not far from Vause's. That the frontier was very exposed and dangerous at this time could also be seen in the fact that most settlers had abandoned their homes (Washington to Dinwiddie, 10 October 1756, Abbot 1984a:432).

In a letter dated 21 July 1756 to Hogg, Washington suggests that there had been many previous complaints about Hogg and that several officers refused to serve with him, and he questioned Hogg's interpretation of payroll policies (Abbot 1984a:269–79). On 8 September 1756, Washington again complained to Hogg about payroll and recruiting issues, asked for more information regarding progress on the fort building, and noted that Dinwiddie desired more information on the fort construction, which Hogg had failed to mention in his last report (Abbot 1984a:401–402). On 24 July 1757, Washington removed Hogg from command, expressing his displeasure in a letter, as follows:

> I have great complaints made concerning your manner of carrying on the works at the Fort you are building. It has cost infinitely more money than ever was intended for it, and by the injudicious spot of

> ground you have chosen to fit it upon, it has caused a general clamour. Mr. Bullet [sic] and Mr. Fleming inform me, that you refuse to do the necessaries belong to it. I therefore desire you will immediately upon receipt of this, deliver up the company, arms, stores, and fort, to the command of the former [Thomas Bullitt]. (Abbot 1984b:325–27)

Hogg was ordered to make an account of the stores that would be turned over to Lieutenant Bullitt.

In a letter to Bullitt, also on 24 July 1757, Washington instructed him to "exert your best endeavors to finish the fort in the most expeditious manner; altho' it should, by that means, be roughly done" (Abbot 1984b:328). Just five days later, Washington ordered Andrew Lewis to send Captain Woodward's company, along with an officer and 25 men from Captain Spotswood's company, to occupy Fort Vause and, as Lewis felt needed, the post on Cuttawba and at Campbell's place (Abbot 1984b:346–47). The number of men actually posted at Fort Vause is uncertain. Orders from Washington to Henry Woodward detail that Woodward was to relieve the company at Fort Vause. Woodward was to receive new kettles and turn in his old ones. Most important were the instructions on the urgency to finish Fort Vause:

> As the Fort which Captn Hogg is building, and to which you are now going, has, either thro' bad conduct in the Director, idleness in the workmen, or thro' some other cause which I can not comprehend, been of infinitely more expense to the country, and much longer about, than was ever expected—You are required to finish it with the upmost dispatch; and in that in any manner, however rough, if it will secure you upon an attack. (Abbot 1984b:351)

Henry Woodward was commander of the Tenth Company of the Virginia Regiment (Goode 2006). Other officers potentially present include Lt. William Daingerfield and Ens. Jethro Sumner (Abbot 1984b:135n3). Perhaps the construction at Vause was completed rapidly under Woodward. On 15 August 1757, Governor Dinwiddie's secretary, Wm. Withers, wrote Lewis that "The Gov'r leaves it to your own Prudence whether or not to abandon Vauss's Fort, as you are on the Spot he says You must be the best Judge" (Goode 2006:26). Lewis felt a much smaller force was all that was needed at Fort Vause, which was now being called Fort Littleton or Lyttelton:

In Answer to a Letter I sent to his honr the governor he writs me to Abandon Fort Lyttleton or Continue the troop as I think proper. As that Fort in time may be of Sume Service I think it Best to Continue one officer with 20 Men at it. Capt. Woodward with 50 at Campbells the Remainder of the Detachment under Capt. Woodward which will be near 30 at old Cloyds. (1 September, Abbot 1984b:393)

These orders may have been changed or not followed, however, since Washington's Return for February 1758 shows a sizeable force listed under Woodward "on Roanoke," which must have been at Vause's Fort. This Return shows a captain, 2 lieutenants, an ensign, 3 sergeants, 2 drummers or corporals, and privates to give a total of 74 fit for duty and a man furloughed, under Woodward, on Roanoke. Two men had been recruited since the previous return (Scottish Records Office n.d.).

The fact that no further mention of Fort Vause or Fort Littleton occurs in the Washington Papers after February 1758 indicates that its importance diminished. Goode (2006) suggests that it likely was used in 1758 for storage of munitions. Detaching Maj. Andrew Lewis to the Forbes campaign against Fort Duquesne in the fall of 1758 would have meant fewer resources were being directed to local forts such as Fort Vause. After Fort Duquesne was abandoned by the French in November 1758, Indian attacks decreased dramatically, and Fort Vause would have become much less essential.

The number of men stationed at Fort Vause seemed to vary over time. The initial proposal was for 70. In an updated statement on the chain of forts after his October 1756 tour, Washington estimated Fort Vause needed 150 men (Proposal for Frontier Forts, Abbot 1984b:11). In May 1757, Governor Dinwiddie recommended 70 men for Fort Vause (Abbot 1984b:154). Washington's Returns for January 1757 list Fort Vause under Captain Hogg, with a captain, a lieutenant, an ensign, 3 sergeants, a drummer, and 31 fit for duty with 19 on command (Abbot 1984b:76). In June the number fit for duty at Vause's was 60 (Memorandum from Washington, 16 June 1757, Abbot 1984b:220–21). As recruitment into both the militia and Virginia Regiment had become very difficult, Washington suggested the need to enlist servants. There is some indication from pay records that at least three servants were recruited to Fort Vause with pay going to their owner (Abbot 1984b:326).

After the likely abandonment of Fort Vause in 1758, no other military occupation is documented. In 1760, Ephraim Vause sold his land in the

Roanoke valley to John Madison. Madison's son sold it to Jacob Kent Jr. in 1790, and it passed through this family until 1897, when the heirs of Sarah Kent Anderson sold the property to J. H. and Ella Crockett. The land then passed to the John Spotte heirs, relatives by marriage of the Crockett family, and to W. H. Basham. In 1903 Basham sold the land on which the second Fort Vause was located to G.W.M. Gardner (Sammons 1966:32). It passed from the Gardner-Sammons family through other owners and eventually to the present owners, Jack and Laree Hinshelwood. Sammons mentioned that a log house on the property in 1903 was torn down by her father, who built the house that stands on the site today, about 50 feet south of the fortifications.

Archaeological Investigations

Archaeologist Ed Heite, of the Virginia Landmarks Commission, conducted preliminary test excavations at the Fort Vause site in 1968. Artifacts, plan views, and profiles from Heite's excavation are curated at the Virginia Department of Historic Resources in Richmond. Heite's excavations consisted of a 10 × 10 ft. unit (Unit A) and an L-shaped trench (Unit B), which showed a zone of yellow fill under the modern topsoil overlying what he labeled as "old ground." The plan view showed an area of burning that may have led Heite to assume the site contained the first Fort Vause.

Our archaeological investigations consisted of excavating 31 shovel test pits and 5 larger excavation units or trenches (figure 7.2). The excavations were directed by the author and W. Stephen McBride, with assistance from Tom Klatka and John Kern, Virginia Department of Historic Resources, in September 2005 and May 2006. David Rotenizer also helped with the excavations, as did a number of other volunteers. Since portions of the earthen bastions can still be seen as raised areas behind the Hinshelwood house, topographic mapping (figure 7.3) was an important component. The southeastern bastion showed up very well, the southwestern bastion moderately so. While the northeastern bastion shows up faintly, the northwestern bastion does not appear. The northwestern bastion would have been located across the modern property line, beyond which mapping did not extend. Since the fort is much eroded, it is hard to tell the precise configuration of the bastions, but it is nearly 100 feet from the center of each bastion's entrance (gorge) to its neighbor. This corresponds to the interior square dimension described by the Council of War's order that the fort be "100 feet square in the clear."

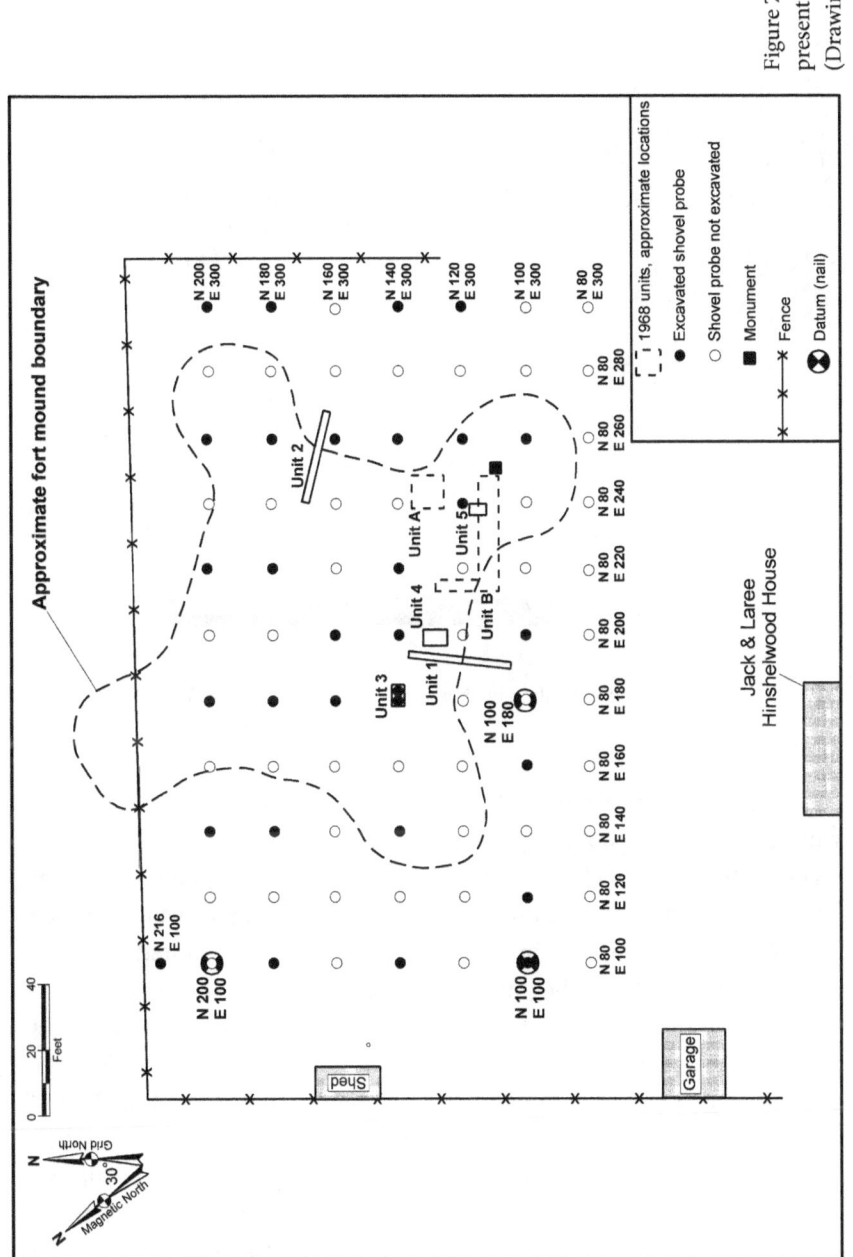

Figure 7.2. Map of present excavations. (Drawing by author.)

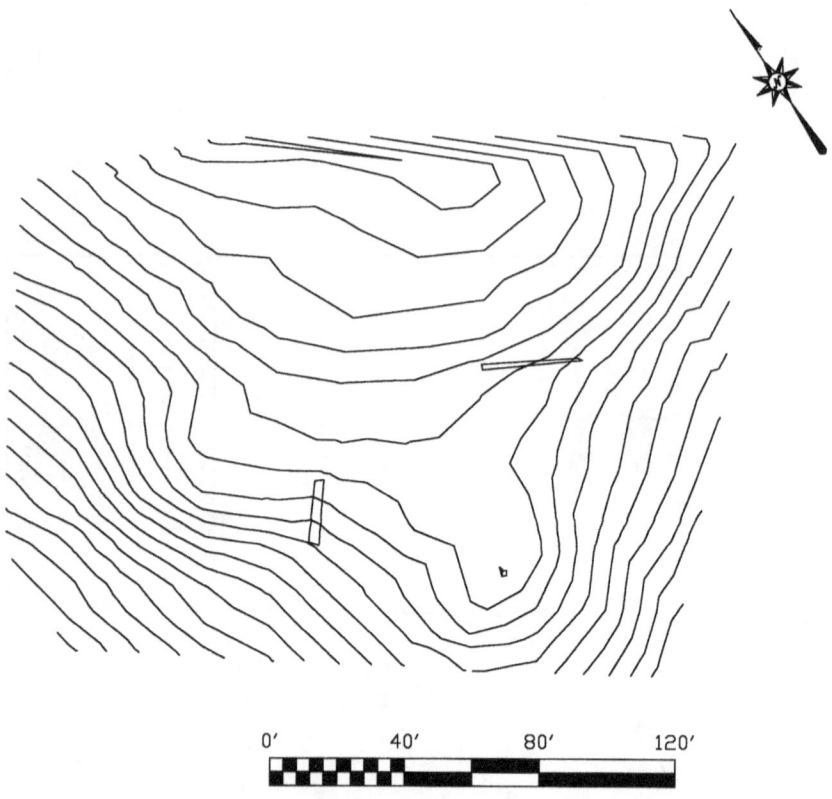

Figure 7.3. Map of topography, showing bastions. (Drawing by author.)

Shovel testing provided initial information on stratigraphic variation within the site. Three main profiles were identified. Profile 1 consisted of medium-brown topsoil to about 5 to 8 in. below surface, followed by yellowish-brown clay subsoil. Profile 2 consisted of the same layers as Type 1, but with a mottled layer of brown silt mixed with orange-tinted clay, typically remnant plowzone, beginning anywhere from 5 to 9 in. below surface, under the initial topsoil and extending to about a foot below surface, at which point subsoil was encountered. Profile 3, potentially the most interesting profile, included a zone of clay fill from fort construction. This fill typically was encountered below the modern topsoil and mottled zone if present. Its depth varied, and in some cases the bottom of the clay fill zone was not reached by the shovel test. In several cases, the clay fill was underlain by an older surface soil of brown silt loam, presumably the surface at

Table 7.1. Profile types as seen in the shovel test pits

Profile 1	Profile 2	Profile 3 (with fort construction clay fill)
N140 E100	N100E120	SE Bastion N100E240 (older surface preserved)
N140E 260	N100E160	N100E260
N160E180	N100E200	N120E240 (older surface preserved)
N160E200	N120E300	N120E260
N160E260	N140E200	NE Bastion N180E260 (did not get below fill)
N180 E100	N140E220	N200 E260 (did not get below fill)
N180E140	N140E300	SW Bastion N140E140
N200 E140	N180E180	N140 E180 (older surface preserved)
N200 E180	N180E220*	N140 E181 (older surface preserved)
N216 E100	N180E300	
	N200E220	
	N200E300	

* Has ash lens.

the time the second Fort Vause was built. In some shovel tests, the construction fill was underlain by the yellowish-brown natural subsoil. The distribution of these profile types is shown in table 7.1.

The type 2 profile was also seen in the long trenches, Units 1 and 2. A middle section of Trench 1 was taken down to about 2.5 ft. below surface, but only natural variations in the subsoil clay were seen. A stain designated as Feature 2 contained wire nails, however, and is not thought to be associated with the fort. Units 1 and 2 were dug in hopes of intersecting curtain walls from the fort. They did not produce any evidence of construction fill clay, post molds, or a stockade trench, as had been hoped.

Unit 3 was a 5 × 5 ft. unit located within the mouth of the southeast bastion area, encompassing two test pits that had the clay fill zone and a buried topsoil. Unit 3 provided a much clearer understanding of the stratigraphy (figure 7.4). This fill was present across the whole unit in the south and west profiles, but only in parts of the north and east profiles, where it appeared to be fading away. Thus this unit was successful in locating the edge of the southeastern bastion construction fill. Several pockets of ash and concentrations of animal bone were found in the buried topsoil underlying the construction fill. The unit contained a rodent-disturbed area in the northwestern corner and along the middle of the western wall.

Unit 4 was a 5 × 7.5 ft. unit located southeast of Unit 3 and in the area where it was thought the fort's south curtain wall might be located. Unit 3 had the Type 2 profile (figure 7.5) with plow scars in the subsoil. A shallow trench-like stain seen in the middle of the unit (designated Feature 2)

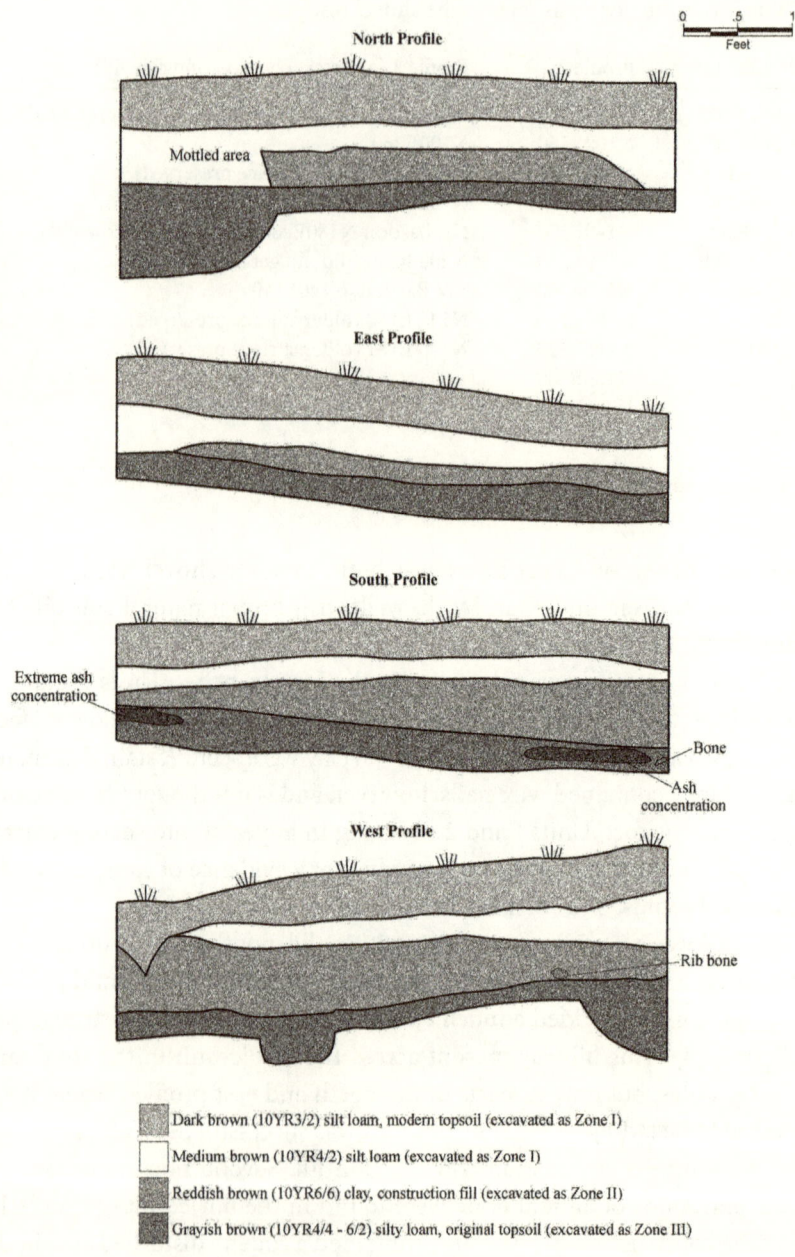

Figure 7.4. Unit 3 profiles. (Drawing by author.)

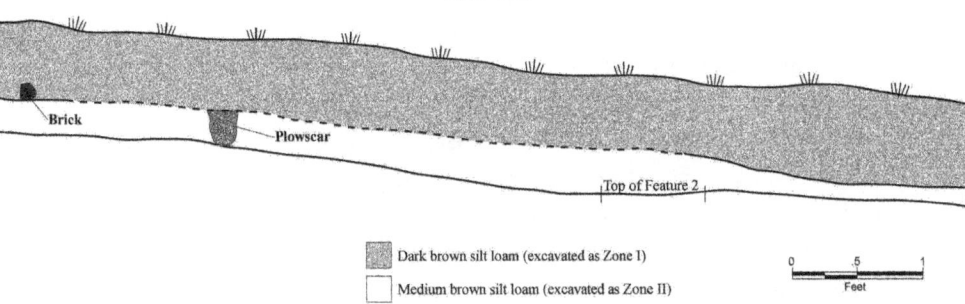

Figure 7.5. Unit 4, east profile. (Drawing by author.)

contained only late nineteenth-century artifacts and may be just a larger than normal plow scar.

Unit 5 was a 3 × 7 ft. unit in the southwest bastion area located to intersect Heite's Unit B excavation. The southern part of the unit revealed backfill from the 1968 excavations, which were conveniently lined with black plastic. These excavations stopped with removal of the clay construction fill and had not penetrated the buried "old surface" shown in Heite's drawings. Our excavation removed this soil zone, as the entire unit was taken down to subsoil. The general profile was the typical Type 3 (figure 7.6). The original surface zone found under the construction fill contained no historic period artifacts. This zone did contain an unusually dense concentration of

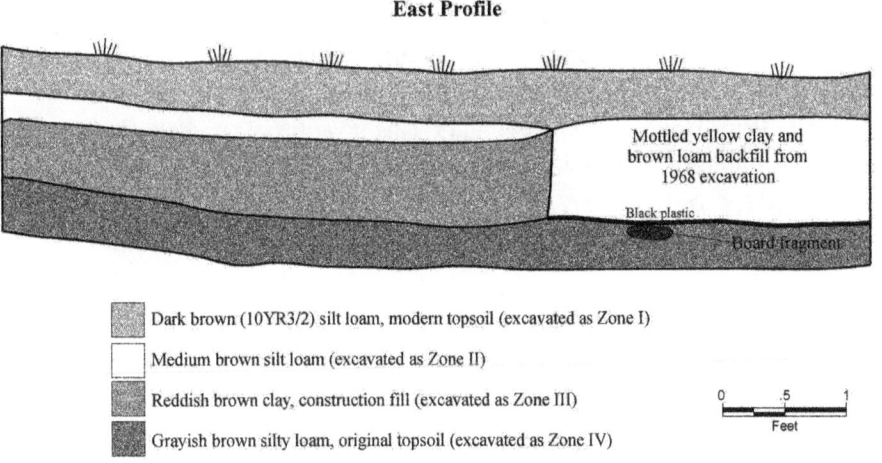

Figure 7.6. Unit 5, east profile. (Drawing by author.)

flint debitage and tools (including Morrow Mountain and Savannah River types) and a cord marked ceramic sherd, indicative of long-term Native American occupation. No fort construction features were found other than the clay zone, and no layer of extensive burning was found. No features or artifacts indicative of the first Fort Vause, or its destruction, were found.

We also conducted limited metal detecting north of the fort and in the adjoining residential property east of the fort, in hopes of finding areas where the men constructing the fort might have been encamped. We did not find any fort period artifacts.

Material Culture Recovered

Much of the artifact assemblage recovered during the excavations was from the post fort occupation, chiefly from the middle to late nineteenth-century to twentieth-century domestic and farm functions. A multicomponent prehistoric occupation is represented by many pieces of debitage and projectile points. A number of artifacts recovered from the fort construction fill zone, or just below it within the original topsoil, date from the fort period. These artifacts have a high probability of being associated with the construction and occupation of Fort Vause. They include wrought nails, clay pipe stems, British Brown stoneware, Scratch Blue salt-glazed stoneware, a cast-iron kettle fragment, a gunflint fragment, hammered lead, lead balls (.30, .39, .69 caliber), and animal bones. Other artifacts, such as bottle glass, could be from the fort occupation, but since they extend so far in time beyond the likely abandonment of the fort in 1757–58, it is more difficult to associate them with the fort occupation.

An interesting perspective on the material culture at the fort is provided by an inventory conducted on 4 August 1757, as the fort was being turned over by Peter Hogg to Thomas Bullitt. This inventory is preserved within the Washington Papers at the Library of Congress (figure 7.7).

Summary

Documentary research confirms that site 44My59 is the location of the second Fort Vause and almost certainly not the first. The first Fort Vause was located a short distance to the east, but more research is needed to establish the exact location. Archaeological investigations showed that despite extensive plowing and a post fort period of domestic occupation, site 44My59 has well-preserved remains from three of the four earthen bastions that

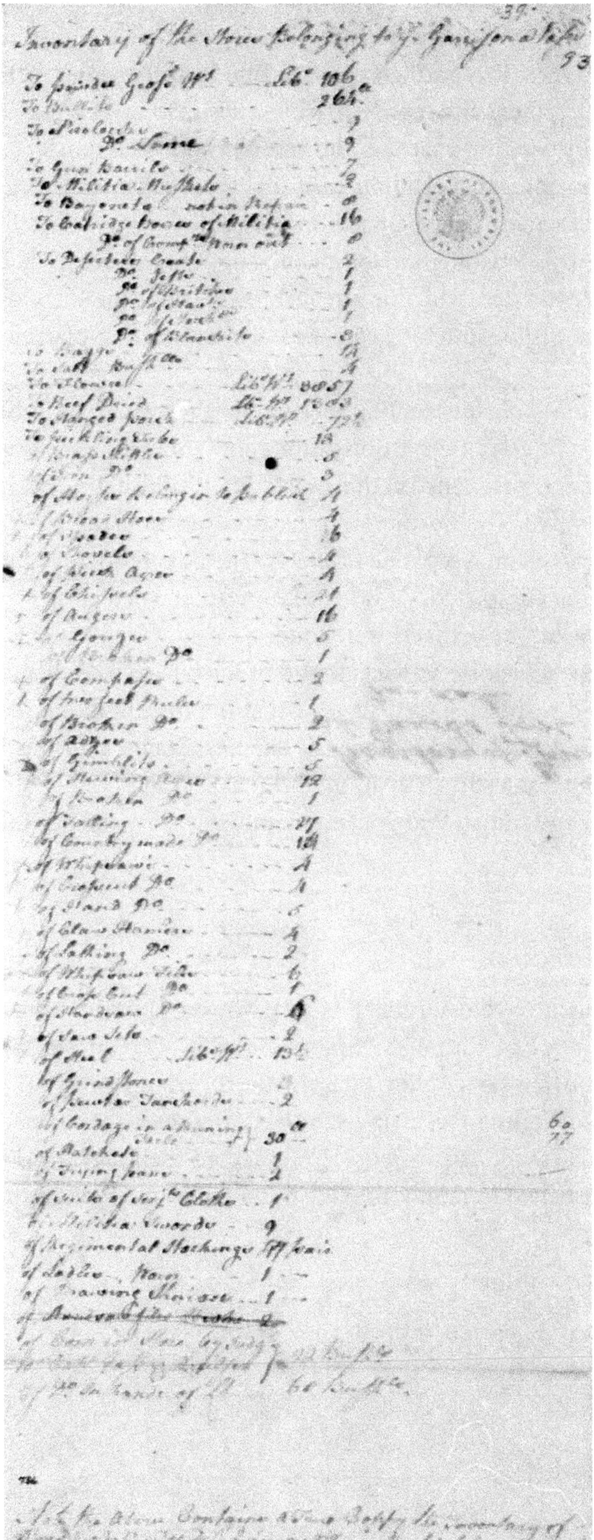

Figure 7.7. Fort Vause inventory. (Library of Congress, Manuscript Division.)

composed the second fort. This earthen construction is unlike other forts built by the Virginia Regiment and may stem from a desire to make it "extra strong," given the severity of the attack on the first fort and the importance of the locale along a major transportation corridor. The earthen construction of the second Fort Vause may be partly responsible for the delays in construction that George Washington complained about. The design is a very typical and academic one, which is not surprising, since the fort was built following orders of Washington, who was also circulating plans as guidance.

No evidence was found of construction methods of the curtain walls or other structures that connected the bastions. Since both units showed clear indications of plowing, if this construction was entirely above ground, it has likely been obliterated. The northeastern bastion was not well represented because it is located on a separate property. The possibility remains that this bastion was not completed. Only very limited metal detecting was conducted in this area, but no artifacts were found.

The general scarcity of historic artifacts found in the buried topsoil and in the construction fill within the fort suggests that the men building the fort were encamped outside the fort. Since the site has a range of artifact types, up to the present domestic occupation, this makes traditional methods of finding French and Indian War encampments, such as metal detecting, more difficult.

Acknowledgments

This chapter owes much to the summary of research on Ephraim Vause provided by Eddie Goode of Virginia's Explore Parks in 2006 and to the published Washington papers (Abbot 1983, 1984a, 1984b). Tom Klatka and John Kern of the Virginia Department of Historic Resources helped in organizing the project, and many people volunteered their time in the excavations. The Hinshelwood family provided assistance and wonderful hospitality.

8

"To Preserve the Forts, and the Families Gathered into Them"

Archaeology of Edwards's Fort, Capon Bridge, West Virginia

W. STEPHEN MCBRIDE

Following the defeat of Gen. Edward Braddock's British and colonial army by the French and Indians in July 1755, Indian raids along the Virginia frontier accelerated in scale and ferocity. These raids depopulated some frontier settlements but also increased defensive measures initiated by the colonial government and private settlers. Actions taken by the Virginia government included deploying ranger companies to patrol the frontier, enlarging their colonial military force, known as the Virginia Regiment, calling out county militia companies, and building forts to garrison troops and militia and to provide a safe haven for settlers. A major goal of these colonial measures was to encourage western settlers to remain and therefore create a buffer or boundary between the French and Indians and the more eastern settlements. The first two colonial forts built were Ashby's and Cocke's Forts along Patterson Creek, a tributary of the Potomac, in far northwestern Virginia (now West Virginia) during October 1755. Virginia Regiment troops also garrisoned Fort Cumberland, which was constructed in spring 1755 following orders from Lt. Gov. Robert Dinwiddie of Virginia and Lt. Gov. Horatio Sharpe of Maryland (Ansel 1995:63).

At this same time, individual settlers, especially prominent ones, began fortifying their own homes in an attempt to defend themselves and their neighbors. One of these fortified homes was Joseph Edwards's Fort along the Cacapon River in present Hampshire County, West Virginia. While it is known from orders, recommendations, and archaeology that the Virginia Regiment forts were, or were supposed to be, rather academic four- or two-bastioned square or rectangular forts, we have no detailed descriptions of the private forts and therefore have little idea of what they looked like or, perhaps more importantly, what their builders' idea of a fort was. For instance, since Joseph Edwards does not appear to have had any military background, what was the source of his knowledge of fort design? Did he learn about forts from books, neighbors, or experience on the frontier, or did British or Germanic settlers include fort design and construction as part of their broad cultural toolkit? Wooden stockaded forts had been built in Virginia and other American colonies since the earliest European settlement. Stone castles and towers were common in the British Isles from medieval times, and the construction of stone fortifications was part of the British colonization of Ireland in the sixteenth and seventeenth centuries (St. George 1990). Horizontal log blockhouses were part of the architectural heritage of both Germany and Scandinavia (Jordan 1985:75).

The archaeological investigations of Edwards's Fort were directed toward answering these questions: Was it an academic, rectangular bastioned fort, or more irregular? Was it strongly stockaded, simply fenced, or just an individual blockhouse? How were Edwards's house and outbuildings incorporated into the fort, if they were at all? Also, were additional militia or military structures or activity areas present in the fort during the time that it was garrisoned? Another research area to be investigated is related to material culture and daily activities at the fort. What do artifacts and features tell us about these activities, and can we separate civilian and military activity areas? Before addressing these archaeological questions, more historical context of the site is necessary to set the stage.

Historical Context

Joseph Edwards's original 400-acre settlement tract on the Cacapon River was first surveyed on 3 May 1748 by surveyor James Genn and conveyed to him on 26 May 1748. Edwards had already settled this property, however. Exactly how many years before is unclear, but he may have been there as early as 1738, when he appears in Orange County, Virginia, records (Quisenberry and Munske 2003:24). In May 1742, Joseph Edwards and Phillip Babbs were appointed as overseers of the road from James Caudy's [adjacent to Edwards's property on Cacapon] to Parkins Mill (Quisenberry and Munske 2003:25). So it is likely that Edwards had settled the fort property by this time.

In 1751, Edwards was appointed justice of the peace for Frederick County, a powerful local political position (Frederick County Order Book 4:101; Gruber 1999). Hampshire County was carved out of Frederick in 1754. He acquired an additional 1,239 acres between 1750 and 1762 (Gruber 1999). By the mid-eighteenth century Joseph and his wife, Sarah, had four children, David, Joseph Jr., Thomas, and Mary, who had grown to adulthood and married.

It is not known exactly when Edwards's Fort was built or what it looked like, but it was certainly an important site when Indian raids began to occur in Hampshire County during the fall of 1755 (Gruber 1999). In October 1755, Edwards is mentioned by Col. George Washington, who ordered two rangers, Captains Cocke and Ashby, to make a stand against raiding Indians, but if they had to withdraw, "to retreat no farther than Joseph Edwards in Cacapehon: where you will be joined by other parties as fast as they can be collected" (Abbot 1983:91). In October 1755, Washington also ordered Capt. William Vance of the Frederick County militia, who had abandoned the South Branch, "to halt at Joseph Edwards's on Cacapehon, until further orders, unless you should be drove from thence by superior force. You will be quickly joined there by numbers sufficient to prevent those insolent invaders from committing such inhuman outrages; and I hope to retaliate their crimes" (Abbot 1983:93). Washington also told Vance: "It would be right to acquaint the Inhabitants, as I doubt not but you may see many of them Retreating, how necessary, and how much it is their Duty and Interest, to Lodge their Families, in some safe place and join our Party in Dislodging the Enemy from their Lurking places" (Abbot 1983:93). In none of these statements is Edwards's place called a fort, although it is certainly probable that it was one, given this military use as a rallying point.

On 7 April 1756, Washington ordered "A subaltern and twenty men to parade immediately to March to Joseph Edwards . . . Lieutenant [John] Blagg for this Command" (Abbot 1983:331–32). Washington told Blagg, "You must endeavor to keep the inhabitants of the place together as much as possible" (Abbot 1983:332). On 12 April, Washington ordered Capt. John Fenton Mercer of the Virginia Regiment "immediately to return to Joseph Edwards's on Great Cape-capon: and there wait with your party, until you receive orders from me" (Abbot 1983:349). Mercer's troops soon returned to Edwards's Fort. That same day, Washington's aide-de-camp George Mercer ordered Sgt. Reuben Vass "to escort a Waggon with provisions, etc to Joseph Edwards's, for the men there" (Abbot 1983:354).

On 18 April, Mercer and 60 men left Edwards's Fort in pursuit of a large force of Indians seen nearby. Mercer and his men were ambushed one and a half miles from the fort and soundly defeated, with the loss of Captain Mercer, Ens. Thomas Carter, and 15 men (Gruber 1999; Abbot 1984a:17–18). The day after the battle, Washington ordered Capt. Henry Harrison of the Virginia Regiment "to repair to Joseph Edwards's Fort, and there to take upon you the command of all those different parties that are at that place" (Abbot 1984a:21). The parties left were the remainder of Mercer's and Blagg's Virginia Regiment commands. On 21 April, Washington ordered Ens. Edward Hubbard of the Virginia Regiment at Enoch's Fort to retreat to Edwards's "if desired" (Abbot 1984a:29). That same day, Washington asked Joseph Edwards to supply provisions to soldiers stationed at this fort, since Washington could not, and he threatened to remove the men if Edwards did not comply (Abbot 1984a:30). Generally provisions were provided by Winchester and included, if Fort Cumberland can be used as an example, salted beef and pork as well as live cattle, pigs, and sheep.

On 23 April, Washington wrote Ensign Hubbard that it was "advisable" to abandon Enoch's and remove to Edwards's, and he also ordered Captain Harrison to return to Winchester, but "You are to have a subaltern, two Sergeants, and 25 rank and file, at Edwards's Fort; unless the inhabitants desire to come down here—if so, you are to take them under escort: and must take care, if they insist on leaving the Fort, to destroy it" (Abbot 1984a:40–41). This quote is particularly interesting, since it mentions the fort's "inhabitants."

A heightened level of anxiety certainly spread throughout the region after the Mercer battle. Colonel Washington worried that "the inhabitants that are there, will more probably fall a sacrifice to the Indians" (Koontz 1925:120). As Gruber (1999:6) stated, "The battle had a sobering effect upon the Virginia legislature, transforming a balky House of Burgesses to a supportive body that appropriated over 20,000 pounds to the war effort." In July 1756, the Virginia Regiment accelerated construction of a chain of forts to protect the frontier.

Edwards's Fort became one of a number of settler forts added to the provincial chain of forts. The choice of Edwards's Fort was somewhat surprising given its eastern position. Most other forts were on the South Branch, plus two older forts were on Patterson's Creek. Edwards's Fort was probably chosen because of its location on the main road between Washington's headquarters in Winchester, the forts on the South Branch, and Fort Cumberland. Edwards's Fort became a major stopover point for convoys moving between Winchester and Fort Cumberland. On 13 July 1756, Washington ordered Capt. Thomas Cocke of the Virginia Regiment "to escort the Waggons sent to you, to Pearsall's Fort; and so soon as you arrive there, inform Captain [William] Baylis it is ordered, that he send a party of the [Prince William County] Militia to guard them to Edwards Fort; where Ensign Milner will receive them and conduct them to Winchester" (Abbot 1984a:266). On 5 August 1756, Washington ordered "Captain Bell to march his company immediately to Cox's Fort . . . to cover and secure all convoys, expresses, etc that are passing and repassing to and from Fort Cumberland; as you [Capt. Robert McKenzie] likewise to do betwixt him and Edwards's" (Abbot 1984a:334).

On 9–10 December 1756, Washington ordered "A Sergeant, and ten men . . . [to] march to Joseph Edwards's to strengthen the party there, and escort the Cattle as far as Pearsalls, and to return here again immediately" (Abbot 1984b:47). That Edwards's Fort continued its importance in convoy defense is noted in a May 1758 letter from Washington where he stated, "A part of the Militia ordered for the [South] Branch, should take post at Edwards's (on Cacapehon) and at Pearsalls, for the security of the convoys passing hence to Fort Cumberland" (Abbot 1988a:158). In April and May 1757, Washington disagreed with Dinwiddie, who wanted to replace the supply route through Edwards's Fort with a more northern one that would pass through Enoch's Fort. Washington preferred stationing more men at Edwards's and Pearsall's and noted, "betwixt whom [inhabitants of the South branch] and the Inhabitants about Fort Loudoun, are not any persons living, save at the Forts which we have built and garrisoned for securing the said communication" (Abbot 1984b:146). Washington also noted that keeping the southern road closed "may also (altho' I can not yet absolutely say) render garrisons at Edwards and Pearsalls, useless—unless it be a few to preserve the Forts, and the families gathered into them" (Abbot 1988a, 158). These statements suggest that the only settlers left west of Fort Loudoun were living "at the Forts" (see also Ward 2003).

Edwards's Fort and Henry Enoch's were also used as bases for "ranging" or searching for Indians. For instance, on 12 August 1756, Washington ordered Lt. John McNeill to range "On this road [between Edwards's and Pearsall's]; and in this manner You are to remain, until your provisions is out; and then repair to Edwards's Fort—where you will receive a sufficiency to bring you to this place [Winchester]" (Abbot 1984a:343).

The documents suggest that Virginia Regiment troops or militia were regularly stationed at Edwards's Fort after the spring or summer of 1756. On 13 July 1756, Washington stated, "I imagine [each garrison] will be from fifteen to thirty men—to be left under the command of a subaltern or trusty

Sergeant" (Abbot 1984a:264). In May 1757, Dinwiddie and the Virginia legislature instructed Washington to station 25 men under a subaltern at Edwards's (Abbot 1984b:154; Koontz 1925:107). A month later Washington and his Council of War reported there were 16 men stationed at Edwards's (Abbot 1984b:221; Koontz 1925:108). On 1 December 1757, there were 9 men stationed there (Abbot 1988a:67).

During John Forbes's June–November 1758 Fort Duquesne campaign, Edwards's Fort gained importance as a place to house sick soldiers as well as soldiers guarding the main supply convoy (Abbot 1988a:208, 211). In July 1758, 17 sick men were at Edwards's (Abbot 1988a:269). Some soldiers also remained behind at the fort, as Washington's 23 and 24 June 1758 letters to Col. William Byrd of the 2nd Virginia Regiment noted:

> One Company of the 2nd Regiment to be stationed at Job Pearsall's on the South Branch and Edwards's till all the Convoys of Provisions have passed and then to Join," and "You will want Provisions at Edwards's and Pearsalls for that Company of Your Regiment Ordered to be left at those places. (Abbot 1988a:211, 237)

There is no description of Edwards's Fort or any records of its construction. It is not clear whether the Virginia Regiment improved the fort at all, and if they did, whether or not they followed Washington's four-bastion fort plan. The exact date of Edwards's Fort demise or dismantling, like its construction, is unknown. With the fall of Fort Duquesne in November 1758, the need for Edwards's Fort, like most of the Virginia chain, was greatly reduced. Occupation by provincial troops likely ended soon after as Indian raids subsided (Ansel 1995; Gruber 1999). When the fear of Indian raids returned with Pontiac's War in 1763–64, the fort may have been regarrisoned with militia, but this is not known. In any case, sometime between 1758 and 1764 Edwards's Fort probably ceased being a fort.

Following the Indian Wars of the 1750s and 1760s, Joseph Edwards continued his career as a farmer. There is no evidence of a fort at Edwards's farm during this time, although the house could have been refortified during Dunmore's War (1774) or the Revolutionary War (1775–83). Following Edwards's death in 1781, the site continued to be operated as a farm by a number of owners and tenants until 1999, when the Fort Edwards Foundation acquired the property. The surviving log house on the property was built in the early nineteenth century, so no above-ground evidence of Joseph Edwards's house or fort remained.

Archaeology

As a private rather than governmental fort, Edwards's offers an opportunity to examine a site that reflects the settlers' own view of neighborhood defense and fortifications. Since there are no descriptions of this fort and few for other private forts of this era, we have to rely on archaeology to understand their design and construction. At Edwards's Fort, archaeological investigations occurred over three seasons, and a variety of methods were utilized (Gardner 1990; McBride 2001; McBride 2005).

Archaeological investigations began in 1990 when Dr. William Gardner attempted to verify the fort's location. Gardner successfully located a number of features, including a mid-eighteenth-century cellar or trash pit (Feature 6) and a section of stockade trench (Feature 7), therefore confirming the location of the fort (Gardner 1990). My investigations of the site occurred over two seasons (2001, 2004) and were funded by the Fort Edwards Foundation of Capon Bridge, West Virginia. These investigations had the broad preservation and research goals of understanding the overall integrity and structure of the site, but with an emphasis on discovering information about its design, construction, and associated structures (McBride 2001, 2005). Methods utilized during 2001 and 2004 included shovel test excavation, metal detecting, test unit excavation, and backhoe trenching and stripping.

The testing helped determine that most of the site had been plowed to subsoil, and some 250 years of artifacts were mixed in the same soil layer. In only one part of the site, the southeastern slope near the spring, were intact stratified deposits located. Here Units 3, 4 and 5 were excavated and produced mid-eighteenth-century artifacts in their lowest soil layers. Other units were placed where eighteenth-century artifact concentrations occurred (Units 1 and 2) or within large features (Units 6 and 7). The most important feature discovered in the test units was a section of the fort's stockade trench (Feature 13, later 81) in Unit 1.

In order to uncover more evidence of the fort and locate additional features, parallel backhoe trenches were excavated. These resulted in the discovery of multiple sections of stockade trench and many other features, including cellars, trash pits, post molds, and burned areas (figure 8.1). Some features were further exposed with the backhoe and hand-excavated to better understand their function and spatial extent. More excavation within features, especially the large cellar features, was conducted in the 2004 season. In the end, 11 sections of stockade trench, one house foundation and

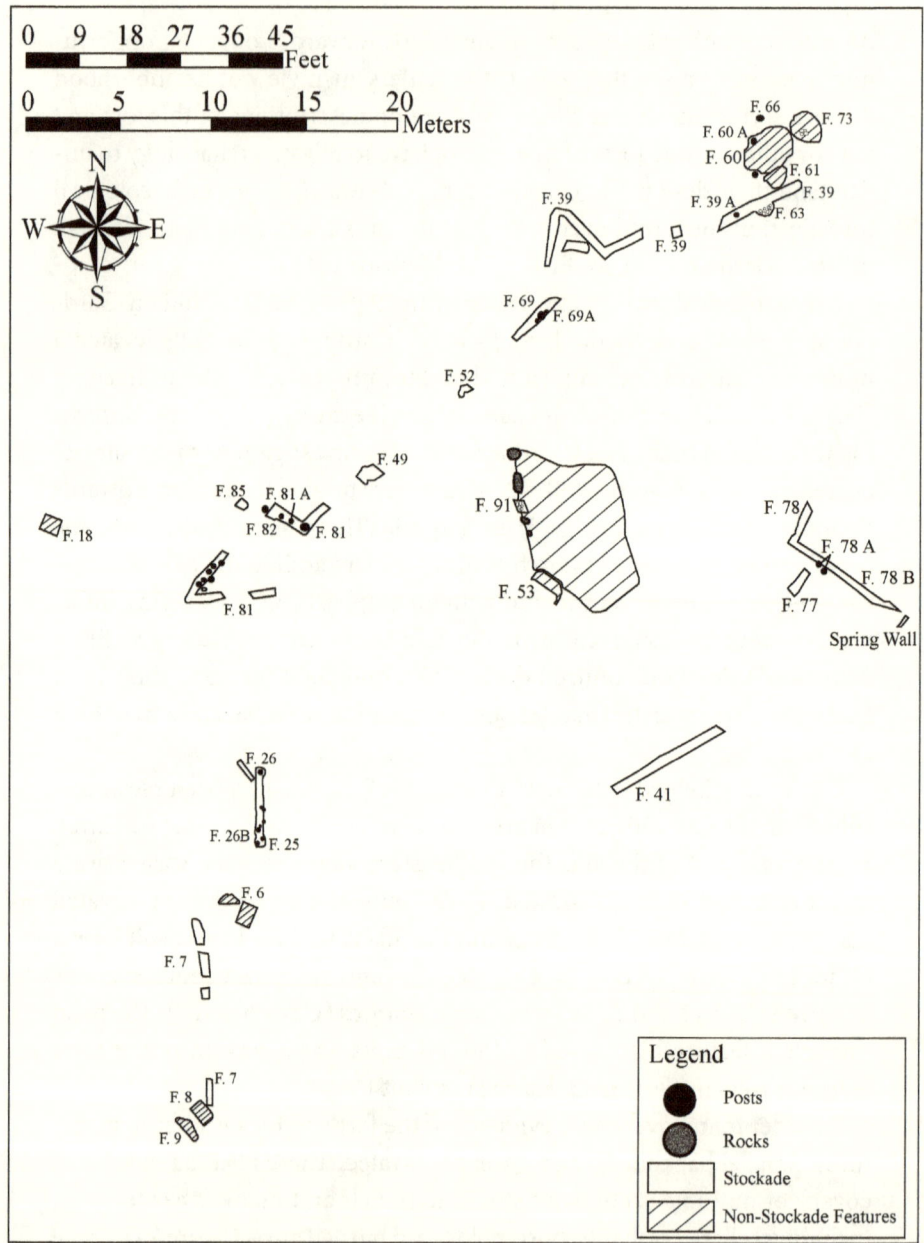

Figure 8.1. Site map showing features. (McBride 2005.)

cellar, two possible hut pits, and three root cellars/trash pits were discovered that date to the mid- to late eighteenth century. These features, along with the lower stratum artifacts from Units 3–5, will be the focus of the remainder of this chapter.

Stockade Trenches

The most exciting discoveries at Edwards's Fort site were the numerous sections of stockade trench that were exposed, some with visible post molds. The stockade sections are associated with the northeastern fort wall (Features 39, 49, 52, and 13/81), the southeastern wall (Features 41 and 77), a possible covered way to the spring (Feature 78), and a possible southern extension (Features 7 and 26). Features 53 and 91 represent Joseph Edwards's house. The gaps between the stockade sections represent unexcavated areas, although the stockade trench stops at the northeastern end of Feature 39 and the northern and southern ends of Features 7 and 26. The reasons for these terminations are unclear, but they may relate to the presence of buildings, gates, or erosion.

The trenches indicate that the fort was constructed of vertical posts set in a trench. The trenches were 1.5 to 2 ft. wide and 2 to 2.5 ft. deep with whole (not split) posts ranging from 4 to 10 in. in diameter, but more commonly 8 to 10 in. Gaps were often present between post molds, suggesting that these were either real gaps, which would not be very defensive, or that there were posts, possibly smaller ones, filling these gaps that did not leave molds. The nature of fort destruction and feature formation is so variable that molds were not always created, particularly if the trench itself collapsed into the mold. In some cases, individual post molds outside the stockade trenches were discovered adjacent to these gaps, suggesting that they were weak points that needed reinforcement. So there may have been fewer posts or smaller posts in these "gaps," and they may not have been placed into the ground.

The fort as now exposed measured roughly 107 ft., east to west, and 71 ft., north to south, excluding the possible southern extension. The northwestern wall contains one corner bastion (Feature 81) and one mid-wall redan (Feature 39). These defensive positions were constructed of vertical stockades, like the main curtain walls, and both contained interior post molds/trench stains that were undoubtedly firing platform supports. The fort probably had other bastions or redans along the southeastern wall and in other corners, but these have not been discovered. The main fort's southwestern corner is under a standing nineteenth-century house and inaccessible.

The fort's northwestern wall is the most clearly understood. The main mystery is why the eastern end (Feature 39) simply stops. Did this wall intersect a building or another structure? Four meters of subsoil east of this feature were exposed without finding evidence of another feature. The southeastern wall contained two sections of stockade curtain wall, Feature 41 and Feature 77, and a perpendicular section of stockade, Feature 78, that led to a spring. This latter wall was likely a "covered way" for people getting water from the spring. The spring is surrounded by a stone wall. Exactly how Features 41 and 77 intersected each other is unclear at present, since the area in between has not been investigated, but the most effective arrangement would be for Feature 41 to lead to the spring and then turn northwestward toward Feature 77.

Features 7 and 26, the southern trenches, are the most irregular element of the fort. Given the location of the northwestern bastion (Feature 81), these trenches would not help and probably would undermine the fort's overall defensibility. When the artifacts from these two stockade trenches and their post molds (Features 25, 26B, and 26C) are examined and compared with the other stockade trenches, a possible explanation for these two stockade trenches emerges (table 8.1). Features 7 and 25 are the only stockade post molds containing pearlware, and Feature 26 is the only stockade trench containing creamware, suggesting that they were constructed and filled at a later date than the other trenches. Diagnostics from the main stockade trenches include delftware and wrought nails and from their post molds, delftware and creamware (table 8.1). The two creamware sherds from Feature 26 suggest that it was constructed after 1762, and the two pearlware sherds suggest that these walls came down after ca. 1775–80. It is possible that the Feature 7/26 walls were constructed during the existence of the main fort, especially since a creamware sherd was found in Feature 81A, a post mold, and simply stood longer, but it is also possible that it was built after the main fort had been dismantled.

Another issue with the Feature 7/26 walls is the gaps between the walls. One possibility is that they may have been related to two nearby small cellar features, Features 6 and 8. If these cellar features had buildings above them, they might explain termination of the stockade trenches as ending at an outbuilding. The southern end of Feature 7 has eroded away, and therefore its stratigraphic relationship with Feature 8 is unclear. However, the presence of delftware and white salt-glazed stoneware and the absence

Table 8.1. Artifacts from Edwards's Fort stockade features

	F7 p.m.	F25 p.m.	F26	F26B p.m.	F26C p.m.	F39	F39a p.m.?	F41	F69	F69A p.m.	F78	F13/81	F81A p.m.
Delftware			3				2	2				1	
White salt-glazed stoneware			1										
Creamware	1		2										1
Pearlware	1	1											
Porcelain							1						
Redware	3	3	13	5	1	1	5	1	1			9	4
Stoneware							1						
Bottle glass	2	2	2	2		1				2			
Table glass	1												
Other kitchen	1												
Window glass	1	1	1	2									
Wrought nails	1	1	1	1		1					1		
Unidentified nails	1	1		1		1		1					
Other architecture													
Mortar												.05g	
Daub				.4g		9g		12.3g		1.8g		2g	
Tool/activity		1	1				2					1 lead	
Gunflint							1				1		
Smoking pipe						1		5					
Bone	10	1	7	26		1	2	51	1	2	2	8	
Shell			3	2									1

Table 8.2. Artifacts from other Edwards's Fort eighteenth-century features and units

	F8	F18	F60	F61	F73	Units 3,4,5
Delftware				1		9
White salt-glazed stoneware						3
Redware		11		2		55
Stoneware						2
Bottle glass		29	19		31	19
Other kitchen						1
Wrought nails						4
Unidentified nails	2	2			1	28
Daub	5.2g	1.7g	65g			132.8g
Mortar	.2g					11.3g
Gunflints	1					
Lead ball						1
Buttons/buckles			1			
Furniture						1
Grid iron			1			
Slate			1			
Game piece			1			
Smoking pipe						9
Bone	33			7	86	605
Shell						5

of creamware or pearlware in Feature 6 suggest that it was filled in the mid-eighteenth century and that makes this argument unlikely (table 8.2). It is possible that a building remained after Feature 6 was backfilled, but there is certainly no evidence of this. Although no diagnostic artifacts were found in Feature 8, it did produce a large (1 7/16 × 1 3/16 in.) musket size French gunflint, a size more commonly found on French and Indian War frontier forts than Revolutionary War frontier forts (McBride et al. 2003).

Chronologically diagnostic artifacts from the main stockade features and documents suggest that Edwards's Fort was built ca. 1755 and dismantled after ca. 1762. This destruction date makes sense given the renewed Indian raids during Pontiac's War of 1762–64. The southern stockade wall was constructed in 1762 or after and stood until ca. 1775. Given that there was peace between Indians and settlers from 1764 until 1774, it is most likely that the southern stockade was built during the Lord Dunmore's War (1774) to Revolutionary War (1775–83) period, rather than standing through a 10-year peaceful era.

Edwards's Fort combines academic and vernacular, or at least irregular, characteristics. The corner bastion and mid-wall redan suggests some knowledge of academic fort design. Whether this knowledge was standard cultural knowledge of mid-eighteenth-century frontier settlers is unclear, but research on frontier forts of the Revolutionary War era strongly indicates that a good understanding of fort design was part of settlers' cultural baggage by the 1770s (McBride et al. 2003; McBride and McBride 2006). It is probable that the 1755 Capon valley settlers had knowledge of nearby four bastioned Fort Cumberland, or earlier, more easterly forts, or even European forts or castles with bastions or corner towers.

The most irregular part of the fort is its overall footprint, particularly the southeastern wall. The termination of Feature 39 at its eastern end is also odd. The orientation of Features 77 and 78, relative to Feature 39, suggests a rather irregular configuration was present on the eastern end. Another bastion, or blockhouse, should be present here for defensive purposes.

Although the entire footprint of Edwards's Fort has not been exposed, it clearly does not conform to the regular two or four bastioned forts recommended by Virginia Regiment commander Col. George Washington or county Councils of War (Abbot 1983:137, 265–66; Koontz 1925:105). It also does not conform to Washington's orders for "hewn" or horizontal log bastions instead of stockaded bastions. Fort Allen, Pennsylvania, which contained two mid-wall redans and two corner demi-bastions, is the most similar to Edwards's Fort (Waddell and Bomberger 1996:32, 82). This fort was rectangular, 125 by 50 ft., and designed by Benjamin Franklin in 1756. Although very similar to Edwards's Fort, Fort Allen was much more regular (figure 8.2).

The archaeological evidence suggests that Edwards's Fort was designed and built by Joseph Edwards, his family, and perhaps neighbors and that

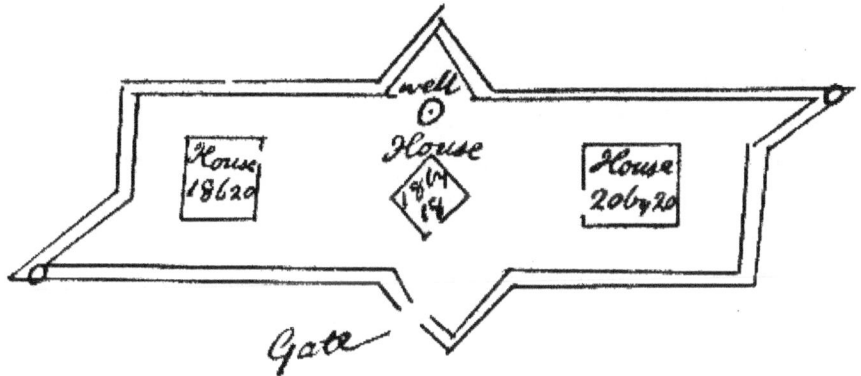

Figure 8.2. Fort Allen, Pennsylvania. (Waddell and Bomberger 1996.)

the fort was probably not altered when it was garrisoned by the Virginia Regiment. The irregular aspect of the fort was probably due to the need to incorporate the Edwards's house and outbuildings within the fort and the topographical variability of the landscape. The slope leading down to the spring was certainly a factor in the irregular nature of the southeastern and eastern sections of the fort.

Other Structures

Archaeological evidence of six possible eighteenth-century structures was found at Edwards's Fort. This evidence consists of a large cellar and foundation for the Edwards's house (F. 53 and 91), three rectangular cellars (Features 6, 8, and 18), and three oval pits (F. 60, 61, and 73) that may be remnants of soldiers' huts. The Edwards's house consists of a roughly 28 by 16 ft. cellar with a limestone foundation. Artifacts within the cellar fill suggest that the house was torn down ca. 1810–20, which fits the estimated construction of the extant house on the property. Flood deposited soils in and around the house cellar may indicate why the house was torn down and another built in a higher location.

The rectangular shape and straight walls of Features 6, 8, and 18 suggest that they were storage cellars rather than simple trash pits. These features were 3.5 to 4 ft. long, 2 to 2.5 ft. wide, and 1 to 2 ft. deep. While there is no evidence that buildings were above these cellars, it is probable that at least small outbuildings were constructed above them. Since all three cellars were located outside the main fort, it was initially thought they were either civilian features or, in the case of Features 6 and 8, possibly associated with the Feature 7/26 stockade. As noted above, this association with Features 7/26 now appears unlikely. Artifacts found within these three cellar features include delftware, white salt-glazed stoneware, redware, wine/rum bottle fragments, the large musket gunflint, and animal bone (Gardner 1990) (table 8.2). These artifacts suggest a mid- to late eighteenth-century filling date, with the absence of creamware and pearlware supporting the former. The gunflint is the only suspected military artifact from these cellars. Excavations at nearby Ashby's Fort, which was occupied by rangers and militia, and Arbuckle's and Warwick's Forts in the Greenbrier Valley of West Virginia, which were built and occupied by militia, suggest a pattern of very low counts for ceramics and bottle glass, moderate architectural items, especially wrought nails, and very high animal bone on non-residential frontier forts (McBride and McBride 1998; McBride et al. 2003;

McBride 2009). Soldiers and militiamen likely had more durable metal and wooden vessels. Therefore, the large volume of ceramics as well as clothing and personal items from Feature 6 suggests that it was most likely a civilian, rather than a military feature (Gardner 1990). Feature 18 had a lower density of artifacts but a large quantity of redware and bottle glass, but it is difficult to designate it as a civilian versus a military feature. The gunflint and lack of ceramics from Feature 8 suggests that this may have been a military feature, although it is difficult to be certain.

Perhaps the most interesting structural features, other than the fort's stockade, were three oval pits discovered on the northeastern edge of the fort. The two larger pits, Features 60 and 73, are of similar size (9 × 8 ft. and 7 × 6 ft.) and shape, with each having a shallow and a deep end, or two levels (figure 8.3). Their similar shapes suggest that they were purposefully excavated. While they may have been storage cellars, comparison

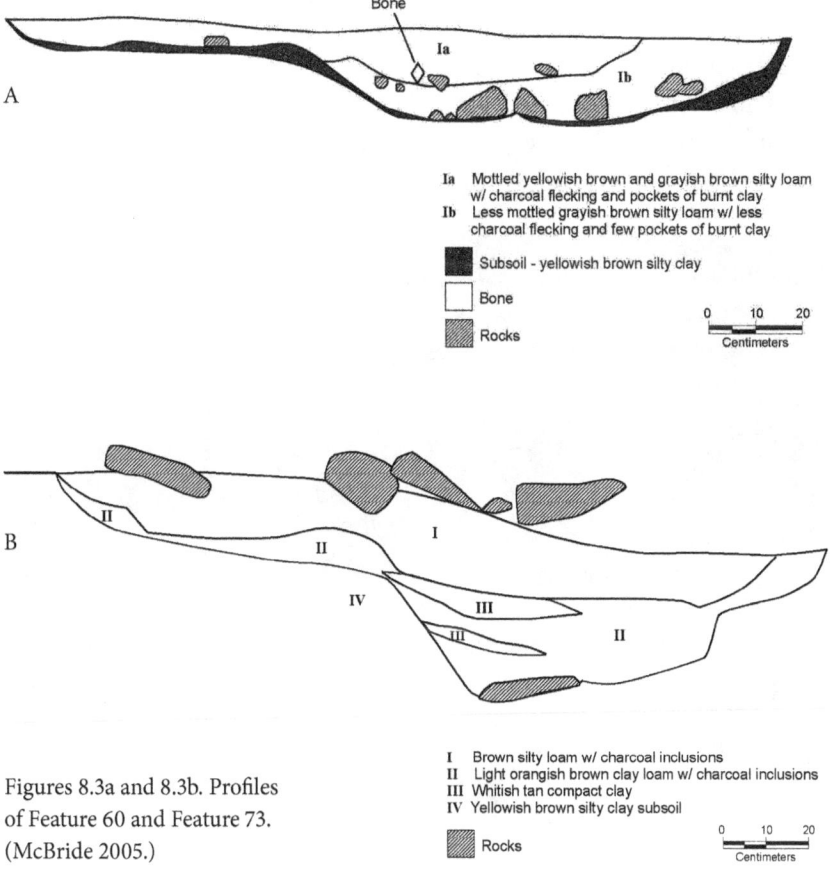

Figures 8.3a and 8.3b. Profiles of Feature 60 and Feature 73. (McBride 2005.)

with semi-subterranean winter huts from Rogers Island, New York, Valley Forge, Pennsylvania, and Sevierville, Tennessee, suggests that these features were more likely military winter huts (Parrington 1979; Starbuck 1999:72–73; Bentz and Kim 1993; Howe 1995). They are all of similar size and shape. Soldiers' tents of the French and Indian War were typically 7 × 5 ft., close in size to these pits (Anderson 1984:90). Floors were dug out in tents and huts for warmth during the winter. The smaller pit, Feature 61, was located adjacent to Feature 60 and contained burned clay, suggesting that it was a hearth or backfilled with hearth soil. The placement of the probable huts outside the fort at first seems odd, but given the fact that by spring 1756 the entire Cacapon neighborhood civilian population lived at this fort, it would have been quite crowded.

Artifacts recovered from these features include one delftware sherd, redware, wine/rum bottle fragments, a lead gaming piece (checker or poker chip), a gridiron, a vented domed button that is South's Type 2, 1726–76 (South 1964:115), an inscribed slate tablet (RBH8A8-?) with a drill hole, and a large assemblage of animal bone. These artifacts date from the mid- to late eighteenth century, but most likely from the middle of the century, since no creamware or pearlware was present. The gaming piece and gridiron are more typical military artifacts and support a military or militia use of these features (figure 8.4). The overall low frequency of ceramics from

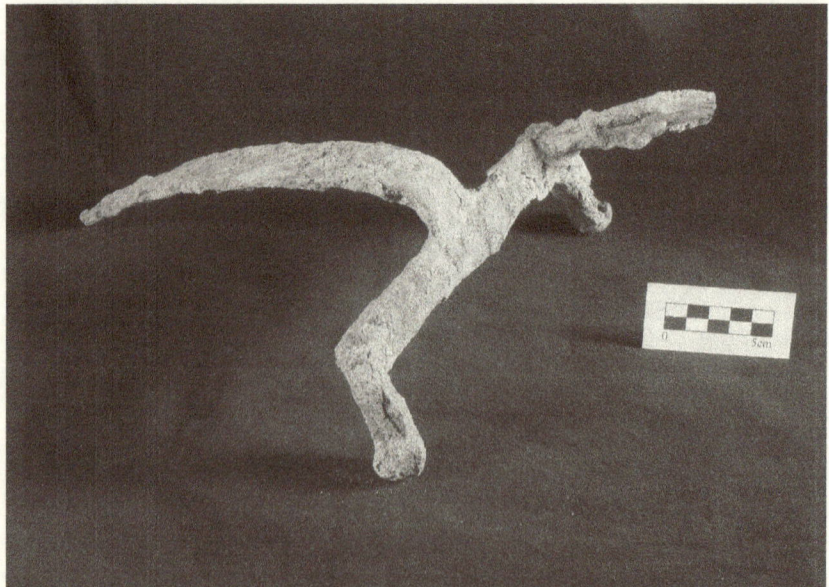

Figure 8.4. Grid iron. (Photo by author.)

Table 8.3. Identified faunal elements from Edwards's Fort

	F26 trench	Main stockade trench	Main stockade post mold	F60	F61	F73	Unit 5
Cattle				14	1	11	5
Pig	1	1	2	5		2	10
Sheep			2	14		1	2
Horse						1	
Deer			2	8		1	7
Bear							1
Chicken							3
Mussel							4

the features also supports a military or militia origin. The stone tablet is quite interesting, and its drilled hole suggests that it may have been used as a gorget or a plaque suspended from a wall.

Table 8.2 lists artifacts recovered from the lowest soil layers of Units 3, 4, and 5. These were all located near the spring just northeast of the fort. This area was the only one that had deeply stratified deposits. Upper soil layers in these units contained late eighteenth- to mid-nineteenth-century artifacts, while these lowest layers were designated middle eighteenth century because of the absence of creamware and presence of delftware and white salt-glazed stoneware. The high frequency of ceramics, low frequency of arms-related artifacts, and absence of military accoutrements or other encampment artifacts suggest these deposits are primarily civilian in origin. The continued use of these areas for refuse disposal following the French and Indian War supports this contention.

Table 8.3 lists the identified faunal remains from mid- to late eighteenth-century deposits excavated in 2004 at Edwards's Fort (Breitburg 2005). The faunal remains from earlier excavations have unfortunately not been analyzed. The faunal results illustrate some interesting patterns, particularly when the larger hut features (Features 60 and 73) are compared with Unit 5. The former have a majority of cattle, with sheep a close second, followed by deer and pig. The dominance of cattle is repeated at the nearby French and Indian War forts Ashby and Loudoun as well as at Fort Ligonier, Pennsylvania, Fort Stanwix, New York, and Fort Loudoun, Tennessee (Breitburg 2005; Clark 2003; Martin and Mallard 2009). Documents also show that large domesticated animals, particularly cattle, were the most common domestic meat source for Virginia's French and Indian War period forts (Abbot 1983:22, 43–45; 1988a:269). The ease with which cattle could be driven and the great quantity of meat per individual were likely factors in this preference.

The Unit 5 faunal remains suggest that pork, venison, and beef were the preferred meats for the Edwards family, but that they also utilized a wider variety of meat sources than did soldiers or militiamen. The preference for pork is a characteristic of Upland South farmers and is also a pattern found on Revolutionary War period frontier forts (Hilliard 1972; Martin and Martin 1993). The Revolutionary War sites were likely supplied more by local farmers and hunters than by military quartermasters as in the French and Indian War (McBride and McBride 1998; Martin and Martin 1993).

Identified faunal remains from the stockade features are fairly sparse, and it is difficult to make firm conclusions. The absence of cattle is rather curious, however. Given that most of the remains came from post molds and therefore date to the end of the stockade period, it is tempting to speculate that perhaps the Edwards family or other civilians deposited most of these food remains.

Conclusion

The archaeological and historical investigation of Edwards's Fort provides an intimate picture of a private settlers' fort of the French and Indian War. This investigation helps to begin an understanding of functional and design variability in the Virginia forts. Edwards's Fort was truly a multifunctional settlement. It was a private residential fort that also garrisoned provincials and militia, acted as a convoy way station, and served as a neighborhood refuge. This complexity is illustrated by the archaeological remains of the fort, the Edwards's house, the soldiers' huts, probable outbuilding cellars, and domestic refuse middens. While the fort footprint was very irregular, it still had academic elements. The refuse deposits show strong differences between the material culture and foodways of soldiers/militia and civilians, which reflect their different statuses and supply systems.

The locations of private forts were more dependent on the settlers' previous settlement patterns, particularly on the more prominent settlers who often built the forts on their property. The location of most military, and perhaps militia, forts was most dependent on three factors: the settlement distribution, transportation routes, and natural setting. Since a major function of the Virginia forts was to protect local settlers, they would be built in population clusters (Abbot 1984a:274; Waddell 1995). As Waddell notes, the Pennsylvania fort system was somewhat different, with some strategic forts being built farther west beyond settlement to attract French and Indian attention. The early (1755) Patterson Creek forts, Cocke's and Ashby's, may have had a similar function, although this is not mentioned explicitly. When Virginia built its organized chain of forts in 1756, none were built west of settled areas. Transportation routes, including mountain gaps, were another important factor in fort location as was the topography and available water sources of the fort site itself (Abbot 1984b:11; McBride et al. 2003; Waddell 1995). A moderately high defensible position with no nearby higher points and a close water source was preferred.

9

Fort Loudoun

A Provincial Fort
on the Mid-Eighteenth-Century Pennsylvania Frontier

STEPHEN G. WARFEL

Motorists on the Pennsylvania Turnpike, between Chambersburg and McConnellsburg, Pennsylvania, see signs for Fort Loudon. Few know that this quiet Franklin County community is named for a nearby French and Indian War fort, built in 1756 to protect settlers from Indian raids. Even fewer are aware that the fort served as an important supply depot during the Forbes Expedition, which drove the French from western Pennsylvania. Unless the travelers are John Wayne movie buffs and have seen *Allegheny Uprising* (1939), it is unlikely they are familiar with a rebellion of local citizens against the British garrison at Fort Loudoun, considered by some historians as the first act of the American Revolution (cf. Swanson 1937; Webster 1964).

This chapter reports on the results of historical and archaeological investigations conducted at the site of Fort Loudoun by the Pennsylvania Historical and Museum Commission between 1977 and 1982. Emphasis is placed on describing structural features and the fort's anatomy. A detailed artifact analysis is not offered; rather, artifacts are referenced with regard to their role in understanding site activity and chronology. A brief narrative concerning the fort's historical context is presented and followed by an examination of the site's archaeological content. Finally, the significance of the findings is evaluated with respect to Fort Loudoun's dynamic history and evolution over time.

Historical Context

The Fort Loudoun story begins in 1755, when Indian attacks on Pennsylvania frontier settlements increased. Pennsylvania's Quaker government was ill-prepared. It had no standing militia or army to protect its interests (Hunter 1971:432). To remedy this situation, the provincial government hastily authorized forts along the eastern foot of the Blue Mountains. These forts were not large enough, nor were there a sufficient number enough to eliminate the threat of attack. They did, however, serve as safe places for settlers during Indian raids.

Fort Loudoun, named for John Campbell, Earl of Loudoun, commander of British military forces in North America, was the southernmost in a chain of Pennsylvania forts built in 1756 (figure 9.1) (Hunter 1960:463). No plans or drawings of Fort Loudoun have been found to date, and only a few documents shed light on the site's history and appearance.

The fort was constructed on land warranted to Matthew Patton on 18 February 1744 (Kent 1978:43). Over an 11-year period, Patton developed a farmstead consisting of a house and barn, which in 1755 were burned during a devastating raid on settlements in the Conococheague valley (Hoban 1935:4929). Like many of their neighbors, the Pattons evacuated the homestead upon learning that an attack was imminent.

Instructed to take advantage of existing structures whenever possible, Col. John Armstrong selected the abandoned Patton farm as the new fort

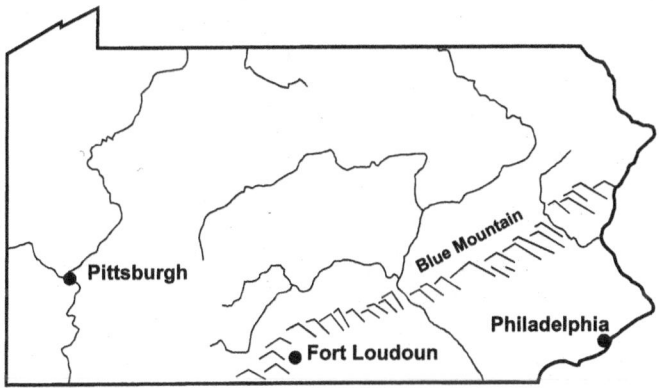

Figure 9.1. Location of Fort Loudoun with respect to Pittsburgh and Philadelphia. (Drawing by author, 2007.)

site in November 1756. In a letter to Pennsylvania governor William Denny on 19 November 1756, Armstrong wrote:

> I'm makeing the best preparation in my power to forward this New Fort, as well as to prepare by Barracks, & c., all the others for the approaching Winter. . . . To-day we begin to Digg a Cellar in the New Fort; the Loggs & Roof of a New House there having been Erected by Patton before the Indians burn'd his Old One. We shall first apprise this House, and then take the benefit of it, either for Officers' Barracks or a Store House. (Hazard 1853a:58)

One month later Armstrong filed the following report:

> The Publick Stores are safely removed from McDowels Mill to Fort Loudon, the barracks for the soldiers are built, and some proficiency made in the Stockade, the finishing of which will doubtless be Retarded by the inclemency of the weather, the Snow with us being upward of a foot deep. (Hazard 1853a:83–84)

The historical account providing the most complete description of the fort is found in the journal of Thomas Barton, an Anglican minister who stayed at Fort Loudoun on 21 July 1758. Barton was serving in the British army under Gen. John Forbes. At this time, the fort was a supply depot for troops moving west toward Fort Duquesne. Barton wrote:

> The Fort is a poor Piece of Work, irregularly built, & badly situated at the Bottom of a Hill Subject to Damps & noxious Vapors. It has something like Bastions supported by Props, which if an Enemy should cut away, down tumbles Men & all. . . . The Fort is properly a square Ridout [redoubt] of 120 feet. Here I found Captain Harding with 380 Royal Americans camped there all Night, & was well treated by the Officers. (Hunter 1971:442)

Fort Loudoun often served as temporary quarters for many more men than could be housed within the palisade. Customarily, tent camps were set up outside the fort to accommodate them. There were occasions, however, when sufficient tents were not available and men were instructed "to make bark shelters, Indian fashion" (Stevens et al. 1951:16).

Some glimpses of living conditions are preserved in the documentary record. On 7 June 1758, Col. Adam Stephen reported to Col. Henry Bouquet, Forbes's second in command:

We have nothing here that is necessary for the Sick, neither Wine, Rice, Barley, Oatmeal, or Butter, I never liv'd in Such scarcity at Fort Cumberland.... There are Several of the Pennsylvania Soldiers at this place [who] are sick & Many with Sore Legs; & they have No Surgeon or Medicines to assist them. (Stevens et al. 1951:53)

A letter written by John Armstrong from Carlisle in 1758 noted that "the Rats are very prejudicial to us here also, yet not so bad as at Fort Loudoun" (Stevens et al. 1951:107). Finally, on 4 July 1758, Lt. Lewis Ourry wrote from Fort Loudoun:

I have a very troublesome Post here, not so much by the Continual fatigue that attends it, as for want of proper Directions how to act in Several Cases, & also the want of necessary Work-men & Tools on very pressing Occasions. We have neither Blacksmiths, Farriers, nor Waggon Makers, nor Tools for either, and every Day Waggons breaking to pieces, & Horses wanting shoes.... The few Nails that I had brought with me are almost expended. (Stevens et al. 1951:160–61)

By November 1758, the Forbes expedition succeeded in forcing the French from Fort Duquesne. Other victories in 1759 and 1760 assured British military control of the entire Ohio Country. With the Treaty of Paris in 1763, Great Britain gained control of Canada, and the frontier was effectively opened for settlement. Ottawa chief Pontiac, a former French ally, did not accept the treaty's conditions. In the summer of 1763, he assembled an alliance of "dislocated" Ohio Country Indian tribes and renewed attacks on British forts and settlements. This rebellion was ended when Indian forces were defeated at the Battle of Bushy Run on 5 and 6 August 1763 (Anderson 1975; Dixon 2003).

Following the Battle of Bushy Run, Fort Loudoun's role changed from military supply post to a checkpoint, designed to ensure that firearms and other contraband were not transported across the Appalachian Mountains for the Indians by unscrupulous traders. Conococheague valley residents took offense to what they perceived to be excessive military control over their business affairs. In November 1765, they besieged the fort for two days and nights in an attempt to force the return of confiscated rifles and muskets. The incident, recognized by some scholars as the first act of the American Revolution, was romanticized in *Allegheny Uprising*.

Allegheny Uprising

The attack on the fort prompted the filing of official reports by Forty-second Royal Highland Regiment officers who had been in the post's garrison. The reports, made a few days after the regiment withdrew from Fort Loudoun on 18 November 1765, provide additional details regarding the fort's composition. In a deposition filed by Lt. Charles Grant, the commanding officer, on 22 November, it is noted that "they . . . fir'd upon all corners of the Fort, so that the Centry's could not stand upright upon the Bastions" (Hazard 1853b:247). Two days later, Capt. William Grant testified that "the Rioters fired some hundreds of Shot at the Stockades . . . many Balls went through Patton's House, and many Lodged in the Stockades of the Fort" (Hazard 1853b:247).

After the Highland Regiment vacated Fort Loudoun, Matthew Patton reoccupied his homestead. In a 1773 will, Patton refers to the property as "his Loudon estate" (Kent 1978:44). The U.S. Direct Tax of 1798 lists his son James as the owner of several buildings on the property—a log kitchen, a log barn, a small log house, and a two-story log dwelling house measuring 28 × 30 ft. with at least nine windows containing 6/6 lights (Kent 1978:44).

Interest in the site and history of Fort Loudoun was sustained through time. In 1915, the Pennsylvania Historical Commission, the Enoch Brown Society, and the citizens of Fort Loudon erected a monument to commemorate the fort. The Pennsylvania Historical and Museum Commission purchased 208 acres of the original Patton tract in 1968 and permitted the property to be worked by a resident tenant farmer. State acquisition of the parcel was the first step in a long-term plan to locate and reconstruct provincial Fort Loudoun (Warfel 1980:7–8).

Archaeological Evidence

A number of unsuccessful attempts to find the fort were made by avocational archaeologists and the Pennsylvania Historical and Museum Commission in the 1950s and 1960s (Kent 1978:44). Armed with sparse historical evidence of the fort's shape and size, State Museum of Pennsylvania archaeologists renewed the search in 1977. Barry C. Kent, state archaeologist, recognized that an existing two-story log farmhouse that stood near the 1915 monument had dimensions nearly identical to the James Patton log house in the 1798 tax list. Kent reasoned that if Patton's son assumed ownership of his father's home, the original farmstead and fort site must be nearby. Test excavations around the monument revealed the remains of a filled cellar, containing "a broken Brown Bess trigger guard, British uniform buttons, gunflints, musket balls, scratch blue salt-glazed stoneware, and numerous other mid-18th century artifacts" (Kent 1978: 45). Elsewhere, evidence of post molds were found and interpreted as the remains of the palisade wall (Kent and Douts 1977; Kent 1978). Apparently, when the stone marker was placed on the site in 1915, the fort's location was known. Yet over a period of 62 years, that knowledge was lost and required rediscovery.

From 1980 through 1982, a complete investigation was conducted (Denton 1980; Joyce 1983; Warfel 1980, 1981). Plow-disturbed topsoil was removed with a bulldozer, and the subsurface was scraped clean with hand tools, exposing telltale stains of fort period construction and habitation. Features were mapped before investigation, and soils were screened through 1/4 in. hardware cloth, permitting the recovery of such small and delicate items as straight pins and buttons. Sometimes a water screen was employed to sort artifacts from heavy clay soils.

Palisade, Gate, and Bastions

Excavation team members quickly determined that removing the top 3–5 in. of palisade trench fill revealed individual post molds, indicating posts set in the trench. The trench was 18 in. wide, U-shaped in profile, and varied from 18 to 30 in. deep.

An archaeological plan, adjusted to show only fort period features, reveals that the fort was nearly square and measured 127 ft. on each side, a finding remarkably close to Reverend Barton's description (figure 9.2). Excavation of the east palisade trench cross-section shows that the walls were, indeed, irregular (figure 9.3). This finding is consistent with John Armstrong's 1756 report, which noted the palisade was constructed when snow was on the ground. Irregularity was also a product of the various ways in which posts were placed in the trench. One section of the east wall trench revealed split logs inserted side-by-side. At various locations full round posts, 8–10 in. diameter, were set in the middle of the trench. At other locations, centrally placed round posts were present and smaller ones, 3–5 in. diameter, were set either to the inside or outside of the trench, filling gaps between larger posts. The concept of "lining" a palisade wall with small posts to fill gaps was traditional customary for the period and necessary to secure a fort from attack. Lining is customarily placed on the inside face of a palisade wall. The unpredictable pattern of lining observed

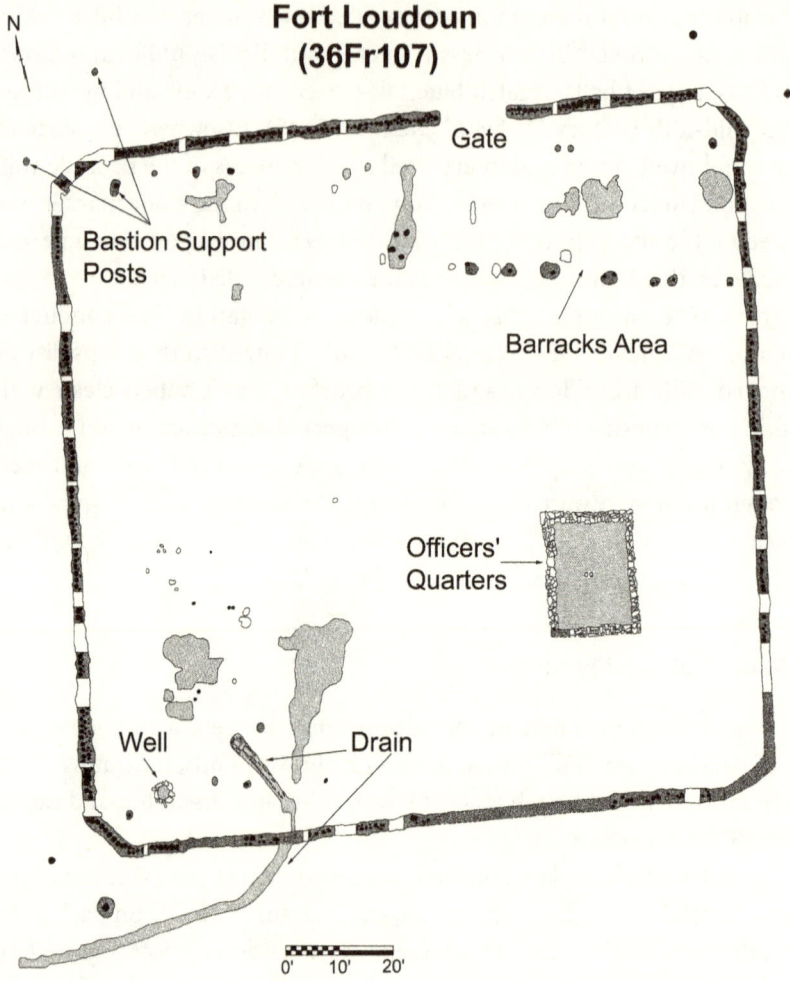

Figure 9.2. Archaeological plan of Fort Loudoun. (Drawing by author, 1982.)

in Fort Loudoun's palisade trench either reflects inconsistent work by the fort's builders or a later remedial effort to plug holes in the fort's walls.

The north palisade trench excavation revealed an intentional 12 ft. wide void in the wall, the location of the fort gate. Today's township road, on the same alignment as the gate, is evidence that the road preserves the course of the original fort road. No indication of a rear gate on the south side of the fort was discovered, though.

Three large postholes set in a triangular configuration were recorded at three of the fort's corners. Evidence of similar postholes on the fort's

Figure 9.3. Post pattern in partially excavated east palisade trench, facing north. (Photograph by author, 1982.)

southeast corner was destroyed when the James Patton log house was built sometime before 1798. Because Lt. Charles Grant's 1765 account notes that rioters "fir'd upon *all* corners of the Fort, so that the Centry's could not stand upright upon the Bastions" [emphasis added] (Hazard 1853b:247), it is deduced that a bastion also protected the southeast corner.

The palisade trench was blunted at each corner, thereby providing support for elevated shooting platforms serving as crude bastions. Two large vertical posts supported each overhanging platform outside the palisade wall (figure 9.4). A third large post provided support inside the fort (figure 9.5). This discovery clarifies Reverend Barton's description of bastions "supported by props" (Hunter 1971:442). Although these projections theoretically permitted soldiers to cover the fort's curtain walls with defensive fire, posts located outside the fort's walls were unprotected and would have been vulnerable to attack.

Figure 9.4. Exterior view of reconstructed northeast bastion, facing east. (Photograph by author, 2006.)

Figure 9.5. Interior view of reconstructed northeast bastion, facing northeast. (Photograph by author, 2006.)

Interior Features

Cellars

In addition to the cellar discovered by Kent in 1977, another cellar, measuring 11 × 25.5 ft., was found during the 1980 west palisade trench excavation. The trench contained well-defined palisade post molds and clearly bisected this pre-fort cellar. It is curious that John Armstrong and his men decided to build the fort's west wall over the cellar. It surely must have been visible and required compacting fill before the palisade wall was erected.

The cellar's fill revealed an intense burn layer near the bottom. Datable artifacts found in and under charred wood boards, such as a 1724 George I halfpenny and a 1738 George II halfpenny, predate the 1755 Indian raid on Conococheague valley settlements and identify the structure as Matthew Patton's burned house. An entire bag of charred flax seeds recovered from the burn layer was likely stored for the next season's planting.

During the 1981 field season, the other cellar was completely excavated. Soil layers in the stone-lined cellar contained a mixture of eighteenth- and early nineteenth-century artifacts representing refuse accumulated around the house before it was demolished and the cellar filled, ca. 1830 (Warfel 1981:13–19). Fort period artifacts confirmed its use by the military. The structure, which measured 17 × 22 ft., must be the one referred to as "Patton's House" by John Armstrong in 1756 and Capt. William Grant in 1765. It is also likely the one listed in the 1798 Direct Tax as a "small log house." Apparently, Matthew Patton was building a new house when the Indian attack occurred. Although his old house and barn were burned, the new house was spared and later finished by Armstrong and his men.

Cellar fill layers produced a variety of mid-eighteenth-century artifacts, including a clipped 1758 silver Spanish coin, fragments of English tableware and teaware, glassware, eating utensils, a clay tobacco pipe, a keg spigot, and a mouth harp. Numerous buckles, buttons, cuff links, straight pins, and thimbles were also present. Many buttons, buckles, and cuff links are thought to come from officers' uniforms, suggesting the structure was an officers' quarters—a finding consistent with Armstrong's 1756 letter.

Another pre-fort feature was discovered in association with the cellars. A stone-lined drain, measuring 110 ft. long × 2 ft. wide × 2½ ft. deep, connected Patton's first house with his second. The feature once conducted water from a source under the second house to and through the first house. Water was then exhausted through an additional 26 ft. long drain on the west side of the first house. The foundation of the second house was clearly constructed to admit the drain, whereas the drain was cut into and through the foundation of the first house. Evidently Mathew Patton planned to create "cold storage" for dairy products in both cellars. There is no evidence that the drain continued to function after the first house was destroyed in 1755.

Barracks

A pattern of large post molds and shallow pits found in the northeast corner of the fort may represent remains of a 25 × 47 ft. post-built barracks. If so, the fort's walls probably doubled as a back and side wall for the barracks (Joyce 1983:12). A similar building may have stood in the southwest corner

Figure 9.6. Hand-blown case bottle with inscribed name. (Photograph by James T. Herbstritt, 1984.)

of the fort, where identical features were recorded. The absence of an intelligible post mold pattern in the southwest corner is attributed to modern farm activity and deep disturbance due to hog pens and wallows.

The barracks area produced objects that were, again, likely associated with officers. The assemblage includes a wrought flat iron, English porcelain saucers, a glass tumbler, clay smoking pipes, and a hand-blown case bottle. The case bottle is remarkable; after reconstruction an inscribed name was visible on its surface a name was visible inscribed on its surface (figure 9.6). The name Bayley was scratched on the bottle to identify it as personal property. This may have belonged to Lt. Alexander Baillie (Bailly or Baily), who was with the Royal Americans at the fort in 1758.

Well and Drain

A 14 ft. deep × 5 ft. diameter (inside dimension), dry-laid stone well was located in the southwest corner of the fort. A protected source of drinking water was essential and typical of eighteenth-century fort construction, even though a fresh water spring and creek lie within a few hundred feet. Careful removal of the well's contents produced thousands of artifacts, deposited in three episodes: 1756–65, debris accumulated during and near the end of the fort's occupation; 1765–70, a period of clean-up following site abandonment by the military; and a 1770–1830 deposition by the Patton family. Organic objects that normally perish were preserved in the damp well fill. The assemblage included a fort period axe with broken handle, a wooden froe club, shingles, spinning wheel pieces, wagon parts, leather footwear and harness pieces, and an oak bucket used to draw water from the well (figure 9.7).

Figure 9.7. Oak bucket recovered from the well. (Photograph by author, 2007.)

More than 1,500 faunal remains were recovered from the well. Those found in the first depositional episode provide a glimpse of the fort period diet. Elements of cow, pig, and sheep dominate the collection (Webster 1982:6–8). It is likely that whole animals were butchered at the site, because all principal parts of the carcass are represented (Webster 1982:7). Wild species, including deer, rabbit, squirrel, turkey, and elk, were also present and contributed to the Fort Loudoun meat diet.

A particularly striking aspect of the assemblage is the way in which a clear attempt was made to "completely exhaust the available animals of their food value" (Webster 1982:8). Webster noted that nearly every element with a marrow-bearing cavity was cracked open, including cow's feet (1982:7). Domestic animals were in their prime or younger. This finding sharply contrasts with evidence recovered from Fort Ligonier in Westmoreland County, Pennsylvania (Grimm 1970). John Guilday notes that Fort Ligonier animals were often past their prime, even senile, and not in good condition when they were butchered (1970:180–84).

Many hundreds of pottery sherds and glassware pieces were recovered from the well. A delicate Chinese-export porcelain teacup, however, best reflects the English character and status of the site's military inhabitants and the importance of the tea ceremony on the frontier where English custom traveled with the British army.

An 18 ft. long × 2 ft. wide stone-lined drain was discovered 16 ft. east of the well. Although its exact purpose is unknown, the drain's proximity to the well suggests that an activity requiring water took place at this location inside the fort. Water from the drain was exhausted through the south palisade wall into a ditch.

Powder Magazine

The James Patton log house, constructed between 1765 and 1798, was positioned precisely over the southeast corner of the fort. No documentary references to a magazine at Fort Loudoun exist. The James Patton log house may have taken advantage of a fort period cellar which served that purpose based on a John Armstrong letter that stated, "To-day we begin to Digg a Cellar in the New Fort" (Hazard 1853a:58). Does Armstrong's note refer to construction of a full cellar under the unfinished Matthew Patton log house, or did his men dig a cellar for use as a magazine in the southeast corner of the fort?

During the 1982 field season, a concrete floor in the basement of the James Patton log house was removed to test the powder magazine hypothesis. An artifact-laden soil layer was discovered, but it contained only nineteenth-century artifacts (Joyce 1983:23). Examination of the point where the stone cellar wall intersected the south palisade trench determined that the wall rests on top of trench fill. Hence the James Patton house cellar walls and floor deposits postdate the fort. Since house construction obliterated all evidence of the fort's southeast corner, it will never be certain if a magazine occupied that space.

Conclusion

Historical archaeology—an often magical blend of history and archaeology—has contributed to our understanding of Fort Loudoun in a way that neither documentary research nor archaeological excavation could do alone. Excavation revealed the fort's anatomy, making it possible to understand how space within the compound was organized and used. Structural evidence indicates John Armstrong was familiar with fortification design. In most respects Fort Loudoun's palisade was typical of traditional picket wall construction (Stotz 1974:34). Yet archaeological evidence shows that Armstrong's fort represents a frontier adaptation. Its structure and form, especially the unusual elevated bastions, were crude and likely conditioned by unskilled workers, readily available materials, difficult weather, and expedience.

The historical record best attests to Fort Loudoun's evolution through time. Its initial purpose was to defend frontier settlements from Indian raids. Following the failed 1755 Braddock campaign, it assumed a new role and became an assembly point for British and provincial troops moving west under Gen. John Forbes in 1758. Because the fort was positioned close to supply sources, it appears to have sporadically enjoyed a supply advantage. Even though historical accounts document a frequent shortage of necessary materials, the site's faunal assemblage demonstrates that fort occupants had access to beef, pigs, and sheep in better condition than those found at posts located farther west.

Following the French abandonment of western Pennsylvania, the fort assumed a final role as a military checkpoint. Conflict between the fort's garrison and local citizens and perceived tension between Crown and Colony are best understood as a result of discourse preserved in documents. Numerous lead shot and musket balls appear in the site's archaeological record, but one could not deduce that they represent a struggle for independence.

Sufficient information concerning the fort's structure was assembled to enable reconstruction of the palisade and bastions in 1993. No interior buildings were rebuilt due to the lack of above-ground details. Fort Loudoun is the only reconstructed example of a Pennsylvania provincial fort, built by a Quaker government to defend frontier settlements. Although reconstructions are difficult and expensive to maintain, they bring history to life and serve as educational settings where visitors can learn about events, objects, and lifeways that shaped our history. They also provide settings for meaningful reenactments or living history experiences.

10

Style Wars in the Wilderness

The Colonial Forts at Crown Point

CHARLES L. FISHER AND PAUL R. HUEY

During the first half of the eighteenth century, the French and later the English built major fortifications at what is now Crown Point, New York (figure 10.1). Situated on a large peninsula at the narrows near the southern end of Lake Champlain, this site was an important location on the water route from Canada to New York. The English name Crown Point presumably is equivalent to its early French name, Pointe à la Chevelure, translated as "scalp point." The *Oxford English Dictionary* lists "head" and the "top part of the skull" as definitions for *crown*, with a reference in 1589 to *crowne* as "the top of a mans head, where the haire windes about." The French word *chevelure* means "head of hair." The name Crown Point was used by the English as early as 1689, while Pointe à la Chevelure first appears in French sources between 1686 and 1689 (O'Callaghan 1855:400; Richter 1982:83; Ramezay 1709). French and English forts were constructed at Crown Point as a result of the struggle between these European powers over control of North America. Although these forts have been viewed as similar in military purpose, they differed in specific structure, function, and location.

Architecture as Statement

Johann Friedrich Specht, a German officer with Burgoyne's army in 1777, remarked that Crown Point "had been alternately constructed by the French and the English with different ideas in mind" (Doblin 1995:50; Strach 1982). This chapter analyzes the French fort from an anthropological perspective in an effort to relate the fortification's physical evidence to the "different ideas" of eighteenth-century builders and occupants of Crown Point.

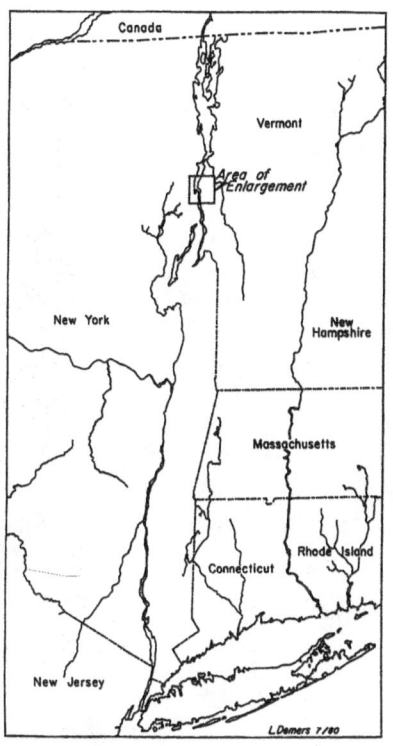

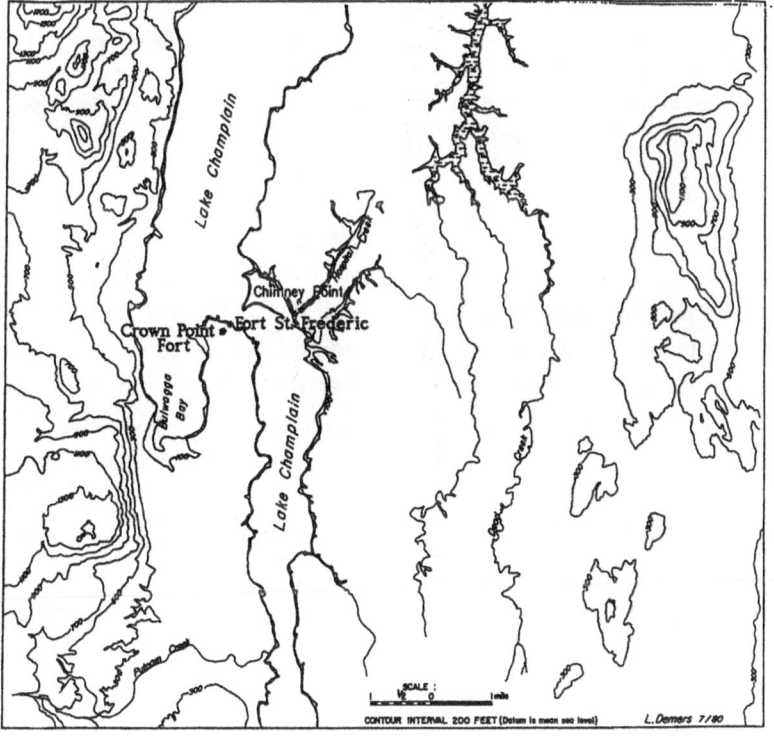

Figure 10.1. Location of Lake Champlain and Crown Point. (Maps by Linda Demers, New York State Office of Parks, Recreation and Historic Preservation.)

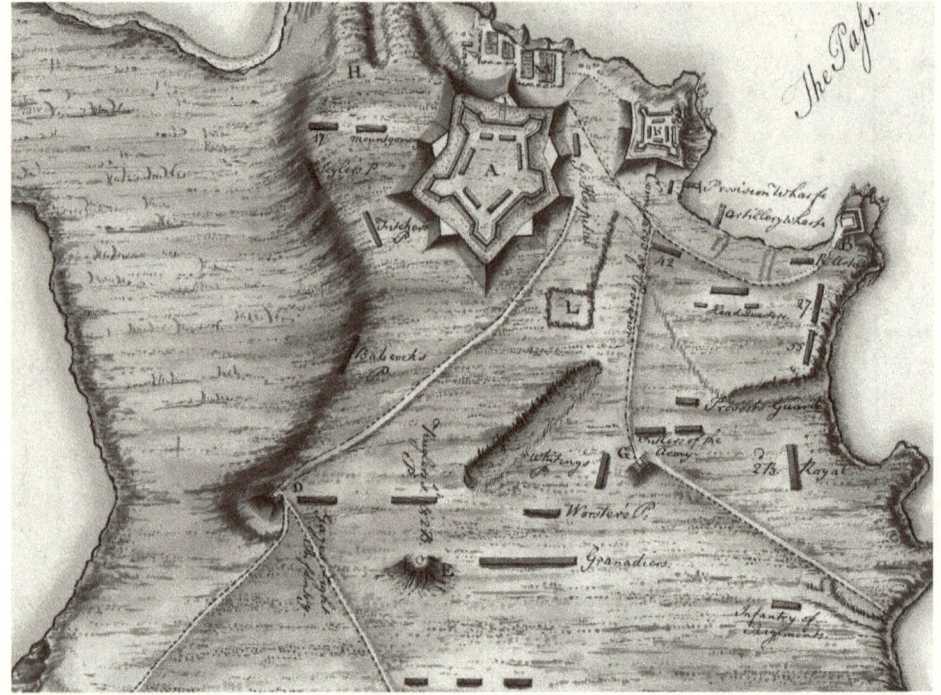

Figure 10.2. Detail from "Plan of the fort and fortress at Crown Point with their environs. With the disposition of the English Army under the command of Genl. Amherst encamp'd there 1759." The main British fort built in 1759 is at the center (A), while the earlier French fort, Fort St. Frédéric, is to the right (K). (Library of Congress, Geography and Map Division, G3804.C92S26 1759. P5 Vault.)

Anthropologists recognize the dual nature of material objects. Material items have an intended function and express the ideas and concepts of their creators. They are products of the social system that produced them. Once constructed, material objects are a component of the social system and serve to reproduce that system as well as transform it. In this manner, architecture, including historic military architecture, provides evidence of the social system that created it. Architecture communicates ideas through the forms employed and relations of these forms to each other and the landscape. Buildings identify the social groups that use them, define the structure of controlling hierarchies, and express this control to everyone. Architecture, particularly in public buildings, displays power and reflects the ideology of the dominant group in the society that created it.

From this perspective, the colonial fortifications at Crown Point were material objects with intended functions and were also material symbols containing information and communicating that information (figure 10.2). Although they were products of social systems that produced them, they became component elements of dynamic social systems once they were constructed. In general, forts are built to maintain a particular social system, but their existence frequently results in major transformations of social, political, and economic systems.

Establishment of the French at Crown Point

The importance of Crown Point in the imperial struggle for North America is evident in late seventeenth-century references. Both England and France claimed the Champlain valley territory, and Dutch, French, and English traders frequently passed Crown Point before 1700. As early as 1681, Louis de Buade, comte de Frontenac et de Palluau, governor general of New France, complained to the king that "certain individuals" were "conveying Beaver to Orange [Albany]" by way of Lake Champlain and were "bringing back money and merchandise" into Canada (O'Callaghan 1855:145). Jean-Frédéric Phélypeaux, comte de Maurepas, the French minister of the marine, attempted to stop all commerce with the English colonies in 1727 with letters patent governing trade, and foreign merchants were forbidden to live in Canada (Barron 1975:45; Pritchard 2004:192; Wraxall 1915:xlvii). The previous year, Crown Point had been selected as the site for a fort to prevent the trade with the English. "The fort at Pointe à la Chevelure will stop the smuggling from the direction of Lake Champlain" (Anonymous 1726).

In 1731, the French constructed a stockade fort on the east side of Lake Champlain opposite Crown Point, ignoring the boundary farther north on the lake that was established by a 1713 treaty between the French and English. This was justified as a necessary response to the presence of English traders from Albany on Lake Champlain by the French. The fort was intended as temporary until a larger stronghold could be built. Gaspard-Joseph Chaussegros de Léry, a trained military engineer born at Toulon, France, had arrived in Canada in 1716 to prepare fortifications. He believed the best fortification for Crown Point would be "a large Machecouli Redoubt having the Floors vaulted and the walls of a good thickness with Embrasures and loop holes, a ditch around it with a covered way well palisaded." He argued against building a conventional fort with four bastions and a wall that could be scaled and thus would require a larger garrison to defend. The winter snow and ice would "bury the Artillery on the Ramparts and prevent their use." The redoubt, on the other hand, was to be a massive, impenetrable stone tower with artillery inside, requiring and containing only an average garrison from which the soldiers would not be able to desert as easily as in a fort (Chaussegros de Léry 1731). The machicouli were projecting galleries on the tower's parapet from which objects or liquids could be dropped on attackers outside the walls.

Construction of the stone redoubt was initiated in 1734 immediately across the lake and opposite the small stockaded 1731 fort. The location was at the north end of Crown Point, and the peninsula was on the west side of the lake. Inspiration for the redoubt's design likely came from the coastal defense towers created by Sébastien le Prestre de Vauban and by Erik Dahlbergh, the "Swedish Vauban," in the seventeenth century. The Tour de Camaret near Brest (figure 10.3) was designed by Vauban and built between 1689 and 1695 within a small battery of artillery designed to defend a harbor against pirates. The tower itself had a cellar and four floors with vertical loopholes for muskets. A similar tower designed by Dahlbergh, however, held artillery (Duffy 1975:155; Toudouze 1954:100). These coastal fortifications could be defended against relatively vulnerable

Figure 10.3. Tour de Camaret near Brest, France, built by Vauban between 1693 and 1696. (Photo by Olivier French, Paris. Used by permission.)

Figure 10.4. Digital reconstruction of the redoubt or citadel at Crown Point, built in 1734. (New York State Office of Parks, Recreation and Historic Preservation.)

warships, while attacks from siege batteries protected by earthworks were unlikely (Langins 2003:58).

The massive redoubt commenced at Crown Point in 1734 was four stories high and had walls that were 10 to 12 ft. thick (figure 10.4). "It contained baking ovens, the fort's stores, a dungeon, an armory, the powder magazine, quarters for some officers, and the commander's quarters. The citadel mounted 20 cannon, mostly pierriers [swivels], and was entered by crossing a drawbridge spanning a ditch" (Titus 1981:3). This redoubt, known to the English as the "citadel" of Fort St. Frédéric, was completed by 1737 with the building of an additional outer wall around the citadel to enclose it (Furness 1984). The fort was named for Jean-Frédéric Phélypeaux, comte de Maurepas. The outer fort was square and contained corner bastions, with the citadel located in the northern corner (figures 10.5, 10.6). Chaussegros de Léry had argued against just such a bastioned fort in 1731, but he then changed his mind (Charbonneau 1990:63–64). Fort St. Frédéric's value as the southernmost French post made Fort Chambly to the north obsolete by the early 1740s (Coolidge 1979:125). Fort St. Frédéric, in turn, remained a position of strategic importance until construction of Fort Carillon in 1755.

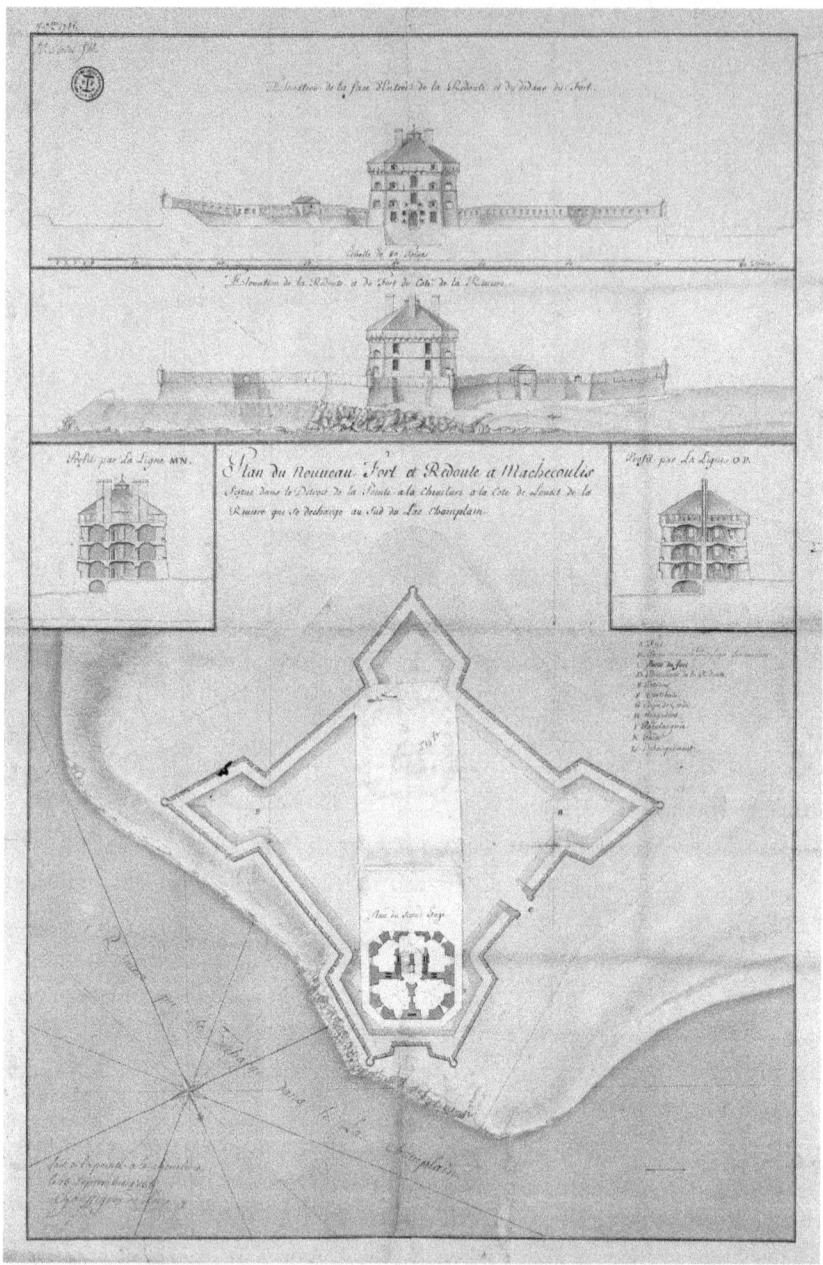

Figure 10.5. "Plan du nouveau Fort et Redoute a Machecoulis Scitué dans le Detroit de la Pointe à la Chevelure a la Cote de Louest de la Riviere qui se decharge au Sud du Lac Champlain" (Plan of the new Fort and Machicolated Redoubt Situated within the Strait at Pointe à la Chevelure on the West Side of the River that discharges Southward from Lake Champlain). The map was drawn on September 15, 1736, at Pointe à la Chevelure by Chaussegros de Léry. (Archives nationales d'outre-mer, FR CAOM 3DFC510A.)

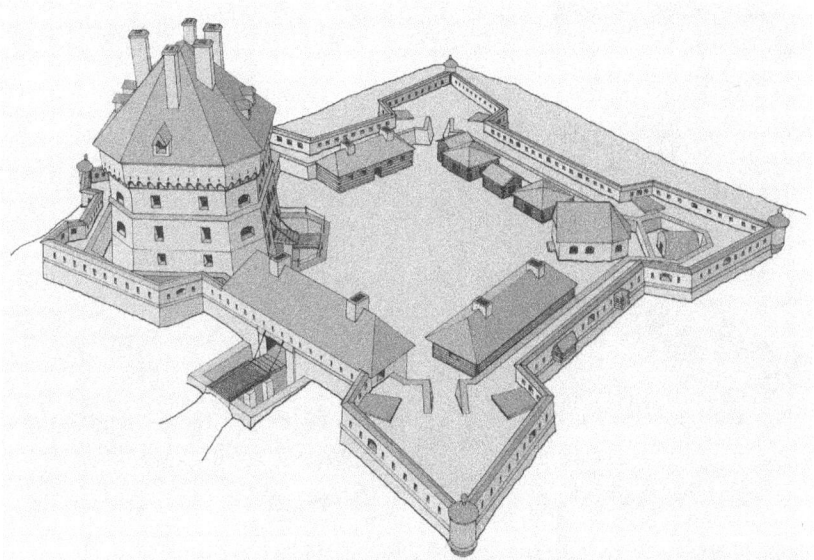

Figure 10.6. Drawing from a model of Fort St. Frédéric. The depiction of some of the structures inside the fort is conjectural. North is to the left. (New York State Office of Parks, Recreation and Historic Preservation.)

In terms of military strategy, the citadel served as the fortification's ultimate defense. Plans called for the outer walls of Fort St. Frédéric to be strong enough to withstand only musket and small artillery fire. Within the outer walls of the fort, guardrooms and storage buildings were also built. The garrison was composed of 120 men, who were augmented by settlers brought to the fort's vicinity. A chapel was built to serve the garrison, civilian settlers, slaves, and Indians. The conversion of Indians to Catholicism was a primary objective of the French, and the fort's register lists Indian baptisms. Outside Fort St. Frédéric to the east, a stone windmill was constructed as a separate redoubt armed with cannons (figure 10.7). This location, with a view up the lake, protected the fort's southern approach. The windmill ground grain for the military and the civilian settlements that were developed around the fort. In 1749, it was noted that at or near Crown Point the French "had erected near 30 small French Houses on both Sides of the Lake" (Chamberlain 1916:265). A separate account said there were 18 houses near Crown Point, while still another report claimed there were 14 farms near the fort (Calloway 1992:27; Coolidge 1979:150).

Figure 10.7. Detail from "Carte du Lac Champlain depuis le Fort Chambly jusqu'à celuyde St. Frédéric, 1740" (Map of Lake Champlain since the building of Fort Chambly to that of St. Frédéric, 1740). (Library of Congress, Geography and Map Division, G3802. C5 1740. R Vault.)

Fatal Flaws

Fort St. Frédéric was an impressive structure, but it was not without problems. Although built with four substantial corner bastions, access to these bastions was obstructed on occasion by interior buildings, which hampered the movement of artillery within the fort. Babits (1981) observed this problem in other eighteenth-century forts. More serious difficulties were noted as early as 1740 when Chevalier Claude de Beauharnois, nephew of the governor, described the fort as having "a well which gives no water . . . ; fortifications without ditches and without ramparts . . . ; no barracks, guard rooms on the third floor, . . . [and] the environs of the fort not sufficiently cleared." In addition, the fort had "an inner court in which one's foot sinks 6 inches when it rains, and which would be worth the trouble to have paved" (Coolidge 1979:123).

The Swedish naturalist Peter Kalm visited the fort in 1749 and commented that it should have been constructed at the windmill site facing English settlements to the south. Kalm believed an attack from that direction would not be visible from the fort (Kalm 1972:377). In 1750, an observer from Crown Point reported to New York governor George Clinton that "the walls are of a considerable height and thickness, and has some 20 pieces of cannon and swivels, mounted on the ramparts and bastions, the largest of which are six-pounders, and but a few of them. I observed the wall cracked from top to bottom in several places" (Coolidge 1979:150).

The French colonial inspector of fortifications, Louis Franquet, recommended a major addition to the fort in 1752. According to Franquet, Fort St. Frédéric had been built in the wrong place. The fort was dominated by higher ground to the south, which had to be incorporated into the fort by either a lunette or a redoubt (Franquet 1974:167). In addition, he found many other defects. "Suffice it to be known," he noted, "that all the revetment walls are in bad condition, although constructed only 6 or 7 years ago, on solid ground and of good materials, they suffer, are cracked, and threaten to fall in ruins." Furthermore, he later reported, most of the fort walls were failing, probably "more from a constructional defect than by the weight of the earth." There was no water in the fort, and if the fort were ever surrounded, it would be necessary to open the gate to go to the lake for water. The stone sentry boxes at the angles of the bastions were too small, and some angles of the flanked bastions were falling into ruins. The frame of the main gate threatened collapse. The drawbridge could not be operated "without risk of it reversing"; the ropes broke while it was being raised. The cabins of the soldiers were in ruins. The roof of the citadel leaked and needed to be covered with shingles or an additional layer of planking (75, 165).

Franquet nevertheless concluded that the redoubt, or citadel, with its separate moat, drawbridge, and thick walls, could resist attack by cannon, and "in this condition would be safe against the Indians and even against any vigorous force; the only fault is lack of water. The purpose of its establishment at the narrow point of the river is to harass all who come down from Lake St. Sacrament [Lake George], from Wood Creek, and all others who emerge from English territory into Lake Champlain" (Franquet 1974:163–64).

Louis Antoine de Bougainville echoed Franquet's opinion of the fort's poor situation during a later visit. Fort St. Frédéric was "badly located, there being several heights which command it." However, he noted, "This place in its present state need fear no sudden attack; it is always something to force the enemy to bring up his artillery . . . but [with] the artillery once in position it would be necessary to surrender" (Hamilton 1964:33, 291). Consequently, in planning an attack on Crown Point in 1755, Massachusetts governor William Shirley directed William Johnson to engage as many Indians as possible and "cause one or more Battery's to be erected upon the

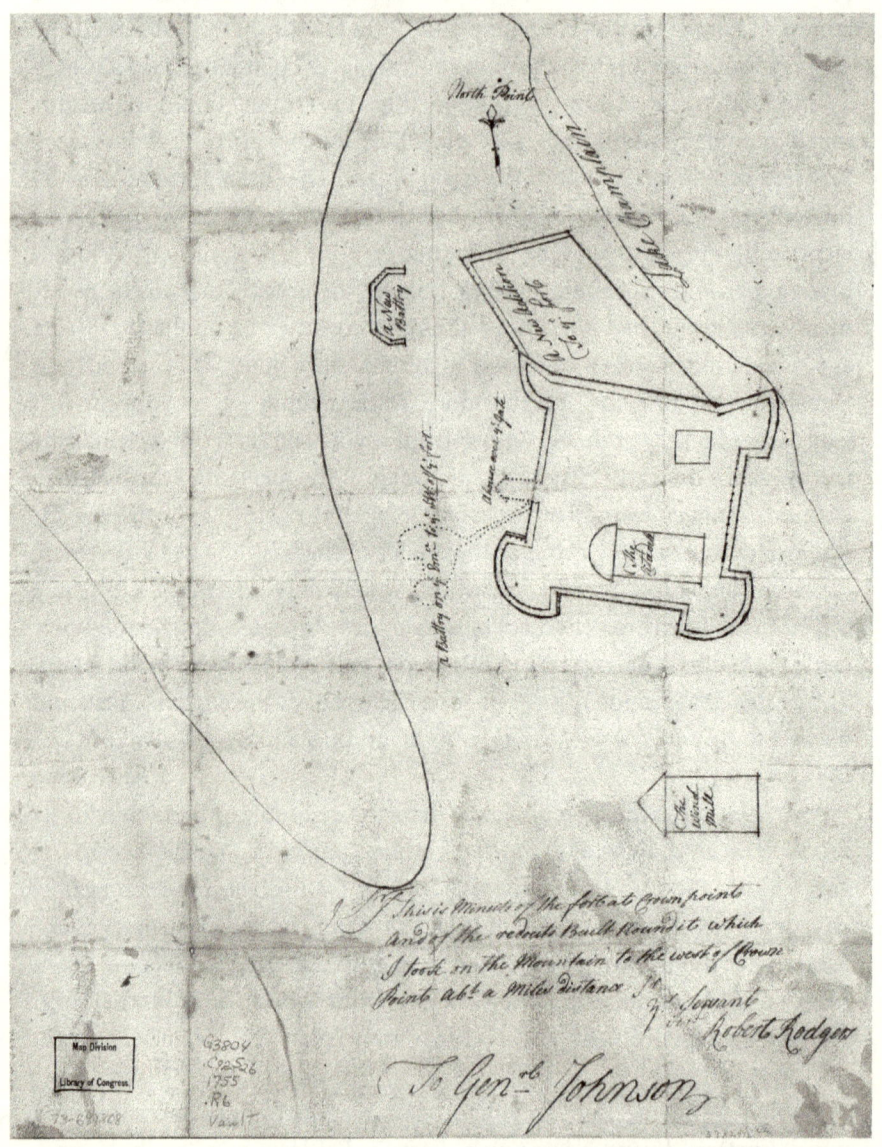

Figure 10.8. Spy map of Crown Point, drawn by Robert Rogers in 1755. Rogers described the hastily drawn, inaccurate sketch as "minuts of the fort at Crown Point and of the redouts built round it; which I took on the mountain to the west of Crown Point abt. 2 miles distance." (Library of Congress, Geography and Map Division, G3804.C92S26 1755. R6 Vault.)

rocky eminence nigh Fort St Frederic, or as near as may be to the said Fort upon the most advantageous ground" (Lewis 1970:412).

Some of Franquet's advice for strengthening the defenses was followed. In 1755, Maj. Robert Rogers spied on the fort for the British and observed that "they were building a battery and had already thrown up an entrenchment" on the southwest side of the fort (Rogers 1961:2). He hastily sketched a crude, inaccurate map of what he could see from a high mountain at least two miles to the west (figure 10.8). The new works were placed on the higher ground to the rear of the fort, connected to the fort by a trench, or covered way. Archaeological excavations in 1979 discovered this trench off the southwest corner of the French fort (Roenke 1979:5, 11).

The improvements did not impress French officers who viewed the fort later. In 1758 Montcalm noted, "St. Frédéric—does not even deserve the name of a bad fort" (Hamilton 1970:396). In 1754, masons at the fort were reluctant to repair the walls, since their poor condition created a dangerous situation. The Canadian artillery commander complained, "The parapets are only two and a half feet thick. The masonry would not be able to sustain the shock of a cannon ball; and the fragments of stone would destroy as many cannoniers as could be placed there" (Casgrain 1890:138). Late in 1758, plans were made for additional strengthening. The fort was to be encompassed by a moat with a palisade in the bottom, and the earth dug from the moat was to form a glacis with a covered way that would also be palisaded (Lévis 1889:156). This work apparently was not completed.

Finally, early in August 1759, a British force of more than 10,000 men under Maj. Gen. Jeffery Amherst advanced northward and took Crown Point without fighting. The French force of approximately 2,300 men blew up the citadel, one bastion, and the windmill upon leaving the fort prior to Amherst's arrival (Parker 1759:596). The British utilized the remains of the French fort while constructing a new fortification. The new British fortress, the largest in British North America, was an artillery fort built on the high ground that commanded the position of the former fort.

The Logic of Fort St. Frédéric

Fort St. Frédéric was constructed as a result of the conflict between European powers. The English and French struggle to control North America resulted in creating material objects, such as the forts at Crown Point. The initial French fort was built specifically in response to the presence of English traders in the Champlain valley. At the same time, its construction intensified the conflict. Fort St. Frédéric enabled the French to extend their influence farther south into colonial New York and northern New England. The extension of French control over the crucial water transportation route between Canada and the English colonies was of critical military and economic importance. The lake and river system was a major invasion route and also both an official and illicit trading route. The location of the French fort is evidence of these concerns. Given the wilderness location, the fort was located without consideration of the possibility of an artillery siege.

This is difficult to understand, since France had developed a corps of formally trained engineers by the late seventeenth century who were regarded as the European experts in military construction. The description of a formal fort or siege required knowledge of the French language. The location and construction of Fort St. Frédéric was not a terrible "mistake" but understandable as a result of a different logic. The strategy evident in locating Fort St. Frédéric is referred to as "positional warfare" (Rothrock 1968), a notion deeply embedded in the ideology of seventeenth-century European society. From this perspective, warfare involved acquisition of territory by establishing a post, maintaining it, and developing a settlement, rather than attempting destruction of the enemy. The military technology and available supply system prevented large field armies and specifically the movement of artillery, which was heavy and required an extensive supply line. Kings, such as Louis XIV (1643–1715) and Louis XV (1715–1774), preferred positional warfare, since the garrisoning of forts was cheaper and politically safer than supporting large, trained field armies (Rothrock 1968). A writer in the *London Chronicle* in 1759, describing Crown Point in 1757, observed that "the great and only security of this, and other forts in the woods of America, is the difficulty of getting at them, and of transporting artillery to attack them; for which and other reasons the situation of those places is of more consequence to consider than their strength" (Anonymous 1759). Writing almost a century earlier, Peter Stuyvesant, the Dutch director-general of New Netherland [later New York] wrote in 1666 that Fort Amsterdam at the south tip of Manhattan Island was "situate in an untenable place, where it was located on the first discovery of New Netherland, for the purpose of resisting any attack of the Barbarians rather than an assault of European arms, having, within pistol shot, on the North and Northeasterly sides, higher ground than that on which it stands, so that, notwithstanding the wall and works are raised the highest on that side, people standing and walking on that high ground can see the soles of the feet of those on the esplanade and bastions of the fort" (O'Callaghan 1858:440). This description matches that of Fort St. Frédéric almost exactly.

The French continued to locate their forts to control water passages and maintain territorial claims and not to take advantage of natural defensive positions. At Crown Point, the French recognized the necessity of fortifying against an artillery siege only because of the renewed British commitment to take North America from the French.

Structural elements of Fort St. Frédéric reflected the ideology of the French in North America. Although the citadel was constructed with thick stone walls, the outer walls were constructed to withstand only musketry and the small artillery fire of skirmish warfare. The absence of a dependable water supply within the fort indicates there was little fear of any substantial, long-term siege. The separate entrance moat and strength of the citadel inside the outer walls provided a second line of defense. This "fort within a fort" was a characteristic of European forts constructed in occupied territories, where the inhabitants of the town were not trusted allies but had access to the interior of a larger fortified area. The citadel was another source of security for the ruling élite, representatives of another ethnic or cultural group. The single entrance and exit, moreover, enabled control over desertion by soldiers.

The castle-like fort was located above the lake with high walls despite the obvious need for low fort walls as a defense against artillery. French engineers were well aware that the use of cannon in warfare changed the medieval defensive strategy based upon height to defense in depth. The citadel's high visibility served to display French imperial power and control (figure 10.9). In turn, visibility up the lake from the fort enabled the sighting of traders who might attempt to go around the fort. The French claim to the territory and the transportation routes was established and communicated through the structure's visibility.

As a military installation, the fort was built to defend against Indian raids rather than a European style siege. The French artillery included a number of pierriers (swivel guns), which were outdated in European warfare by this time but were effective in discouraging Indian attacks. The intimidating physical appearance of this substantial stone structure with multiple lines of defense would by itself have inhibited such attacks. As early as 1721, Pierre de Charlevoix suggested that French settlement should spread to Lake Champlain, where "the inhabitants will have for neighbours, the Iroquois, who are, at bottom, a good sort of people enough, who will,

Figure 10.9. View of Fort St. Frédéric from the south. (Drawing by Leonard F. Tantillo, New York State Office of Parks, Recreation and Historic Preservation.)

probably, never think of coming to a rupture with us, after they shall see us in such a condition as not to fear them, and who, in my opinion, would like us much better for neighbours than the people of New York" (Charlevoix 1761:232). At the same time, the French strength and power exhibited by the elegant construction of the fortress would have attracted Indian allies to the French (Fisher 1985). This was a place for impressive demonstrations and ceremony to cement French alliances with the Indians. It must have been a grand spectacle on 10 June 1747, for example, when there "arrived at Crownpoint about 300 Canoes with French and Indians the major part Indians with two large white flaggs & Drumms beating & . . . the Fort saluted them with 12 guns which they returned with small arms" (Miner and Miner 1915:5). An English writer in 1759, writing after the fort had been captured, commented that "this fort was also a beautiful building, and strongly and judiciously finished" (Parker 1759:596).

Numerous raids by the French and Indians on English settlements in colonial New York and New England were staged from Fort St. Frédéric, earning it a reputation among the English as "greater than its strength merited" (Coolidge 1979:151). Bands of Indians provisioned and aided by the French at Fort St. Frédéric burned military targets, such as the blockhouse at Saratoga, and civilian settlements, such as the houses and barns full of grain at Hoosick. The regulation of trade was a difficult assignment, and there is some evidence that those appointed to regulate trade were themselves guilty of yielding to temptation. Although French officers at Fort St.

Frédéric were offered the full value of any goods seized from smugglers "in the woods," illicit trade continued, even within the fort itself (Demos 1994:184). Franquet in 1752 discovered that the wife of the fort's commander "had a stock of all kinds of merchandise, even contraband articles, that she obtained from New England by way of the Indians" and sold at her exclusive shop in the fort (Franquet 1974:67).

The raids on English colonies led to demands for protection from the French. Fort St. Frédéric, as the origin of these raids, became the objective of several British military expeditions during the Seven Years' War. When Governor Shirley explained his choice of William Johnson as leader of the 1755 expedition, he claimed that "one of the principal things we have in view, in the expedition, is to retain such of those [Iroquois] Castles, as are not yet gone over to the French, in the English interest" (Hamilton 1970:410).

Conclusion

The French constructed Fort St. Frédéric in reaction to the entry of English traders in the Champlain valley. The location and structure of this fort reflect the colonial conflict of the European powers in North America. The role of Indians in this conflict is evident in the presence of the structure at Crown Point, the type of defensive work built, and the presence of the interior chapel. The style is indicative of seventeenth-century European positional warfare, demonstrating the French belief in territorial expansion through invasion and occupation without concern for withstanding an enemy's artillery siege. The stone windmill physically demonstrated that their occupation extended to the civilian sphere, further legitimizing their territorial claim.

The construction of Fort St. Frédéric as a material symbol of the French presence served to attract Indian allies, who maintained French power over this territory by raids on English settlements. These raids, in turn, united the English colonies in an effort to take Fort St. Frédéric and remove the French threat with repeated military expeditions. The importance of maintaining the Iroquois alliance with the British was crucial to the selection of William Johnson as commander of the 1755 expedition. As a material artifact of seventeenth-century French society caught up in an eighteenth-century colonial conflict, Fort St. Frédéric expressed the ideology of that society. This structure established a territorial claim, since it identified the group that built it and physically portrayed their power. The economic and political ideology of positional warfare was evident in the location and type of construction.

Once built, Fort St. Frédéric was an active component in the social system. Both documentary and archaeological evidence indicate that the illicit trade between Canada and the English colonies continued despite the fort. But it was the success of this fort as the point of origin of the many terrifying French and Indian raids on the English colonies that ironically led to its ultimate destruction and abandonment by the French in 1759, transforming the colonial system in North America.

Acknowledgments

This article is revised from the paper written by Charles L. Fisher and presented 13 January 2007 at the Society for Historical Archaeology Annual Conference at Williamsburg, Virginia. A previous version was presented on 10 January 1985 at the Society for Historical Archaeology Annual Conference at Boston.

The authors are indebted to Michael Roets, State Historic Sites Archeologist of the Division for Historic Preservation in the New York State Office of Parks, Recreation and Historic Preservation, for help with the illustrations.

Sadly, Chuck Fisher passed away in February 2007 at the age of 57.

11

Fort Frontenac, Kingston, Ontario, Canada

SUSAN M. BAZELY

The remnants of French Fort Frontenac, located in present-day Kingston, are situated on the north shore of the eastern end of Lake Ontario. The fort exists only in the archaeological record, although extensive investigations from 1982 to 1985 led to a partial reconstruction of the northwest bastion, west, and north curtain walls (figure 11.1). Subsequent utility installation, road widening, and safety upgrades to existing buildings allowed further archaeological examination. The significance of Fort Frontenac was recognized through its designation as a National Historic Site of Canada in 1923.

Excavating to find evidence of the fort began as early as 1938 when the commandant of the Royal Canadian Horse Artillery facility had parts of the parade square trenched. The collection of summarized and translated documents reproduced in *Royal Fort Frontenac* (Preston and Lamontagne 1958) has been an invaluable resource for those who have excavated there. Part of the area once occupied by the fort and areas settled near it remain in military use, while the rest is covered by roads, condominiums, an arena, and a plethora of nineteenth- and twentieth-century buildings and parking lots.

Construction of the First Three Forts

Fort Frontenac was a necessary part of the western trade route of New France long before the French and Indian War erupted in 1754. The recommendation for its establishment came as early as 1670, but was not carried out for some years. Most likely, the fort's establishment was only due to the advantages presented to the fur trade by protecting the Indian allies and keeping the Five Nations Iroquois in check (Preston and Lamontagne 1958:1–19). In 1673, Governor Louis Buade, comte de Frontenac, traveled

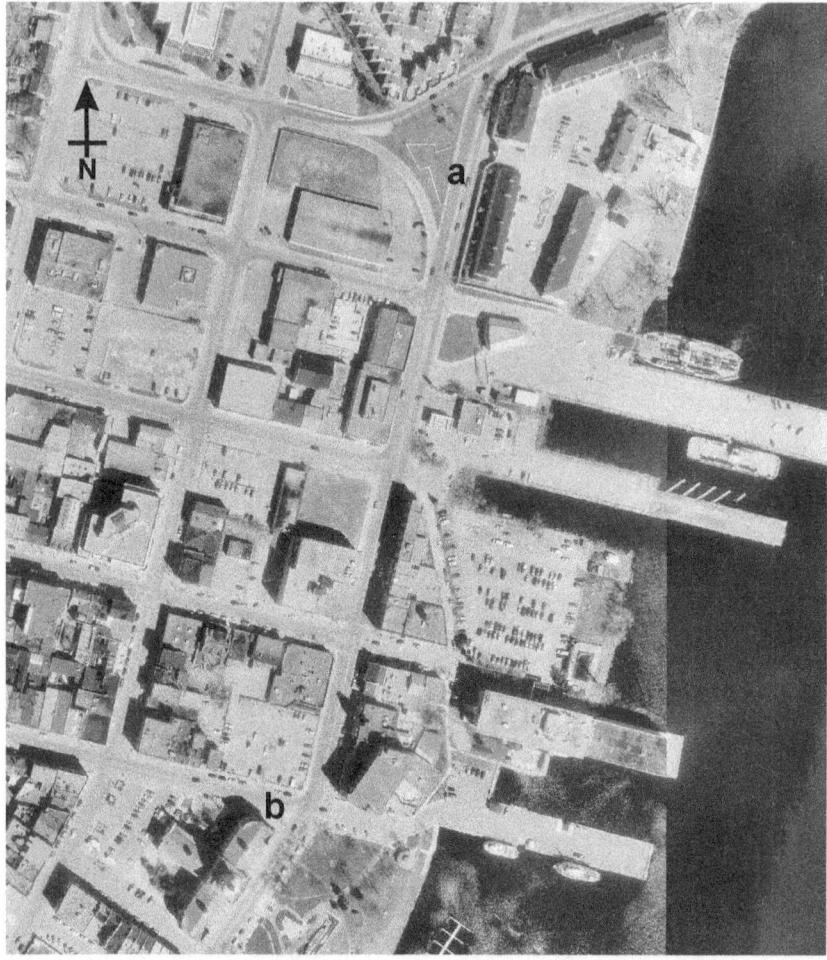

Figure 11.1. (a) Location of Fort Frontenac surrounded by landfill and covered by roads and buildings in present-day downtown Kingston, Ontario, with city hall and the marketplace (b) to the south at the location of the 1755 outer defenses. (Courtesy of the City of Kingston.)

by bateau from Québec to build a fort on Lake Ontario's north shore. A detailed but unsigned journal provides a firsthand view of what Frontenac found and the activities that were undertaken at the mouth of the Cataraqui River. Whether or not the fort was to serve a military capacity as a defensive structure from its first inception is debatable; it was nevertheless intended to provide a reminder of the French presence and perhaps a determination to command the land, its resources, and inhabitants.

Since there already was a mission west of Cataraqui attended by the Sulpician order, Frontenac's reasons for stopping and building where he did must relate in part to the geographic location and perceived benefits of the topography as both strategic and defensible. Construction commenced on 13 July 1673 and was completed by 19 July, as Frontenac reported:

> 12 July. . . . they . . . led him through the mouth of the Cataraqui River into a bay about a cannon shot from the entrance, which forms one of the finest and most pleasant harbors in the world, since it could hold one hundred of the largest ships, having there sufficient water at the mouth and in the basin whose bottom is only mud, and which is so secure from every wind that cables would scarcely be needed for mooring them. . . .
>
> 13 July. . . . Sieur Rendin was working to lay out the fort on the site that the Count had chosen following the plan that he had fixed upon with him; . . . they ordered men to work at the trench where the stakes were to be planted. . . .
>
> 15 & 16 July. . . . The Indians were astonished to see the great clearing of felled trees that had been made and that on one side some were squaring timber, and others bringing stakes, others digging trenches, and that divers works were advancing at the same time.
>
> 19 July. Finished enclosing the fort. (Pritchard 1973:23–55)

The inner harbor of the Cataraqui River is, even today, sheltered and the approach to the bay and harbor itself is clear of rocky shoals, unlike the treacherous waters of the adjacent St. Lawrence River. A spit of land, now absorbed as fill forming the current land mass, projected northward into the river. The good anchorage is consistently mentioned by individuals who visited or were stationed at the fort during the seventeenth and eighteenth centuries (Charlevoix 1761; Hennepin 1880) and thus appears to be a key to the location's selection. Additionally, natural resources for food, farming, fuel, and building materials were plentiful and were likely another primary consideration. The abundance of resources is noted throughout the fort's occupation by Baron Lahontan in 1684 (1735), Reverend Father Emanuel Crespel in 1731 (1754), by Peter Kalm in 1748, and by Reverend Pierre Francois Xavier de Charlevoix in 1761.

There are few details on the first fort, but Robert Cavalier, sieur de La Salle, was the first commandant and seigneur of Cataraqui in 1675. Louis XIV granted La Salle Fort Frontenac and adjacent lands by letters patent of concession for his own profit. It is not clear how much repair work or additional construction was undertaken by the new owner, but La Salle incurred expenses for "new fortifications, clearings, and works" between

1675 and 1677 (Preston and Lamontagne 1958:120–22). It has generally been interpreted and accepted that La Salle immediately demolished and rebuilt Frontenac's fort (Bazely 2007:4; Burleigh 1979:12; Preston and Lamontagne 1958:32), although archaeological investigations in the area have not revealed any definitive evidence of the first fort.

A number of individuals who were at the fort during this early period provided written descriptions with similar characteristics. The Recollet missionary, Father Hennepin, was at Fort Frontenac with La Salle between 1675 and 1678 and described it as "surrounded by a Rampart, great Stakes and Palisado's, and four Bastions." He then noted that in only two years, changes were made to enlarge and strengthen the fort "to the circumference of Three hundred and sixty Toises . . . and is now adorn'd with Free-Stone" (Hennepin 1880). An anonymous report of 1679 to 1681 described the first fort as a small palisade that La Salle had demolished and replaced with a larger fort "with four bastions faced with masonry revetments" and a moat dug across the landside. Clearly a transformation occurred during this time, and Nicolas de La Salle, who traveled to Fort Frontenac in 1682, gives a good description:

> Fort Frontenac is a square with four bastions which measures 15 toises from one corner to the other. Three quarters of it are of masonry of hardstone, the wall is three feet thick and twelve high. There is one place where it is only four feet, not being completed. The remainder is closed in with stakes. There is inside a house of squared logs, a hundred feet long. There is also a blacksmith's shop, a guard house, a house for the officers, a well, and a cow-house. The ditches are fifteen feet wide. . . . there is a barn for storing the harvest. There are near the fort several French houses, an Iroquois village, a convent, and a Recollet church. (La Salle 1898)

Baron Lahontan, at Fort Frontenac ca. 1684, presented some contradictory evidence: "This fort was a Square, consisting of large Curtains flanked with four little Bastions; . . . and the walls were so low, that one might easily climb upon 'em without a Ladder" (Lahontan 1735). Nicolas de La Salle's description most closely relates to a 1685 plan (NMC 4755) that supports the works as being in a state of transition—no longer the hurriedly built wooden stockade (figure 11.2). The 1685 map may have been produced from La Salle's description, as the wall heights are the same, and therefore it may prove problematic for detailed archaeological use (Bazely 1988). Despite potential problems with maps being drawn by individuals who had never

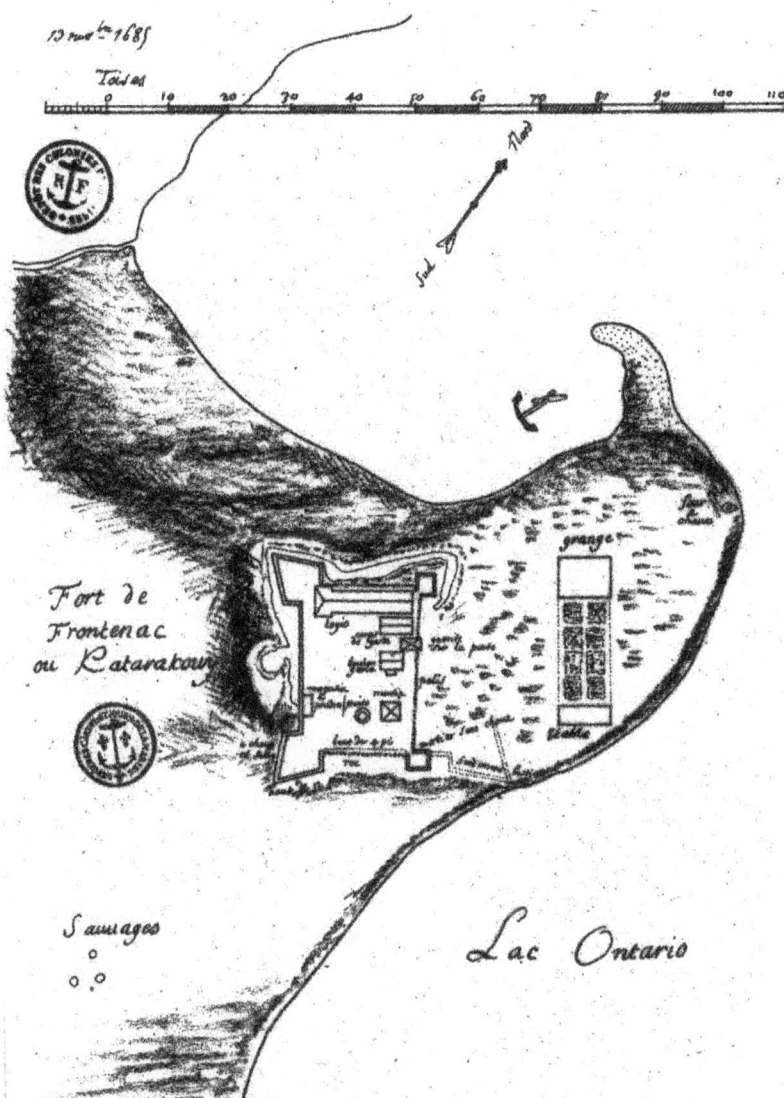

Figure 11.2. Plan of 1685 depicting the transition from the second Fort Frontenac of 1675 to the third by 1687. (NMC 4755 National Map Collection, Library and Archives Canada.)

seen the area, the 1685 plan indicates that La Salle was attempting to utilize state-of-the-art military technology. The fort was transformed from a wooden palisade to one with stone bastions and then to a complete masonry construction. The plan also confirms that a diverse community was developing near Fort Frontenac.

By the time the third Fort Frontenac was under construction, French military engineer Sébastien le Prestre de Vauban had revolutionized fortification design using zigzag trenches, ricochet, flanking fire, and a variety of complex geometric shapes (Brice 1990). Clearly, Fort Frontenac was a simple form of a Vauban style fort with curtain walls flanked by bastions and a ditch on most of the landward side. From an archaeological perspective, there are several elements that relate to both second and third Fort Frontenac transitions. During investigations in 1984 and 1985, fragments of the north stockade posts were identified aligned immediately south of or inside the later stone north curtain wall. It is possible that these posts were also part of the original 1673 construction, but there is no accurate way to determine this, even if datable archaeological material were present in the trench. Subsequent construction and limited excavation space did not allow the corresponding west stockade to be located. The eastern two-thirds of Fort Frontenac is inaccessible, as it lies beneath an existing road and within the modern Canadian Land Force Command and Staff College. Finding any traces of the 1673 fort would be nearly impossible.

Only limited evidence of the west and north ditch was identified during 1983–85 archaeological work as later activities, including nineteenth-century domestic buildings and twentieth-century utilities, obliterated any portions of the fort in these areas (figure 11.3). Remnants of the *logis* or barracks (Bazely 2007:5), a large log house "a hundred feet long" (La Salle 1898) of ca. 1682–89 were identified inside the north stockade, but consisted only of the stone foundations. The masonry walls forming the west curtain and northwest bastion, Bastion Saint Michel, evident on the 1685 plan and in La Salle's 1682 description, exist below the surface to a height of just less than 1.00 m. These foundations have an average width of 0.70 m and are built on limestone bedrock (Stewart 1985:42). A small portion of what is likely the southwest bastion of the third fort was identified during 2006 investigations adjacent to the modern sidewalk. Here the foundation was only 0.25 m below the existing surface (Sheldon 2007).

The last transformation to complete the Vauban style fort was adding the north, east, and south curtain stone walls, joining the northeast and southeast bastions to provide flanking fire. Governor Denonville outlined these last details in a letter to the marquis de Seignelay, minister of colonies, in November 1686. He indicated that Vauban would be sent information to decide what must be done to Fort Frontenac. In the interim he stressed that it is "necessary to lift the walls which are too low and to make one where there are still palings." Denonville went on, "I have this year had a

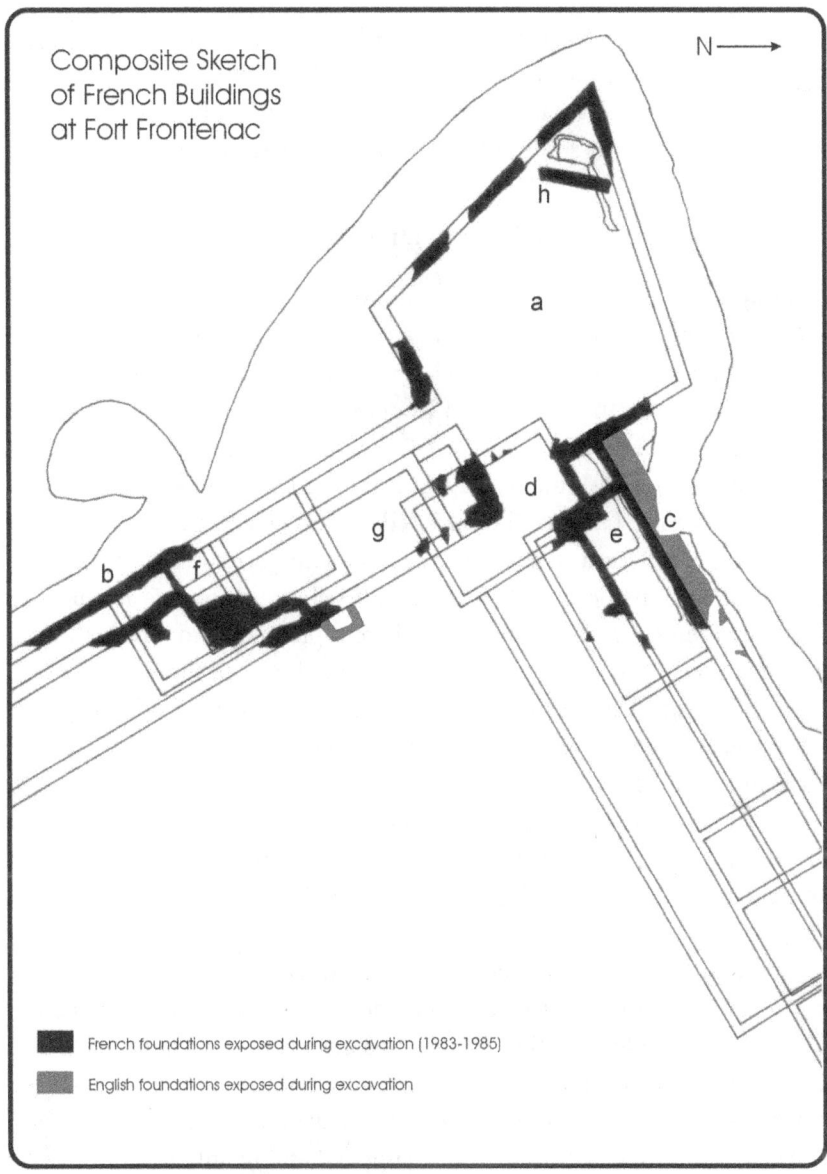

Figure 11.3. Foundations uncovered during archaeological research at Fort Frontenac between 1983 and 1985 including (a) northwest bastion, (b) west and (c) north curtain walls, (d) logis, (e) traders' quarters, (f) trade store, (g) barracks, and (h) *terreplein* or platform support wall. (Cataraqui Archaeological Research Foundation.)

wall made behind the house [*logis* or barracks] in place of the palings which were there" (Denonville 1686). This is the north wall area. The stone fort was completed over the winter of 1686–87. Part of the stone north curtain wall was archaeologically excavated in 1984–85. In 2003, a small portion of the east curtain wall, located within the Canadian Land Force Command and Staff College, was recorded (Bazely 2007:12; Bazely and Brooks 2004).

Siege, Abandonment, and Reoccupation

Although La Salle, as owner of Fort Frontenac, initiated its transformation into a larger and more durable structure, he was seldom at the fort and died on an expedition in 1687 (Preston and Lamontagne 1958:477). Relations between the French and Iroquois were tenuous throughout the construction and rebuilding of Fort Frontenac and continued to deteriorate. The situation eventually erupted into a series of raids and attacks by both sides. Father Lamberville recorded a naval engagement near the fort in September 1687 and an attempted attack on the garrison the next month. Governor Denonville used Father Lamberville to encourage Iroquois to visit Fort Frontenac, where they were then imprisoned and sent to the galleys in France. Denonville also led an attack on the south shore of Lake Ontario and burned Iroquois settlements, villages, and crops. Raids continued into 1688, and French prisoners were taken at Fort Frontenac (Preston and Lamontagne 1958:47–51).

Revenge was on the minds of the Iroquois when they laid siege to Fort Frontenac during the winter of 1688–89. The garrison was short of supplies and decimated by scurvy. Father Lamberville (1695) provided a firsthand account of this episode at Fort Frontenac: "the Iroquois having pressed us so closely so that we had neither wood, nor water, nor refreshment, scurvy infected the garrison, which carried off about a hundred." Despite the use of contemporary fortification theory, it is clear that the garrison was not adequately prepared for a winter siege. Fort Frontenac did not have the necessary stores of food, heating fuel, or safe drinking water.

Since Fort Frontenac could not be supplied and maintained or relieved without great risk and cost, Governor Denonville ordered its destruction (Lahontan 1735; Preston and Lamontagne 1958:51). On 24 September 1689, he wrote his instructions to Commandant Valrennes:

> You will see if you can succeed in mining the walls . . . before embarking. For the magazine which you will blow up will not do much

to cause the walls to fall down by shaking them. I would have rather decided not to burn the house and only knock down what I have made of new masonry, leaving entire all that M. de la Salle built. But as I fear that the English may occupy this post, that is what causes me to tell you to spare nothing if you can manage it. (Denonville 1689)

Governor Denonville, unsure of the destruction that would take place if only the magazine were ignited, was explicit as to what must be done. Count Frontenac was displeased with the order for destruction and determined to return and rebuild Fort Frontenac because he believed it was vital for negotiations with the Iroquois. His reappointment as governor, replacing Denonville, was well received (Preston and Lamontagne 1958:51–52).

Evidence of the 1688–89 siege was first identified during excavations of the *logis* in 1985. A deposit of ash and charcoal was found within the structure's foundations (Stewart 1985:43). Further evidence was uncovered during archaeological investigations within the Canadian Land Force and Staff College during 2003 and 2004 (Bazely and Brooks 2004; Gromoff 2005) and in 2006 under the sidewalk road that cuts through the center of Fort Frontenac (Sheldon 2007). Situated on bedrock in the east ditch near the fort entrance was a layer of burnt, silty clay and large amounts of mammal and bird bone. Similar deposits were identified further west where several buildings were located. Burnt wood, identified as flooring, is likely from the guard house structure or possibly the gatehouse. The locations of these finds match closely with those buildings on the 1685 plan. Although the masonry east curtain wall and new entrance were located further to the east, existing structures probably remained. Artifacts recovered from these areas provide a convincing link to the period. Below the burnt floor, Gromoff (2005) identified trade and rosary beads, carbonized beans, and various sizes of birdshot and musket balls. There were also honey (or blond) colored, spall-type gunflints present. Directly on the floor were forged nails with large heads and a piece of Saintonge pottery. Along with large amounts of bird and mammal bone, Sheldon (2007) identified bone and glass beads, a fragment of copper kettle rim, a clay smoking pipe bowl with a crown on the spur, forged nails, and a "Jesuit" ring with an embossed image, possibly Mary. These deposits range from 0.50 to 0.90 m below the modern surface and clearly indicate that remnants of the earliest Fort Frontenac occupation still exist.

Count Frontenac returned to the Cataraqui River, but could not stop Denonville's order to destroy Fort Frontenac. The Iroquois and French continued to raid each other, and Frontenac was more convinced of the importance of reestablishing the fort despite the lack of government support (Preston and Lamontagne 1958:52–59). Opposition to holding Fort Frontenac was strong as indicated in two letters from Champigny, the intendant of New France, to the minister in October 1694 and August 1695: "this establishment should be looked upon as useless, since the enemy can pass within gun-shot without being afraid of the garrison, nor can we go there in wartime to revictual it without totally exposing those who are sent on this task," and then "I had wished . . . M. le Comte de Frontenac had not thought of re-establishing the fort at Cataracouy and that 700 men, as many soldiers as *habitants* and Indians which he sent on this expedition had been employed on another more useful one." Frontenac took the opportunity to defend himself and his decision to maintain the fort by writing to the minister in October 1696:

> the more I have found that it was an essential thing if one wants to reduce the Iroquois into the condition which you show you wish to put them; for without wishing to study to combat the contrary arguments, those who advanced them could not sustain them before people who have been to the places, and who have some knowledge of them, and less still that I have ever planned to use this excuse to establish there a trade for my own profit as someone has wished adroitly, or rather maliciously, to insinuate to you.

Restoration work is substantiated in a 27 October 1695 letter from Callières, governor of New France during Frontenac's absence, to the minister that stated, "A party with thirty-six officers, three hundred soldiers, one hundred and sixty *habitants* and nearly two hundred Indians . . . remained there eight [days], repairing the breaches with masonry and having building timber brought in for the barracks and firewood for the garrison" (Callières 1695).

By November 1696, a considerable amount of new work had been conducted. New provisions were provided to the garrison and assistance was given in cutting firewood and material for construction. This account, made by an unidentified individual, indicates:

> The masons . . . had built . . . a building 12 feet [high] along one of the curtain walls which is not as high on that side as the parapet. The framework is attached there and loopholes run along the attic as in the rest of the fort. This long building contains a chapel, the lodging of

the officers, a bakehouse, magazines which are now filled with provisions to supply the garrison for more than 18 months.

Since maps of the first half of the eighteenth century identify similar uses for a building spanning the length of the north curtain wall, this new construction replaced the *logis* or barracks that was burned either during the siege or upon the garrison's departure. The archaeological evidence shows the new building was constructed on different foundations, much more substantial than those of the ca. 1682 structure (figure 11.3). Stewart (1985:44) notes that there was a fireplace in the western wall and a small section of an interior partition wall. This western section was later identified in the historical record as the traders' quarters, but this is not mentioned in the 1696 account. Correspondence from the king to Frontenac in April 1697 and May 1698 speaks negatively about trade and recommends abandonment of Fort Frontenac after peace is made with the Iroquois. It is more likely that this westerly section was used for the garrison's provisions. Although Frontenac was able to rebuild and garrison the fort, there would not be peace until the next century.

Fort Frontenac and Trade in the First Half of the Eighteenth Century

Count Frontenac would never experience the peace; he died on 28 November 1698 (Preston and Lamontagne 1958:473). By 1700, the Iroquois were keen to begin trading again, particularly at Fort Frontenac, and the commandant there obtained goods to trade for the Natives' furs strictly against the interdict of the governor (Preston and Lamontagne 1958:61–63). Once again Fort Frontenac was at the center of conflict, but this time directly related to trading activities. It was in the ideal position to act as a regulation point, and in order for France to see any benefits from the fur trade there would need to be strict control. This was not really what the king wanted. The royal plan for the French colony was to concentrate settlement along the central and lower shores of the St. Lawrence River and Acadia, while putting land under cultivation, developing a sustainable economy, and focusing the fur trade around major centers (Preston and Lamontagne 1958:60). If Fort Frontenac was never really part of the overall plan, why did it continue to be repaired and garrisoned at the expense of the Crown? With Frontenac no longer there to champion its cause, several themes were driving its continued existence: threats of conflict and a new war, supremacy of one group over another, and economics all likely contributed to legalizing trade at Fort Frontenac.

Although trade goods again flowed through the gates of the fort, there was still controversy as to whether it was profitable. The king wished to give trading rights to the company formed at Québec (King of France 1701), but the company was unsure of the expense compared with any gains from trade (Company Directors 1701). Even the cost of religious ministrations was questioned as mentioned in a 1702 letter from Callières, who had become the governor, and Beauharnois, the intendant, to the minister:

> We beg you, Monseigneur, to rule whether the two Recollets who are at Fort Frontenac and Detroit will be maintained by His Majesty or by the Company of the Colony. We believe that as this company has the profit of these two forts, it is up to it to have the expenses, as M. de la Salle had them for Fort Frontenac.

The chapel and lodgings for the priest were located in the large stone building constructed along the north curtain wall toward the end of the seventeenth century. Archaeological excavations were undertaken immediately west of the chapel, as the current street configuration does not allow access to the chapel site. Religious items were identified within the nearby northwest bastion and the area west of the chapel. They include a double-barred cross of Lorraine and rosary beads. Several rings set with stones and embossed images were also uncovered, but they are not necessarily of a religious nature.

Reestablishing trade at Fort Frontenac seemed almost as difficult as its rebuilding. Although an agent was stationed there by 1708, the supervisor of Fort Frontenac and other forts, d'Aigremont, provided a long list of complaints to the secretary of state about the trade (d'Aigremont 1708). Although likely, it is not clear if the trader had his own quarters in the building along the north curtain wall or whether a dedicated trade store had been constructed along the west curtain, as shown on a 1720 plan (NMC C15989). This store is shown in two forms on different plans, the first in 1720 as a single square building against the center of the west curtain wall. In the 1726 plan (NMC 4987), the square is further north, and there is a rectangular addition on the south side. Archaeological investigations identified the southern and eastern addition's walls along with a small section of the main structure's east wall. Stewart (1985:45–46) noted that the exposed foundations consisted of dry-laid stones of a small and irregular nature and that the structures utilized the west curtain as the fourth wall.

During excavations, both exposed walls were resting on the underlying limestone bedrock; however, a small section of natural, undisturbed clay containing varves confirmed that only the inside of the structure was dug down. This would have provided more storage space within the trade store. These dedicated structures confirm that trade was somewhat valued within the confines and activities of the fort.

Quantities of trade goods survive in the archaeological record, but do not closely match items described from earlier fort periods. Baron Lahontan, at Fort Frontenac ca. 1684, mentioned exchanging a variety of natural resources "for needles, knives, powder and ball" (Lahontan 1735). The 1723 statement of provisions, munitions, and goods traded at Fort Frontenac and other posts provides a comprehensive listing of items and their value. This list includes signet rings, red and yellow copper cauldrons, large, medium, and small axes, copper medals, leadshot and leadballs, gunflints, and large and small glass beads. These are the types that dominate many French period deposits uncovered along the north curtain wall near the traders' quarters and the west curtain wall where the trade store stood. These also represent the most typical objects that survive best in the ground, given the heavy clay soils of the Kingston region (figures 11.4a-d). There are many more perishable items including cloth and other textiles and finer metals such as brass thread, listed in the statement, that have not survived in the archaeological record. Lead bale seals that were attached to goods and supplies were also found at the traders' quarters and trade store (Bazely 1986:14).

Other fort buildings and facilities during the 1720s included a forge, infirmary, two guard houses, a large storehouse in the form of a two-story tower, bakery, well, and a powder magazine. The division of the large structure situated along the north curtain was, from west to east, the traders' quarters, chapel, priest's quarters, officers' quarters, and commandant's quarters (Bazely 1988:27). These facilities related primarily to housing the garrison and the necessary provisions for their health and well-being (figures 11.4e, 11.4f). Beyond the fort walls were a few facilities, including stables and a limekiln. Unlike the earlier period, when settlement by French *habitants* was encouraged and actually resulted in a small village, a Native settlement, and cultivated land, the early eighteenth century saw little civilian desire to live on the frontier (Preston and Lamontage 1958:32–33, 66). Again, the 1720 plan depicts only a small number of *cabannes des sauvages* (NMC C15989) adjacent to Fort Frontenac and no indication of a civilian population at all. The focus seemed to be on controlling a profitable trade

204 · Susan M. Bazely

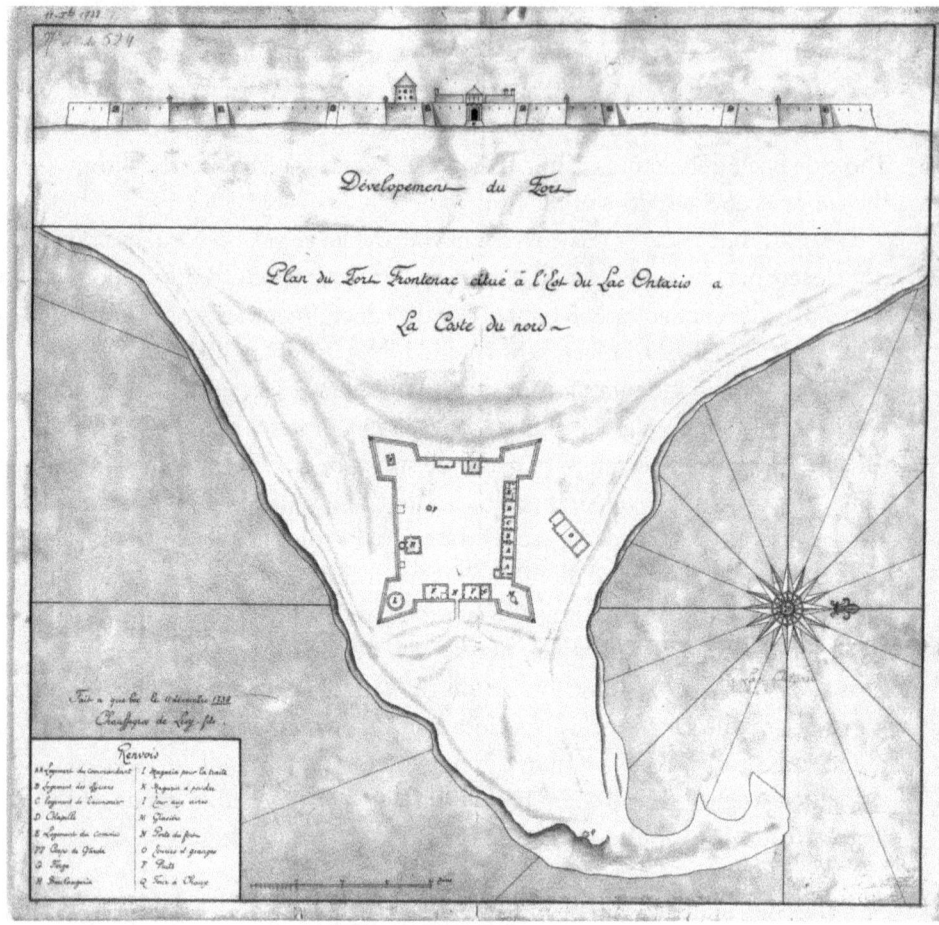

Figure 11.4. Plan of Fort Frontenac, 1738, by Chaussegros de Léry fils, depicting the elevation of the fort. (NMC 22954 National Map Collection, Library and Archives Canada.)

business through maintaining good relations with various Native groups and preventing trade between them, illegal traders, and the British. Any desire of establishing a post with a balanced settlement of colonists and Native people was completely abandoned at Fort Frontenac.

A detailed plan of Fort Frontenac was created in 1726 (NMC 4987). This was executed under Gaspard Joseph Chaussegros de Léry. As the first military engineer in Canada, Léry was responsible for military fortifications and public building between 1716 and 1751 (Preston and Lamontagne 1958:471). Fort Frontenac was presumably examined during the 1720s in order for such a plan to be produced. Since there is a difference between the 1720 and 1726 plans, it can be concluded that additional monies were put into expanding the fort, although it is not known whether the trading company or the military provided funding. The only change between the two plans is the enlargement of the trade store. This alteration suggests support for the fur trade industry rather than military priorities.

Various correspondence throughout the 1730s indicate that trading activities at Fort Frontenac operated at a financial loss in most years. In 1736, Beauharnois and Hocquart, the intendant, reported to the minister, "As for the trade done today at Fort Frontenac and Niagara, it becomes from year to year a smaller business, taking into account the expenses which the king bears there." The king of France, Louis XV, was rather displeased with the affairs of the fur trade, since it was not a benefit to the colonial or royal purses. His frustration is clear in a letter to Beauharnois and Hocquart in 1738: "It is annoying that this trade diminishes every year. The Srs de Beauharnois and Hocquart attribute this decline to three causes: to the suppression of the brandy trade with the Indians, to the bad quality of the woolen material, and to the low price of beaver [fur]." It is ironic that 1738 was also the year that Gaspard Joseph Chaussegros de Léry, the son of the chief military engineer, put together the most detailed plan yet of Fort Frontenac (NMC 22954) (figure 11.5). The younger de Léry was also a military engineer, and it is not surprising that the overall plan is rather similar to that of 1726. The key difference is the illustration of the elevation of the fort depicted across the top where it appears as a flat "cut-out," with an ice house in the northeast bastion (Bazely 1988:27). The most intriguing details from the elevation drawing illustrate the position of loopholes in the curtain walls and face of each bastion, embrasures in the bastion flanks, the sentry boxes in the bastion salient angles, and the elaborate gate house and drawbridge. Did these construction characteristics really exist in what was essentially a fur trade post, or were they aspects of standard military engineering drawings?

Abysmal Condition and Final Improvements

During the fourth decade of the eighteenth century, details of the true conditions of Fort Frontenac come to light. While it is difficult to clearly interpret whether various repairs and changes made at this time were ongoing requirements in response to the necessity of maintaining the fort for trade, it is certain that there was now a concern for defensible integrity. At this point it was probable that hostile activities from the Natives were feared.

Combinations of official visits and inspections and accounts of officers garrisoned at Fort Frontenac provide conflicting reports on its condition and usefulness. The first indication of the situation and the probable work is in a September 1742 letter from Hocquart to the minister. He proposed

> to send M. De Lery to Fort Frontenac and Niagara next spring to effect the necessary repairs and to restore the curtain wall at Fort Frontenac if that work is essential. No work has been done this year in these two forts except for some minor repairs which did not amount to much, and for which a carpenter was left there, who has been especially employed in finishing the platforms of the bastions at Fort Frontenac. (Hocquart 1742a)

Barely a month later, Beauharnois and Hocquart (1742a) sent another letter to the minister confirming that they would send Monsieur de Léry to Fort Frontenac the following spring "to restore the curtain wall which is in danger of collapse." Repairs to masonry buildings are an ongoing requirement due to the Canadian climate and the limited longevity of lime mortar. Some 40 to 60 years had elapsed since construction of the masonry curtain walls and bastions, and without any regular maintenance they would be in dire condition. From Hocquart and Beauharnois's indication, it would appear that the curtain walls may have already collapsed. British military engineers were to grapple with the same issues 100 years later at Fort Henry, Kingston, where even the strictest maintenance and repair program could not sufficiently slow deterioration caused by moisture and harsh Canadian winters (Garcia 2006; Last 2006a). More interesting than the masonry repairs at Fort Frontenac is the carpentry work in the bastions. Platforms were necessary for the garrison to access musket loopholes in the bastion faces and embrasures in the bastion flanks for the guns to provide flanking fire along the curtain walls. Yet, almost in the same breath, it is agreed by all parties including the trader that the garrison can be reduced to only 15 with two officers (Beauharnois and Hocquart 1742b; Hocquart 1742b). This suggests the only perceived threat was from Natives and not a British attack using cannon.

The contest for controlling the fur trade and the vast territories of the Great Lakes, Ohio, and Acadia kept the two colonial empires of France and Britain in conflict. Frontier forts like Fort Frontenac were invariably an important part of the rivalry (Preston and Lamontagne 1958:70). Within the context of rapidly approaching conflict, the visit to Fort Frontenac by the military engineer Chaussegros de Léry should be viewed in light of the

Figure 11.5. Trade and domestic items recovered during archaeological investigations at Fort Frontenac between 1983 and 2006. *Left to right*: (a) beads—fritcore blue-black and white, blue faceted, blue raspberry, black and white stripe, red with black center; (b) copper tinkle cones; (c) ring with embossed image; (d) honey-colored spall flints and lead shot; (e) tin-glazed earthenware with black and blue decoration typical of Rouen; (f) flacon and wine bottle neck and finish. (Cataraqui Archaeological Research Foundation.)

defense strategy. In his 1744 report to the minister, he stated, "I have visited Fort Frontenac. The fortification is in good condition. I only had some loopholes opened where they were lacking and an open palisade [built] outside the walls to prevent anyone from coming suddenly to scale the walls into this fort." It would seem from this comment that Fort Frontenac was in a better state of repair than previously reported. Or it could be surmised that the engineer did not think much of the structure at all and only reported on what he thought was best for the situation. Regardless of the physical condition, the lessee of the trade license was continually discouraged by the lack of profits the company was making and attempted on more than one occasion to dissolve the lease (Preston and Lamontagne 1958:68–69). The fur trade was obviously in a state of decline, and it is perhaps at this point that Fort Frontenac finally takes on a truly military role.

By 1747, trade at Fort Frontenac had virtually ceased and the lessee had abandoned the post. Hocquart outlined the situation in October and indicated that there were trade goods remaining at the fort that had not yet been liquidated. It is unknown whether the merchandise was distributed among the garrison and the Natives still living around the fort. Excavations within the northwest bastion, where there were never any buildings, produced large quantities of trade materials including fragments of copper kettles, iron fishing spears, rings, an axe head, glass beads in varying sizes and colors, and a small cross (figure 11.4). These were found in layers of French period fill, perhaps an attempt to dispose of items for later use, trade, and sale.

Some distance beyond the northeast bastion, 12 burials were archaeologically excavated in 1989. A number of these burials contained trade goods including copper alloy annular brooch pins, glass seed beads, and an iron clasp knife. Adams (1989) identified the burials as being from the 1740s and 1750s by linking some with the parish register of St. Francis, Fort Royal of Frontenac. The register was begun in November 1747. Four of the burials were aboriginal; all but one were interred in wooden coffins (Adams 1989). Whether these trade items were part of the last legitimate trading activities conducted at Fort Frontenac or from the final phase of asset liquidation is unknown.

The son of military engineer Chaussegros de Léry was an advocate of Fort Frontenac. His message for maintaining the fort relates more to the importance of the harbor:

> Fort Frontenac will always be a great refuge for our barks since it is the only harbor on Lake Ontario where we can place them in security. It would be advantageous to make other posts but it is necessary to maintain Fort Frontenac. In earlier times it was abandoned, but we were compelled to go back to it. [I was] very happy to find a tower still there which the mines had not been able to destroy when the other buildings were blown up. (Chaussegros de Léry Jr. 1749)

Blowing up the buildings refers to the intentional destruction in 1689. This letter, which implies an actual visit to Fort Frontenac, suggests that the tower (located in the southeast bastion) was in good condition, and perhaps there was some thought given to fortifying it. Both father and son military engineers spoke in a positive way about Fort Frontenac, and each was responsible for producing a detailed plan. There is almost a sentimental tone to their correspondence. It is, nevertheless, difficult to comment from an archaeological perspective on the robustness of the tower and southeast bastion. The "excavations" that exposed its foundations were not archaeological but carried out by Commandant Brigadier General Kitching in 1952 (Bazely 2007:9; Kitching 1953). The foundations that are now exposed in a sunken garden have been repointed and stones replaced on numerous occasions. Based on structural evidence from archaeological excavations at the fort over the past 25 years, it is unlikely that any of the tower and exposed sections of the southeast bastion are of seventeenth-century French construction.

Some individuals believed that changes were indeed necessary at Fort Frontenac. The transition from trade post to military supply depot is obvious in a letter from La Jonquière, the governor-general of New France, to the minister in 1750:

> Fort Frontenac is not in truth placed in a position to defend the colony from the north, as I had the honor to give you an account by one of my letters last year. But I have recognized since that time that its harbor is very good and very useful for the transport of the effects of the King by bateaux. . . . This post is used as a warehouse and there are two barks which are safe there even during the winter, upon which the said goods can be sent to Niagara at little expense, without delay. Besides, planks and joists are continually being made there to supply the needs of Niagara and other neighboring posts. I think, then, Monseigneur, that it is fitting to preserve it, that it will be sufficient to do some indispensable repairs there and reduce the garrison, which I am going to do.

In addition to highlighting the positive attributes of the fort, La Jonquière pointed out the negative as well. Some repairs were necessary, and the fort stood in a poor defensive position. While reducing the garrison again seemed ongoing, there must have been some laborers at Fort Frontenac to carry out the work. The ships had to be maintained in good order if they were to be of any use; raw materials had to be processed, cut, and sawed to appropriate or manageable sizes. The good harbor was located immediately north of the fort, and archaeological investigations prior to condominium development gave access to the filled land. A series of vertical cedar posts that extended from the French period shoreline out into the bay were interpreted as a wharf or jetty used for loading and unloading boats (Adams

1985:13–14). The shallow waters of the bay could easily accommodate the barks, but no archaeological evidence to date has been found of any French period vessels.

The continued use of Fort Frontenac as a staging ground for troops to assemble supplies, arms, and ammunition in preparation for renewed hostilities was of utmost importance to New France. In 1753, the new governor, Duquesne, increased the garrison at Fort Frontenac by sending a detachment of 70 soldiers along with 80 bateaux full of supplies, and ordered three new barks built there (Preston and Lamontage 1958:71). This action was part of the major fort-building expedition planned for securing the Ohio River, a key access route to the interior lands (Stephenson 2006:1–2). The increased numbers were woefully inadequate to mount any offense attack or an adequate defense of Fort Frontenac. There needed to be improvements to the fort's defensive structure, and a larger garrison would necessitate construction of additional accommodations, as the long building adjacent to the north curtain could not house all the troops.

Captain Malartic, adjutant of the Béarn Regiment, was stationed at Fort Frontenac during this critical period (Preston and Lamontagne 1958:73, 479). He kept an account of what transpired at the fort and made critical comments on the situation of the existing works as well as new work that was undertaken by both the Béarn and the Guyenne Regiments in 1755:

> Fort Frontenac, which is esteemed the strongest in the country, and consists only of four small stone bastions, the faces of which are no more than six toises, the flanks two, and the curtains twelve. The walls are not two feet thick and have neither revetments nor terraces. The terreplain of the rampart is built of plank and masonry; when one of the guns on it is discharged the whole fort shakes. Generally speaking, its situation is very bad, as also is its construction, and it is of no use except for stores. . . .
>
> 19th A shipbuilder arrived from Montreal to work on a schooner for the navigation of the lake, in addition to the two already in the bay, and for the protection of our bateaux against the English sloops that are cruising the lake.
>
> 20th Traced out a grand redoubt at the head of the camp of the regiment of Guyenne, two at that of Bearn, joined to the one of Guyenne by a curtain and breastwork on the bank of the river which the two regiments commenced and completed. . . .

When we arrived at this post, for which much apprehension was felt, there was not a single piece of artillery in good condition; or any of the equipment necessary for moving and loading them. We are lucky that the English were not prepared to come. (Malartic 1755)

It is not difficult to see all the potential weaknesses of Fort Frontenac, especially from the perspective of this professional soldier. Archaeological remnants of the masonry support wall for the *terreplein* were identified in the northwest bastion. This wall was similar in width to that of the curtain and bastion walls, only 0.70 m, or 2 ft., on average. This dimension is a good match for Malartic's description, and although the wall was constructed on the bedrock, it did not appear particularly substantial. Subsequent nineteenth- and twentieth-century utility line construction destroyed the relationship between the *terreplein* support wall and the bastion walls. Without this relationship, it is difficult to understand how the later masonry construction was linked and, more importantly, anchored. The reported state of the artillery is at a minimum appalling and certainly frightening for those expected to fight. In contrast, recognizing the importance of vessels on the lakes to counter the English is a sharp appreciation of the tactical situation. New works consisted of three redoubts, a curtain, and breastwork (Last 2006b:78–79). They included an entrenchment constructed well beyond the fort. The *ravelin*, outside the main gate, may have been part of this construction. Two plans dating to 1758 (NMC 16333; NL 135 R68 1765) show these new works, although in a rather stylized fashion. Estimates based on these and other historic plans place part of the works near the current Kingston City Hall, built in 1842, and the marketplace. Captain Jacques Viger (1895) wrote in his memoirs of the War of 1812 that "the remains of a moat or ditch, also of a glacis constructed by the French, can still be seen in the public square." Recent archaeological work behind City Hall revealed indications of a retaining wall and ditch, but analysis has not yet determined whether any part of it may relate to the 1755 French outer works. The south corner of the *ravelin* was exposed during utility upgrades (Bazely and Brooks 2004).

A critic of the new redoubts and entrenchments was the adjutant of the Guyenne Regiment, La Pause. In his observations on Fort Frontenac in 1756 he pointed out the deficiencies of this work, noting that "these trenches are too extended to be defended by less than 1,500 men" and that "the parapet is good, but not high, the trenches are not deep, since rock was reached at two

Figure 11.6. Excavations along the west curtain of Fort Frontenac demonstrate later nineteenth- and twentieth-century impacts to the (a) curtain wall, (b) trade store, and (c) 1756 barracks and confirm wall thickness and construction technique. (Cataraqui Archaeological Research Foundation.)

or three feet." He provided a complete outline of all the inadequacies and how they could be improved upon. With apparently little but well thought-out work, Fort Frontenac could indeed have a serviceable defense.

It was not until 1756 that more permanent quarters were built for the enlarged garrison. During the winter months a schooner was constructed at Fort Frontenac and quarters were prepared for the soldiers (Preston and Lamontagne 1958:73). La Pause (1756–57) provided only a brief note on these new facilities, stating, "Last winter, barracks for the accommodation of land forces were built in the area (KK)." He is referring to an, as of now, unavailable plan, so there is no way to tell exactly where or how many barracks were constructed. The two 1758 plans (NMC 16333; NL 135 R68 1765) depict a long narrow structure adjacent to the west curtain wall. A new building in this location would require demolition of the trade store, suggesting increased military needs (Stewart 1985:47). Archaeological excavations uncovered several sections of this new building along the west curtain (figure 11.6). The north wall of the barracks extended to the east–west line of the south flank of the northwest bastion. This would have left only a small opening into that bastion, as the corner of the new barracks came very close (less than 2.00 m) to the corner of the north curtain building. An area representing approximately two-thirds of the building footprint from north to south was investigated, but the southern third extends below the present street. With foundations built directly onto the bedrock, the barracks measured an average of 5.20 m in width and was positioned 1.50 m away from the curtain wall (Stewart 1985:47). There was little evidence of French period barracks occupation, primarily due to the impact of constructing a large 1830s building and use of the barracks structure by the British military in the 1780s. Most of what was uncovered consisted of below-grade foundations, including a stone fireplace and chimney base.

La Pause (1756–57) provided a narrative description of Fort Frontenac that, although critical, gives some explanation for the layout of the barracks:

> The fort has a simple revetment of masonry, with poor foundations of small stones badly set, and the lime is bad; one could easily damage it with a sledge or a pick. The wall is about three to three and a half feet thick at the bottom and two at the top. . . . The walls are from 20 to 25 feet high; there are no moats . . . a wooden scaffold has been built all around except along the north curtain . . . where the buildings are against the wall. . . . There are some places where the scaffold and even the wall would not stand cannon-fire long. The embrasures are

badly placed; the steps to ascend into the bastions are too narrow. (La Pause 1756–57)

The new barracks construction on the west curtain accommodated a wooden scaffold. Perhaps the narrowness of the steps into the bastion was the result of the closeness of the two buildings with a gap of less than 2.00 m. There are some confirmed inaccuracies in La Pause's observations including wall thickness, which archaeological excavation has determined to be an average of only 0.7 m, or about 2 ft., at the base. A wall height of 20 to 25 ft., as La Pause indicates, would certainly be unstable during cannon fire; a greater height could be achieved if depth of the ditch were included, but he suggests that none existed, unless he uses the term *moat* in the very specific sense of containing water. It can therefore be assumed that the walls were only about 12 ft. in height as earlier sources indicated (Lahontan 1735; La Salle 1898; NMC 4755; Unidentified 1696). Even Montcalm, commander of French forces in Canada, had something to say about Fort Frontenac. He noted that it was a place where the least work had been done and that engineers must make an entrenched camp to command the ill-located fort, which needed to be preserved only because it existed (Preston and Lamontage 1958:74).

There is no doubt from the historical record and the archaeological evidence that none of the final proposals for improving Fort Frontenac were ever undertaken. Despite the various successes of the French forces, the English put a plan of attack in motion that would give Fort Frontenac its final test. In August 1758, a force of about 3,000 British regular and colonial troops, including Natives, set out from the south shore of Lake Ontario at Oswego (Andrews 2004:14–15, 18; Preston and Lamontagne 1958:79–80). Their aim was to destroy Fort Frontenac and make it impossible for the French to reoccupy it, thus cutting off all supplies to the other French Great Lake posts. The worst fears of the fort's critics, in particular La Pause's (1756–57) comments about its indefensible nature, were realized in Bradstreet's attack. Artillery was set up on the high ground west of the fort, and the French outer defensive works to the south, constructed exactly three years earlier, were turned to British advantage (Andrews 2004:19–20; Bradstreet 1759; Preston and Lamontage 1958:79). Archaeological evidence of the attack is limited. Two pieces of solid cannon shot possibly relating to the British bombardment from the west were found, one within the northwest bastion against the interior wall and the other approximately 80 m west of the fort. Structurally, there was no evidence of this siege. Activities related to the British use of Fort Frontenac 25 years later, as well as nineteenth- and twentieth-century land use, seem to have eradicated evidence of most of the final period of French use.

The many and varied individuals who were responsible for or reliant upon Fort Frontenac had what can best be described as a love-hate relationship with it, from its first construction to the final days. There is no doubt the fort played a significant role in building New France and its frontier expansion, but if it were not Fort Frontenac, then some other post would have been constructed nearby. Perhaps if all the advice for an alternate location or for additional defensive works were followed, the final outcome might have been different. This would have required a significant investment in resources, time, and ultimately money. Few recommendations were carried through and Fort Frontenac was besieged twice, abandoned once, and reoccupied twice. Surely, based on this continued willingness to settle at Cataraqui, Count Frontenac had done something right. Fort Frontenac was beneficial in the fur trade and as a supply post. It provided a base for new exploration and military attack. It was indeed a useful tool to be exploited, and in so doing it did provide a livelihood for the garrison and French settlers as well as the Native populations who flocked to its walls.

Acknowledgments

Copies of all material cited are held by the Cataraqui Archaeological Research Foundation. Its staff assisted in a variety of tasks in order to prepare this chapter, especially Lindsay Dales and Helen Moore, who retrieved specific artifacts from the collections and Jonas Fernandez, who labeled the images.

12

Michilimackinac, a Civilian Fort

LYNN L. M. EVANS

Fort Michilimackinac, built on the south shore of the Straits of Mackinac about 1715, was one of a series of forts built to control this strategic location during the colonial period. Although military, it was much more a fortified trading post. Archaeological excavations have taken place at Michilimackinac every summer since 1959, and approximately two-thirds of the fort has been excavated.

The Straits of Mackinac are formed by the junction of Lakes Michigan and Huron. As early as 1670, Father Claude Dablon wrote:

> Missilimackinac is an Island of note in these regions . . . situated exactly in the strait connecting the Lake of the Hurons and that of the Illinois [Lake Michigan], and forms the key and the door, so to speak, for all the peoples of the South, as does the Sault for those of the North; for in these regions there are only those two passages by water for very many Nations. (Thwaites 1959:157)

Mackinac Island was the site of the first European settlement in the straits area, but the cultural history of the region goes back over a thousand years. The Anishnabeg (the Odawa, the Ojibwa, and their ancestors) came every summer to fish for whitefish and lake trout. The seasonal concentration of Native people brought Jesuit missionaries to the area, including Father Dablon. He spent the winter of 1670–71 on Mackinac Island. After discovering that the island was too rocky to support horticulture, Father Jacques Marquette moved the mission north of the straits, establishing the Mission of St. Ignace in 1671. The mission served not only local Indians but also a number of Huron people who were following the Jesuits during their diaspora fleeing the Iroquois.

Michilimackinac, a Civilian Fort · 217

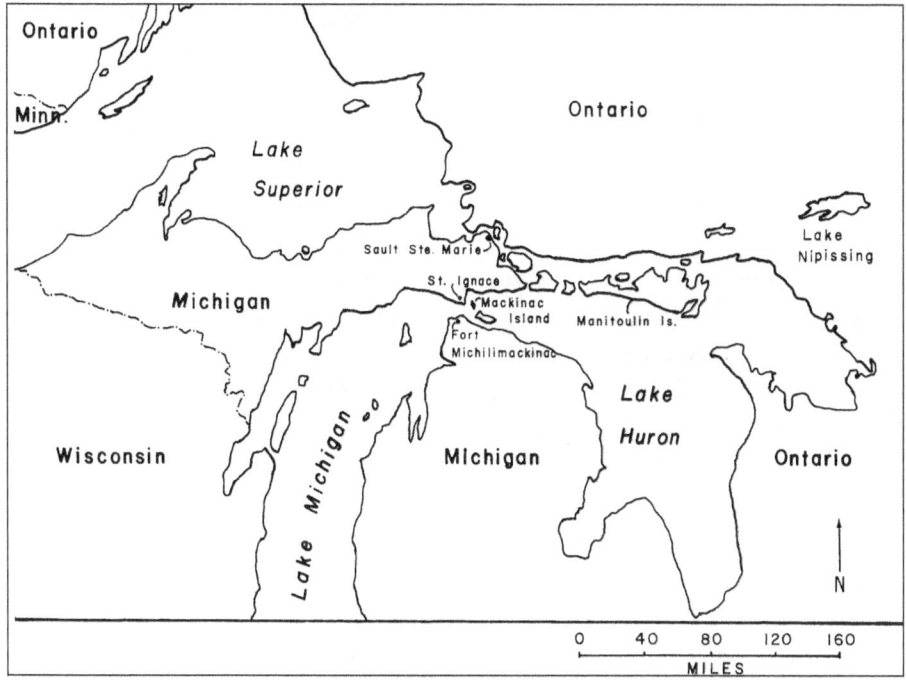

Figure 12.1. The upper Great Lakes. (Mackinac State Historic Parks Collection.)

Huron and Odawa villages located on a major water route were appealing not just to missionaries but to fur traders as well, and a French trading community soon developed. Baron Louis-Armand de Lom d'Arce Lahontan's 1684 map shows a French village, the Jesuits' house, the Huron village, the Odawa village, and Indian fields. Conflicts between traders and priests, and recognition of the commercial and strategic importance of the Straits of Mackinac, led to establishing Fort de Buade by 1690. The fort was abandoned in 1697, as part of a general reorganization of New France. Some of the region's Indians, missionaries, and traders moved their activities to Detroit when that post was founded in 1701; others remained.

About 1715, the French officially reestablished their presence in the Straits of Mackinac, this time on the south shore, where the Odawa and Jesuits now resided. The new post of Michilimackinac was established by Constant Le Marchand de Lignery as part of the French campaign against the Mesquakie (Fox) Indians and to prevent British incursions into the area. The caption on an anonymous map ca. 1717 states that the fort on the south side had a commandant, a few settlers, and some French women.

Not much is known about the physical characteristics of this first fort. There are no extant plans or drawings; only a sketchy description survives. In a 1720 memorial to Count Toulouse, seeking reimbursement for his expenses during the Fox War, de Lignery listed: "Having, also, before departure, had a new Establishment created for the Outavois and the French, on the other Side of the River; a fort for the garrison, with two guardhouses, and a 40-foot house—all at his own expense" (Thwaites 1888–1911, 16:387). A few sections of "DeLignery's Fort" survived under later versions of Michilimackinac and have been identified over the years. Archaeologists extrapolating from these remains estimate it to have been roughly 150 sq. ft., enclosing a mission and around 20 houses (Heldman 1991:13).

In the 1730s, New France flourished with the fur trade, and Michilimackinac flourished along with it. The missionary function of the post decreased, as the Jesuits established a new mission at the Odawa village of L'Arbre Croche, some 20 miles down the Lake Michigan coast. As more traders came to Michilimackinac, it underwent its largest expansion and reconstruction. Its purpose was largely as an *entrepôt* for the fur trade of the *pays d'en haut*, the western Great Lakes. The soldiers garrisoned at the fort policed this trade and also invested a great deal of time in Indian diplomacy, aiming to keep various nations allied with the French and at peace with each other.

The first expansion is generally agreed to have happened in the mid-1730s. Archaeological evidence indicates the serviceable life of wood structures at the fort is 15 to 20 years (Maxwell and Binford 1961:31; Heldman 1991:26). Counting forward from 1715 gives a date of 1730–35 when the original structures would need major repair, a logical time to expand. In 1731, Gaspard-Joseph Chaussegros de Léry, chief engineer of New France, submitted plans for a stone "redoubt" to be built at Michilimackinac (Dunnigan 2008:79). The king thought this too expensive, and the plan was rejected in 1732 (Halchin 1985:14), but a wooden expansion took place. Writing in 1749, French Canadian military engineer Michel Chartier de Lotbinière described the fort as "badly built" (Gérin-Lajoie 1976:4). If this is because it was falling down again, one can count back 15 to 20 years and come up with a construction date of 1729–34. Combining these sources yields an approximate construction date of 1733–34.

During this expansion the settlement pattern for the remainder of the fort's existence was established, including the familiar row houses. The regularity of the lot sizes suggests that it was all laid out at one time (Heldman 1991:27). Ideally, one could look at the artifacts found in the lower levels of these houses to date their construction. Unfortunately, in some cases these layers were destroyed by repair and reconstruction later in the eighteenth century (Heldman 1977:80; Reck 2004:219). In places where French occupation layers do survive, diagnostic artifacts support a 1730s construction date (Stone 1974; Heldman 1977, 1978; Halchin 1985; Evans 2001; Reck 2004). It is interesting to note that an early attempt to use pipe stem dating formulae at Michilimackinac came up with an initial date of 1733 (Maxwell and Binford 1961:108). Knowing that the initial date was really 1715, Maxwell and Binford suggested the discrepancy was a "function of the increased population at the fort in the later years" (1961:109). The increased population and the expansion are directly linked.

The era of peace and prosperity did not last long. Continual tensions between European powers erupted into the War of Austrian Succession in Europe in 1740. This war spread to the northern North American colonies as King George's War in 1744. Defensive measures were taken to strengthen Michilimackinac as a result of these hostilities. A second palisade was erected six or seven feet outside the existing one, and the space in between was designated the *chemin de ronde*, or sentry beat (Gérin-Lajoie 1976:6). This may also be the time when a triangular outwork was constructed on the fort's west side (Heldman 1991:49). Michilimackinac has none of the more traditional earthworks or ditches surrounding it because it stood on an unstable sandy beach. Later, a British officer described the sand dunes around the fort as follows: "The Drifts from these Hills are like snow Drifts, which we are after every storm obliged to remove" (Michigan Pioneer and Historical Society 1886:387). The triangular enclosure ran 132 ft. north–south along the west palisade. The point of the triangle extended 66 ft. out from the palisade wall. Test excavations in 1973 found upright logs in a footing ditch 6 ft. below the current surface (Heldman 1991:52).

The best map and description of Fort Michilimackinac comes from the military engineer Lotbinière in 1749, just after King George's War ended. Lotbinière was sent from Québec City by Governor de La Galissonière to survey the route from Montreal to Michilimackinac. He arrived at Michilimackinac on 22 September 1749 and spent 11 days at the post. He was not particularly impressed, as his description indicates:

> I will say right away that this fort is very badly built; it is square or just about, with four bastions, that is to say, what they call bastions. The sides measure from forty-seven *toises* [282 French feet] up to fifty-three [318 French feet] outside dimensions. The bastions have faces

of eighteen and twenty feet and flanks of eight. The lines of defence in some places are fichantes; one or two take their covering fire from the shoulder of the neighboring bastion. (Gérin-Lajoie 1976:4, 6)

The term *fichante* was used "to describe flanking fire, that is, directed from the flank of a bastion to impinge on the face of an opposite bastion" (Gérin-Lajoie 1976:11). This attention to having all exterior curtain walls defended by flanking fire is a reflection of the influence of Vauban on European fortifications. Lotbinière's description continues:

This fort is built of Cedar posts 12 feet high above ground. It has two doors; one facing landward is a double door, the other facing the water is a smaller single door; both are made of Oak wood; there is a third one giving entrance to the missionary's yard of triangular shape; the key for this door is at his disposal in daytime; it is handed over to the Commandant in the evening. (Gérin-Lajoie 1976:6)

At this time, the triangular enclosure had a civilian function. The structures inside it were an icehouse, a bake oven, and a post of the meridian. Outside the fort to the north were Mr. Langlade's stables and two more bake ovens. Returning to Lotbinière's description:

[The] *chemin de ronde* . . . is interrupted by the street which runs across from one door to the other and by the powder magazine situated near the East bastion. On the flanked angle of this bastion, as well as on the West bastion near the water diagonally opposite to it, is a square sentry box 5 feet long by 3½ feet wide. The powder magazine is buried and covered with turf. (Gérin-Lajoie 1976:6)

Lotbinière also described the civilian buildings of the fort:

This fort contains 40 houses all very badly built; I do not include in this number either the Church or the missionary's house. Most of the houses are built of upright posts caulked inside and outside with clay with cob. Many are still covered with bark. The others as well as the Church are built of squared timbers and are covered with boards. (Gérin-Lajoie 1976:6)

One particularly useful feature of Lotbinière's map is the inclusion of names for the residences. This detail connects people with particular houses at one point in time, but whether as owners or occupants is not always clear. Incomplete notary records from the fort can then be used to trace some

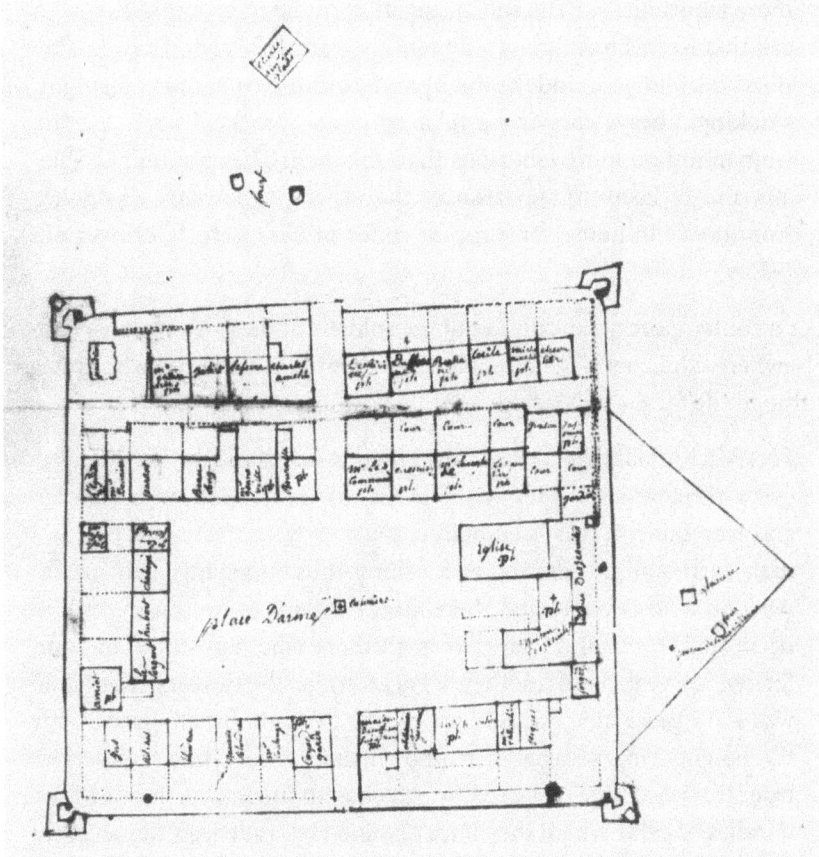

Figure 12.2. Lotbinière map of 1749. North is at bottom of map. (Michel Chartier de Lotbinière, 1749, Library and Archives Canada.)

property transfers. The vast majority of the space within the palisade walls was taken up by civilian homes. The notary records indicate that even the powder magazine was privately owned (Heldman and Minnerly 1977:7). In terms of building placement, the Lotbinière map has proven the most accurate of all known historic maps. It is also the only French period map of Michilimackinac currently identified.

Lotbinière was not any more impressed with the inhabitants of the fort than he was with their buildings:

> There are ten French families in the fort among whom three are mixed blood; although this piece of land is quite barren they could nevertheless give themselves some of the comforts of life if they were

more laborious. . . . The sole occupation of the men at this post who call themselves merchants although they are only plain Coureurs de Bois is strolling around the fort's parade ground from morn till night, smoking, always carrying a tobacco pouch on their arm. . . . The women are no more laborious than the men. They put on lady-like airs and to keep up appearances they spend time every day going from house to house for a cup of coffee or chocolate. (Gérin-Lajoie 1976:9)

For a contemporary description of the soldiers at the post, we have to look elsewhere. "Jolicoeur" Charles Bonin was a French marine who traveled through the Straits of Mackinac with a 1754 expedition.

Fort Michilimakinac . . . has thirty men in garrison who are changed every three years, if they wish. Their only remuneration is powder and lead bullets. This is enough because they cultivate maize or Indian corn, and go hunting and fishing thus supplying their needs. Anyone who is contented there, and asks not to be transferred, is permitted to remain. I saw two men there who had stayed on, one for twenty years, and another, a Parisian, for thirty years. The latter was sixty years old. The soldiers of this garrison usually trade with the neighboring savages. It is known that some, when transferred from this post, have collected and taken with them, two, three or four bundles of pelts, which they have obtained by trade with the savages. (Gallup 1993:64–65)

In his September 1751 report to the French minister regarding the northern posts, Governor General La Jonquière reported that the

guard-house of fort Missilimakinack has been destroyed by fire caused by smokers. The damage has been repaired, and each voyageur has supplied a stake for the purpose. As the fort is in need of many repairs, I have permitted the Sieur Duplessis to have it enlarged on the Lake side, to have a new guard-house built, and some other repairs made which will cost the King nothing, as I have given the said Sieur Duplessis orders to employ therefore the proceeds of the sale of some building lots, and if such moneys be insufficient, he will make the voyageurs contribute in equal shares. (Thwaites 1888–1911, 18:82–83)

The 1751 alteration may be the origin of the fort's final roughly hexagonal shape, with dimensions of 380 ft. north–south and 360 ft. east–west. The

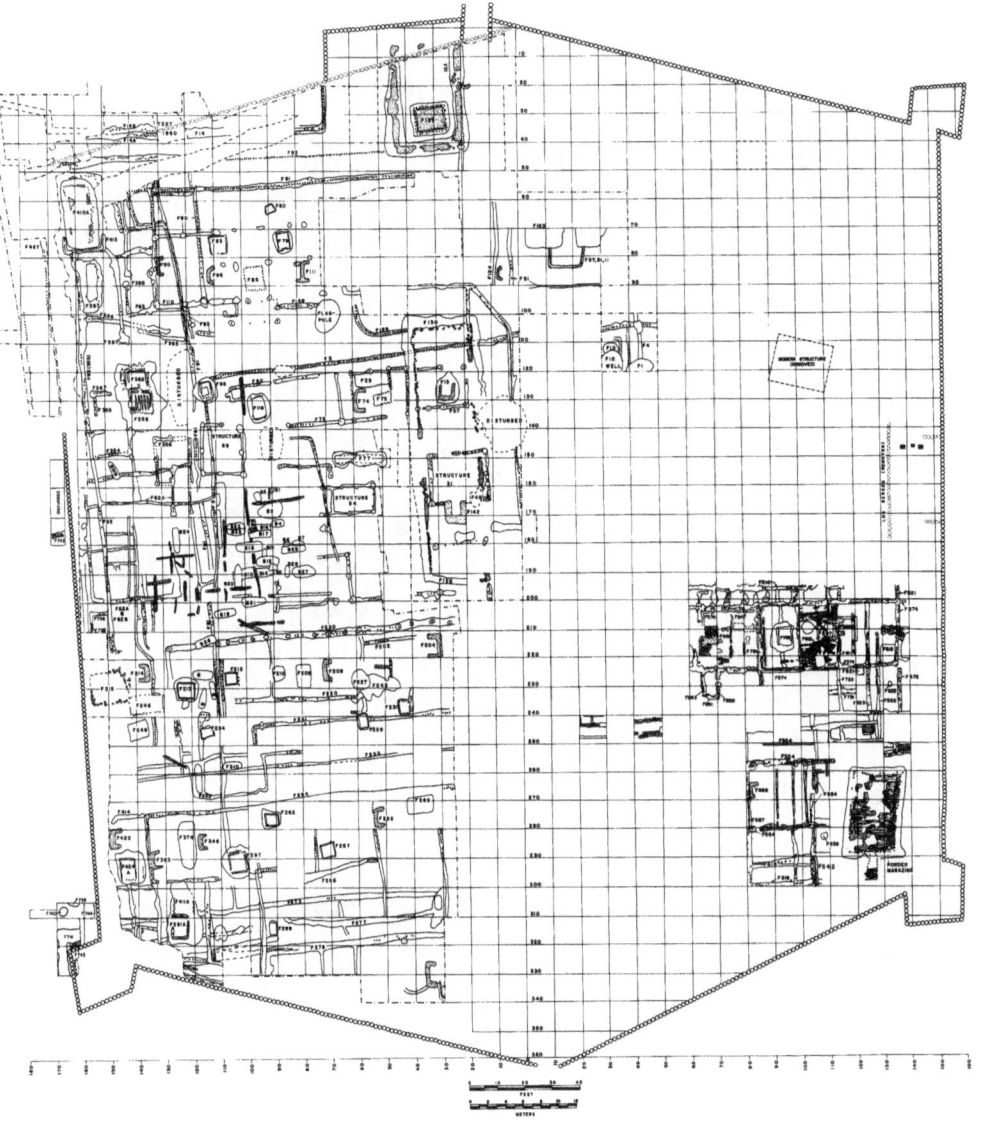

Figure 12.3. Michilimackinac Archaeological Master Map, 1959–97. (Mackinac State Historic Parks Collection.)

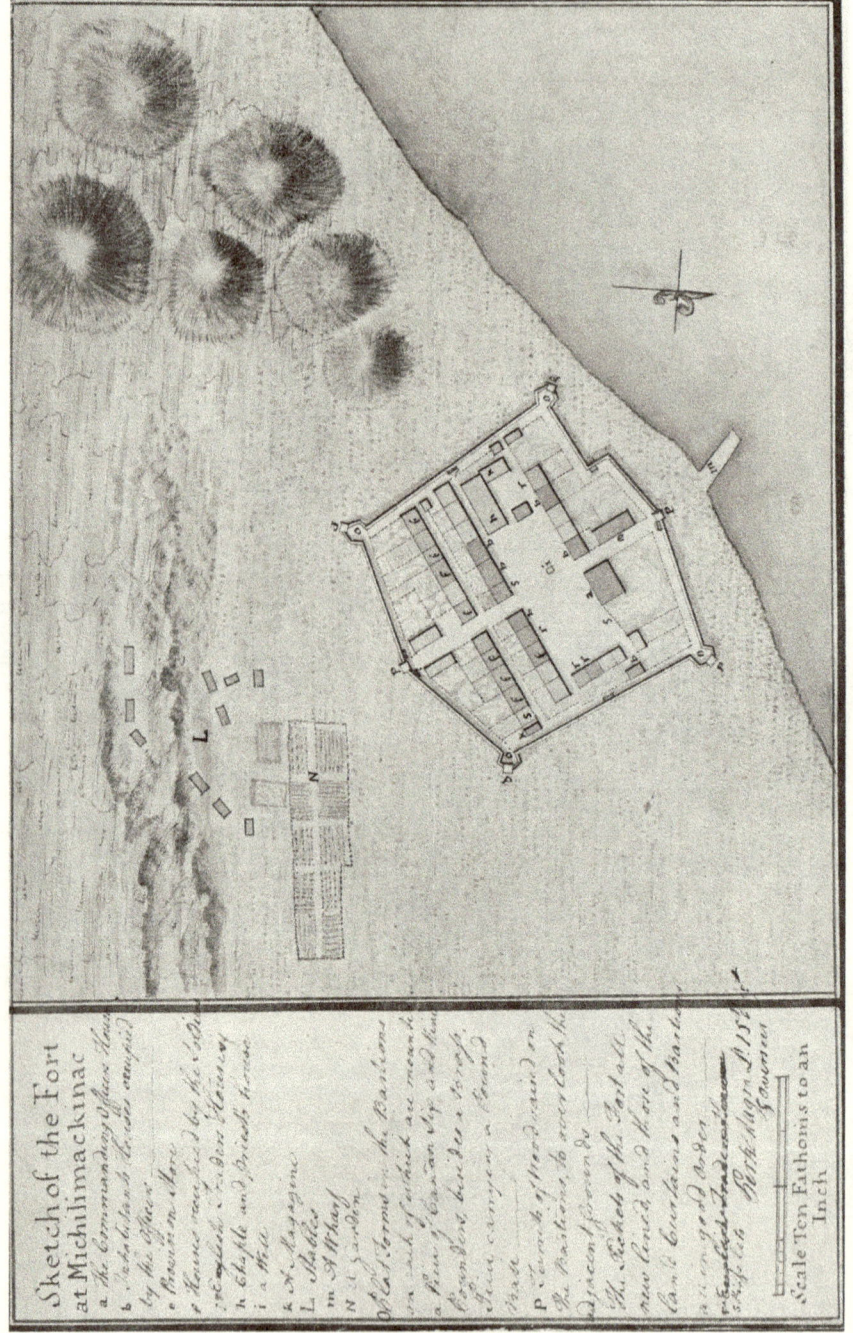

Figure 12.4. Perkins Magra map of 1765. North is at bottom of map. (William L. Clements Library, University of Michigan, Ann Arbor.)

guardhouse destroyed by fire is shown on the Lotbinière map immediately southeast of the water gate. Areas adjacent to the land and water gates were expanded, as shown on British maps of the 1760s. The north expansion contained a storehouse while the southern expansion contained traders' houses. Newly created lots may be the ones Duplessis was authorized to sell, since the Lotbinière map does not show other crown lots that would be available for sale.

The date of the hexagonal expansion has been a long-standing question in the archaeological literature on Michilimackinac (Binford 1961:37; Heldman 1979:8-12). Recent research by Brian Dunnigan (2008:46-69) has shown that a plan of Michilimackinac drawn by Lt. Perkins Magra, long believed to date to 1766, actually dates to 1765 and is more likely the Gordon map.

The Gordon map, a plan drawn up in 1765 to illustrate the situation and deficiencies of Michilimackinac for Gen. Thomas Gage, commander in chief of British forces in North America, is the map named for engineer Capt. Harry Gordon. It was mentioned in an October 1765 letter from John Campbell, commander at Detroit, to Gage (Gage 1762-76: Campbell to Gage, Detroit, October 14, 1765). In a subsequent letter, Campbell sent a long list of necessary projects to be completed at Michilimackinac (Gage 1762-76: Campbell to Gage, Detroit, October 31, 1765). Thus the Gordon map is seen as illustrating the fort essentially as the British received it from the French and prior to the massive renovations that began in 1766 and continued until the garrison was moved (Heldman and Grange 1981:33; Heldman 1991:73). The map shows the palisade walls in their final form. In addition to a few outbuildings, the sand dunes to the west are prominently shown. Although the buildings were used differently in 1765 (for example, Magra indicates which houses were rented out to British foot soldiers), the outline is that of Michilimackinac during the French and Indian War.

During the technically peaceful year of 1752, Charles Langlade led a party of Odawa and Ojibwa from Michilimackinac on a successful raid against English traders and Miami Indians at Pickawillany in the Ohio country. This raid is considered one of the contributing factors to the French and Indian War. Charles Michel de Langlade was probably the most notable person to come from Michilimackinac. He was born there in May 1729 to Augustin Mouet de Moras, a French fur trader, and his wife, Domitilde, an Odawa woman. When he was only 10, he accompanied his uncle, Nissowaquet, on an expedition against the Chickasaw. His father purchased a place for him as a cadet in the king's service in 1750. After the raid on Pickawillany, he received an appointment as Indian agent (Zipperer 1999). Langlade's ability to work in the cultures of both parents was a tremendous asset to his military career. He was frequently put in charge of raising and leading parties of Native warriors allied with the French.

In 1755, militia and allied warriors from Michilimackinac and other upper Great Lakes posts, under the command of Beaujeu and Langlade, traveled east to help the French defend the Ohio Country posts. While there they helped defeat General Braddock at the Battle of Monongahela in Pennsylvania. In 1756 another party went east, this time under Repentigny and Langlade, to assist in the Fort Oswego campaign. Some of the men, including Langlade, remained in the east that fall, traveling to Montreal and then on to "harass" Fort William Henry and other New York posts. In January 1757, members of this party engaged and defeated Robert Rogers (Kent 2004, 2:373–74). The following summer, 1757, hundreds of western warriors participated in Montcalm's capture of Fort William Henry. Tragically, when they returned to the straits that fall, they carried smallpox with them.

A smaller party of warriors went east in 1758, this time without Langlade, to defend Fort Carillon. In 1759, a party went east and helped defend the St. Lawrence settlements; troops from Michilimackinac were present at the fall of Québec and also were present the following year when Montreal fell, but they were sent home before the final surrender of New France.

The marquis de Vaudreuil, governor general of New France, was able to secure terms favorable to Michilimackinac's inhabitants in the Articles of Capitulation, as he described in a letter to Langlade:

> In short, the terms preserve to them all the free exercise of their religion, and leaves them in possession of their goods, furniture, real estate and peltries. They have also reserved to them a free commerce, the same as is enjoyed by the proper subjects of the king of Great Britain. (Thwaites 1888–1911, 8:216)

Regular French troops left Michilimackinac in October 1760, but the British army did not arrive until September 1761. Several British traders preceded them that summer, including Alexander Henry, who described the settlement as:

> Garrisoned with a small number of militia, who, having families, soon became less soldiers than settlers. Most of those, whom I found

in the fort, had originally served in the French army.... Within the stockade, are thirty houses, neat in their appearance, and tolerably commodious, and a church.... The number of families may be nearly equal to that of the houses; and the subsistence is derived from the Indian traders, who assemble here, in their voyages to and from Montreal. (Henry 1969:40–41)

British attitudes and trade policies were less accommodating to traditional Native American trading practices than those of the French. These provide a short explanation for Pontiac's Revolt, a series of coordinated attacks on all British forts west of the Allegheny Mountains in June 1763. The uprising began with the capture of Michilimackinac on 2 June 1763. Several visiting and local Indians staged a baggatiway (lacrosse) game outside the palisade wall, and the soldiers came out to watch. When the ball went near the fort entrance, the soldiers let the players into the fort to retrieve it, and the Indians, whose wives had been concealing weapons under their blankets, stormed the fort. This was the only battle actually fought at Michilimackinac, and it was over in minutes. Ultimately, Pontiac's plan failed because he could not take Forts Detroit, Niagara, or Pitt, and the British regarrisoned Michilimackinac in 1764. Trade policies were loosened, but the British also brought in twice as many soldiers as before. The civilian population increased as trade licenses became easier to obtain and generally peaceful conditions prevailed for a few years.

With the increased population of British soldiers and civilians, lodgings were in demand and the fort was in desperate need of repair. The British began a renovation project that would last 15 years, until they abandoned the post. Unfortunately, the renovation activity wiped out most traces of the French-era occupations.

The terms of the Articles of Capitulation became very important. The British Crown did not own the fort outright; French Canadian civilians owned most of the houses and land within the palisade. The Crown was forced to rent run-down row houses to house their foot soldiers until a barracks could be built. Three maps survive from this era, probably all drawn to demonstrate the need for barracks to the eastern military establishment. Due to a variety of delays inherent in being at the end of the military supply line, the barracks was not constructed until 1769 and does not appear on any of the historic maps.

A civilian trading village gradually sprang up outside the fort. In April 1778 John Askin, a wealthy merchant at Michilimackinac, wrote a friend in Montreal, "You would be Surprized to see how this place grows, there is near one hundred houses in the Subarbs" (Quaife 1928:69).

The American Revolution brought an end to Fort Michilimackinac. The British feared that the success of Col. George Rogers Clark in the Illinois Country would inspire local French Canadians and Native Americans to revolt. One of their first measures was to construct a series of fences controlling access to the powder magazine (Heldman and Grange 1981). This was, however, only a stopgap measure. Lieutenant Governor Patrick Sinclair decided to move the entire settlement to nearby Mackinac Island. Beginning in 1779, he ordered construction of stone Fort Mackinac, on an island hill, with the civilians in a town below. The move took two years. What was left of Fort Michilimackinac was then destroyed by the British to prevent it from being used as a staging area for attacks on the island.

While not the ideal fort from a military standpoint, Michilimackinac was a success at its primary function, a rendezvous point for the fur trade. The presence of large numbers of traders and Native Americans, while unpredictable from a defensive point of view, made it ideal for conducting the negotiations crucial for maintaining peace in the west and raising allied militias for battles in the east. For these reasons, both the French and British governments invested substantial sums of money in this outpost of empire.

13

War and the Colonial Frontier

Fort de Chartres in the Illinois Country

DAVID J. KEENE

Until excavations in the 1970s and 1980s began to recover artifacts and expose construction elements of the third Fort de Chartres, most literature and popular belief assumed that this fort was built as a fur trade outpost in a network of outposts on the margins of the French colonial empire in North America (Keene 2002:6). Analysis of the data generated by these excavations has changed the understanding of the region's history.

Early on, excavations at Fort de Chartres failed to yield archaeological materials similar to those found at fur trade outposts. Analysis of archaeological and architectural information from Fort de Chartres provided an opportunity to reexamine historic documents in order to assist in explaining the archaeological record and the role this site played in the eighteenth-century colonial empire of France.

Historical Background

There were three Forts de Chartres. The first was built in 1719 by Pierre Duque, sieur de Boisbriant, the newly appointed commander of the Illinois Country. Upon his arrival at the village of Kaskaskia in 1718, he organized a land distribution system, separated the native inhabitants from the French, and erected a fort to serve as the seat of government (Palm 1931:50). The fort was 10 miles north of Kaskaskia on the Mississippi River, where the river was deeper and better able to facilitate the shipping of goods. Immediately, colonists began to settle around the fort in an area that became known as the village of Chartres.

In 1723, Diron d'Artaquiette, the inspector general for the Company of the West, which held a royal charter to develop Louisiana, described the fort and village during an official inspection of the Illinois Country:

> Fort de Chartres is a fort of piles the size of one's leg, square in shape, having two bastions, which command all of the curtains. There are two companies in garrison commanded by M. de Boisbriant, Knight of the Military order of St. Louis, first royal lieutenant of the province. There is a church outside the fort and some dwellings a half league lower down on the same side as well as half a league above as far as the little village of the Illinois where there are two Jesuit fathers, missionaries who have a dwelling and a church. This little village is called Mechiquamias [Michigamea] and numbers perhaps about 200 warriors. (Mereness 1916:69)

This first Fort de Chartres, which was square with two bastions and a wooden palisade, suffered from the deleterious effects of natural forces. By 1726, the floodwaters of the Mississippi had destroyed much of this fort built by Boisbriant (Belting 1948:18).

Documentary sources are unclear about what actually took place after the deterioration of the first fort, but there appears to have been a second Fort de Chartres constructed. In 1732, the Compagnie des Indes made an inventory of its property. This inventory described the fort as

> falling to pieces, was 160 feet square with four bastions in which there were five cannons. On each of the scaffolds was hung a bell. Inside the palisade was the house of the commandant and garde magazin, a frame building 50' by 30'. Another building of the same size housed the garrison and the armorer's forge; there was a third house of posts in the ground, 30' by 20'. In one of the bastions was the prison, in one the hen house, and in another, a stable. (Belting 1948:18)

Whereas the first fort had only two bastions, the second had four. It is unclear whether the first fort was repaired and two bastions were added or an entirely new fort was built immediately after the destruction by floodwaters. A land description dating to 1726 (Brown and Dean 1977:355) suggests that there already was an "old Fort" distinct from that occupied at the time of the land transaction (Price 1980:2–3). Nevertheless, as the description above attests, the second palisade fort was in terrible condition in 1732.

By this time the Illinois Country was becoming important to the Compagnie des Indes for its production of wheat and salt (Surrey 1916:289). The economy of the French in Illinois did include some fur trading and mining, but for the vast majority of the inhabitants farming was the chief occupation during most of the year.

> The convoys from the Illinois country carried to the Gulf settlements, in 1748, 800,000 pounds of flour alone. Besides the flour the cargoes were made up of corn, bacon, hams from the bear as well as the hog, salt pork, buffalo meat, tallow, hides, tobacco, lead, copper, small quantities of buffalo wool, venison, bear's oil, tongues, poultry and peltry, chiefly, however, the loads were made up of pork and flour. (Surrey 1916:293)

In 1752 the shipment from Illinois to New Orleans was reported as "unusually large" (Surrey 1916:297). By the middle of the 1750s and well into the French and Indian War, Illinois supplied grain not only to Louisiana and the Caribbean but also to the Ohio River valley posts. These included Fort Ouiatenon, Massac, and Fort Duquesne (Pease and Jenison 1940:892–93).

Building the third and last Fort de Chartres proved problematic. As early as 1733, Jean-Baptiste Le Moyne de Bienville, governor of Louisiana from 1733 to 1742, initiated plans to erect a stone fortification in the Illinois Country. Native American uprisings during the ensuing years interfered with construction plans. In addition, there was considerable bickering between officials as to the appropriate location of this stone fortification. Some wanted it located on bluffs overlooking Kaskaskia, while others wanted the new fort built near the location of the first two.

Not until 1750, when the current governor of Louisiana, Pierre de Rigaud de Vaudreuil de Cavagnial, appointed Jean-Jacques Macarty as commandant of the Illinois Country, was the location resolved. The shallowness of the Kaskaskia River convinced Macarty not to locate the fort at Kaskaskia. He was concerned about shipment of grain and the availability of enough good land for population growth. Vaudreuil, however, remained adamant. He wanted the post located at Kaskaskia. Macarty, though respectful, became more vehement in voicing the disadvantages of the Kaskaskia site:

> All that I can tell you of the Kaskaskia River since I have been here, is that it has not been possible to take an empty boat up it until a few days ago, and that a loaded boat could not have been sent off for New Orleans without risk since the month of August. The experience of M. Girardeau proves it. This river is not a resource for wood, which will be scarce at this post in a few years, as it has neither current nor

water three-quarters of the year. Its environs are nothing but marsh, and its water much complained of as causing frequent sickness. I have even observed the frequent colic it occasions in the troops. (Pease and Jenison 1940:557)

Each appears to have held firm in his conviction of the appropriate location of the fort until Vaudreuil was called back to France in 1753. He would not return to America until appointed governor of New France in 1755. A new governor, Louis Billouart Kerlerec, was assigned to the post in Louisiana. He immediately reviewed the plans and cost projections, made some revisions, and agreed with Macarty on the location of the stone fortification.

By the time George Washington built Fort Necessity in late spring of 1754 at the Great Meadows some 60 miles from the forks of the Monongahela and the Allegheny Rivers, the third Fort de Chartres was complete.

Archaeological Investigations

The location of the second Fort de Chartres is still undiscovered. The locations of the first and third Forts de Chartres are within a quarter mile of each other. The third fort, made of limestone mined from nearby bluffs overlooking the Mississippi River valley, has always been known. The ruins of the fort were so massive that neither the Mississippi's periodic flooding nor pillaging of the limestone by local inhabitants could completely erase its footprint. The location of the first fort, built totally of wooden pickets, was lost until its discovery in the early 1980s (Jelks et al. 1989).

The first excavations at the third Fort de Chartres began in the mid-1970s under the direction of Margaret Kimball Brown. In the 1980s, prompted by an initiative to reconstruct various elements of the stone wall and fortification features, intensive archaeological excavations were conducted by this author (Keene 1988). Archaeological material recovered from these excavations formed a substantial portion of a dissertation (Keene 2002).

Artifacts were organized in categories developed by Stone in his research on Fort Michilimackinac (Stone 1974). This facilitated comparison of artifact assemblages from the third Fort de Chartres, Fort Michilimackinac, and Fort Ouiatenon. Fort Michilimackinac is located along the Straits of Mackinac between the northern and lower peninsulas of Michigan. It was the most important French fur trade outpost in the Great Lakes region during the eighteenth century. Archaeological excavations have been taking place at Fort Michilimackinac almost continuously since the 1960s.

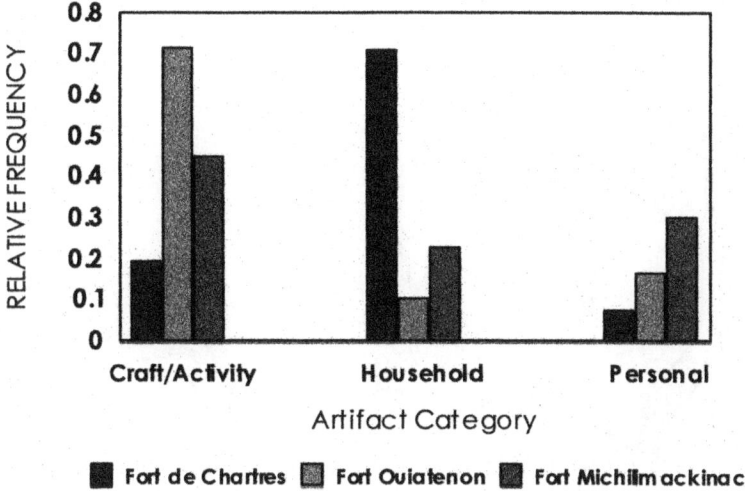

Figure 13.1. The relative frequency of artifacts by category for each site. (Graph by author.)

Fort Ouiatenon is located on the Wabash River near present-day Lafayette, Indiana. It functioned as one of the fur trade outposts associated with Fort Michilimackinac. Extensive excavations were conducted at Fort Ouiatenon during the 1970s by Tordoff (1983) and Noble (1983).

For the purpose of this essay, artifacts from these three sites were grouped into three main categories based on the system devised by Stone. The results are summarized in figure 13.1.

The category "Craft/Activity" contains all artifacts related to economic activity. This includes trade beads, baling seals, coins, fish hooks, and gun hardware. The category "Household" contains artifacts related to food preparation, consumption, and storage. The category "Personal" would include items such as pipes, buttons, gaming pieces, and combs.

Figure 13.1 suggests some profound differences in the relative frequencies of artifacts among the three sites and, consequently, differences in cultural activities at the forts. Over 70 percent of the artifacts recovered at Fort de Chartres fall within the Household category. At first glance this may appear peculiar because the population that Fort de Chartres served, except for some of the soldiers, lived outside the fort. This contrasts with the colonists at Fort Michilimackinac and Ouiatenon, who lived within the fort walls.

Two possible explanations may account for this discrepancy. The first and most obvious is simply statistical. Because most of the population lived

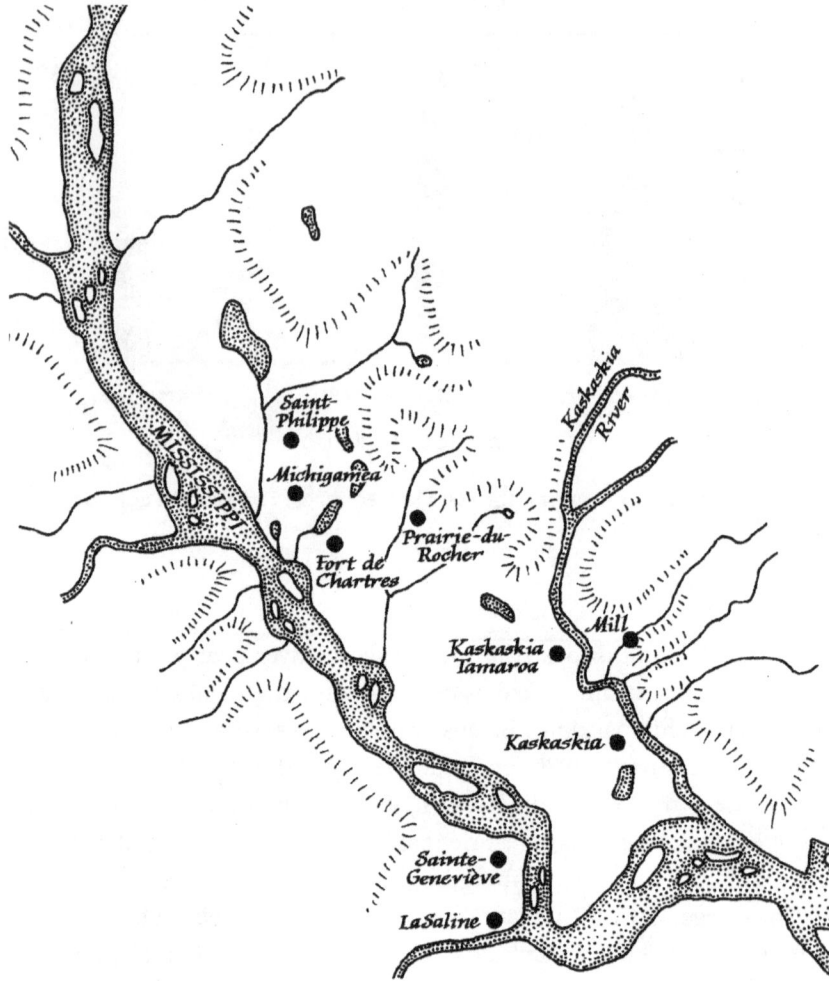

Figure 13.2. Fort de Chartres and surroundings. (Map by author, with assistance from Jack Scott.)

outside Fort de Chartres, other artifact categories well represented at the other two forts are poorly represented. Though the actual count of household artifacts is smaller at Fort de Chartres than at Michilimackinac and Ouiatenon, it commands a higher percentage of the total assemblage, since the other artifact contexts are so poorly represented.

Another explanation, however, must be considered. Fort de Chartres did not serve as a residential compound. It served as a social and economic center for the entire colony. As pointed out by Noble (1997:70), the ceramic assemblage at Fort de Chartres contains a greater variety of high quality ceramics than found at the other two forts. Fort de Chartres, as the economic and governmental center of the colony, would have been the place where the colonists met for social and economic activities—in many cases, this would have been within the context of prepared meals.

Fort de Chartres was the center of economic activity in the Illinois County. Figure 13.2 illustrates the relationship of the fort to the French villages under its sphere of influence. All of these villages were engaged in agricultural production. Their surplus products were brought to Fort de Chartres for shipping, where they were given credit against past or future purchases of goods shipped from New Orleans. The fort served as the *entrepôt* for the colony. All goods moving to and from the Illinois Country passed through Fort de Chartres. Colonists brought their agricultural produce to the fort where it was made ready for shipment down the Mississippi. Goods coming up the river from New Orleans were unloaded from *bateaux* and brought into the fort for distribution to colonists.

Structural Evidence

Excavations in the 1980s focused primarily on the structural remains of the third Fort de Chartres. The state of Illinois was embarking on an active construction campaign at the fort with the goal of reconstructing many of the original elements. Particular attention was given to the walls. Though a number of attempts had been made in the past to locate copies of the original engineering drawings of the fort (Price 1980), none had been found. As a result, project architects and engineers were at a disadvantage in determining the height and thickness of the wall, the size of the ditch, and the volume and structure of the banquette.

Excavations focused first on understanding the techniques used by the French to construct the wall at Fort de Chartres. During the 1980s, excavations exposed large segments of the curtain wall revealing three distinct episodes of wall construction: the eighteenth-century foundation, a portion of the eighteenth-century wall, and a short wall built atop the exposed remains in the 1910s (figure 13.3). Archaeological evidence suggests that, after the builders' trench was excavated to a depth approximately 1 m below the eighteenth-century ground surface, a footing of mortar was poured. (It should be noted that the bottom of the builders' trench follows the contour of the eighteenth-century ground surface and is not a level plane.) After the footing dried, large limestone blocks and additional mortar were poured into the trench until filled. The wall was built on top of these large blocks.

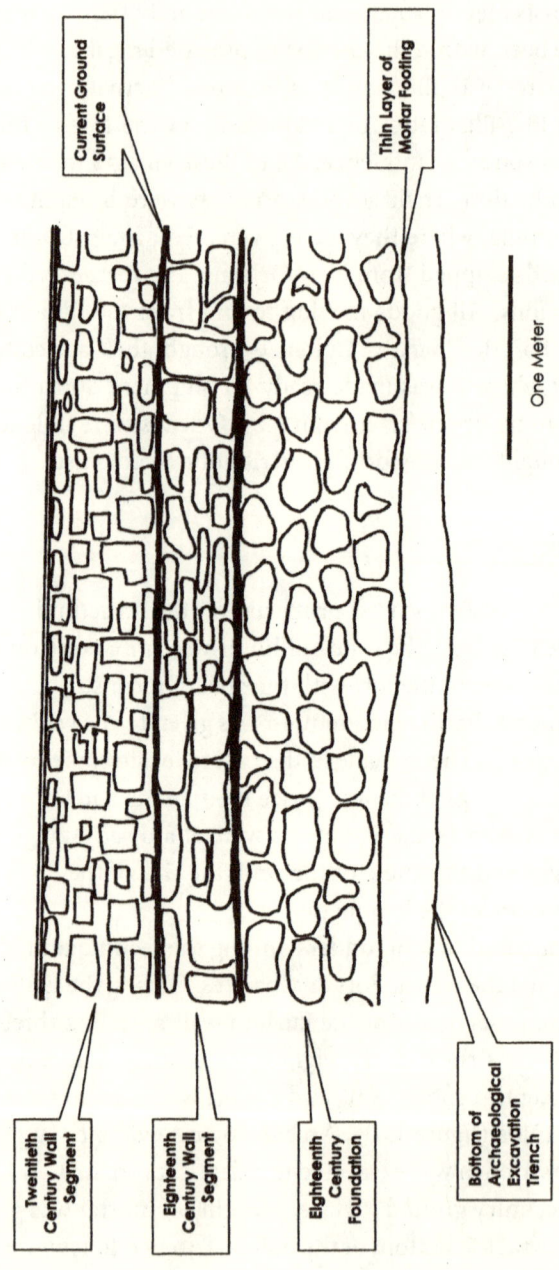

Figure 13.3. Profile of a typical wall at Fort de Chartres. (Drawing by author.)

Historic accounts are not in agreement about the wall's actual height (Orser 1977:38). Formulas, however, for the height of walls are known from eighteenth-century engineering manuals (Hart, this volume). A key to using these formulas required knowledge of the depth and dimensions of the ditch that surrounded the fort.

Examination of the ditch structure was accomplished by digging backhoe trenches around the fort's exterior. The primary function of a fortification ditch was to act as a barrier to advancing offensive troops as they approached the rampart. In constructing the ditch around the powder magazine side of the fort, the French excavated a little over 1 m deep with a slight slope for drainage. They found the soil extremely sandy and cut a *cuvette* in the bottom of the ditch.

> The drainage of rainwater from a dry ditch could be effected by tilting the floor gently downwards in the direction of the enceinte, and leading the water away by a small ditch which followed the curve of the revetment. A common alternative was to cut a cuvette, a V-sectioned trench which ran round the fortress in the centre of the ditch. (Duffy 1975:60)

Soils on the western half, around the north bastion, were firmer and more claylike. No cuvette was needed here as rainwater would flow easily along the hard clay floor of the ditch toward the river due to a slight pitch. The ditch was essentially bowl shaped with a more gradual slope on the curtain wall side than on the outer or *glacis* side (the scarp) of the ditch.

After the fort dimensions were laid out by the engineer, excavations began on the ditch and builders' trenches. Soil from these excavations was piled inside the fort's trace, or enceinte, to form the banquette. Once complete, the bottom of the builders' trench was lined with a limestone mortar footing upon which limestone blocks of uniform size composing the wall foundation were placed. These blocks were unfinished and like rubble in form. The depth of the builders' trench below the eighteenth-century ground surface was uniform. In other words, as the ground surface elevation varied, so varied the builders' trench. The ditch depth also varied deliberately to facilitate movement of water that might collect in the ditch. Once the foundation was complete, dressed limestone blocks were placed to a height of approximately 18 ft. There was some variation, since the wall height is measured from the bottom of the ditch, not the foundation. The bottom of the ditch was not on a level plane; depending on where

Figure 13.4. View of the reconstructed wall and ditch. (Photo by author.)

in the ditch you measured, the height of the wall would vary. Figure 13.4 illustrates a portion of the completed wall and ditch.

Conclusion

As an *entrepôt*, Fort de Chartres provided a vital link between the Illinois Country and the larger French empire. Its primary role was to organize economic activity in the colony and facilitate the movement of goods between the colony and France. But it also played a colonial military role by providing protection from hostile natives as well as administering justice within the colony itself.

As a military outpost, Fort de Chartres played an important part early in the French and Indian War. Capt. François Coulon de Villiers was stationed at Fort de Chartres when his brother Joseph Coulon de Villiers de Jumonville was killed in May 1754 by the detachment led by George Washington. Over the following years, Coulon de Villiers led parties of soldiers from Fort de Chartres on raids against British outposts in the Virginia Territory (*Dictionary of Canadian Biography*, vol. 4).

Conclusion

LAWRENCE E. BABITS

As historian William Hunter pointed out in 1960, eighteenth-century forts fall into three generalized categories: those built by an imperial government, those ordered by colonial (or provincial) governments, and those generated by local needs. All three types are covered in this text. The chief distinction appears to be the funding source to build and maintain the forts, with other differences including the variety of people who garrisoned the fort and the distance they came to do so.

These forts were built on the frontier, but they were not, as a rule, devoid of tactical sophistication. Even locally built forts were often planned with practical considerations for drainage, flanking fire, and protective lines. This is well expressed by Charbonneau, who noted for the works on Île aux Noix that the

> establishment of the exact trace of a work, compared to the models used at the period, produces an evaluation of the type of defence planned and carried out. Further, a fortification's defensive effectiveness and power of resistance are to be measured by an examination of its profile. The study of the French fortification at Île aux Noix is susceptible of this model of analysis, even though it involves a so-called field fortification, that is, one erected during a period of active warfare. Though geometrical regularity and the stability of the revetments are not the primary concerns of an engineer tasked with erecting a temporary fortification, it remains true that the work should reflect the defensive theories being taught at the time as much as the so-called permanent fortification does. (Charbonneau 1994:24)

Dr. James Hart provides a basis for understanding the forts by pointing out that there were available manuals and officers who had read them.

Military engineers were available on site at most imperial forts and provided advice for colonial efforts. Two British engineers, Henry Gordon and Patrick McKellar, turn up repeatedly when specific details are sought for posts as far apart as Fort Frederick, Maryland, Fort Ontario, Fort Ligonier, and Fort Michilimackinac. They were responsible for assisting in defensive planning and providing maps (Babits 1981:126; Evans, this volume). Largely unknown today, these two men are representative of the major role undertaken in fortifying the British Empire's North American frontier.

The eighteenth century used several systems to design and construct fortifications. In New France, engineers built fortification lines in the St. Lawrence and Richelieu valleys adapted to local conditions and very different from those in Europe. These fortifications were not designed to withstand European sieges, although European warfare came to North America in 1755. What resulted were traits found at most forts and some very impressive works, especially along the New York frontier and Lake Champlain.

Farther south, there was less concern about being attacked by artillery, so fortifications tended to be "softer" in the sense that defense in depth, while present, was not as obvious. More important, a fort's outer defensive lines were seemingly less effective than a core defense in height as a wall or multistory building. As seen in this study, this initial impression does not stand up to closer examination.

Fort Prince George was a South Carolina colonial fort situated in a flood plain near a creek junction. Downstream and across the river sat a Cherokee town; other Cherokee towns lay within 15 miles. The fort was built in 1753 and garrisoned by British regulars and American provincials until 1768, when the garrison was sent to New York and Boston. The fort then became a trading post until abandoned. These geographical and historical considerations suggest why the fort was located where it was. The longer occupation allowed for successive rebuilding, changes that reflected an appreciation for correcting earlier deficiencies.

South Carolina's Fort Loudoun was located west of the Appalachians in modern Tennessee. Built to solidify Overhill Cherokee alliances, it also served as an imperial outpost against potential French encroachment from Alabama. Fort Loudoun's defenses were perhaps the largest and most unique of the southern frontier forts considered here. Construction, as planned and executed, contrasts somewhat with other French and Indian War frontier forts, especially Fort Prince George, east of the Appalachians. Unlike many forts, Fort Loudoun was besieged and eventually fell. While Fort Loudoun was discussed here in terms of contemporary fort design, artifacts were also summarized. Distributions of several artifact categories illustrated refuse disposal patterns inside and outside the fort. The overall artifact assemblage was then compared to the means and expected ranges of both the Carolina and Frontier Patterns, South's seminal analytical tools initially designed for Carolina sites. Modification of the Frontier Artifact/Architecture Pattern, was suggested and the case made for a separate French and Indian War Fort Pattern that would aid in explaining similarities and differences among period forts.

Fort Dobbs was North Carolina's French and Indian War fort. Possibly designed by the governor, it had obvious stone antecedents on another British frontier, the Scottish Highlands. Fort Dobbs was funded by North Carolina and manned by provincial troops who were often called to serve in other colonies. The temporary duty allowed cross-fertilization, but the fort's basic design seems to fit an earlier style of post found in the Scottish Highlands where marauding Scottish Jacobites threatened British dominance. Fort Dobbs likewise provided a base for patrols demonstrating British ownership and served as a refuge for settlers who threatened native inhabitants. Driven by local forces, a move to reconstruct the fort resulted in locating the site, its excavation, and analysis of minimal data to generate architectural drawings that revealed a tactically sophisticated wooden fortification demonstrating British claims to the Carolina Piedmont.

Fort Loudoun, Virginia, is one of at least three period forts named after Lord Loudoun, commander of British troops in North America. The fort was designed and constructed by Col. George Washington in 1756–58 to serve as Virginia's frontier command center and supply depot. Never attacked, troops who garrisoned the fort participated in the 1758 Forbes expedition against Fort Duquesne and an unsuccessful 1760 expedition to relieve the Cherokee siege of Fort Loudoun, Tennessee. The fort provides evidence of difficulties that impacted construction in the proper style.

Fort Vause was a 1756 post within modern Shawsville, Montgomery County, Virginia. It blocked a key raiding route. Fort Vause represents the only known civilian earthen work in George Washington's chain of French and Indian War forts guarding the Virginia frontier. The earthen construction may reflect the impact of an attack that destroyed an earlier Fort Vause. The more labor intensive earthen works may explain construction delays. Not surprisingly, given available manuals and assistance, Fort Vause has a standardized trace that fits well within period fortifications.

Following Braddock's Defeat, increasing raids by Native American war parties led to depopulating some frontier areas but increased defensive measures initiated by the colonial government and private settlers, especially prominent ones who could raise local resources. This feature of local leadership has not been emphasized but is certainly a major factor in frontier fort locations and not only because local elites fortified their own homes in an attempt to defend themselves and their neighbors. The fort commanders were charged with protecting their sectors of the frontier using local militias augmented by Provincial troops from the Virginia Regiment. The landowners were able to build the forts and patrol their neighborhoods because they drew upon the local populace as part of the growing frontier social network.

One Virginia fortified homestead was Joseph Edwards's fort along the Cacapon River in present Hampshire County, West Virginia. Although Virginia Regiment forts were supposed to be standardized as four- or two-bastioned rectangular forts, we know little about their appearance or their builders' concepts of a proper fortification. The archaeological investigation of Edwards's Fort was directed toward learning whether it was a formal or irregular bastioned fort. Along with that question, there was an attempt to learn how well it was built and how the existing house and outbuildings were incorporated into the defenses. It is also probable that the 1755 Capon Valley settlers knew of nearby four-bastioned Fort Cumberland or earlier forts with bastions or corner towers.

The archaeology revealed that Edwards's Fort combined academic and vernacular characteristics. The corner bastions and mid-wall redan suggest an academic fort design, while the fort's overall footprint is very irregular and does not appear to have followed standardized Virginia plans very closely, if at all, even though it does have generalized similarities to at least one Pennsylvania fort.

Pennsylvania's Fort Loudoun represents a third fort named after the British Empire's North American commander. It was built in 1756 by a Quaker government to defend frontier settlements. The study provided clues about how space within the compound was organized and used. Structural evidence indicates John Armstrong was familiar with fortification design. While Fort Loudoun's palisade was typical vertical log construction, archaeology shows a frontier adaptation. Structurally it was somewhat crude in form, especially the elevated bastions with external supports, possibly representing unskilled workers, difficult weather, and expedient shortcuts.

The colonial forts at Crown Point, New York, were situated to cover a narrows on southern Lake Champlain but north of the forts (Carillon and Ticonderoga) guarding the waterway to Lake George. Occupied at different times by French, British, and American troops beginning in 1731, this location controlled the trade route between New York and Montreal. Unlike most forts in this study, Crown Point's two forts were built of stone. When garrisoned by the British, Crown Point was one of the largest British forts in North America and enclosed some six acres. While both French and British forts at Crown Point were erected for similar strategic reasons, the forts differed in structure, function, and location.

Fort Frontenac was a French fort located at the confluence of eastern Lake Ontario and the St. Lawrence River. It experienced its share of attacks from both Native American populations and imperial military forces from its 1673 founding to 1758. The combination of historical records and archaeological evidence supports understanding of the establishment and ongoing refurbishment of the fort for fur trading and military activity. Archaeological details are presented within the context of the historical record, which includes comments from military engineers and officers inspecting or stationed at Fort Frontenac, as well as those responsible for it. The fort, seemingly typical of most frontier forts, was described in terms both disparaging and praising, depending on the author's needs. These comments were tested and found generally true, depending on what the author intended. The site's examination thus provides an opportunity to examine multivocality and look at the nuances of textual meaning (Olsson 2008:94–99, 111–24; Babits and Howard 2009:xii–xiv), while serving as a warning about using historical documents alone when dealing with frontier situations.

Michilimackinac was initially a civilian trading post at a strategic location in the upper Great Lakes. Described as "the key and the door," it was built as a mission and fur trading post. During the French and Indian War, colonial forces did not attack it. Although built for basically civilian purposes, the structural history of Michilimackinac, from its construction by the French in 1714 to its deliberate destruction by the British in 1781, reveals contrasts between trading posts and forts built for military purposes.

Fort des Chartres was an eighteenth-century French colonial fort located near modern Prairie du Rocher, Illinois. Extensive archaeological excavations were conducted on the massive limestone walls, interior drains, and exterior earthen defensive features to avoid damaging archaeological information during reconstruction. The excavations, in conjunction with architectural questions generated by reconstruction planners, provided valuable information on engineering and construction techniques used by the French. The artifacts and structural evidence, in comparison with two contemporary trading posts, suggest the fort was not built primarily as a defensive structure, despite the effort expended by using limestone. The combined evidence allowed reexamination of the documentary sources and a new understanding of the fort's construction and role as an entrepôt.

Through the range of forts and differing locations there is still some overall similarity. They generally used readily available local materials. Colonial and local forts were invariably built with a heavy reliance on timber, except Fort Frederick, Maryland, while imperial forts often utilized stone, especially in the north. Where there was any possibility of artillery being brought against a fort, the defenses were usually heavily built and incorporated stone or earth walls. Throughout, the forts were erected with a sense of tactical acumen.

While it might be said that the Vauban system had a trickledown effect that reached the colonial frontiers, it is just as likely that, under an officer's direction, local citizens built the forts. The officer was usually experienced in the practicalities of frontier fighting and incorporated that experience in the defensive works that usually had little dead space and denied attackers cover within musket range. In some cases, the fort builder, or its designer, may have been advised by British military engineers who did meet with Maryland's governor Horatio Sharpe and provided him with plans for a four bastion fort that might be something of a standard format (Babits 1981:126; Kimmel 1973:8; Jolley, this volume). A good understanding of fort design was seemingly part of settlers' cultural baggage, especially after the French and Indian War. Antecedents were present or developed and reinforced by experiences between 1755 and 1763. For example, coverage of exterior walls could be provided from the wall with loopholes and platforms, as well as by various forms of flankers that allowed protective fire along the wall's face. While there was a general assumption that loopholes should be 5 ft. 4 in. high, with a firing step on the inside, from the outside the loopholes were much higher above ground level to avoid horizontal firing into the fort.

A fort's location often depended on decisions by local elites who, not unreasonably, opted to build fortifications incorporating their own property or who built in close proximity to their existing homes. Local leaders were men whose perceived status, wealth, and military abilities would encourage participation and support by their neighbors, both for erecting fortifications and for defending them when the time came. In some cases, a leader's position was formally verified by awarding militia rank with ascribed status commensurate with the existing achieved status. In other cases, especially provincial service, awarding of rank depended, in large measure, on the number of men raised or political connections, something that was documented repeatedly in the Revolutionary War (Babits 1981:105, 109; Babits 1998:29–30; Babits and Howard 2009:59–60, 65–67).

Forts were repeatedly located on the same, or a nearby, site (Frontenac, Michilimackinac, des Chartres, Carillon/Ticonderoga, St. Frédéric/Crown Point, and Loudoun, Tennessee) or subjected to repeated rebuilding (Prince George, Michilimackinac). These longer service posts were often utilized for diplomatic or economic purposes as well as a defensive structure. They contrast with the single episode, short-term occupations for a particular campaign or war (Vause, Loudoun, Pennsylvania, Loudoun, Virginia, and Dobbs).

Fort wall construction varied from stone (St. Frédéric, Crown Point, Carillon, Ticonderoga, des Chartres) to cribbed earth (Loudoun, Virginia) to palisades (Edwards, Loudoun, Pennsylvania). At long-term posts, an almost predictable sequence was followed of using timber first and stone later, especially if stone were regularly available as at Fort Frontenac. Using extant buildings as part of the defensive walls (Loudoun, Pennsylvania, Edwards) or, conversely, using an existing fort wall as part of an interior building (Frontenac) seems to have been a common practice. At Fort Vause, the bastions were earthen, while it is possible that the curtain walls were palisaded. The Fort Prince George palisade walls were seemingly erected in parapets after the earth was thrown up, a manner of construction that was totally unsatisfactory. Fort Loudoun, Tennessee, initially had something similar, but the palisade timbers were removed and then placed against the interior side of the raised earthen parapet. Other forts had the more traditional vertical logs placed in trenches in a variety of fashions (Loudoun, Pennsylvania, Edwards, Michilimackinac). Some stockades were created using whole logs, and others were split logs; in any case, stockade posts abutted each other while palisade posts were from 4 to 9 in. apart (Simes 1768; Robinson 1977:204–205). From a combination of documentary and archaeological information, timbers were placed in trenches at varied depths, ranging from 1 to 4 ft., and widths from 1.5 to 2 ft., depending on the planned height above ground as shown by Benjamin Franklin's note that posts 18 ft. long were buried 3 ft. deep to create a wall 15 ft. high (Franklin 1756:38; Stotz 1974:34).

Additions to fort walls included redans (Vause), corner blockhouses (Loudoun, Pennsylvania), and bastions (Vause, Edwards, Prince George, Frontenac) and placing smaller timbers between stockade posts to fill in gaps (Prince George). Irregular traces (Edwards's, Michilimackinac) were usually the result of coping with terrain to provide drainage or tactically to provide coverage against anticipated attack from cover or higher ground. Fort Dobbs provided evidence of a heavily built barracks, fortified with flankers and with only abatis as an outer defense. The Rocque plats showing northern fortifications provide similar flanker equipped buildings, in this case blockhouses, provided with ditches, palisades, covered way, and a glacis (Rocque 1765).

Food, as evidenced by surviving bone, was collected to provide the maximum amount of nutrition by brining in larger, meatier portions (haunches) while abandoning less desirable parts such as lower limbs and vertebrae at some forts (Loudoun, Pa., Dobbs). This contrasts with the manner in which meat was treated at major supply depots such as Fort Ligonier (Guilday 1970) and Fort Loudoun, Virginia (Jolley, this volume). At Fort Dobbs, meat was apparently brought in as quarters, without vertebrae or skulls, although lower jaws were present, perhaps for the tongue. The same treatment was applied to all large quadrupeds at Fort Dobbs, both wild and domestic (Babits and Pecoraro 2008:131–32). Beef was the preferred British meat (Guilday 1970:181), although pork, sheep, and game animals were nearly always present and treated in much the same fashion at militia and Provincial posts (Edwards's, Dobbs, Loudoun, Pennsylvania). At Fort Dobbs and Fort Loudoun, Virginia, most butchering was done by hacking, possibly with axes (Babits & Pecoraro 2008:133–34; Jolley, this volume).

Ceramics were linked with social distinctions at several forts (Fort Dobbs, Ligonier, Warfel at Fort Loudoun, Pennsylvania, this volume). Generally speaking, the finer imported wares were in different areas of the forts and usually interpreted as officers' possessions, used to validate their status through tea-related ritual behavior (Roth 1961). In some cases, the finer ceramics were also associated with more elaborate or expensive clothing (buttons) or household furnishings. An intriguing subplot for the ceramic distinctions can be suggested for Fort Dobbs, where only imported ball clay smoking pipes were found despite a nearby source for reed stem pipes at Bethabara (Babits and Pecoraro 2008:225–27). If the finer imported ceramics were associated with officers, then were only officers smoking?

The McBrides, drawing from several forts, noted:

> Excavations at nearby Ashby's Fort, which was occupied by rangers and militia, and Arbuckle's and Warwick's Forts in the Greenbrier Valley of West Virginia, which were built and occupied by militia,

suggest a pattern of very low counts for ceramics and bottle glass, moderate architectural items, especially wrought nails, and very high animal bone on nonresidential frontier forts." (McBride and McBride 1998; McBride et al. 2003; McBride 2009)

This pattern was also noted at Fort Dobbs, a North Carolina provincial fort (Babits, this volume).

Munitions were not addressed to any great extent here. However, the various reports clearly indicate clusters of ammunition sizes indicating that supply was effective and, even for individually made rifles, regularized with uniform calibers. Shot sizes from Prince George, Ligonier, Virginia's Fort Loudoun, Fort Vause, and Fort Dobbs reflect some basic commonalities and differences. Along with musket balls for standard British military muskets in the .69 to .72 range, there were many musket balls in the .55–.60 range. These shot are almost certainly for trade guns used by Indians, although they may also have been used as grape shot in the swivel guns or as rifle bullets (Callaway 1758). Fort Dobbs and Fort Vause personnel used smaller buckshot and larger birdshot than at Fort Ligonier. There may be an interpretive error regarding Fort Loudoun where 150 pounds of swan shot were reported but no buckshot. It may be that swan shot was utilized as buckshot. Fort Dobbs, Fort Ligonier, and Fort Loudoun also reported shot around .44 caliber. Too small for the period's rifles, these bullets are too large for what is usually considered buckshot. Their use may have been for case shot in swivel guns or extremely heavy buckshot.

Plain pewter buttons with a "PN" back mark have been found at several French and Indian War fort sites. The back mark is important, both as a chronological marker for the period and because it may signify British stores issued to Provincial officers or to soldiers. The "PN" buttons seem to be a British hallmark of an as yet unknown firm or maker of the French and Indian War period, suggesting that coat buttons were standardized or fit into roughly acceptable patterns. This is interesting considering that all these forts suffered from financial shortages, partially due to their location on the empire's outer fringes and thus the far end of supply lines.

Back marked buttons are quite rare for the 1750s (Albert 1976:464–65). The first representatives documented turned up at Fort Ligonier where two types were noted: the first a one-piece, cast eye type, with a bulb on the mold seam, and the second a two-piece, hollow cast button (Grimm 1970:59, 63). Two were recovered at Fort Dobbs, both are one-piece, cast eye type, 0.9 in. in diameter, and 0.06 in. thick, for use on a coat. A "PN" button found at Fort Stanwix, Rome, New York, was the smaller, 0.69 in. waistcoat size (Hanson and Hsu 1975:86). Another coat button was found at the Judge Maurice Moore house site in Brunswick Town, North Carolina. Six "PN" coat buttons were found at Fort Loudoun, Tennessee (Kuttruff 2010:572-573; Babits 1982:35–36). Similar buttons have also been reported near Fort Moultrie, Johnson's Island, South Carolina, and Orangeburg, South Carolina (Paul Chance, personal communication, September 1981). A final cluster of these buttons has been reported from military sites near Pensacola, Florida. These were allegedly from a Spanish context, but the Spanish obtained much military materiel from British sources, and the British did occupy Pensacola during the Revolution (Powell 1994:10).

Stanley South has asserted that an archaeologist's first responsibility is to recognize patterns within the archaeological record (South 1977a:43). According to South, predictive models should be employed to aid this recognition. The function of a model is to organize data "in such a way that hypotheses can conveniently be tested, accepted, modified, or rejected" (Flannery in South 1977b:89). In 1977, South published two seminal works, *Method and Theory in Historical Archaeology* and *Research Strategies in Historical Archaeology*. Both texts contained information about observed patterning on southeastern archaeological sites. South proposed two basic patterns, the mainstream Carolina Artifact Pattern (CAP) and the Frontier Artifact Pattern, later renamed the Frontier/Architecture Pattern (FAP) to reflect a predominance of architectural remains over Kitchen Group artifacts.

South abstracted quantified data to try and identify artifact distribution patterns that could be used to create predictive models for eighteenth-century British colonial sites. The CAP and FAP patterning represents predictive models that suggest behavioral differences. Broadly speaking, South's comparative analysis of eight sites defined two basic patterns. The CAP reflected mainstream Anglo-American, or British colonial American, material culture found on eighteenth-century sites. The corollary pattern, the FAP, had an inverse ratio between the Kitchen and Architecture groups (South 1977a:143). The FAP is "generally associated with military and trading post sites on the periphery of or beyond the limits of the actual area of colonization" (Lewis 1976:110). By stating these patterns, South created a situation where archaeologists had to arrange their own data in the same format to challenge their validity.

Working from an assumption that each site represents part of a larger system (South 1977a:86), South postulated that a level of uniformity can be

Table C.1. The Carolina artifact pattern

Artifact group	Mean %	% Range
Kitchen	63.1	51.8–69.2
Architecture	25.5	19.7–31.4
Furniture	0.2	0.1–0.6
Arms	0.5	0.1–1.2
Clothing	3.0	0.6–5.4
Personal	0.2	0.1–0.5
Tobacco pipes	5.8	1.8–13.9
Activities	1.7	0.9–2.7

Source: South 1977a:107.

identified through a comparative examination of artifact distribution ratios between sites. The model identified eight generalized groups of artifacts within a given assemblage: Kitchen, Architecture, Furniture, Arms, Clothing, Personal, Tobacco Pipes, and Activities. Each group is then further divided into artifact class and individual type. The CAP and the FAP are identifiable by ratios developed at the group level. They have an inverse ratio relationship between Kitchen and Architecture-related artifacts (South 1977a:146). That is, CAP assemblages contain an overwhelmingly large ratio of Kitchen group artifacts. In terms of the overall assemblage, Kitchen related artifacts typically fall within a range of 51.8 to 69.2 percent of the total, as indicated by tables C.1 and C.2.

In contrast, the FAP assemblages are defined by a large percentage of Architecture-related artifacts. The FAP Kitchen-related artifact ratio is reduced to approximately one-quarter of the assemblage, similar to the corresponding Architecture ratio in the CAP. A comparison between South's

Table C.2. South's adjusted frontier pattern mean and range, with standard deviation and predicted range for the next site

Artifact group	Mean %	Pattern range	Standard deviation	Predicted range (95%)
Kitchen	27.6	22.7–34.5	6.15	10.2–45.0
Architecture	52.0	43.0–57.5	7.88	29.7–74.3
Furniture	0.2	0.1–0.3	0.10	0–0.5
Arms	5.4	1.4–8.4	3.60	0–15.6
Clothing	1.7	0.3–3.8	1.85	0–6.9
Personal	0.2	0.1–0.4	0.17	0–0.7
Tobacco pipes	9.1	1.9–14.0	6.39	0–27.1
Activities	3.7	0.7–6.4	2.87	0–11.8

Source: South 1977a:145, table 16.

Table C.3. FAP comparison with contemporary forts

Artifact group	Fort Loudon, Virginia	Fort Ligonier, Pennsylvania	Fort Prince George, South Carolina	Fort Frederick, Maryland	Fort Dobbs, North Carolina	Range
Kitchen	39.8	25.6	22.7	28.5	34	10–45
Architecture	39.0	55.6	57.5	53.4	7	29.7–74.3
Furniture	0	0.2	0.1	0.1	0	0–0.5
Arms	2.8	8.4	6.4	0.7	11	0–15.6
Clothing	2.6	3.8	1.85	1.4	1	0–6.9
Personal	0.4	0.4	0.1	0.1	0.1	0–0.7
Tobacco pipes	6.1	1.9	11.5	1.6	0.23	0–27.1
Activities	9.3	4.1	0.7	1.6	0.01	0–11.8
Unclassified	1.9					

Source: Jolley 2005:96.

tables (C.1 and C.2) demonstrates the inverse relationship between the two artifact groups. The FAP does have a much wider predictive range than the CAP (South 1977a:145). The FAP predicted range was adjusted to explain the large amount of Cherokee Indian pottery recovered from Fort Prince George. The adjustment was intended to maintain South's focus on finding predictive patterns about British colonial assemblages. Therefore, artifacts representing specialized, or ethnic, activity were not considered germane (South 1977:143–45).

While the various chapters did not present their artifact data in one consistent fashion, preliminary comparison of available assemblages suggests that the CAP and FAP results at Fort Dobbs were different when compared with contemporary fortifications. Unlike the other forts, Fort Dobbs does not have the predicted inverse ratio between the Kitchen and Architecture Groups. The Fort Dobbs Arms Group percentage is the highest of the five forts despite being the smallest fort. Skewing observable in table C.3 may be the result of dismantling the building, because this activity would obviously affect architectural percentages.

A statistical factor should be considered when using the Frontier/Architecture Pattern. To define the Frontier/Architecture and Carolina Artifact Patterns, South drew from only eight sites; this may have skewed his data, since there is no record that he corrected for this small number. At Fort Dobbs there was a very low architectural artifact count. It may be that the buildings were logs—a building type that does not require many nails compared with a frame structure. It is also possible the buildings were recycled after abandonment in 1764 (Rockwell 1876).

At other frontier fort sites, a ratio similar to the mainstream Carolina Artifact Pattern occurs. The inverse relationship between Kitchen Group and Architecture Group artifacts appears related to occupational duration. That is, more Kitchen-related materials would build up over time while Architectural materials were present soon after structures were erected. Sites demonstrating the CAP typically represent longer settlement, allowing artifact accumulation. This is shown by the high ratio of Kitchen Group artifacts. Items in this category reflect daily household activity and produce a steady accumulation over time. In contrast, the FAP represents shorter-term settlements that are transitional in nature. The high number of Architecture Group artifacts reflects an emphasis on structural, rather than domestic, activities that, over time, produce secondary midden deposits. Further, as all three South frontier sites were forts rather than fortified home sites, the FAP also has higher percentages of both the Arms and Tobacco Pipes group, indicating specialized activities occurring at these sites.

The fort research has suggested many possible avenues for future research, either because several sites had similar attributes and artifacts or because new questions were derived from rereading, or reworking, older data. There are far too many possibilities to discuss in a conclusion. As so often happens in an edited work, a succinct commentary was provided as incidental comment by a contributor. In this case, Carl Kuttruff provided a summary, both of the text and future directions.

> At this time, we now have a considerable body of information on French and Indian War fortifications and associated artifact assemblages, from both English and French North American sites. We may have comparable information from Revolutionary War and Federal Period fortifications of the late eighteenth and early nineteenth centuries. For future directions, I would suggest some possibilities. First, in relation to this collection of papers, it might be appropriate to suggest a reevaluation of what the entire artifact assemblages from French and Indian War forts represent, or even individual classes of artifactual remains, as I have tried to do here with two artifact groups. This will allow a more comprehensive evaluation of any patterning that may or may not be present among forts of this period and explanations for the differences that are determined. It may be that defining the differences present among many fortified sites may be more important for explaining those occupations than determining the

normative aspects common to all the sites. While it may be interesting and often constructive to compare or contrast assemblages from frontier fortifications with domestic sites, there is usually no need to use artifact assemblages to determine that a site was a fortification as opposed to a domestic or other type of occupation, since there is most often, if not always, available historic documentation about the fortifications. Similar examination of assemblages at opposing French fortifications may provide an interesting, if not significant, comparison or contrast of two nations' frontier adaptations. Likewise, the present ability to compare large numbers of fortifications and patterns from succeeding military endeavors should produce an interesting work on the development of fortifications and their occupations by differing powers in eastern North America throughout the last half of the eighteenth century. (Kuttruff 2009)

Kuttruff's comments were seconded by Jolley, who pointed out: "Given the rarity, importance, and fragility of French and Indian War military sites, additional archaeological work conducted at Fort Loudoun or other period military sites should address research questions designed to obtain specific types of comparative data. As evidenced by Farry's 2005 recent study, there is much data that can be extracted from those forts that have already been excavated."

Glossary

Abatis. Structure "formed by cutting down many entire trees, the branches of which are turned towards an enemy, and as much as possible entangled one into another. They are made either before redoubts, or other works, to render the attacks difficult" (Duane 1810:1). "A row of obstructions made up of closely spaced, felled trees with branches trimmed to points and interlaced" (Robinson 1977:197).

Backcountry. The interior zone between the coast and the frontier. This was a thinly settled zone of small farms and few towns. The term is used more for the southern colonies than for the mid-Atlantic and northern colonies.

Barracks. "Places erected for both officers and men to lodge in; they are built different ways, according to their different situations" (Duane 1810:33).

Bastion. "A projection in the enceinte, made up of two faces and two flanks, which enabled the garrison to defend the ground adjacent to the enceinte" (Robinson 1977:197). "A Bastion is a part of the inner inclosure of a fortification, making an angle towards the field, and consists of two faces, two flanks, and an opening towards the center of the place, called the Gorge" (Simes 1768).

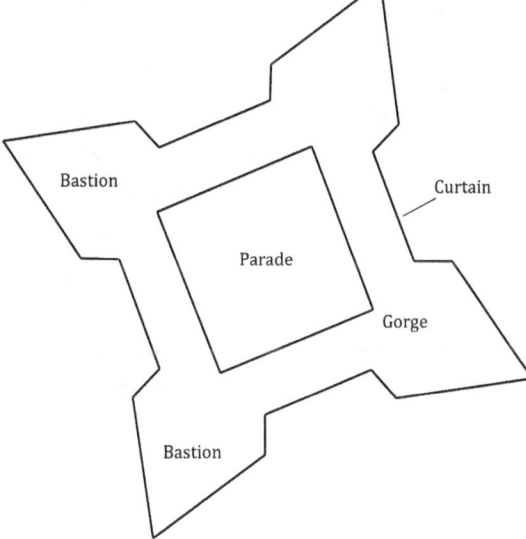

G.1. Outline of a four-bastion fortification.

Bateau. The French word for "boat." A flat-bottomed work boat used for a variety of purposes including troop and supply transport. In eighteenth-century Canada, *bateau* was a "term given to a rowboat" with "sharp ends; flat bottom, sheer swept up at ends" (Parry 2000:51).

Bayonet. "Kind of triangular dagger, made with a hollow handle, and a shoulder, to fix on the muzzle of a firelock or musket, so that neither the charging nor firing is prevented by its being fixed on the piece" (Duane 1810:52). A long, pointed blade mounted on the end of a musket. The bayonet allowed men to attack and defend themselves when their muskets were unloaded.

Berm. "Narrow, level space between the exterior slope and the scarp which functioned to prevent earth of the rampart from sliding into the ditch" (Robinson 1977:197).

Blockhouse. "Small fortified building used as a place of retreat or as a flanking device in forts. It was generally constructed from logs, although other materials, such as earth and stone, were commonly used in conjunction with wood" (Robinson 1977:197).

Company. In eighteenth-century military organizations, the company was a smaller unit within a battalion. It was usually commanded by a captain and numbered from 25 to 80 men. "A small body of foot, or artillery, the number of which is never fixed, but is generally from 50 to 120, commanded by a captain" (Duane 1810:101).

Counterscarp. "Outside of a ditch, opposite to the parapet of the work, behind the ditch" (Simes 1768). "The exterior side of the ditch—the side away from the body of the place" (Robinson 1977:198).

Covered way. "Road . . . protected from enemy fire by a parapet" (Robinson 1977:198).

Cresset. "Any great light upon a beach, light-house, or watch-tower" (Duane 1810:110).

Curtain. "That part of the rampart of a place, which is between the flanks of two [sic] bastions, and is the best defended of any part of the rampart" (Simes 1768). "Section of a bastioned fortification that lies between two bastions" (Robinson 1977:198).

Ditch. In fortification, a ditch is a "large deep trench made round each work" (Duane 1810:176) or a "wide, deep trench around a defensive work, the material from the excavation of which was used to form the ramparts" (Robinson 1977:198). *Fosse* is another term for "ditch."

Flank. "Section of a bastion lying between the face and the curtain from which the ditch in front of the adjacent curtain and the flank and face of the opposite bastion were defended" (Robinson 1977:198).

Fort. "Small fortification, made in a pass near a river, or at some distance from a fortified town, to guard the pass, or to prevent the approach of ships, or an enemy by land: they are made of different figures, some made small, and some greater" (Simes 1768).

Fortification. "Art of building works for defense or attack which . . . enabled their occupants to resist assaults by superior forces" (Robinson 1977:203).

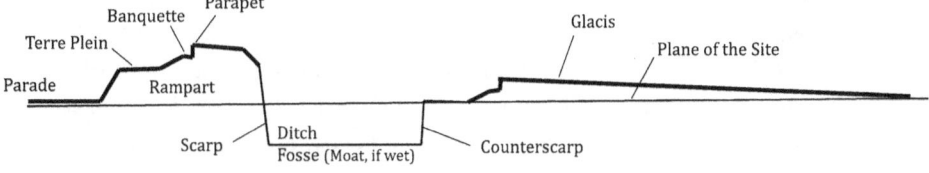

G.2. Cross-sectional view of an entrenched fortification.

Fosse. "A work established for the defense of a land or maritime frontier, of an approach to a town, or of a pass or river" (Robinson 1977:203). Also **Ditch** or **Moat**.

Fraise. "A kind of stakes of palisades, placed horizontally on the outward slope of a rampart of turf, to prevent the work being taken by surprise" (Simes 1768). "A row of palisades planted horizontally or obliquely in the ground at the edge of a ditch or other earthwork" (Robinson 1977:203).

Glacis. "That part of a fortification, beyond the covert-way, to which it serves as a parapet, and terminates towards the field in an easy slope" (Simes 1768).

Hornwork. "Composed of a front and 2 branches; the front is made into 2 half bastions and a curtain. . . . The use of horn-works in general is to take possession of some rising ground advanced from the fortification" (Duane 1810:178; Lochee 1783:77–77, plate V, figure 3).

Loophole. "Square or oblong holes made in the wall to fire through with muskets" (Simes 1768). "They are generally 8 or 9 inches long, 6 or 7 inches wide within, and 2 or 3 feet without; so that every man may fire from them direct in front, or obliquely to right or left" (Duane 1810:178).

Magazine. "Place for the storage of gunpowder, arms, provisions, or goods" (Robinson 1977:203).

Machicoulis. Projecting galleries on the exterior of a parapet or tower from which defenders could drop, pour, or shoot weaponry at attackers. "Machicoulis is an old word, sometimes applied to projections in old castles, and over gates of towns, left open above, to throw down stones, &c. on the approaching enemy" (Smith 1779:151).

Militia. Initially, the colonial self-defense force. During the Revolution, militias were placed in classes called up (drafted) for service as needed. They usually served for short periods, such as six weeks or three months. In emergencies, they might be called out for only a few days. Generally, militias were not well trained and did not turn out in great numbers or in a timely fashion.

Moat. "Depth or trench round the rampart of a place to defend it and prevent surprises. The brink of the moat next to the rampart is called the scarp; and that opposite, on the other side, is called the counterscarp, which forms a re-entering angle before the center of the curtain. A dry moat round a place that is large and has a strong garrison, is preferable to one full of water, because the passage may be disputed inch by inch" (Simes 1768). See **Fosse**.

Muskets. "The most commodious and useful firearms used in the army: they carry a ball at the rate of twenty-nine to two pound of lead" (Simes 1768). The musket was the most common shoulder arm of the French and Indian War. This was a smoothbore weapon that also used a bayonet. The musket was easier and faster to load than a rifle, but its accurate range was only about 50 yards. It had a smooth bore (interior barrel) and ranged in caliber from .62 to .75 inch. A common name for the British musket today is the Brown Bess.

Opposite angles. This term is not defined in contemporary manuals. From written descriptions and fort plans, it can be shown that these were the corners opposite each other across the parade.

Outwork. "A work inside the glacis but outside the body of the place" (Robinson 1977:204).

Palisade. "Kind of stakes made of strong split wood, of about nine feet long, three feet deep in the round, in rows about six inches asunder. They are placed in the covert-way, at three feet from, and parallel to the parapet or side of the glacis, to secure it from being surprised" (Simes 1768). "A high fence, for defensive enclosure, made of poles or palings planted in the ground from six to nine inches apart" (Robinson 1977:204).

Parade. "Now used in a military sense to signify any place where troops assemble" (Duane 1810:505). "The place where troops assemble to go upon guard, or any other duty" (Simes 1768).

Parapet. "Elevation of earth, designed for covering the solders from the enemy's cannon, or small shot; wherefore, its thickness is from eighteen to twenty foot, its height is six on the inside, and four or five on the side next the country. It is raised on the rampart, and has a slope, called the superior talas, to the glacis of the parapet.... The height of the parapet being six foot on the inside, it has a banquet or two for the soldier[s] who defend it, to mount upon, that they discover the country better; as likewise the foss and counterscarp, to fire as they find occasion" (Simes 1768). "In fortification, a work of earth or masonry forming a protective wall over which defenders fired their weapons" (Robinson 1977:204).

Provincial. Colonist who served in an American military unit on a full-time basis, usually under colonial authority and pay. Provincials were intended to serve within a colony's borders but frequently were sent to serve with armies operating in a major campaign.

Rampart. "Elevation of earth raised along the faces of any work of 10 or 15 feet high, to cover the inner part of that work against the fire of an enemy" (Simes 1768). "A mass of earth, usually formed with material excavated from the ditch, to protect the enclosed area from artillery fire and to elevate defenders to a commanding position overlooking the approaches to a fort" (Robinson 1977:204).

Ranger. During the French and Indian War, "Independent Companies, called Rangers . . . were very different from the average Militia. . . . Their role in these campaigns was to form the screen covering the advance of the more regular units, to carry out long distance raids to secure information of the enemy's strength and movements, and to execute the ruthless destruction of the enemy's supplies and material" (Lawson 1974:212–13).

Redoubt. Also called "castle" or "donjon." "A place more particularly intrenched, and separated from the rest by a fosse. There is generally in each of them a high tower, from whence the country round the place may be discovered" (Simes 1768). "An enclosed fortification without bastions" (Robinson 1977:204).

Reentering or reentrant angle. "An angle pointing toward the interior part of a fortification" (Robinson 1977:204).

Regular. In the eighteenth century, this term referred to the British soldier. These men were enlisted for long service and were generally well trained and disciplined.

Salient angle. "An angle pointing outward" (Robinson 1977:204).

Scarp. "That whose points turn from the centre of the place" (Simes 1768). "The interior side of the ditch" (Robinson 1977:204). In fortification, the term is used to "express the outside of the rampart of any work next to the ditch" (Duane 1810:179).

Stockade. "A defensive work—usually eight or more feet high—composed of timbers planted tightly together in the ground. Stockades were generally provided with loopholes, and since these openings were often in the upper part of the fence, banquettes or elevated walks were often necessary parts of the wall" (Robinson 1977:204–205).

References Cited

Abbot, W. W. (editor)
1983 *The Papers of George Washington: Colonial Series.* Vol. 2, *August 1755–April 1756.* University Press of Virginia, Charlottesville.
1984a *The Papers of George Washington: Colonial Series.* Vol. 3, *April–November 1756.* University Press of Virginia, Charlottesville.
1984b *The Papers of George Washington: Colonial Series.* Vol. 4, *November 1756–October 1757.* University Press of Virginia, Charlottesville.
1988a *The Papers of George Washington: Colonial Series.* Vol. 5, *October 1757–September 1758.* University Press of Virginia, Charlottesville.
1988b *The Papers of George Washington: Colonial Series.* Vol. 3, *September 1758–December 1760.* University Press of Virginia, Charlottesville.

Adams, Nick
1985 Excavations at the Frontenac Village Site. *Newsletter of the Cataraqui Archaeological Research Foundation* 2(1):1–17. Kingston, Ont.
1989 An Archaeological Study of Human Graves at Fort Frontenac (CFB Kingston) City of Kingston, Ont. Report to Canadian Forces Base Kingston from Mayer, Poulton and Associates, London, ON.

Adams, William H., and Linda P. Gaw
1977 A Model for Determining Time Lag of Ceramic Artifacts. *Northwest Anthropological Research Notes* 11:218–31.

d'Aigremont, François-Clairambault
1708 Clairambault d'Aigremont to Pontchartran. Library and Archives Canada, C11A 29, pp. 25–102; Québec Seminary Archives, Viger, *Ma Saberdache* IV. In *Royal Fort Frontenac,* edited by Preston and Lamontagne, pp. 164–69.

Albert, Alphaeus H.
1976 *Record of American Uniform and Historical Buttons.* Alphaeus H. Albert, Heightstown, NJ.

Alden, John Richard
1944 *John Stuart and the Southern Colonial Frontier.* University of Michigan Press, Ann Arbor.

Anburey, Thomas
1791 *Travels through the Interior Parts of America.* London.

Anderson, Fred
1984 *A People's Army.* University of North Carolina Press, Chapel Hill.

2000   *Crucible of War: The Seven Years' War and the Fate of Empire in British North America, 1754–1766.* Alfred A. Knopf, New York.
2005   *The War That Made America: A Short History of the French and Indian War.* Viking Penguin, New York.

Anderson, Niles
1975   *The Battle of Bushy Run.* Pennsylvania Historical and Museum Commission, Harrisburg.

Andrews, Robert J.
2004   John Bradstreet's Raid: An Account of the Expedition Mounted against Fort Frontenac in August–September 1758. *Historic Kingston* 52:10–38.

Ansel, William H., Jr.
1984   *Frontier Forts along the Potomac and Its Tributaries.* McLain Printing Company, Parsons, WV.

Anonymous
1726   Liste d'endroits où it faut poster des gardes pour empêcher le commerce avec les Anglais. Collection de la famille Beauharnois, MSS1553, Library and Archives Canada, Ottawa.
1759   A Just Estimate of the Importance of Having Reduced Crown Point and Niagara. *London Chronicle; or, Universal Evening Post,* Thursday, 6 September, to Saturday, 8 September 1759.

Ansel, William H.
1995   *Frontier Forts along the Potomac and Its Tributaries.* McClain Printing, Parsons, WV.

Assembly
1754b Reports of the Committee of Public Claims held at Wilmington, 6 December 1754. In *Colonial Records of North Carolina,* vol. 6, edited by Saunders and Daniels, pp. 209-215, State of North Carolina, Raleigh.

Babits, Lawrence
1981   *Military Documents and Archaeological Sites: Methodological Contributions to Historical Archaeology.* PhD dissertation, Brown University, and University Microfilms, Ann Arbor.
1982   French and Indian War Button Backmarks: A Clue to Movements after June 1758. *Military Collector and Historian* 34(1):35–36.
1998   *A Devil of a Whipping.* University of North Carolina Press, Chapel Hill.

Babits, Lawrence E., and Joshua B. Howard
2009   *Long, Obstinate, and Bloody: The Battle of Guilford Courthouse.* University of North Carolina Press, Chapel Hill.

Babits, Lawrence E., and Tiffany A. Pecoraro
2008   Fort Dobbs (Id1) 1756–1763, Iredell County, North Carolina: An Archaeological Study. Manuscript on file, Fort Dobbs Alliance, Statesville, NC.

Babson, Jane F.
1968   The Architecture of Early Illinois Forts. *Journal of the Illinois State Historical Society* 61(1):9–40. Springfield.

Bailey, Lynn R.
1966   Preliminary Archaeological and Feasibility Study, Fort Massac, Illinois. Report on file, Southern Illinois University Museum, Carbondale.

Bandyopādhyāya, Śekhara
2004   *From Plassey to Partition: A History of Modern India.* Orient Blackswan, Andhra Pradesh, India.
Barron, Bill
1975   *The Vaudreuil Papers.* Polyanthos, New Orleans.
Bazely, Susan M.
1986   Selected Artifacts: Bale Seal. *Newsletter of the Cataraqui Archaeological Research Foundation* 3(2):11.
1988   Historical Maps of Fort Frontenac. *Historic Kingston* 36:26–32.
2007   *Fort Frontenac: A French Stronghold on the Great Lakes.* Cataraqui Archaeological Research Foundation, Kingston, ON.
Bazely, Susan M., and Rachel Brooks
2003   Fort Frontenac BbGc-8: Archaeological Monitoring Fort Frontenac Waterline Installation. Report to Defence Construction Canada from the Cataraqui Archaeological Research Foundation, Kingston, ON.
Beauharnois, Charles de la Boische, marquis de, and Gilles Hocquart
1736   Beauharnois and Hocquart to the Minister. Library and Archives Canada, C11A 65, pp. 17–44. In *Royal Fort Frontenac,* edited by Preston and Lamontagne, p. 224.
1742a   Beauharnois and Hocquart to the Minister. Library and Archives Canada, C11A 77, pp. 28–30. In *Royal Fort Frontenac,* edited by Preston and Lamontagne, p. 227.
1742b   Beauharnois and Hocquart to the Minister. Library and Archives Canada, C11A 77, pp. 32–35. In *Royal Fort Frontenac,* edited by Preston and Lamontagne, p. 228.
Bélidor, Bernard Forest de
1729   *La Science des Ingénieurs dans la Conduite des travaux de fortification et d'architecture civile.* Claude Jombert, Paris.
1755   *Dictionnaire portatif de l'ingénieur et de l'artilleur.* Paris.
Bellico, Russell P.
1992   *Sails and Steam in the Mountains.* Purple Mountain Press, Fleischmanns, NY.
Belting, Natalia Maree
1948   *Kaskaskia under the French Regime.* University of Illinois Press, Urbana. Reprinted 1975, Polyanthos, New Orleans.
Bentz, Charles, and Yong W. Kim
1993   *The Sevierville Hill Site: A Civil War Union Encampment on the Southern Heights of Knoxville, Tennessee.* Tennessee Anthropological Association Miscellaneous Paper 17 and the University of Tennessee Transportation Center Report of Investigations 1. Knoxville.
Bibliothèque et Archives nationales du Québec
1780–81 *Inventaire des meubles et effets de feue Humbertine Franquet, soeur de l'ingénieur Louis Franquet, 1780–1781.* Bibliothèque et Archives nationales du Québec, Québec Centre, Cote: P1000,S3,D1378. http://pistard.banq.qc.ca/unite_chercheurs/description_fonds?p_anqsid=20070727132339549&p_classe=P&p_fonds=1000&p_centre=03Q&p_numunide=3059. Accessed 16 August 2007.
1762   *Dictionnaire de L'Académie française.* 4th ed. http://colet.uchicago.edu/cgi-bin/dicolook.pl?strippedhw=elemens. Accessed 16 August 2007.

Binford, Lewis R.
1961 Preliminary Report: Archaeological Investigations at Fort Michilimackinac, 1961 Season. Manuscript on file, Mackinac State Historic Parks' Petersen Center, Mackinaw City, MI.
1972 The "Binford" Pipe Stem Formula: A Return from the Grave. *Conference on Historic Sites Archaeology Papers 1971* 6(2):230–53.
Bougainville, Louis Antoine de
1924 La mission de M. de Bougainville en France en 1758–1759. *Rapport de l'Archiviste de la Province de Québec, 1923–24*. Québec.
1964 *Adventure in the Wilderness: The American Journals of Louis Antoine de Bougainville, 1756–1760*, edited and translated by Edward P. Hamilton. University of Oklahoma Press, Norman.
Boyd, Varna G.
2001 Archaeological Investigations Report: Fort Frederick State Park, Washington County, Maryland. Report submitted to the State of Maryland, Department of General Services, Annapolis.
Bradstreet, John
1759 An Impartial Account of Lieut. Col. Bradstreet's Expedition to Fort Frontenac. In *Kingston! Oh Kingston!* edited by A. B. Smith, pp. 49–55.
Breitburg, Emanuel
1983 Bone Discardment Patterns and Meat Procurement Strategies at British Fort Loudoun (Tennessee), 1756–1760. Master's thesis, Department of Anthropology, Vanderbilt University, Nashville.
2005 Faunal Remains from Fort Edwards, Hampshire County, West Virginia. In *Report of the 2004 Archaeological Investigations at Fort Edwards (46Hm75), Hampshire County, West Virginia*, by W. Stephen McBride, pp. C1-C10. McBride Preservation Services, Lexington, KY.
Brice, Martin H.
1990 *Forts and Fortresses: From the Hillforts of Prehistory to Modern Time*. Facts on File, New York.
Brock, R. A.
1883 Official Records of Robert Dinwiddie in the Collections of the Virginia Historical Society. Vol. 3. Richmond, VA.
Brown, Elsworth
1965 The Fort Loudoun People: A Provisional Directory Based on Evidence of Residence at the Fort between October 4, 1756, and August 9, 1760. Report on file, Fort Loudoun Association and the M. C. McClung Historical Collection, Lawson McGhee Library, Knox County Public Library System, Knoxville, TN.
Brown, Margaret K.
1971 Glass from Fort Michilimackinac: A Classification for Eighteenth-Century Glass. *Michigan Archaeologist* 17(3–4).
Brown, Margaret K., and L. Dean
1977 *The Village of Chartres in Colonial Illinois, 1720–1765*. Polyanthos, New Orleans.
Brumwell, Stephen
2002 *Redcoats: The British Soldier and War in the Americas, 1755–1763*. Cambridge University Press, Cambridge.

Burleigh, Herbert Clarence
1979   *The Romance of Fort Frontenac, Kingston, Ontario*. Mastercraft Print & Graphics, Kingston.

Burnaby, Rev. Andrew
n.d.   *Travels through the Middle Settlements in North America. In the Years 1759 and 1760. With Observations upon the State of the Colonies*. 2nd ed. Great Seal Books, Ithaca, NY.

Byrd, William
1735–72 Letters. Library of Virginia, Richmond.
1760   Papers. Virginia Historical Society, Richmond.

Callières, Louis-Hector
1695   Callières to the Minister. Library and Archives Canada, C11A 13, pp. 449–79. In *Royal Fort Frontenac*, edited by Preston and Lamontagne, pp. 164–69.

Callières, Louis-Hector, and Charles de la Boische, Marquis de Beauharnois
1702   Callières and Beauharnois to the Minister. Library and Archives Canada, C11A 20, pp. 13–57. In *Royal Fort Frontenac*, edited by Preston and Lamontagne, pp. 164–69.

Callaway, Joseph
1758   Return of Ammunition at Fort Loudoun [South Carolina], 24 February 1758. *Colonial Records of South Carolina Series 2: Documents Relating to Indian Affairs, 1754–1765*. Edited by W. L. McDowell Jr., pp. 448–49. South Carolina Department of Archives and History, University of South Carolina Press, Columbia (1970).

Calloway, Colin G. (compiler)
1992   *North Country Captives: Selected Narratives of Indian Captivity from Vermont and New Hampshire*. University Press of New England, Hanover, NH.

Casgrain, H. R. (editor)
1890   *Extraits des Archives des Ministères de la Marine de la Guerre à Paris: Correspondence Générale, MM. Duquesne et Vaudreuil, Gouverneurs-Généraux, 1755–1760*. Vol. 1. Imprimerie de L-J Demers & Frère, Québec.
1889–95 *Collection des Manuscrits du Marechal de Lévi*. 12 vols. Chez L-J Demers & Frère, Québec.

Caswell, Richard, and Francis Brown
1756   Report on Fort Dobbs. In *Colonial Records of North Carolina*, vol. 5, edited by Saunders and Daniels, p. 849.

Cawthorn, J. E., and V. S. Jenkins
1964   *Soil Survey: Iredell County, North Carolina*. U.S. Department of Agriculture, Soil Conservation Services Series, no. 14. Government Printing Office, Washington, DC.

Chamberlain, George Walter
1916   The Redeemed Captives of 1747. *New England Historical and Genealogical Register* 70(2):260–65.

Charbonneau, André
1990   The Redoubt in New France: A Contribution to the History of Fortification in North America. *Fort: The International Journal of Fortification and Military Architecture* 18:43–67.
1994   *Fortifications of Ile Aux Noix*. Minister of Supply and Services, Department of Canadian Heritage, Ottawa.

Charbonneau, André, Yvon Desloges, and Marc Lefranc
1982 *Québec: Ville fortifiée du XVIIe au XIX siècle.* Parcs Canada, Québec. English translation: *Québec: The Fortified City from the 17th to the 19th Century.* Parks Canada, Québec.

Charlevoix, Pierre Francois Xavier de
1761 Journal of a Voyage to North America. In *Kingston! Oh Kingston!* edited by A. B. Smith (1987), p. 2.

Chaussegros de Léry, Gaspard-Joseph
1731 Mémoire, Québec, October 25. Archives nationales d'outre-mer, COL C11A 54, pp. 344–45.
1744 Chaussegros de Léry to the Minister. Library and Archives Canada, C11A 82, pp. 62–71. In *Royal Fort Frontenac,* edited by Preston and Lamontagne, p. 231.

Chaussegros de Léry, Gaspard Joseph, Jr.
1749 Chaussegros de Léry Junior to the Minister. Library and Archives Canada, C11A 94-1, pp. 16–18. In *Royal Fort Frontenac,* edited by Preston and Lamontagne, p. 244.

Churchill, Winston
1956 *A History of the English-Speaking Peoples.* Vol. 3, *The Age of Revolutions.* Dodd, Mead, New York.

Clark, David T.
2003 An Analysis of Faunal Remains from the Excavations at Fort Loudoun (44FK593), a French and Indian War Period Site. Report prepared for the Virginia Department of Historic Resources, Richmond.

Coe, Michael D.
2006 *The Line of Forts: Historical Archaeology on the Colonial Frontier of Massachusetts.* University Press of New England, Hanover, NH.

Company Directors
1701 Directors of the Company of Canada to the Minister. Library and Archives Canada, C11A 19, pp. 221–41. In *Royal Fort Frontenac,* edited by Preston and Lamontagne, p. 197.

Coolidge, Guy Omeron
1979 *The French Occupation of the Champlain Valley from 1609 to 1759.* Harbor Hill Books, Harrison, NY.

Cowley, Robert, and Geoffrey Parker (editors)
1996 *The Reader's Companion to Military History.* Houghton Mifflin, New York.

Coytmore, Richard
1759a Richard Coytmore to Governor Lyttelton, 9 April. Lyttelton Papers, box 10.
1759b Richard Coytmore to Governor Lyttelton, 3 August. Lyttelton Papers, box 11.
1759c Richard Coytmore to Governor Lyttelton, 21 November. Lyttelton Papers, box 13.
1760 Richard Coytmore to Governor Lyttelton, 28 January. Lyttelton Papers, box 14.

Deetz, James
1973 Ceramics from Plymouth, 1620-1835: The Archaeological Evidence. In *Ceramics in America,* edited by Ian M. G. Quimby pp. 15–40. University Press of Virginia, Charlottesville.
1977 *In Small Things Forgotten: The Archaeology of Early American Life.* Anchor Books, Garden City, NY.

Deidier, Abbé
1734   *Le parfait ingénieur françois, ou la fortification offensive et défensive.* Claude Jombert, Paris.

Demos, John
1994   *The Unredeemed Captive: A Family Story from Early America.* Alfred A. Knopf, New York.

Denonville, Jacques René de Brisay de
1686   Denonville to Seignelay. Library and Archives Canada, C11A 8, pp. 192–226. In *Royal Fort Frontenac,* edited by Preston and Lamontagne, pp. 158–60.
1689   Denonville to Valrennes. Library and Archives Canada, C11A 10, pp. 326–36. In *Royal Fort Frontenac,* edited by Preston and Lamontagne, pp. 176–79.

Denton, Mark
1980   Site Field Report of the 1980 Field Excavation at Fort Loudoun (36Fr107). Manuscript, Section of Archaeology, State Museum of Pennsylvania, Harrisburg.

Desbarats, Catherine, and Alan Greer
2007   The Seven Years' War in Canadian History and Memory. In *Cultures in Conflict: The Seven Years' War in North America,* edited by Warren Hofstra. Rowman and Littlefield, Lanham, MD.

De Vorsey, Louis, Jr.
1971   *DeBrahm's Report of the General Survey in the Southern District of North America.* University of South Carolina Press, Columbia.

Distretti, Joe P., and Carl Kuttruff
2004   Reconstruction, Interpretation, and Public Education at Fort Loudoun. In *The Reconstructed Past: Reconstructions in the Public Interpretation of Archaeology and History,* edited by John H. Jameson Jr., pp. 167–76. AltaMira Press, Walnut Creek, CA.

Dixon, David
2003   *Bushy Run Battlefield: Pennsylvania Trail of History Guide.* Stackpole Books, Mechanicsburg, PA.

Dobbs, Arthur
1754   Arthur Dobbs to Board of Trade, 19 December. In *Colonial Records of North Carolina,* vol. 5, edited by Saunders and Daniels, pp. 153–57.
1755a   Arthur Dobbs to Board of Trade, 1 January. In *Colonial Records of North Carolina,* vol. 5, edited by Saunders and Daniels, pp. 312–13.
1755b   Arthur Dobbs to Board of Trade, 24 August. In *Colonial Records of North Carolina,* vol. 5, edited by Saunders and Daniels, pp. 353–64.
1755c   Arthur Dobbs to Board of Trade, 25 September. In *Colonial Records of North Carolina,* vol. 5, edited by Saunders and Daniels, pp. 495–98.
1755d   Arthur Dobbs to Board of Trade, 26 December. In *Colonial Records of North Carolina,* vol. 5, edited by Saunders and Daniels, pp. 461–79.
1756a   Arthur Dobbs to Board of Trade, 15 March. In *Colonial Records of North Carolina,* vol. 5, edited by Saunders and Daniels, pp. 570–75.
1756b   Arthur Dobbs to Board of Trade, May. In *Colonial Records of North Carolina,* Vol. 5, edited by Saunders and Daniels, p. 672.

Doblin, Helga (translator)
1995   *The Specht Journal: A Military Journal of the Burgoyne Campaign*, edited by Mary C. Lynn. Greenwood Press, Westport, CT.

Duane, William
1810   *Military Dictionary*. Philadelphia.

Duffy, Christopher
1975   *Fire and Stone: The Science of Fortress Warfare, 1660–1860*. Hippocrene Books, New York.
1979   *Siege Warfare: The Fortress in the Early Modern World, 1494–1660*. Routledge and Kegan Paul, London.
1985>*Siege Warfare: The Fortress in the Age of Vauban and Frederick the Great, 1660–1789*. Routledge and Kegan Paul, London.

Dunnigan, Brian Leigh
1989   *Forts within a Fort: Niagara's Redoubts*. Old Fort Niagara Association, Youngstown, NY.
1996   *Siege 1759: The Campaign against Niagara*. Old Fort Niagara Association, Youngstown, NY.
2008   *A Picturesque Situation: Mackinac before Photography, 1615–1860*. Wayne State University Press, Detroit.

Dunnigan, Brian L., and Patricia K. Scott
1991   *Old Fort Niagara in Four Centuries: A History of Its Development*. Old Fort Niagara Association, Youngstown, NY.

Dupre (Dupree), Daniel
1756   The Public of North Carolina to Daniel Dupree. Treasurer and Comptroller Papers, Military Papers, box 1, Archives of North Carolina, Raleigh.

Eliason, Minnie Hampton
1976   Fort Dobbs. In *Iredell County Landmarks: A Pictorial History of Iredell County*, edited by Virginia Fraser Evans, 19–34. Iredell County American Revolution Bicentennial Commission, Statesville, NC.

Evans, Lynn L. M.
2001   *House D of the Southeast Row House: Excavations at Fort Michilimackinac, 1989–1997*. Archaeological Completion Report Series, no. 17. Mackinac State Historic Parks, Mackinac Island, MI.

Farry, Andrew
2005   Regulars and "Irregulars": British and Provincial Variability among Eighteenth-Century Military Frontiers. *Historical Archaeology* 39(2):16–32.

Feister, Lois M.
1984   Building Materials Indicative of Status Differentiation at Crown Point Barracks. *Historical Archaeology* 18(1):103–7.

Feister, Lois M., and Paul R. Huey.
1985   Archaeological Testing at Fort Gage, a Provincial Redoubt of 1758 at Fort George, New York. *Bulletin and Journal of Archaeology for New York* 90:40–59.

Fer, Nicolas de
1693   *Introduction à la Fortification*. Paris.

Fisher, Charles L.
1985   Style Wars in the Wilderness: A New Look at the Colonial Forts at Crown Point. Paper presented at the Society for Historical Archaeology annual meeting, Boston.
1991   A Report on the 1977 Archaeological Test Excavations at Fort St. Frédéric, Crown Point State Historic Site, Essex County, New York. New York State Parks, Recreation, and Historic Preservation, Bureau of Historic Sites, Waterford, NY.
1995   The Archaeology of Provincial Officers' Huts at Crown Point State Historic Site. Northeast Historical Archaeology 24:65–86.
Fitzpatrick, John C. (editor)
1925   The Diaries of George Washington, 1748–1799. Houghton Mifflin, Boston.
Forbes, John.
1758   Papers relating to the expedition against Fort Duquesne in 1758. Department of Special Collections, University of Virginia Library. Charlottesville.
Fortier, John B.
1969   New Light on Fort Massac. In Frenchmen and French Ways, edited by John Francis McDermott, pp. 57–71. University of Illinois Press, Urbana.
Fowler, William H.
2005   Empires at War: The Seven Years' War and the Struggle for North America. Douglas and McIntyre, Vancouver, BC.
Franklin, Benjamin
1756   Account of Building Fort Allen. Cited in Outposts of the War for Empire, by Charles M. Stotz, p. 38. University of Pittsburgh Press, Pittsburgh, 1985.
Franquet, Louis
1974   Voyages et mémoires sur le Canada par Franquet. Éditions Élysée, Montréal. Originally published in 1889 by Imprimerie générale A. Coté et cie., Québec.
1924   Le Voyage de Franquet aux îles Royale et Saint-Jean. Rapport de l'Archiviste de la province de Québec, 1923–24. Québec.
Frederick County, VA
n.d.   Order Book 4-5. Frederick County Courthouse, Winchester, VA.
Fries, Adelaide L. (editor)
1922   Records of the Moravians in North Carolina. Department of Cultural Resources, Raleigh, NC.
Frontenac, Louis Baude, comte de Palluau et de
1696   Frontenac to the Minister. Library and Archives Canada, C11A 14, pp. 246–77. In Royal Fort Frontenac, edited by Preston and Lamontagne, p. 195.
Fry, Bruce
1984   "An Appearance of Strength": The Fortifications of Louisbourg. 2 vols. Parks Canada, Ottawa.
Furness, Gregory
1984   Gregory Furness to Paul Huey, 23 January. Manuscript on file, New York State Office of Parks, Recreation and Historic Preservation, Waterford, NY.
Furness, Gregory, and Timothy Titus
1985   Master Plan for Crown Point State Historic Site. New York State Parks, Recreation, and Historic Preservation, Bureau of Historic Sites, Waterford, NY.

Gage, Thomas
1762–76 Papers. William L. Clements Library, University of Michigan, Ann Arbor.
Gale, R. R.
2007 "A Soldier-like Way" Material Culture of the British Infantry, 1751–1768. Track of the Wolf, Elk River, MN.
Gallup, Andrew (editor)
1993 Memoir of a French and Indian War Soldier: "Jolicoeur" Charles Bonin. Heritage Books, Bowie, MD.
Garcia, Bob
2003 The Pivot of Defence of Upper Canada: An Overview and Structural History of Fort Henry. *Ontario Archaeology* 76:54–63.
Gardner, William M.
1990 In Search of the Stockade: Archaeological Testing at Fort Edwards, Hampshire County, West Virginia. Thunderbird Archaeological Associates, Woodstock, VA.
Gélinas, Cyrille
1983 The Role of Fort Chambly in the Development of New France, 1665–1760. Parks Canada, Ottawa.
Gérin-Lajoie, Marie (translator and editor)
1976 Fort Michilimackinac in 1749: Lotbinière's Plan and Description. *Mackinac History* 2:5. Mackinac Island State Park Commission, Mackinac Island, MI.
Gipson, Lawrence H.
1949 The Great War for the Empire: The Victorious Years, 1758–1760. Alfred A. Knopf, New York.
1954 The Great War for the Empire: The Culmination, 1760–1763. Alfred A. Knopf, New York.
Glassie, Henry
1976 Folk Housing in Middle Virginia. University of Tennessee Press, Knoxville.
Glen, James
1754 Governor James Glen to the Privy Council, 26 August. Public Records Office, Privy Council, vol. 25, p. 347. National Archives, London.
Goode, Eddie
2006 Fortifying the Frontier: Ephraim Vause and Fort Vause of Augusta County, Virginia, 1755–1758. Original manuscript on file with the author, Virginia's Explore Park, Roanoke.
Grimm, Jacob L.
1970 Archaeological Investigation of Fort Ligonier, 1960–1965. Annals of Carnegie Museum 42, Pittsburgh.
Gromoff, Nick
2005 Fort Frontenac (BbGc-8) Stage 4 Excavations for the Installation of Fire Escapes at the DeNoyan and LaSalle Buildings, Fort Frontenac, CFB Kingston. Report to Defence Construction Canada from the Cataraqui Archaeological Research Foundation, Kingston, Ont.
Gruber, Terry
1999 Early History of the Fort Edwards Site. In *Historical and Archaeological Investigations of the Fort Edwards Properties*, by W. Stephen McBride, pp. 3–8. Wilbur

Smith Associates, Lexington, KY, for the Fort Edwards Foundation, Capon Bridge, WV.

Guilday, John E.
1970   Animal Remains from Archaeological Excavations at Fort Ligonier. In *Archaeological Investigation of Fort Ligonier, 1960–1965,* by Jacob L. Grimm, pp. 177–86. Annals of Carnegie Museum 42, Pittsburgh.

Hagerty, Gilbert
1971   *Massacre at Fort Bull, the De Léry Expedition against Oneida Carry—1756.* Mowbray, Providence, RI.

Halchin, Jill Y.
1985   *Excavations at Fort Michilimackinac, 1983–1985: House C of the Southeast Row House, the Solomon-Levy-Parant House.* Archaeological Completion Report Series, no. 11. Mackinac Island State Park Commission [MISPC], Mackinac Island, MI.

Hale, John Peter
1886   *Trans-Allegheny Pioneers: Historical Sketches of the First White Settlers West of the Alleghenies, 1748 and After.* Graphic Press, Cincinnati.

Hamer, Philip M.
1925   Anglo-French Rivalry in the Cherokee Country, 1754–1757. *North Carolina Historical Review* 2(3):303–22.

Hamer, Philip M. (editor)
1972   *The Papers of Henry Laurens.* Vol. 3. University of South Carolina Press, Columbia.

Hamilton, Edward P. (translator and editor)
1959   *Lake Champlain and the Upper Hudson Valley.* Fort Ticonderoga Association, Ticonderoga, NY.
1962   *The French and Indian Wars.* Doubleday, New York.
1964   *Adventure in the Wilderness: The American Journals of Louis Antoine de Bougainville, 1756–1760.* University of Oklahoma Press, Norman.
1970   The French Colonial Forts at Crown Point Strait. *Bulletin of the Fort Ticonderoga Museum* 12(6):393–99.
1995   *Fort Ticonderoga: Key to a Continent.* Fort Ticonderoga, Ticonderoga, NY.

Hamilton, T. M.
1976   *Firearms on the Frontier: Guns at Fort Michilimackinac, 1715–1781.* Reports in Mackinac History and Archaeology 5. Mackinac Island State Park Commission. Pendall Printing, Midland, MI.
1980   *Colonial Frontier Guns.* Fur Press, Chadron, NE.

Hanson, Lee, and Dick Ping Hsu
1975   *Casemates and Cannonballs: Archaeological Investigations at Fort Stanwix, Rome, New York.* U.S. Department of the Interior, National Park Service, Publications in Archaeology 14, Government Printing Office, Washington, DC.

Harrington, J. C.
1970   *New Light on Washington's Fort Necessity.* Eastern National Park and Monument Association, Richmond, VA.

Hatley, Tom
1993   *The Dividing Paths: Cherokees and South Carolinians through the Era of Revolution.* Oxford University Press, Oxford.

Hazard, Samuel (editor)
1853a   *Pennsylvania Archives,* series 1, vol. 3. Joseph Severns, Philadelphia.
1853b   *Pennsylvania Archives,* series 1, vol. 4. Joseph Severns, Philadelphia.

Heighton, Robert F., and Kathleen A. Deagan
1972   A New Formula for Dating Kaolin Clay Pipestems. *Conference on Historic Site Archaeology Papers 1971* 6(2):220–29.

Heldman, Donald P.
1973   *Archaeological Investigations of Fort Toulouse.* Alabama Historical Commission and National Park Service, Montgomery.
1977   *Excavations at Fort Michilimackinac, 1976: The Southeast and South Southeast Row Houses.* Archaeological Completion Report Series, no. 1. Mackinac Island State Park Commission, Mackinac Island, MI.
1978   *Excavations at Fort Michilimackinac, 1977: House One of the South Southeast Row House.* Archaeological Completion Report Series, no. 2. Mackinac Island State Park Commission, Mackinac Island, MI.
1979   Archaeological Preservation at Michilimackinac: The First Twenty Years. Paper presented at the 12th Conference on Historical and Underwater Archaeology, Nashville, TN.
1991   Archaeology and Exhibits at Colonial Michilimackinac. Manuscript on file, MISPC Petersen Center, Mackinaw City, MI.

Heldman, Donald P., and Roger T. Grange Jr.
1981   *Excavations at Fort Michilimackinac 1978–79: The Rue de la Babillarde.* Archaeological Completion Report Series, no. 3. MISPC, Mackinac Island, MI.

Heldman, Donald P., and William L. Minnerly
1977   *The Powder Magazine at Fort Michilimackinac: Excavation Report.* Reports in Mackinac History and Archaeology, no. 6. MISPC, Mackinac Island, MI.

Hening, William Walker
1819   *Virginia's Statutes at Large.* Richmond, VA.

Hennepin, Jean-Louis
1880   Voyages and New Discoveries of a Very Great Country in America. In *Kingston! Oh Kingston!* edited by A. B. Smith, pp. 3–7.

Henry, Alexander
1969   *Travels and Adventures in Canada and the Indian Territories between the Years 1760 and 1776.* Edited by James Bain. Charles E. Tuttle Co., Rutland, VT.

Hilliard, Sam Bowers
1972   *Hog Meat and Hoecake: Food Supply in the Old South, 1840–1860.* Southern Illinois University Press, Carbondale.

Hillman, Benjamin J.
1966   *Executive Journals of the Council of Colonial Virginia.* Vol. 6, *June 20, 1754–May 3, 1775.* Virginia State Library, Richmond.

Hoban, Charles F. (editor)
1935   *Pennsylvania Archives,* series 8, vol. 6. State Library, Harrisburg, PA.

Hocquart, Gilles
1742a   Hocquart to the Minister. Library and Archives Canada, C11A 77, pp. 362–67. In *Royal Fort Frontenac,* edited by Preston and Lamontagne, p. 227.
1742b   Hocquart to the Minister. Library and Archives Canada, C11A 78, pp. 20–21. In *Royal Fort Frontenac,* edited by Preston and Lamontagne, p. 195.
1747   Hocquart to the Minister. Library and Archives Canada, C11A 88, pp. 126–55. In *Royal Fort Frontenac,* edited by Preston and Lamontagne, p. 236.

Howe, Dennis E.
1995   The Archaeological Investigations of 18th-Century Temporary Military Shelters. In *Archaeology in Fort Edward,* edited by David R. Starbuck. Adirondack Community College, Queensbury, NY.

Hunter, William A.
1960   *Forts on the Pennsylvania Frontier, 1753–1758.* Pennsylvania Historical and Museum Commission, Harrisburg.
1971   Thomas Barton and the Forbes Expedition. *Pennsylvania Magazine of History and Biography* 95(4):431–83.

Israel, Stephen
1971a   Archaeological Research at Fort Dobbs, a French and Indian War Fort on the Carolina Frontier, 1755–1765, Iredell County, North Carolina. Manuscript on file, Office of State Archaeology, Raleigh, NC.
1971b   Excavation map on file, Office of State Archaeology, Raleigh, NC.

James, Alfred P., and Charles M. Stotz
1958   *Drums in the Forest: Decision at the Forks, Defense in the Wilderness.* Historical Society of Western Pennsylvania, Pittsburgh.

Jelks, Edward B., Carl J. Eckberg, and Terrance J. Martin
1989   *Archaeological Explorations at the Laurens Site: Probable Location of Fort de Chartres I.* Studies in Illinois Archaeology 5. Illinois Historic Preservation Agency, Springfield.

Jolley, Robert L.
2005   Archaeological Investigations at Fort Loudoun (44FK 593): A French and Indian War Period Fortification, Winchester, Virginia. *Quarterly Bulletin of the Archaeological Society of Virginia* 60(2):67–106.

Jones, Olive R., and E. Ann Smith
1985   *Glass of the British Military ca. 1755–1820.* Studies in Archaeology, Architecture, and History, National Parks and Sites Branch, Parks Canada, Environment Canada, Ottawa.

Jordan, Terry G.
1985   *American Log Buildings: An Old World Heritage.* University of North Carolina Press, Chapel Hill.

Joyce, Dee Dee
1983   The 1982 Field Season at Fort Loudoun (36Fr107). Manuscript on file, Section of Archaeology, State Museum of Pennsylvania, Harrisburg.

Kalm, Peter
1748   *Travels in North America,* English translation, Warrington, 1771. In *Kingston! Oh Kingston!* edited by A. B. Smith (1987), pp. 41–48.

1972 *Travels into North America.* Translated by John Reinhold Forster. Imprint Society, Barre, MA.

Kars, Marjolene

2002 *Breaking Loose Together.* University of North Carolina Press, Chapel Hill.

Keene, David

2002 Beyond Fur Trade: The Eighteenth-Century Colonial Economy of French North America as Seen from Fort de Chartres in the Illinois County. PhD dissertation, University of Wisconsin, Madison.

Keesecker, Guy L., and Geraldine Keesecker

1972–82 Major General Adam Stephen: Letters to, from, and about Him, 1718–91, Founder of Martinsburg, VA. Manuscript on file, Martinsburg Public Library, Martinsburg, WV.

Keever, Homer

1976 *Iredell Piedmont County.* Iredell County Revolutionary War Bicentennial Commission, Statesville, NC.

Kegley, F. B.

1938 *Virginia Frontier.* Southwest Virginia Historical Society, Roanoke.

Kelley, Paul

1961a *Historic Fort Loudoun.* Fort Loudoun Association, Vonore, TN.

1961b Fort Loudoun: The After Years, 1760–1960. *Tennessee Historical Quarterly* 20:303–22.

Kent, Barry C.

1978 Discovery of Fort Loudoun, Franklin County, Pennsylvania. *Pennsylvania Archaeologist* 48(3):42–47.

Kent, Barry C., and Charles Douts Jr.

1977 Exploratory Excavations at the Site of Fort Loudoun, Peters Township, Franklin County, Pennsylvania. Manuscript on file, Section of Archaeology, State Museum of Pennsylvania, Harrisburg.

Kent, Donald H., Louis M. Waddell, and Autumn L. Leonard (editors)

1976 *The Papers of Henry Bouquet.* Vol. 3, *January 1, 1759–August 31, 1759.* Pennsylvania Historical and Museum Commission, Harrisonburg.

Kent, Timothy J.

2004 *Rendezvous at the Straits: Fur Trade and Military Activities at Fort de Buade and Fort Michilimackinac, 1669–1781.* Vol. 2. Silver Fox Enterprises, Ossineke, MI.

Kimmel, Ross M.

1973 Fort Frederick Restoration: Report on Historical Research. Report on file, Maryland Park Services, Annapolis, MD.

King of France

1697 Louis XIV to Frontenac and Champigny. Library and Archives Canada, B19-3, pp. 304–37. In *Royal Fort Frontenac,* edited by Preston and Lamontagne, pp. 196–97.

1698 Louis XIV to Frontenac. Library and Archives Canada, B20-1, p. 196. In *Royal Fort Frontenac,* edited by Preston and Lamontagne, p. 197.

1701 Louis XIV to Callières. Library and Archives Canada, B22-4, pp. 268–312. In *Royal Fort Frontenac,* edited by Preston and Lamontagne, p. 197.

1738   Louis XV to Beauharnois and Hocquart. Library and Archives Canada, C11A 69, pp. 6–53. In *Royal Fort Frontenac*, edited by Preston and Lamontagne, p. 225.

Kitching, G.
1953   Recent Excavations at Fort Frontenac. *Historic Kingston* 2:26.

Koontz, L. K.
1925   *The Virginia Frontier, 1754–1763*. Johns Hopkins University Studies in Historical and Political Science 43(2). Johns Hopkins University Press, Baltimore.

Kopperman, Paul
1977   *Braddock at the Monongahela*. University of Pittsburgh Press, Pittsburgh.

Kummerow, Burton K., Christine H. O'Toole, and R. Scott Stephenson
2008   *Pennsylvania's Forbes Trail*. Taylor Trade, New York.

Kuttruff, Carl
1990   Fort Loudoun, Tennessee, a Mid-18th-Century British Fortification: A Case Study in Research Archaeology, Reconstruction, and Interpretive Exhibits. In *The Politics of the Past*, edited by Peter Gathercole and David Lowenthal, pp. 265–83. Unwin Hyman, London.
2007   Fort Loudoun in Tennessee, 1756–1760: History, Archaeology, Replication, Exhibits, and Interpretation. Report on file, Tennessee Historical Commission, Nashville.
2009   Karl Kuttruff to L. Babits, 2009.
2010   Fort Loudoun in Tennessee 1756–1760: History, Archaeology, Replication, Exhibits, and Interpretation. Report of the Tennessee Wars Commission and Tennessee Division of Archaeology, Nashville.

Lahontan, Louis-Armand de Lom d'Arce
1735   New Voyages to North America. In *Kingston! Oh Kingston!* edited by A. B. Smith, pp. 9–16.

La Jonquière, Pierre Jacques de Taffanel, marquis de
1750   La Jonquière to the Minister. Library and Archives Canada, C11A 95, pp. 229–30. In *Royal Fort Frontenac*, edited by Preston and Lamontagne, pp. 246–47.

Lambert, Phyllis (editor)
1992   *Opening the Gates of Eighteenth-Century Montréal*. Canadian Centre for Architecture, Montréal.

Lamberville, Jean
1687   An Account of a Naval Engagement between a Small French Bark and the Iroquois Army near the Fort of Frontenac, Called Cataraqui by Father Lamberville, S.J. In *Royal Fort Frontenac*, edited by Preston and Lamontagne, pp. 164–69.
1695   Father Lamberville to my Reverend Father in Christ. British Museum, Add MSS 16913, ff. 173–80v. In *Royal Fort Frontenac*, edited by Preston and Lamontagne, pp. 172–74.

Langins, Janis
2004   *Conserving the Enlightenment: French Military Engineering from Vauban to the Revolution*. MIT Press, Cambridge.

La Pause, Charles de Plantavit, chevalier de
1756–57 La Pause's Observations and Notes on Fort Frontenac. Rapport de l'archiviste de la Province de Québec pour 1933–1934, Papiers La Pause, pp. 84–87. In *Royal Fort Frontenac*, edited by Preston and Lamontagne, pp. 250–53.

La Salle, Nicolas de
1898 Relation of the Discovery of the Mississippi River, 1681–82. In *Kingston! Oh Kingston!* edited by A. B. Smith, p. 23.

Laurens, John
1763 John Laurens to Henry Laurens. In *The Papers of Henry Laurens,* vol. 3, edited by Philip M. Hamer, p. 321. University of South Carolina Press, Columbia.

Lawson, Cecil C. P.
1974 *A History of the Uniforms of the British Army.* Vol. 3. Kaye and Ward, London.

Leach, Douglas Edward
1973 *Arms for Empire: A Military History of the British Colonies in North America, 1607–1763.* Macmillan, New York.
1986 *Roots of Conflict: British Armed Forces and the Colonial Americans, 1667–1763.* University of North Carolina Press, Chapel Hill.

Le Blond, Guillaume
1756 *Élémens de fortification: Contenant Les Principes & la description raisonnée des differens ouvrage qu'on employe à la Fortification des Places; les Systêmes des principaux Ingénieurs, la Fortification irréguliere, &c.* Chez Charles-Antoine Jombert, Paris.
1757 Fortification. In *Encyclopédie ou Dictionnaire raisonned des sciences, des arts et des meitiers,* vol. 7, edited by Denis Diderot. Paris. Facsimile ed. 1966, Bad Cannstatt, Frommann, Stuttgart.

Lévis, François Gaston
1889 *Journal des Campagnes du Chevalier de Lévis en Canada de 1756 à 1760.* Edited by H. R. Casgrain. C. O. Beauchemin & Fils, Montréal.

Lewis, Kenneth
1976 *Camden, a Frontier Town.* Anthropological Studies 2. Institute of Archaeology and Anthropology, University of South Carolina, Columbia.

Lewis, Theodore Burnham, Jr.
1970 The Crown Point Campaign, 1755. *Bulletin of the Fort Ticonderoga Museum* 12(6):400–415.

Lochee, Lewis
1783 *Elements of Field Fortification.* T. Cadell, Charing Cross, London. Facsimile copy by Kings Arms Press, Oldwick, NJ.

Loth, Calder (editor)
2000 *The Virginia Landmarks Register.* 4th ed. University of Virginia Press, Charlottesville.

Louis-Philippe, King of France
1977 *Diary of My Travels in America.* Delacorte Press, New York.

Lyttelton, William Henry
1730–1806   Papers. William L. Clements Library, University of Michigan, Ann Arbor.

Maass, John R.
2002 All This Poor Province Could Do: North Carolina and the Seven Years' War, 1757–1762. *North Carolina Historical Review* 79(1):50–89.

Mackintosh, Lachlan
1758a Lachlan Mackintosh to Governor Lyttelton, 21 August. Lyttelton Papers, box 8.
1758b Lachlan Mackintosh to Governor Lyttelton, 19 September. Lyttelton Papers, box 8.
1758c Lachlan Mackintosh to Governor Lyttelton, 16 October. Lyttelton Papers, box 8.
Malartic, Anne-Joseph-Hippolyte Maurès, comte de
1755   Adjutant Malartic to Count d'Argenson, Camp at Cataracoui, 6 October. Library and Archives Canada, Archives anciennes, Ministère de la Guerre, Correspondance, vol. 3405, pièce 119, pp. 211–24. In *Royal Fort Frontenac*, edited by Preston and Lamontagne, pp. 248–49.
Martin, Terrance J., and Angela M. Mallard
2009   Animal Remains from the Fort Ashby Site (46Mi58), Mineral County, West Virginia. In *Report of the 2007–2008 Archaeological Investigations at Ashby's Fort (46Mi58), Mineral County, West Virginia*, by W. Stephen McBride. McBride Preservation Services, LLC, Lexington, KY.
Martin, Terrance J., and Claire Fuller Martin
1993   Animal Remains from Arbuckle's Fort (46Bg13), Greenbrier County, West Virginia. Illinois State Museum Society Technical Report 93–000–15. Springfield.
Maxwell, Moreau S., and Lewis Binford
1961   *Excavations at Fort Michilimackinac, Mackinac City, Michigan, 1959 Season*. Publications of the Museum, Michigan State University, Cultural Series, vol. 1, no. 1. Lansing, MI.
McBride, W. Stephen
1998   "For the Protection of Your Lives and Fortunes...": *Archaeological Explorations at Fort Edwards, Hampshire County, West Virginia*. Wilbur Smith Associates, Lexington, KY.
2005   *Report of the 2004 Archaeological Investigations at Fort Edwards (46Hm75), Hampshire County, West Virginia*. McBride Preservation Services, LLC, Lexington, KY.
2009   *Report of the 2007–2008 Archaeological Investigations at Ashby's Fort (46Mi58), Mineral County, West Virginia*. McBride Preservation Services, LLC, Lexington, KY.
McBride, W., Stephen and Kim Arbogast McBride
1998   Archaeological Investigations of Fort Arbuckle. *Journal of the Greenbrier Historical Society* 6(6):15–45.
2006   Archaeological Investigations of Fort Donnally. *Journal of the Greenbrier Historical Society* 8(2):21–36.
McBride, W. Stephen, Kim A. McBride, and Greg Adamson
2003   *Frontier Forts in West Virginia: Historical and Archaeological Explorations*. West Virginia Department of Culture and History, Charleston.
McDowell, William L., Jr. (editor)
1970   *Documents Relating to Indian Affairs*. University of South Carolina Press, Columbia.
McLennan, J. S.
1918   *Louisbourg from Its Foundation to Its Fall, 1713–1758*. Macmillan, London.
MacLeod, D. Peter
1996   *The Canadian Iroquois and the Seven Years' War*. Dundurn Press, Toronto.

Mereness, N. D.
1916 *Travels in the American Colonies.* Macmillan, New York.

Michigan Pioneer and Historical Society
1886 *Historical Collections.* Vol. 9. State Printers, Lansing, MI.

Merrell, James H.
1989 *The Indians' New World: Catawbas and Their Neighbors from European Contact through the Era of Removal.* University of North Carolina Press, Chapel Hill.

Miles, Lion G.
1988 The Winchester Hessian Barracks. *Winchester-Frederick County Historical Society Journal* 3:19–65.

Miller, J. Jefferson, II, and Lyle M. Stone
1970 *Eighteenth-Century Ceramics from Fort Michilimackinac: A Study in Historical Archaeology.* Smithsonian Institution Press, Washington, DC.

Miln, Alexander
1760 Ensign Alexander Miln to Governor Lyttelton, 28 February 1760. Lyttelton Papers, box 14.

Miner, Frank Denison, and Hannah Miner (editors)
1915 *The Diary of Manasseh Minor, Stonington, Conn., 1696–1720.* Frank Denison Miner, Jersey City, NJ.

Moneypenny, Alexander
1761 Diary of Alexander Moneypenny. Microfilm on file, South Carolina State Archives, Columbia.

Muller, John
1746 *A Treatise Containing the Elementary Part of Fortification, Regular and Irregular.* J. Norse, London. Reprinted in 1968 by Museum Restoration Service, Ottawa.

Myers, James P.
1999 Pennsylvania's Awakening: The Kittanning Raid of 1756. *Pennsylvania History* 66(3):399–420.

NL 135 R68 1765.
1758 Plan of Fort Frontenac. Edward E. Ayer Collection 135 R68 1765, Newberry Library, Chicago.

NMC 16333
1758 Vue de Frontenac ou Kataracoui. Library and Archives Canada, National Map Collection, Ottawa.

NMC 22954
1738 Plan du Fort Frontenac citué à l'Est du Lac Ontario a la Coste du Nord. Library and Archives Canada, National Map Collection, Ottawa.

NMC 4755
1685 Fort de Frontenac ou Katatakouy. Archives Nationales, section Outre-Mer, Depot des Fortifications des colonies, Amerique septentrionale. 552c. Paris. Copy held by Library and Archives Canada, National Map Collection, Ottawa.

NMC 4987
1726 Plan du Fort Frontenac. Library and Archives Canada, National Map Collection, Ottawa.

NMC C15989
1720   Plan du Fort Frontenac ou Cataracouy. Edward E. Ayer Collection MS Map 30, no. 108, Newberry Library, Chicago. Copy held by Library and Archives Canada, National Map Collection, Ottawa.

Noble, Vergil E.
1983   Functional Classification and Intra-Site Analysis in Historical Archaeology: A Case Study from Fort Ouiatenon. PhD dissertation, Michigan State University, Lansing.
1997   Eighteenth-Century Ceramics from Fort de Chartres III. *Illinois Archaeology* 9:36-78.

Noel Hume, Ivor
1969   *A Guide to Artifacts of Colonial America*. Alfred A. Knopf, New York.

O'Callaghan, E. B. (editor)
1855   *Documents Relative to the Colonial History of the State of New-York*. Vol. 9. Weed, Parsons, Printers, Albany, NY.
1858   *Documents Relative to the Colonial History of the State of New-York*. Vol. 2. Weed, Parsons, Printers, Albany, NY.

Oliphant, John
2001   *Peace and War on the Anglo-Cherokee Frontier, 1756-63*. Louisiana State University Press, Baton Rouge.

Olsson, John
2008   *Forensic Linguistics*. Continuum International, London.

Orser, Charles E.
1977   The 1975 Season of Archaeological Investigations at Fort de Chartres, Randolph County, Illinois. *Southern Illinois Studies* 16. Southern Illinois University Museum, Carbondale.

Osborne, Alexander
1759   The Publick of North Carolina to Alexander Osborne. In Frontier Scouting and Indian Wars, 1758-1788, box 1, Military Collection, North Carolina State Archives, Raleigh.

Pargellis, Stanley M.
1966   *Lord Loudoun in North America*. Archon Books, North Haven, CT. Originally printed 1933.

Parish Register
1747   Register of the Baptisms, Marriages, and Burials of the Parish of St. Francis, Fort Royal of Frontenac. Archives of the Church of Notre Dame, Montreal. In *Royal Fort Frontenac*, edited by Preston and Lamontagne, pp. 236-43.

Parker, James
1759   *The New American Magazine: No. XX. For August, 1759*. Printed and Sold by James Parker, Woodbridge, NJ.

Parkman, Francis
1995   *Montcalm and Wolfe: The French and Indian War*. Da Capo Press, New York.
1892   *A Half-Century of Conflict*. Little, Brown, Boston.
1885   *France and England in North America*. Reprint ed. Little, Brown, Boston.

Parrington, Michael
1979   Revolutionary War Archaeology at Valley Forge, Pennsylvania. *North American Archaeologist* 1(2):161–76.

Parry, Muriel H.
2000   *Aak to Zumbra: A Dictionary of the World's Watercraft*. Mariners' Museum, Newport News, VA.

Pease, T. C., and E. Jenison
1940   *Illinois on the Eve of the Seven Years' War 1747–1755*. Collections of the Illinois State Historical Library, vol. 29, Illinois State Historical Library, Springfield.

Peckham, Howard H.
1947   *Pontiac and the Indian Uprising*. Princeton University Press, Princeton, NJ.

Pell, S.H.P.
1978   *Fort Ticonderoga: A Short History*. Fort Ticonderoga Museum, Ticonderoga, NY.

Pendleton, Lee
n.d.   Fort Vause and Its Traditions. Typescript on file, Virginia Department of Historic Resources, Richmond.

Pilling, Arnold R.
1976   Arnold R. Pilling to Stanley South, 29 May 1967. Manuscript on file, Office of State Archaeology, Raleigh, NC.

Polhemus, Richard R.
1979   *Archaeological Investigation of the Tellico Blockhouse Site: A Federal Military and Trade Complex*. University of Tennessee, Department of Anthropology, Report of Investigations 26, and Tennessee Valley Authority Reports in Anthropology 16. Knoxville.

Preston, Richard A., and Leopold Lamontagne (editors)
1958   *Royal Fort Frontenac*. University of Toronto Press, Toronto.

Price, Anna
1980   French Outpost on the Mississippi. *Historic Illinois* 3(1):1–4.

Pritchard, James S.
1973   *Journey of My Lord Count Frontenac*. Downtown Kingston Business Association, Kingston, ON.
2004   *In Search of Empire: The French in the Americas, 1670–1730*. Cambridge University Press, Cambridge.

Privy Council
1748   Privy Council to Governor James Glen, 9 June 1748. British Public Records Office, Privy Council, vol. 27, p. 147. National Archives, London.

Quaife, Milo M. (editor)
1928   *The John Askin Papers, 1747–1795*. Vol. 1. Burton Historical Records, Detroit Library Commission, Detroit.

Quarles, Garland
1974   *George Washington and Winchester, Virginia, 1748–1758*. Vol. 8. Winchester–Frederick County Historical Society Papers, Winchester.

Quisenberry, Marie E., and Roberta R. Munske
2003   *Joseph Edwards*. Fort Edwards Foundation, Capon Bridge, WV.

References Cited · 281

Rackerby, Frank
1971   Preliminary Report of the 1970 Archaeological Excavations at Fort Massac. Report on file, Southern Illinois University Museum. Carbondale.
Ramezay, Claude de
1709   Letter to Pierre François de Rigaud, marquis de Vaudreuil-Cavagnal, Montreal, 19 October. Archives nationales d'outre-mer, COL C11A 30/fol. 93–96v, Paris.
Ramsey, Robert W.
1964   *Carolina Cradle: Settlement of the Northwest Carolina Frontier, 1747–1762*. University of North Carolina Press, Chapel Hill.
Reck, Todd M.
2004   Reexcavating Michilimackinac: Use of Harris Matrices to Analyze Stratigraphy for the Purpose of Studying French Canadians Living in the South Southwest Rowhouse of Fort Michilimackinac. PhD dissertation, Department of Archaeology, Boston University.
Reese, George (editor)
1980   *The Official Papers of Francis Fauquier, Lieutenant Governor of Virginia, 1758–1768*. Vol. 1, *1758–1760*. University Press of Virginia, Charlottesville.
1981   *The Official Papers of Francis Fauquier, Lieutenant Governor of Virginia, 1758–1768*. Vol. 2, *1761–1763*. University of Virginia, Charlottesville.
1983   *Official Papers of Francis Fauquier, Lieutenant Governor of Virginia, 1758–1768*. Vol. 3, *1764–1768*. University of Virginia, Charlottesville.
Richter, Daniel K.
1982   Rediscovered Links in the Covenant Chain: Previously Unpublished Transcripts of New York Indian Treaty Minutes. *Proceedings of the American Antiquarian Society* 29(1):45–85.
Robert, Jean-Claude (editor)
1994   *Atlas Historique de Montreal*. Libre Expression, Outremont, Québec.
Robinson, Kenneth, and William Terrell
2006   *Revisiting Fort Dobbs: A North Carolina French and Indian War Site 2006 Archaeological Excavations*. Report on file, Wake Forest University Archaeology Laboratories, Winston-Salem, NC.
Robinson, Willard B.
1977   *American Forts: Architectural Form and Function*. University of Illinois Press, Urbana.
Rockwell, E. F.
1876   Iredell County: Historical Address Delivered by Rev. E. F. Rockwell in Statesville on the 4th Day of July, 1876. *Landmark*, 11 July 1876, Statesville, NC.
Rocque, Mary Ann
1765   *A Set of Plans and Forts in America Reduced from Actual Surveys*. London.
Roenke, Karl
1979   Field Report on the 1979 Archaeological Excavations at Crown Point State Historic Site (Fort St. Frédéric), Town of Crown Point, Essex County, New York. Manuscript on file, New York State Office of Parks, Recreation and Historic Preservation, Waterford, NY.
Rogers, Col. H. C. B.
1975   *A History of Artillery*. Citadel Press, Secaucus, NJ.

Rogers, Robert
1961   *Journals of Major Robert Rogers.* Corinth Books, New York.
Roth, Rodis
1961   *Tea Drinking in 18th-Century America: Its Etiquette and Equipage.* Contributions from the Museum of History and Technology 14. Smithsonian Institution, Washington, DC.
Rothrock, George A. (translator)
1968   *A Manuel of Siegecraft and Fortification by Sebastien le Prestre de Vauban.* University of Michigan Press, Ann Arbor.
Roy, Pierre Georges
1946   *Hommes et choses du Fort Saint-Frédéric.* Editions des Dix, Montréal.
Sammons, Lena Gardner
1966   Fort Vause: The Site and the Story. *Journal of the Roanoke Historical Society* 2(2):23–33.
Saunders, William L., and Josephus Daniels (editors)
1886–90   *The Colonial Records of North Carolina.* 10 vols. P. M. Hale, State Printer, Raleigh.
Schuyler, Robert L.
1978   *Historical Archaeology: A Guide to Substantive and Theoretical Contributions.* Baywood, Farmingdale, NY.
Schwartz, Seymour I.
1994   *The French and Indian War, 1754–1763: The Imperial Struggle for North America.* Simon and Schuster, New York.
Scottish Records Office
n.d.   Monthly return for the regiment commanded by Colonel George Washington, 1 March 1758, GD45/2/83. Scottish Records Office Offprint 3, Scottish Records Office, Edinburgh.
Selesky, Harold
1990   *War and Society in Colonial Connecticut.* Yale University Press, New Haven.
Shaw, Lachlan
1757   Shaw to Governor Lyttelton, 19 October. Lyttelton Papers, box 6.
Sheldon, Helen
2007   *Stages 2 & 3 Archaeological Assessment Place d'Armes Re-alignment Kingston, Ontario.* Report to the City of Kingston from the Cataraqui Archaeological Research Foundation, Kingston, Ont.
Simes, Thomas, Esq.
1768   *Military Medley.* London.
Skaggs, David Curtis, and Larry Lee Nelson (editors)
2001   *The Sixty Years' War for the Great Lakes, 1754–1814.* Michigan State University Press, Lansing.
Smith, Arthur Britton (editor)
1987   *Kingston! Oh Kingston!* Kingston, Ont.
Smith, George
1779   *An Universal Military Dictionary.* J. Millan, London. Reprinted in 1969 by Museum Restoration Service, Ottawa.
Smith, Samuel D., and Benjamin C. Nance
2000   *An Archaeological Interpretation of the Site of Fort Blount, a 1790s Territorial Militia*

and Federal Military Post, Jackson County, TN. Tennessee Department of Environment and Conservation, Division of Archaeology, Research Series 12. Nashville.

Snyder, Louis Leo, and Ida Mae Brown
1968   *Frederick the Great: Prussian Warrior and Statesman.* F. Watts, New York.

Soldier
1756   Account of anonymous soldier. British Public Records Office 27:312.

South Carolina Gazette
1760   Soldier's letter, September 20–27.

South, Stanley
1964   Analysis of Buttons from Brunswick Town and Fort Fisher. *Florida Anthropologist* 17:113–33.
1977a *Method and Theory in Historical Archeology.* Academic Press, New York.
1977b *Research Strategies in Historical Archeology.* Academic Press, New York.

St. George, Robert Blair
1990   Bawns and Beliefs. *Winterthur Portfolio* 24(5): 241–87.

Stacey, C. P.
1959   *Québec, 1759: The Siege and the Battle.* Macmillan, Toronto.

Starbuck, David R.
1999   *The Great Warpath: British Military Sites from Albany to Crown Point.* University Press of New England, Hanover, NH.
2002   *Massacre at Fort William Henry.* University Press of New England, Hanover, NH.

Statement of Provisions
1723   Statement of Provisions, Munitions, and Trade Goods Which Have Been Traded at Fort Frontenac, at Niagara at the Head of Lake Ontario, and at the Bay of Quinte during the Years 1722 and 1723. Library and Archives Canada, C11A 45, pp. 195–202. In *Royal Fort Frontenac,* edited by Preston and Lamontagne, pp. 211–14.

Steele, Ian K.
1990   Betrayals: Fort William Henry and the "Massacre." Oxford University Press, New York.

Stell, G.
1973   Highland Garrisons, 1717–1723, Bernera Barracks. *Post-Medieval Archaeology* 7: 20–30.

Stephen, Adam
1749–1849   Papers. Library of Congress Archival Manuscript Material, Washington, DC.

Stephenson, R. Scott
1995   Pennsylvania Provincial Soldiers in the Seven Years' War. *Pennsylvania History* 62(2): 196–212.
2006   *Clash of Empires: The British, French & Indian War, 1754–1763.* Senator John Heinz Pittsburgh Regional History Center, Pittsburgh.

Stevens, S. K., Donald H. Kent, and Autumn L. Leonard (editors)
1951   The Forbes Expedition. In *Papers of Henry Bouquet,* vol. 2. Pennsylvania Historical and Museum Commission, Harrisburg.

Stewart, W. Bruce
1985   The Structural Evolution of Fort Frontenac. *Northeast Historical Archaeology* 14:38–49.

Stone, Garry W.
1974 Garry Stone to Larry Babits, 12 November. Manuscript on file, Office of State Archaeology, Raleigh, NC.

Stone, Lyle M.
1974 *Fort Michilimackinac, 1715–1781: An Archaeological Perspective on the Revolutionary Frontier.* Anthropological Series, vol. 2. Michigan State University, East Lansing (in cooperation with Mackinac Island State Park Commission).

Stotz, Charles M.
1974 The Reconstruction of Fort Ligonier: The Anatomy of a Frontier Fort. *Bulletin of the Association for Preservation Technology* 6(4): 1–104.
1985 *Outposts of the War for Empire.* University of Pittsburgh Press, Pittsburgh.

Strach, Stephen G.
1982 Letter to Paul Huey, 15 November. Manuscript on file, New York State Office of Parks, Recreation and Historic Preservation, Waterford, NY.

Surrey, Nancy M. Miller
1916 *The Commerce of Louisiana during the French Regime, 1699–1763.* Columbia University Press, New York.

Swanson, Neil H.
1937 *The First Rebel.* Farrar and Rinehart, New York.

Thackeray, William Makepeace
1898 *The Memoirs of Barry Lyndon, Esq., Written by Himself.* In *The Works of William Makepeace Thackeray, with Biographical Introductions by His Daughter, Anne Ritchie,* 4:56–57. Harper and Brothers, New York.

Thomas, Daniel H.
1929 Fort Toulouse and Its Subsequent History. Master's thesis, University of Alabama, Tuscaloosa.
1959 Fort Toulouse in Tradition and Fact. *Alabama Review* 12(4): 248–54.
1960a Fort Toulouse in Tradition and Fact. *Alabama Review* 13(4): 243–57.
1960b Fort Toulouse: The French Outpost at the Alibamos on the Coosa. *Alabama Historical Quarterly* 22(3): 135–230.

Thorpe, F. J.
1974 Louis Franquet. In *Dictionary of Canadian Biography,* vol. 2, edited by Frances G. Halpenny, Jean Hamelin, and Ramsay Cook. University of Toronto Press, Toronto.

Thwaites, Reuben Gold (editor)
1888–1911 *Wisconsin Historical Collections.* 20 vols. State Historical Society of Wisconsin, Madison.
1959 *The Jesuit Relations and Allied Documents: Travels and Explorations of the Jesuit Missionaries in New France, 1610–1791.* Vol. 55, *Lower Canada, Iroquois, Ottawas, 1670–1672.* Pageant Book, New York.

Tinling, Marion (editor)
1977 *The Correspondence of the Three William Byrds of Westover, Virginia, 1684–1776.* Vol. 2. University of Virginia, Charlottesville.

Titus, Timothy D.
1981 *Crown Point State Historic Site: An Historical Introduction.* Crown Point State His-

toric Site, Bureau of Historic Sites, New York State Office of Parks, Recreation and Historic Preservation, Crown Point.

Todish, Tim
2002 *America's First First World War: The French and Indian War, 1754–1763*. Purple Mountain Press, Fleischmanns, NY.

Tordoff, Judith Dunn
1983 An Archaeological Perspective on the Organization of the Fur Trade in Eighteenth-Century New France. PhD dissertation, Michigan State University, Lansing.

Trudel, Marcel
1968 *Introduction to New France*. Holt, Rinehart and Winston of Canada, Toronto.

Unidentified
1696 Relation of the Most Remarkable Events Which Happened in Canada from the Departure of the Vessels of 1695 to the Commencement of November 1696. Library and Archives Canada, C11A 14, pp. 38–94. In *Royal Fort Frontenac*, edited by Preston and Lamontagne, pp. 195–96.

Vachon, André
1982 *Taking Root: Canada from 1700 to 1760*. Canadian Government Publishing Centre, Ottawa.

Vauban, Sébastien le Prestre de
1968 *A Manual of Siegecraft and Fortification by Sebastien Le Prestre de Vauban*, translated by George A. Rothrock. University of Michigan Press, Ann Arbor.

Viger, Jacques
1895 Reminiscences of the War of 1812–14. Translated by J. L. Hubert Neilson, M.D., Kingston. In *Kingston! Oh Kingston!* edited by A. B. Smith, pp. 186–91.

Waddell, Alfred M.
1890 *A Colonial Officer and His Times, 1754–1773*. Edwards and Broughton, Raleigh, NC.

Waddell, Hugh
1760 Hugh Waddell to Arthur Dobbs, 1 March. In *Colonial Records of North Carolina*, vol. 6, edited by Saunders and Daniels, p. 229.

Waddell, Louis M.
1995 Defending the Long Perimeter: Forts on the Pennsylvania, Maryland, and Virginia Frontier, 1755–1765. *Pennsylvania History* 62(2):171–95.

Waddell, Louis M., and Bruce D. Bomberger
1996 *The French and Indian War in Pennsylvania, 1753–1763: Fortification and Struggle during the War for Empire*. Pennsylvania Historical and Museum Commission, Harrisburg.

Waddell, Louis M., John L. Tottenham, and Donald H. Kent (editors)
1978 *Papers of Henry Bouquet*. Vol. 4, *September 1, 1759–August 31, 1760*. Pennsylvania Historical and Museum Commission, Harrisburg.

Wade, Mason (editor)
1947 *The Journals of Francis Parkman*. 2 vols. Harper, New York.

Ward, Harry M.

1989 *Major General Adam Stephen and the Cause of American Liberty.* University Press of Virginia, Charlottesville.

Ward, Matthew C.
2003 *Breaking the Backcountry: The Seven Years' War in Virginia and Pennsylvania, 1754–1765.* University of Pittsburgh Press, Pittsburgh.

Warfel, Stephen G.
1980 Excavations at Fort Loudoun: The Archaeology of a Provincial Fort on the Pennsylvania Frontier. Manuscript on file, Section of Archaeology, State Museum of Pennsylvania, Harrisburg.
1981 Archaeology at Fort Loudoun (36Fr107): The 1981 Field Season. Manuscript on file, Section of Archaeology, State Museum of Pennsylvania, Harrisburg.

Waselkov, Gregory A.
1984 *Fort Toulouse Studies.* Auburn University Archaeological Monograph 9. Auburn University, Montgomery, AL.

Waselkov, Gregory A., Brian M. Wood, and Joseph M. Herbert
1982 *Colonization and Conquest: The 1980 Archaeological Excavations at Fort Toulouse and Fort Jackson, Alabama.* Auburn University Archaeological Monograph 4. Auburn University, Montgomery, AL.

Washington, George
1741–99 Papers, series 4, General Correspondence. Library of Congress, Washington, DC.

Webster, Eleanor M.
1964 Insurrection at Fort Loudoun in 1765. *Western Pennsylvania Historical Magazine* 47(2):125–40.

Webster, Gary S.
1982 An Analysis of Faunal Materials from the Well at Fort Loudoun, Penna. Manuscript on file, Section of Archaeology, State Museum of Pennsylvania, Harrisburg.

Weiderhold, Andreas
1777 A Plan of the Small Town of Winchester. Special Collections Department, University Libraries, University of Pennsylvania, Philadelphia.

Wells, Louise
n.d. The Voss Family of Virginia. Typescript on file, Virginia Department of Historic Resources, Richmond.

Williams, Samuel Cole
1948 *The Memoirs of Lieut. Henry Timberlake, 1756–1765.* Continental Book Company, Marietta, GA. Originally published in 1927 by Watauga Press, Johnson City, TN.

Wraxall, Peter
1915 *An Abridgment of the Indian Affairs.* Edited by Charles Howard McIlwain. Harvard University Press, Cambridge.

Young, Richard J.
1979 *Blockhouses in Canada, 1749–1841: A Comparative Report and Catalogue.* Canadian Historic Sites Occasional Papers in Archaeology and History 23. Minister of Supply and Services, Québec.

Zipperer, Sandra J.
1999 Sieur Charles Michel de Langlade: Lost Cause, Lost Culture. *Voyageur: Historical Review of Brown County and Northeast Wisconsin* (Winter/Spring). Accessed at www.uwgb.edu/wisfrench/library/articles/langlade, December 12, 2006.

Contributors

Lawrence E. Babits is now retired. In an earlier life, he was director of the Program in Maritime Studies, East Carolina University. He is still active in a variety of archaeological and historical teaching and research endeavors and writes extensively on eighteenth- and nineteenth-century military topics when not shooting period weapons or playing rugby.

Susan M. Bazely is a consulting archaeologist in Kingston, Ontario. As senior archaeologist with the Cataraqui Archaeological Research Foundation for 28 years, she directed investigations at the Fort Frontenac National Historic Site of Canada and other Kingston military sites, including the Royal Naval Dockyard and Fort Henry Garrison Hospital, both also national historic sites and part of the Rideau Canal World Heritage Site. She is author of *Fort Frontenac: A French Stronghold on the Great Lakes* and *Fort Frontenac: Bastion of the British* and editor of *Fields of Fire: Fortified Works of Kingston Harbour*.

Lynn L. M. Evans is curator of archaeology for Mackinac State Historic Parks, a position she has held since 1996. She began excavating at Michilimackinac in 1989. She holds a BA in anthropology and museum studies from Beloit College and a PhD in American civilization and historical archaeology from the University of Pennsylvania.

Charles L. Fisher was born in 1949 in Champaign, Illinois. He attended the State University of New York at New Paltz as an undergraduate and received his PhD in anthropology in 1983 from the University at Albany. From 1981 until 1995 he worked as an archaeologist in the Bureau of Historic Sites of the New York State Office of Parks, Recreation and Historic Preservation, the agency which administers the Crown Point State Historic Site. From 1995 until his death in 2007 from melanoma, he served as the first curator of historical archaeology at the New York State Museum. He edited *"The Most Advantageous Situation in the Highlands": An Archaeological Study of Fort Montgomery State Historic Site* (2004) and *People, Places, and Material Things: Historical Archaeology of Albany, New York* (2003), plus *Nineteenth- and Early Twentieth-Century Domestic Site Archaeology in New York State* (2000), which he coedited with John P. Hart.

Stephanie Gandulla is a maritime archaeologist and media coordinator at Thunder Bay National Marine Sanctuary.

James L. Hart is a writer and researcher affiliated with Archaeological Research, Inc. His interests include fortifications of the early modern period, the history of French and British colonial America, and the American Civil War. He is translating journals and inspection reports on the defenses of New France just before the French and Indian War. He lives in Baltimore.

Paul R. Huey, now retired, developed and directed the archaeology program of the Bureau of Historic Sites in the New York State Office of Parks, Recreation and Historic Preservation for more than 40 years. He instituted a program of research and resource management for the archaeological resources for which his agency is responsible. His research has focused on the Dutch of seventeenth-century New Netherland and the French and English of late seventeenth- and eighteenth-century New York, while his interests also extend through the nineteenth century to the early twentieth century.

Robert L. Jolley is a regional archaeologist for the Commonwealth of Virginia's Department of Historic Resources. He received his MA in anthropology from Vanderbilt University. He has published reports of investigations on military sites dating from the French and Indian War to the Civil War.

David J. Keene is founder and president of Archaeological Research, Inc., with offices in Illinois and Wisconsin. He first became interested in eighteenth-century fortifications while working on French colonial sites in Illinois.

Carl Kuttruff is adjunct assistant professor at Louisiana State University and works as an independent archaeologist and researcher. He is actively involved in a number of prehistoric and historic archaeological projects and has a wide range of research interests and experience, including military sites and battlefield archaeology.

Kim A. McBride is codirector of the Kentucky Archaeological Survey. She has a BA in anthropology from Beloit College and an MA and PhD in anthropology from Michigan State University. She has directed historical research and archaeological excavations on a number of sites, including many frontier forts.

W. Stephen McBride is director of interpretation and archaeology at Camp Nelson Civil War Heritage Park and manager of McBride Preservation Services, LLC. His main interest is military archaeology, and he has conducted extensive historical and archaeological research on French and Indian War, Revolutionary War, and Civil War sites.

R. Scott Stephenson is director of collections and interpretation for the American Revolution Center (www.americanrevolutioncenter.org). He received his MA and PhD in American history from the University of Virginia and was curator of the international traveling exhibition "Clash of Empires: The British, French, and Indian War, 1754–1763."

Stephen G. Warfel has conducted archaeological investigations on prehistoric and historic sites for the past forty years. He was the State Museum of Pennsylvania's senior curator of archaeology from 1980 until retirement in June 2007. Warfel recently assisted the Shippensburg Historical Society with the discovery of Fort Morris, a French and Indian War fort site in Shippensburg, Pennsylvania.

Marshall W. Williams, retired now for many years, worked as a volunteer on many archaeological projects with both the University of Georgia and the University of South Carolina.

Index

Page numbers in italics refer to illustrations (i) or tables (t).

Abatis: at Fort Dobbs, *90i*, 90–93, 101, 248; at Fort Loudoun (Tenn.), 77; at Fort Loudoun (Va.), 119
Abenaki, 13
Abercromby, James (British gen.), 15
Algonquian, 14
Allegheny Mountains, 11, 123, 227
Allegheny River, 11, 13, 232
Allegheny uprising, 161, 162
Allegheny Uprising (movie), 158, 161–62
American Revolution, 1, 10; first act of, 158, 161; and Fort Michilimackinac, end of, 228; "way of war" and, 1, 50
Amherst, Jeffrey (British Gen.), 49–50, 176; and Crown Point, taking of, 15, 185; and Louisbourg, attack on, 51
Ammunition, 249
—musket balls: commonalties across forts, 249; at Fort Dobbs, 97, 100; at Fort Frontenac, 199, 210; at Fort Ligonier, 100; at Fort Loudoun (Pa.), 163, 172; at Fort Loudoun (Tenn.), 99; at Fort Loudoun (Va.), 106, 114; at Fort Prince George, 57, 59; at Fort Vause, 136
—rifle balls, 249; at Fort Dobbs, 100
—buckshot/birdshot, 249; at Fort Frontenac, 199; at Fort Loudoun (Pa.), 161, 172; at Fort Loudoun (Va.), 114; at Fort Vause, 136
—grape shot, 249; at Fort Loudoun (Va.), 106, 116, 249

—solid shot, 106; at Fort Frontenac, 214; at Fort Loudoun (Va.), 116
Arbuckle's. *See* Fort Arbuckle
Architecture Hydraulique L'Art de Conduire (Bélidor), 19
Armstrong, John (Pa. col.), 159–61, 163, 167–68; fort design, familiarity with, 172, 244
—and Fort Loudoun (Pa.): rats at, 161; rebuilding of, 167, 171; reports on, 163, 169; site selection of, 159
Artifact patterns: archaeological, 5, 117–18, 249
—CAP (Carolina Artifact Pattern), 5, 78, 250–53, *251t*; at Fort Loudoun (Tenn.), 78, 242; at Fort Prince George, 79
—FAP (Frontier Artifact Pattern), 5, *77i*, 77, 250–52, *252t*; at Fort Dobbs, 78, *81t*, 252, *252t* ; at Fort Ligonier, 78, *81t*, *118t*; *252t*; at Fort Loudoun (Tenn.), 78–83, *80t*, *118t*, 242; at Fort Loudoun (Va.), 78, *81t*, 118, *118t*; *252t*; at Fort Prince George, 78–79, *80t*, *118t*, *252t*
Artillery, 22, 24, 26, 37–38, 40; and defense in depth, 37, *39i*, 39
—siege cannon, 47, 50; at Fort Chambly, 44, 48; at Fort des Chartres, 230; at Fort Frontenac, 206; at Fort Michilimackinac, 230; at Fort St. Frederic, 47–48, 179, 183
—swivel guns, at Fort Dobbs, 85; at Fort Loudoun (Tenn.), 76; at Fort Loudoun

(Va.), 105–6, 116; at Fort Prince George, 55–57, 67; at Fort St. Frederic, 6, 178–79, 181, 183, 187
Ashby's. *See* Fort Ashby
Augusta Courthouse (Va.), 126–27; Council of War at, 125

Backcountry, 11–13, 107–9, 256
Baillie, Alexander (Lt., 42nd Foot), 169
Banquet: at Fort des Chartres, 235, 237; at Fort Prince George, 54–55, 67
Barracks, 85; at Fort des Chartres, 230; at Fort Dobbs, 84–85, 100–101, 248; at Fort Frontenac, 196, 198, 200–201, 213–14; at Fort Loudoun (Pa.), 160, 168–69; at Fort Loudoun (Tenn.), 70, 74, 76; at Fort Loudoun (Va.), 103–6, 111–12, 116, 119–20; at Fort Michilimackinac, 227; at Fort Prince George, 56–59, 61–63 65–66; at Fort St. Frederic, 41–42, 48, 182; at Fort Stanwix, 116; Ruthven Barracks, 98–99
Bastion, 22, 24–28, 32–34, 35, 37, 86; dead space covered by, 25; flankers compared to, 86; systems, 23; towers replaced by, 24
—construction and design, 24–36; cannon mounted in, 76, 103, 105, 109; at Crown Point, 7; earth-filled crib construction, 6, 110; at Edwards's Fort, 147–48, 150–51, 244; elevated, 70, 73–75, 244; flat, 34, 43, 45, 183; at Fort Chambly, 43; at Fort des Chartres, 230, 235, 237; at Fort Frontenac, 187, 191, 194, 202, 205, 210–11, 214; at Fort Loudoun (Pa.), 160, 163, 166, 172; four-bastion forts, Washington's plans for, 144, 151, 244; hewn log instead of stockade, ordered by Washington, 151; at Montreal, *46i*; reconstructed, 7
—with gun platform, 60–61, 67; extant, 130; at Fort St. Frederic, 177, 179, 182–83; at Fort Vause, 125–26, 133, 135, 138, 247
—stone, 104, 119, 195–96, 206; at Fort Michilimackinac, 219–20; at Montreal, 43; at Fort Prince George, 54–57, 63, 65
Bayonet, 15, 87; at Fort Dobbs, 99; at Fort Loudoun (Va.), 107, 116–17; scabbard finials at Fort Dobbs, 99
Beads: at Fort des Chartres, 233; in Fort Frontenac burials, 208; at Fort Loudoun (Va.), 117, 120; at Fort Michilimackinac, 233; at Fort Ouiatenon, 233; at Fort Frontenac, 199, 203, 208; rosary, at Fort Frontenac, 199, 202
Beef: cattle at French and Indian War forts, 155, 248; at Edwards's Fort, 142, 155–56; at Fort Cumberland, 142; at Fort Loudoun (Pa.), 172; at Fort Loudoun (Tenn.), *75i*, 77, 82; at Fort Loudoun (Va.), 108; as rations, 108
Belestre, Francois-Marie Picot de, 124
Bélidor, Bernard Forest de (engineer), 19–20, 38; dictionary by, 47; on flanking defense, 22; on machicoulis, 47; manual by, 19
Bienville, Jean-Baptiste Le Moyne de, 231
Blockhouse, 140, 248; corner, at Fort Loudoun (Pa.), 247; with flankers, ditches, and palisade known, 248; at Fort Dobbs, 92, 96; possible, at Edwards's Fort, 151; at Saratoga, 188; Tellico, 72
Bonin, Charles (French marine), 222
Bougainville, Louis Antoine de, 50, 183
Bouquet, Henry (British col., 60th Foot), 106, 108, 160
Braddock, Edward (British gen.), 11, 15; campaign, 15, 172; defeat, 5, 12–13, 139, 243; and Fort Michilimackinac, 226
Brown, Francis, 85–86
Brunswick Pattern of Refuse Disposal: at Fort Loudoun (Tenn.), 77, 242
Buade, Louis de. *See* Frontenac, Louis de Buade, Comte de
Bullets. *See* Ammunition
Bullitt, Thomas, 128, 136
Burgoyne, John (British gen.), 174
Bushy Run, Battle of, 161
Buttons, 233, 248; at Edwards's Fort, 150,

154; at Fort des Chartres, 233; at Fort Loudoun (Pa.), 169; at Fort Loudoun (Va.), 115; at Fort Michilimackinac, 233; at Fort Ouiatenon, 233; at Fort Prince George, 59.
— "PN" buttons, 249–50; at Fort Dobbs, 99; at Fort Ligonier, 99; at Fort Loudoun (Pa.), 168; at Fort Loudoun (Tenn.), 99; at Fort Loudoun (Va.), 163; at Fort Stanwix, 99

Byrd, William, III, 102; 1st Va. Regt., offered command of, 108; Fort Loudoun, commander of, 106; 2nd Virginia Regt., commander of, 107, 144

Campbell, John (commander at Detroit), 225
Campbell, John, Earl of Loudoun, 15, 102, 159
Campbell's place. *See* Fort Campbell
Carolina Artifact Pattern. *See* Artifact patterns, CAP
Caswell, Richard, 85–86
Cataraqui River, 199; fine harbor, 193; settlement at, 199, 215
Catawba, 11, 13; at Fort Loudoun (Va.), 107
Cellar: at Fort Loudoun (Pa.), 160, 163, 167–68, 171–72; at Fort Prince George, 59, 61, 65; Fort St. Frederic, 178
—at Fort Dobbs, 92–95; post mold in, 96–98; artifact distribution in, 99–101
—at Edwards's Fort, 145–46, 148, 152; possible hut floors, 155–56; root, 147
Ceramics: at Fort Loudoun (Va.), 113; Cherokee, 76, 78; militia forts, low counts at, 152; social distinctions, as expression of, 248
Chain of forts (Va.), 122, 125
Charlevoix, Pierre de, 187–88, 193
Cherokee, 11, 13, 52, 54, 58, 69, 120, 242; ceramics, 76–82, 252; at Fort Loudoun (Va.), 107–8; Fort Prince George, attack on, 57; structures at Fort Loudoun (Tenn.), *71i*, 74
—Ceramics, 76, 78; at Fort Loudoun (Tenn.), *75i*, 79, 81; at Fort Loudoun (Va.), 120; at Fort Prince George, 79; at Fort Frontenac, 199
—Overhill Cherokee, 5, 69–70, 108, 242; siege of Forts Prince George and Loudoun (Tenn.), 70, 72–73, 78, 102, 243

Cloyd's. *See* Fort Cloyd
Cocke's. *See* Fort Cocke
Coehoorn, Menno van, 19
Coins, 233; at Fort Loudoun (Pa.), 168
Colono-ware: at Fort Prince George, 79
Combes, John, 58, 63
Conococheague Valley, 159; Indian raid on, 159, 168; residents object to military control, 161; uprising, 161
Counterscarp: at Fort Dobbs, 88, 91–92; at Fort Loudoun (Tenn.), 77
Covered way, 248; at Edwards's fort, 147–48; at Fort St. Frederic, 177, 185
Coytmore, Richard (British lt.): ambush and death of, 57; Fort Prince George, commander of, 57, 67–68; grave of, 61
Creamware: absence of, 154–55; Cresset, at Fort Dobbs, 97, 101; at Edwards's Fort, 148, 150, 152
Crown Point, N.Y., 6, 15, 174, *175i*, *176i*; capture by British, 15, 185; forts at, 176–77; French at, 176, 178–79, *180i*, 181. *See also* Fort Crown Point
Cumberland, Md. *See* Wills Creek
Curtain (fort wall), 26–29, 247; design of, 34–38, 45; at Edwards's Fort, 147–48; at Fort des Chartres, 230, 235, 237; at Fort Dobbs, 99; at Fort Frontenac, 7, 191, 194, 198–200, 202–3, 205–6, 210–11, 213–14; at Fort St. Frederic, 43, 47; at Fort Vause, 126, 133, 138; terrain's influence on, 46
—Stone curtain, 196; earth-holding cribs, built with, 105; at Fort Loudoun (Pa.), 166; at Fort Loudoun (Tenn.), *71i*, 73, 75; at Fort Loudoun (Va.), 103, 105–6, 111; at Fort Michilimackinac, 220; at Fort Prince George, 55, 57, 61, 66–67, 73

Dahlbergh, Erik, 178
Dead space, 4, 246; eliminated by, 25, *29i*; at square towers, *24i*, 24–25
de Brahm, John William Gerard (engineer), 70
Deer: at Edwards's Fort, 155–56; at Fort Ligonier, 171; at Fort Loudoun (Pa.), 171; at Fort Loudoun (Va.), 117
Deetz, James, 86
Defense: convoy, 143; in depth, 21, 37, *39i*, 187, 242, 248; flanking, 21–24, 43; in height, 21, *23i*, 37; incorporating existing buildings into, 244; local, 125, 145; siting for defensive purpose, 123; towers, 178; ultimate (citadel), 181
de Fer, Nicolas (French cartographer), 19, 23
Delaware, at Kittanning, 13
Delft: at Edwards's Fort, 148–50, 152, 154–55; at Fort Loudoun (Tenn.), 113; at Fort Loudoun (Va.), 113
Demere, Paul, 70
Demere, Raymond, 54–55, 70
Denonville, Jacques Rene de Brisay de (Canadian gov.), 196, 199; and Fort Frontenac, destruction of, 198–99
Detroit, 202, 217, 225; Pontiac's War, not captured in, 227
Diderot's *Encyclopedia*, 20
Dinwiddie, Lt. Gov. Robert (Va.), 11, 106–7; on Edwards's Fort, 143–44; and Fauquier, replaced by, 198; Fort Cumberland, orders troops to, 139; on Fort Loudoun, 104–7; on Fort Vause, 126–29
Ditch, 38; at Fort Dobbs, 87–88, *89i*, *90i*; at Fort Frontenac, 199, 211; at Fort Loudoun (Tenn.), 70, 73, 75; at Fort Loudoun (Va.), 105, 111–12; at Fort Prince George, 54, 67; at Fort St. Frederic, 177, 179, 182. *See also* Fosse
Dobbs, Gov. Arthur (N.C.), 84–85, 243
Drains and drainage, 241, 245, 248; at Fort des Chartres, 237; at Fort Dobbs, 92; at Fort Loudoun (Pa.), 168, 170–71; at Fort Loudoun (Tenn.), 76; at Fort Loudoun (Va.), 112, 119; at Fort Prince George, 60; at Fort St. Frederic, 182
Dunmore's War, 144, 150

Earthenware: at Edwards's Fort, 153; at Fort Frontenac, 207; at Fort Loudoun (Va.), 113; at Fort Prince George, 80
Edwards's Fort, 5–6; abandonment, 144; archaeology, 145–56, *146i*, *153i*; artifacts from, *149t*, *154i*; as base for rangers, 143; battle near, 141–42; buildings at, 145, 152; ceramics at, 150, 152; characteristics of, academic and vernacular, 244; defenses of, 140, 145; Edwards family and, 156; Henry Harrison to command, 142; history of, 139–44; huts at, semi-subterranean, 154; location of, between Winchester and Cumberland, 142; metal detection at, 145; militia posted at, 143; as rangers' retreat, 141; rations at, 142; stockade at, *146i*, 147, 153; as supply point, Forbes Expedition, 144; Va. Regt. garrisons, 152
Élémens de fortification (Le Blond), 19, 31
Element de fortification (Le Blond?), 20
Elites (social), 5, 8, 91, 187, 244, 246; at Fort Dobbs, 248; at Fort Loudoun (Pa.), 248; at Fort Loudoun (Tenn.), 82; at Fort Loudoun (Va.), 110, 119; at Fort St. Frederic, 187; and private forts, building of, 244, 246
Elk, at Fort Loudoun (Pa.), 171
Engineering manuals, 19–22, 39–40, 237; at Fort Michilimackinac, 218–19, 225
Engineers, 4, 22, 32, 37–38, 49, 241–42
—British, 242; at Crown Point, 186–87; and Fort Frederick, design of, 246; at Fort Loudoun (Tenn.), 70; at Fort Michilimackinac, 225; and Fort William Henry, layout of, 15
—French, 17–20, 47, 186–87, 245; at Fort des Chartres, 235, 237; fort evaluations of, 48; at Fort Frontenac, 196,

204–5, 209, 214; at Fort St. Frederic, *42i*, 186–87; at Ile aux Noix, 241
Enoch's. *See* Fort Enoch

Fairfax, Gov. William (Va.), 104–5, 116
Fauna: at Edwards's Fort, 155–56; at Fort Dobbs, 91; at Fort Loudoun (Pa.), 171–72; at Fort Loudoun (Tenn.), 76–77; at Fort Loudoun (Va.), 117, 120
Fauquier, Lt. Gov. Francis (Va.): replaces Gov. Dinwiddie, 108; on Fort Loudoun (Va.), 108; during Pontiac's War, 109; disbands Va. Regt., 109
Fish: at Fort des Chartres, 233; at Fort Frontenac, 208; at Fort Loudoun (Va.), 117; at Fort Michilimackinac, 222; at Straits of Mackinac, 216
Flanking: angles (interior), 33, 43; defense, 21–25, 37, 43, 45; fire, 26, 196, 206, 220, 241; at Fort Dobbs, 86, 93, 101, 248; at Fort Frontenac, 194, 196, 210; at Fort Michilimackinac, 220; at Fort Vause, 126; at Fort St. Frederic, 183; and protective fire, 246; at Ruthven, 99; theories of, 21–36
Forbes, John (British gen.), 12, 107, 160, 172
Forbes Expedition, 6, 12, 91, 102, 106–7, 144, 158, 160, 243; Fort Duquesne, French forced from, 161; and Indian allies, 107; Virginia troops detached to, 129
Forks of the Ohio, 10–11
Fort Allen, Pa., 151; designed by Franklin, 151; redans at, *151t*, 151
Fort Amsterdam, N.Y., 186
Fort Arbuckle (Va.), 248; occupied by militia, 152; west of settled area, 157
Fort Ashby (Va.), 139, 141, 155; occupied by militia and rangers, 152, 248; west of settled area, 157
Fort Beausejour (N.S.), 15, 18
Fort Bull (N.Y.), 3
Fort Campbell (Va.), 50, 128, 129
Fort Carillon (N.Y.), 15, 40, 244, 247;

attack on, 15; construction outmoded by Fort St. Frederic, 179; defended by Fort Michilimackinac Indians, 226; Fort Ticonderoga, built on same site as, 15. *See also* Fort Ticonderoga
Fort Chambly (P.Q.), 3, 41–43, 45; faced European armies, 49–51; Franquet's inspection of, 48; Franquet's plan of, 43, *44i*; made obsolete by Fort St. Frederic, 179
Fort Cloyd (Va.), 129
Fort Cocke (Va.), 139
Fort Crown Point (N.Y.), 6, 15, 182, 244, 245; adjacent to Fort St. Frederic site, 6–7; multiple occupations, 245; stone construction, 245
Fort Cumberland (Wills Creek, Md.), 105; Council of War and, 125; knowledge of, 151; rations at, 108, 142; Va. Regt, garrisoned by, 139
Fort de Buade, 217
Fort des Chartres (Ill.), 7, 229–40, *234i*; archaeology, 232–37; artifacts from, 232; buildings at, 230; ceramic use at, 235; compared to Fort Ouiatenon and Fort Michilimackinac, 230, 232, *233i*; curtain wall, 235, *236i*, *238i*; descriptions of first and second forts, 230; defenses of, 230, 232; as economic center, 234; and farming, 231; fur trade at, 229; garrison of, 230; history of, 229–32; magazine of, 230; 1754 completion, 232; stone, plans to convert to, 231, 245; three forts at site, 229
Fort Dobbs (N.C.), 5, 72; abatis as outer defense, *90i*, 248; archaeology, 87–98, *94i*; bastion ditch, 93, 96; buildings at, 93, 95–97, 101; defenses of, 87–93, 101; description, 86, *100i*; history of, 84–87; related to British forts in Scottish highlands, 243; tactical sophistication of, 243; well at, 97
Fort Duquesne (Pa.), 11–12, 15, 103, 160, 231; as base for Indian raids, 13; Gen.

Index · 295

296 · Index

Braddock's march against, 11, 15; British fort built on ruins of, 15, 108; capture of, 13, 108, 161; destruction of by garrison, 12, 144; Forbes expedition sent against, 6, 12, 102–3, 106–7, 160, 243; at Forks of the Ohio, 11–12; Va. troops sent to, 129

Fort Edwards (Va.). *See* Edwards's fort

Fort Enoch (Va.): as base for rangers, 143; and Va. Regt., 142; supply routes through, 143

Fort Frederick (Md.), 242; artifact patterns at, *118t*; ceramics similar to those at Fort Loudoun (Va.), 113; engineers on, 242, 246; stone construction, 246

Fort Frontenac (Ont.) 7, 16, 191–215, *192i*; archaeology, 196, *197i*, 199–200, 203, *207i*, 209, 211; artillery, poor condition of, 211; barracks described, 213–14; buildings at, 194, 196, 200, 202–3; burials at, 208; chapel, 200–203; curtain and bastion walls similar, 211, *212i*; defenses described, 194, *195i*, 196, *204i*, 206, 210–11; masonry facing of, 194–95; fur trade as reason for siting, 245; granted to La Salle, 193; history of, 191–206; and Iroquois control, 190; natural resources surrounding, 193; naval engagement near, 198; opposition to holding, 200; repairs, continual because of climate, 206; ship building at, 201–10; siege unreadiness of, 198; as supply depot, 209; three forts at site, 191; trade goods documented and found at, 203; and Vauban's defense theories, 196

Fort Gage (N.Y.), 3

Fortifications and forts: fort design, local knowledge of, 151; repeatedly built on same sites, 247; variations and irregularities due to frontier conditions, 172, 244; terrain-related variations, 4, 21, 29, *30i*, *31i*, 31–32, 33–34, 46, 49, 248; water passage and territorial control, built for by French, 186

Fort Le Boeuf (Pa.), 103

Fort Ligonier (Pa.), 3, 72, *73t*, 78–79, 119, 242; archaeology, 3, 120; butchering patterns at, 117, 171; ceramics similar to those at Fort Loudoun (Va.), 113, 248; iron shot similar to that at Fort Loudoun (Va.), 116; "PN" buttons found at, 99; shot similar to that at other forts, 100, 116, 249; size similar to that of Fort Loudoun (Va.), 119

Fort Loudoun (Pa.), 6, 72, *73t*, 108, 158–73, *159i*; archaeology, 162–72, *164i*; buildings at, 162, 167–69; defenses of, 164–68, *165i*, 172; history of, 159–62; reports on, 169; shot penetrates, 162

Fort Loudoun (Tenn.), 5, 69–83, *73t*, 102, 108; archaeology, *71i*, 74; buildings at, 74; and Cherokee, built for alliance with, 242; Cherokee buildings at, 74; defenses of, 73–76; history of, 69–72; refuse disposal at, 76–78; siege at, 70; surrender of, 70; uniqueness among forts, 72–74

Fort Loudoun (Va.), 6; archaeology, *110i*, *111i*, *112i*, 110–18; artifacts from, 113–17; artillery at, 116; buildings at, 104, 111; buttons found at, 115; ceramics, mean date for, 114; defenses of, 103, 110; description of, 105; designed by George Washington, 102, *103i*, 111, 243; Forbes Expedition, support base for, 243; Fort Loudoun (Tenn.), relief base for, 243; garrison of, 105–6, 109; history of, 102–10; stone bastion of, 119; Washington at, 103; Winchester, referred to as, 108, *109i*

Fort Lyttelton or Littleton (Va.) *See* Fort Vause

Fort Mackinac (Ont.): built on Mackinac Island, 228; Fort Michilimackinac settlement moved to, 228

Fort Massac (Ill.), 69

Fort Michilimackinac (Mich.), 3, 7, *73t*, 73, 216–28, *224i*, 242; archaeology, 219, *223i*, 225; artifacts compared with forts

Ouiateon and des Chartres, 232–33, 233i; buildings at, 219, 220, 226; buttons found at, 115; capture during Pontiac's War, 227; ceramics similar to those of Fort Loudoun (Tenn.), 113; defenses of, 219; Delignery's fort beneath, 218; ditches and earthworks, absence of, 219; engineers at, 242; expansion of, 225; fur trade, hub for, 228, 245; guard house at, 222; history of, 113, 218–26; row houses at, 218, 221i; as mission, 245; outwork (in front of gate), 219–20; pipe stem found at, dating of, 219; poor construction of, 218; second palisade (cedar), 219–20

Fort Necessity (Pa.), 3, 11, 232

Fort Niagara (N.Y.), 3, 12, 15, 16; attack resistance, 50; and Pontiac's War, not captured during, 227; as staging point for troops, 210; as supply destination for Fort Frontenac, 209;

Fort Ninety-Six (S.C.), 69

Fort Ontario (N.Y.), 242

Fort Oswego (N.Y.), 15; British reoccupation of, 16; Fort Frontenac, British march on from, 214; Fort Niagara, march on from, 16; Fort Michilimackinac garrison attacks, 226; falls to French and Indian siege, 16

Fort Ouiatenon (Ill.): archaeology, 233; artifacts compared to forts Des Chartres and Michilimackinac, 232–34, 233i; as fur trade outpost, 233; grain from Fort des Chartres to, 231; located on Wabash River, 233

Fort Pearsall (Va.): cattle and wagons moved to, 143; characterization as "useless," 143; and company from 2nd Va. Regt., 144

Fort Pitt (Pa.): earth and brick construction, 12; and Pontiac's War, not captured during, 227; Va. troops return from, 109

Fort Prince George (S.C.), 5, 52–69, 72, 73t, 88, 92, 242; archaeology, 58–68; buildings at, 56, 59, 61–66; defenses of, 54, 66–67; garrisoned by British regulars and S.C. provincials, 242; history of, 52–58; prisoners returned to, 72; trading post after military use, 242

Fort St. Frederic (N.Y.), 4, 6–7, 41, 42i, 43, 45, 174–90, 176i, 181i, 182i; abandonment by French, 185; archaeology, 185; barracks, absence of, 182; buildings at, 178–79, 181i, 187, 188i; citadel, British name for redoubt, 179i, 179; defense in depth, 37, 39i, 187, 178–80, 183; fatal flaws of, 182–85, 187; Franquet inspection of, 48, 183; history of, 174–81; moat with palisade, 185; outer walls, penetrability of, 181, 183, 186; parapets, weakness of, 185; plank roof of citadel, 183; raids based from, 187; redoubt, 47; Rogers spies on, 184i; stone construction of, 245; siege, vulnerability to, 50, 183, 185; water supply of, 183, 187; windmill at, 181, 182i, 182

Fort Stanwix (N.Y.), 3, 72, 73t; ceramics similar to those of Fort Loudoun (Va.), 113; shot similar to that at Fort Loudoun (Va.), 116

Fort Ticonderoga (N.Y.), 4, 244; archaeology, 3; built by British, 15; on same site as Fort Carillon, 15, 40, 247; stone construction, 247

Fort Toulouse (Ala.), 73t, archaeology, 3; French encroachments from, 5, 69

Fort Vause (Va.), 5–6; abandonment, 129; archaeology, 130, 131i, 133t, 134i, 135i; attack on, 124, 243; as block to key raiding route, 243; defenses of, 12, 125–26, 132i; description of, 125–26; earthen fortification at, 122; also called Fort Lyttelton (Littleton), 128; garrison at, 129; history of, 122–38; "very important," characterization as, 125

Fort Warwick (Va.), 248; militia occupation, 152

Fort William Henry (N.Y.): archaeology, 3; built by provincials, 15; captured by Montcalm, 15, 226; harassed by troops from Michilimackinac, 244
Fort Wood Creek (N.Y.), 183
Fosse, at Fort Dobbs, 85, 87–88, *90i*, 90–91, 98. *See also* Ditch; Moat
Fox Indians (Mesquakie), 217–18
Franklin, Benjamin: and Fort Allen, designer of, 151; on palisade post depths, 247; rise of, 1
Franquet, Louis (French engineer), 17–18; on American fortifications, 40, 46–49; Canadian defenses evaluated by, 20; at Fort Chambly, 41, 48; at Fort St. Frederic, 42i, 43, 47–48, 183, 185; illicit trade discovered by, 189; inspections conducted by, 41, 43; library of, 18; at Louisbourg, 18, 51; at Montreal 43, 46i, 48; at Quebec, 49
Frontenac, Louis de Buade, Comte de (Gov. Gen. of Canada), 177, 191, 199–200; builds fort on Lake Ontario, 191–92, 201
Frontier Artifact Pattern. *See* Artifact patterns, FAP

Garrison: militia, 226; British, 227; French, 226; paid in powder and shot, 222
Gate: at Edwards's Fort, 147; at Fort Dobbs, 99, 101; at Fort Frontenac, 199, 205, 211; at Fort Loudoun (Pa.), 163–64; at Fort Loudoun (Tenn.), 75–77; at Fort Loudoun (Va.), 103, 119; at Fort Michilimackinac, 225; at Fort Prince George, 55–56, 59, 61–62, 65, 67; at Fort St. Frederic, 183; at Montreal, 45
Georgian mindset, 86
Glacis, 38; blockhouses with, 248; at Fort des Chartres, 237; at Fort Dobbs, 85, 92; at Fort Frontenac, 211; with palisade at Fort St. Frederic, 185
Glass, 77
—bottle glass: at Edwards's Fort, 149–50, 153; at Fort Loudoun (Pa.), 168–69, 171; at Fort Loudoun (Va.), 113–14, 119–20; at Fort Vause, 136; at militia forts, low counts of, 249
—window glass, at Fort Loudoun (Va.), 114, 117
—jewelry, 115; at Fort Frontenac, 199, 203, 208
Glassie, Henry, 86
Glen, Gov. James (S.C.), 54–55, 66
Gordon, Capt. Harry (British engineer), 242; and Fort Michilimackinac, map of, 225
Grant, Lt. Charles: at Fort Loudoun (Pa.), 162; and Col. James, digs well with, 63, 68; and Fort Prince George, rebuilds, 58, 62–63, 65; report on Fort Loudoun (Pa.), 162
Grant, Charles (British lt.), at Fort Loudoun (Pa.), 162
Grant, James (British col.), at Fort Prince George, 58, 62–63, 65, 68
Grant, William (British Capt.): report on Fort Loudoun (Pa.), 162, 168
GreatLakes, *217i*
Great Meadows (Pa.). *See* Fort Necessity
Gunflint, 106: at Edwards's Fort, 149–50, 152–53; at Fort Frontenac, 199, 203, 207; at Fort Loudoun (Pa.), 163; at Fort Loudoun (Va.), 106, 114–15, 117; at Fort Vause, 136
Gun parts: at Fort Loudoun (Pa.), 163; at Fort Loudoun (Va.), 114–15; at Fort Prince George, 59
Gun powder, invention of, 24; at Fort Prince George, 63; at Fort Loudoun (Va.), 106; used to pay Fort Michilimackinac garrison, 222; as trade goods at Fort Frontenac, 203

Harrington, J. C., 3
Hogg, Peter (Va. capt.), 6, 129; building of Fort Vause, 125, 128; inventory of Fort Vause, 128, 136, *137i*; officers refuse to serve with, 127; tools and pay sought by, 126

Hornwork, 37; at Fort Loudoun (Tenn.), 70, 73, 75
Huron, 216–17

Introduction à la Fortification (de Fer), 19
Introduction de la Fortification avec les Cartes et plans, (de Fer?), 19, 23
Iroquois, 14–15, 17, 216, 187, 191; alliance with British, 189; attack on Fort Frontenac, 198; and contraband fur trade, 41; relations with French, 198–201; village at Fort Frontenac, 194
Israel, Stephen, 88, 91

Johnson, William (British trader, Indian agent): and Indians, 183; New England army, leader of, 15, 189
"Jolicoeur." *See* Bonin, Charles

Kalm, Peter: and Fort Frontenac resources, 193; at Fort St. Frederic, 182
Kaskaskia, 229, 231
Keowee, S.C., 52, 57
Kingston, Ont. *See* Fort Frontenac

Lahontan, Louis-Armand de Lom d'Arce, Baron: at Fort Frontenac, 193–94; Straits of Mackinac, map of, 217; on trade goods at Fort Frontenac, 203
Lake Champlain, 174, *175i*, 183, 187, 242; choke point, 4, 6, 41, 50, 244; corridor, 3, 14, 41; forts on, 15, 17, 41, 177, 242; and French settlement, 187; illegal trade on, 177; valley of, 17
Lake George, 15, 244; battle of, 15; Lake George–Lake Champlain corridor, 14–15; called Lake St. Sacrament by French, 183
Lake Ontario, 15–16, 190, 192, 245; Fort Frontenac on northern shore, 7, 191–92, 208, 245; French attack on southern shore, 198; and Mohawk River corridor, 14, 16; Oswego on southern shore, 214
Langlade, Charles Michel de (French Indian agent), 226; at Braddock's defeat, 226; and Pickawillany, Michilimackinac raid against, 225; stables at Fort Michilimackinac, 220
La Salle, Robert de (René-Robert Cavelier, Sieur de La Salle), 202; Fort Frontenac, first commandant of, 193–94, 198; and military technology, state-of-the-art, 195
Laurens, John, 58
Le Blond, Guillaume (French engineer): on angles (re-entrant), 46; on curtains and bastions, design of, 25, 27, *29i*, *30i*, 32–39; on defense in depth, 37–38, *39i*; on flanking fire, 27, 29; on flat bastions, 45; fortification, definition and design of, 40; on high ground, importance of, 22; on "honorable defense," 40; manuals by, 2; on parapet thickness, 37–38; on terrain, use of, 45; theories of, 20–22, 23–25, 29–31, 35–36, 38; on Vauban, 26, 32
Léry, Gaspard-Joseph Chaussegros de, Sr. (French engineer), 177; argument against bastioned fort, 179; plan of Fort Frontenac, 204–6
Léry, Gaspard-Joseph Chaussegros de, Jr.: advocate for Fort Frontenac, 208; plan of Fort Frontenac, 205; sent to Fort Frontenac and Fort Niagara, 206–7; and stone redoubt for Fort Michilimackinac, 218
Lewis, Andrew (capt., maj., Va. Regt.), 128, 129
Loophole, 246; set height for, 246; at Fort Dobbs, 98, 101; at Fort Frontenac, 200, 205–7; at Fort Prince George, 55, 67; at Fort St. Frederic, 177–78; at Ruthven Barracks, 98–99
Lord Dunmore's War. *See* Dunmore's War
Lotbinière, Michel Chartier de (French engineer): and Fort Michilimackinac, 218–20, 221, 225
Loudoun, Earl of. *See* Campbell, John

Louisbourg, Cape Breton Island (N.S.), 3; fortress town, 18; Franquet at, 18, 51; 1758 attack on, 51

Lunette, 38; and Fort St. Frederic, control of high ground at, *42i*, 48–49, 183

Lyttelton, Gov. William Henry (S.C.), 54, 56–57

Machicoulis, 24; planned for Fort St. Frederic, 177–78; obsolescence of, 47

MacIntosh, Lachlan (S.C. provincial), 56–57, 67

Mackinac, Straits of, 7, 216–17, 222

Magazine: at Fort des Chartres, 237; at Fort Frontenac, 198–99, 201, 203; at Fort Loudoun (Pa.), 171; at Fort Loudoun (Tenn.), 70, 74–76; at Fort Loudoun (Va.), 103, 105–6; at Fort Michilimackinac, 220–21, 227–28, 230; at Fort Prince George, 56–58, 61, 63, 68; at Fort St. Frederic, 47, 179

Maurepas, Jean-Frédéric Phélypeaux, Comte de (French minister of the marine), 177; Fort St. Frederic named for, 179

McKellar, Patrick (British capt., engineer), 242

Mercer, John F. (capt. Va. Regt.), 105, 141, 142

Metal detection, 4; at Edwards's Fort, 145; at Fort Vause, 136, 138

Method and Theory in Historical Archaeology (South), 250

Midden, 253; at Edwards's Fort, 156; at Fort Dobbs, 88; at Fort Loudoun (Tenn.), 76–77; at Fort Loudoun (Va.), 111, 118

Military units. *See* Militia; Provincials; Regulars

Militia: Canadian, 15; French, at Fort Michilimackinac, 226; New England, 15; New York, 15; North Carolina, at Fort Loudoun (Va.), 106; Pennsylvania, at Fort Loudoun (Pa.), 161; South Carolina, 70; Virginia, 102, 139. *See also* Virginia militia

Miln, Alexander (British ensign), 57–58, 67

Moat: at Fort Frontenac, 194, 211, 213–14; at Fort Loudoun (Va.), 119; at Fort Prince George, 66; at Fort St. Frederic, 47, 183, 185, 187. *See also* Ditch; Fosse

Mohawk Indians, 14–15

Mohawk River, 14, 16; and Lake Ontario corridor, 14–15; valley, 14–15

Moneypenny, Alexander (British maj.), 58, 62

Monongahela, Battle of. *See* Braddock, Edward, defeat

Monongahela River, 11

Montcalm, Louis-Joseph de (French gen.), 15; and Fort William Henry, capture of, 15; Fort St. Frederic, reported as "bad fort" by, 185; Plains of Abraham, fights British on, 50; at Quebec, 50

Montgomery, James (British col.), at Fort Prince George, 58

Montreal, P.Q., 16–17, 41; defenses of, 43; Franquet's inspection of, *46i*, 47; surrenders, 51; weaknesses, 44

Muller, John, 29

Musket, 26, 87, 246, 249; bastion positioning of, 23, 26, 34; musket-only attack, 40, 48–49; range of, 34, 48 50

—Covering fire, 34; at Fort Dobbs, 86–87; at Fort Frontenac, 206; at Fort Loudoun (Pa.), 161; at Fort Loudoun (Va.), 107, 114–15; at Fort St. Frederic, 178, 181, 187

Nails, 249, 252; at Edwards's Fort, 148, 150, 152; at Fort Dobbs, 99; at Fort Frontenac, 199; at Fort Loudoun (Pa.), 161; at Fort Loudoun (Va.), 114; at Fort Prince George, 56–57, 59, 62; at Fort Vause, 133, 136

Nottaway, at Fort Loudoun (Va.), 107

Odawa, 216–17

Ohio Country (Ohio Territory), 11, 16, 161, 206, 225–26; Valley, 10–12, 16, 231

Ohio River, 10–11, 69, 210, 231; upper called Allegheny, 11
Ojibwa, 216–17
Opposite angles: at Fort des Chartres, 230; at Fort Dobbs, 86
Osborne, Alexander (N.C. militia officer), 86
Outwork, 38: at Fort Dobbs, 5; at Fort Michilimackinac, 219

Palisade, 85, 119; at Fort des Chartres, 230; at Fort Dobbs, 87–88, 92–93, 101; at Fort Frontenac, 194; at Fort Loudoun (Pa.), 163–64, 172; at Fort Loudoun (Tenn.), 71i, 74, 76; at Fort Michilimackinac, 219, 225; at Fort Prince George, 66–67; planned for Fort St. Frederic, 177; posts, 247. *See also* Stockade
Parapet, 24, 37–38; at Fort Dobbs, 88, 91–92, 99; at Fort Frontenac, 200, 211; at Fort Loudoun (Tenn.), 70, 72–76, 247; at Fort Loudoun (Va.), 104–5; at Fort Prince George, 54–55, 66–67, 247; at Fort St. Frederic, 178, 185; thickness of, 37–38
Patten, Matthew, 159, 168
Patterns. *See* Artifact patterns
Pearlware: at Edwards's Fort, 148, 150, 152, 154
Pearsall's. *See* Fort Pearsall
Phelypeaux, Jean-Frederic. *See* Maurepas
Pig: at Fort des Chartres, 231; at Edwards's Fort, 156; at Fort Loudoun (Pa.), 171; at Fort Loudoun (Tenn.), 77; at Fort Loudoun (Va.), 117; mention of, as rations, 108
Pipes/pipe stems, 253; at Fort des Chartres, 233; at Fort Dobbs, 248; at Fort Frontenac, 199; at Fort Loudoun (Pa.), 168–69; at Fort Loudoun (Va.), 115–16; at Fort Michilimackinac, 233; at Fort Ouiatenon, 233; at Fort Prince George, 59; at Fort Vause, 133, 136
Pitt, William, 10
Pittsburgh, Pa. *See* Fort Duquesne; Fort Pitt
Plains of Abraham, Battle of, 50
Pontiac's Rebellion, 16, 109, 144, 150, 161, 227; attack on Fort Michilimackinac begins, 227; battle of Bushy Run ends, 161
Porcelain: Chinese, at Fort Loudoun (Pa.), 171; at Fort Loudoun (Va.), 113; at Fort Prince George, 80
Powder magazine. *See* Magazine
Provincials: North Carolina, 242; South Carolina, 242; Virginia, 102
—1st Virginia (also called the Virginia Regiment), 5–6; at Edwards's Fort, 141, 152; at Fort Loudoun (Va.), 106; at Fort Vause, 124, 128, 138, 244; expanded, 139; payment to, 127; Washington resigns as commander of, 108
—2nd Virginia (William Byrd commanding), 107; at Fort Loudoun (Va.), 106; Indian dress suggested for troops, 106; troop postings to southwestern Va. and western Pa., 108

Rampart, 23, 37–38, 41; at Fort des Chartres, 237; at Fort Dobbs, 88, 92; at Fort Frontenac, 194; at Fort St. Frederic, 178, 182–83; plank and masonry construction, 210
Rangers, 139; at Edwards's Fort, 141; at Fort Loudoun (Va.), 106; at Fort Vause, 124
Ravelin, 38, 48; at Fort Frontenac, 211; at Fort Loudoun (Tenn.), 71i, 73; at Fort Prince George, 55; at Fort St. Frederic, 183
Redan: at Edwards's Fort, 147, 150; at Fort Allen, 151; at Fort Vause, 247
Redoubt: and control of high ground, 183; at Fort Frontenac, 210, 211; at Fort Loudoun (Pa.), 160; at Fort St. Frederic, 42i, 47, 178
Reentering (or re-entrant) angle, 36, 45
Regulars: British, at Fort Prince George, 242; 42nd Foot at Fort Loudoun (Pa.), 162; French leave Fort Michilimackinac, 226; 60th Foot at Fort Loudoun (Pa.), 160, 169; Regiment of Bearn, 210; Regiment of Guyenne, 210–11; versus provincials, 121

Relic hunters. *See* Metal detection
Research Strategies in Historical Archaeology (South), 250
Revolutionary War, 110, 144, 150–51, 156, 247, 253; gunflints used in, 150
Richelieu River, 14, 17, 41; Chambly Rapids on, 43; forts along, 17
Rocque, Mary Ann, 2
Rogers, Robert (New England provincial maj.), 226; Fort St. Frederick, spies on, *184i*, 184–85
Rogers Island, N.Y.: semi-subterranean huts at, 154
Ruthven Barracks (Kingussie, Scotland), 98–99

La Science des ingénieurs dans la conduite des travaux de fortification et d'architecture civile (Bélidor), 19
Salient angle, 36; at Fort Frontenac, 205; at Fort Prince George, 54
Saponi, at Fort Loudoun (Va.), 107
Scarp: at Fort des Chartres, 237; at Fort Dobbs, 91–92
Sharpe, Gov. Horatio (Md.), 139; contact with engineers, 246
Shaw, Lachlan: at Fort Prince George, 55; on swivel guns at Fort Prince George, 67
Shawnee, 6
Sheep, 248; at Edwards's Fort, 142, 155; at Fort Loudoun (Pa.), 171–72; at Fort Loudoun (Va.), 108, 117
Shirley, Gov. William (Mass.), 183
Siege, 40, 49; artillery, Braddock's, 11; artillery, forts not designed to resist, 242; at Fort Frontenac, 198–99, 201, 214–15; at Fort Loudoun (Pa.), 161; at Fort Loudoun (Tenn.), 60, 70–72, 78, 102, 243; at Fort Niagara, 12, 16; at Fort Prince George, 57–58; at Fort St. Frederic, unlikelihood of, 47–48, 179, 186–87; French and Indian, Fort Oswego falls to, 16; knowledge of French essential for planning, 186; Lake Champlain, artillery siege unanticipated in, 186, 189; St. Lawrence Valley, artillery siege unanticipated in, 49, 185–86, 242; tactics, 37–38; Vauban and, 18
Smith, Charles: writes Washington about Fort Loudoun (Va.), 103–4, 106
Smith, John (Va. regt. capt.): at Fort Vause, 123
South, Stanley, 69, 250; archaeologist at Fort Dobbs, 87–88; button types identified by, 115, 154; artifact patterns named by, 77–79, 113, 115, 243, 250–53; South's artifact patterns found at Fort Loudoun (Va.), 117–18, 120
Specht, Johann Friedrich (German officer), 174
Squirrel: at Fort Loudoun (Pa.), 171
St. Ignace mission, 216
Stand of arms, 87, 99
Stanwix, John (British col., gen.), 106, 108, 115
Stephen, Adam (Va. provincial): commander of 1st Va. Regt., 108; at Fort Loudoun (Pa.), 160; during Pontiac's War, 109
Stockade, 247; at Edwards's Fort, 147; at Fort Dobbs, 85; at Fort Loudoun (Pa.), 160, 162; at Fort Prince George, 55, 66–68; at Fort Vause, 125, 133; at French fort on Lake Champlain, 177. *See also* Palisade
Stone, Garry W., 87–88, 91
Stoneware: at Fort Loudoun (Va.), Rhenish and salt glazed, 113; at Fort Loudoun (Pa.), scratch blue, 163; at Fort Vause, brown and scratch blue, 136
Straits of Mackinac, 7, 216–17, 222, 232
Sumner, Jethro (Va. provincial ensign), 128

Tea ceremony: at Fort Dobbs, 91; at Fort Loudoun (Pa.), 171; at Fort Loudoun (Va.), 120
Tellico Blockhouse (Tenn.), 72
Toise (French unit of measure): and defenses, used for laying out of, 25–28,

33–36; at Fort Frontenac, 194, 210; at Fort Michilimackinac, 219; at Fort St. Frederic, 43, 48; at Montreal, 45
Tour de Camaret, *178i*
Toys, gaming pieces: at Edwards's Fort, 154; at Fort des Chartres, 233; at Fort Michilimackinac, 233; at Fort Ouiatenon, 233; marble at Fort Loudoun (Va.), 117
Trade: fur, 7, 188, 201, 218; garrison, at Fort Michilimackinac, 222; illegal, 188–89, 204
—Fort Frontenac, 201–3, 207; cessation of at, 208; trade losses at, 205
—Trade goods, 11; at Fort Loudoun (Va.), 120; Indian expectation of, 107; knives, powder, and shot, 203; need for, 108
—Traders: Fort St. Frederic built in response to, 185–86; French, at Straits of Mackinac, 217
Treatise Containing the Elementary Part of Fortification, Regular and Irregular (Muller), 22
Turkey: at Fort Loudoun (Pa.), 171; at Fort Loudoun (Va.), 117
Tuscarora: at Fort Loudoun (Va.), 107

Vauban, Sébastien le Prestre de (French marshal and engineer): on bastions, *29i*, 47; on defense in height, 21, *23i*, 37; flanking fire at Fort Michilimackinac, influence on, 220; redoubt at Fort St. Frederic, inspiration for, 178
—Fortification: frontier, trickledown effect of theories on, 246; revolutionary of, 196; systems of, 4, 25–26, *26i*, *27i*, 32; theories of, 18–20, 38, 196
Virginia militia, 102, 139; as carpenters, 126; at Edwards's Fort, 141; at Fort Vause, 124, 244; payment to, 127; during Pontiac's War, 109; as wagon escort, 143

Waddell, Hugh (N.C. provincial officer), 85, 87; as "captain of the fort," 85
Waggener, Thomas (Va. provincial officer), 125
Wagons, 11–12, 56, 58, 141, 143, 161, 170
Warwick's. *See* Fort Warwick
Washington, George (Va. provincial col.), 1, 5, 11, 13, 232; at Fort le Boeuf, 1–3; at Fort Cumberland, 105; Fort des Chartres, kills brother of French capt. stationed at, 239; Fort Loudoun (Va.), designer of, 102, 104; Fort Loudoun (Va.) design plans, sends to William Fairfax, 104; fort plans created by, 104, *124i*, 119, 123, 125–26; Fort Vause, complains of construction delays at, 138; Pearsall's Fort, orders Va. Regt. cattle escort to, 143; and rangers, orders retreat to Edwards's Fort, 141; resigns commission, 108; and Va. Regt. troops, orders to Edwards's Fort, 143; window glass, orders for Fort Loudoun (Va.), 114
Well: at Fort Dobbs, 97; at Fort Frontenac, 194; at Fort Loudoun (Pa.), 170; at Fort Loudoun (Va.), 104–5, 111; at Fort Prince George, 68
Will's Creek, Md., 11. *See also* Fort Cumberland
Winchester, Va., 102, *109i*; alternate name for Fort Loudoun (Va.), 108. *See also* Fort Loudoun (Va.)
Wolfe, James (British gen.), 50
Woodward, Henry (Va. Regt. capt.), at Fort Vause, 128–29; at Campbell's Fort, 129

www.ingramcontent.com/pod-product-compliance
Lightning Source LLC
Chambersburg PA
CBHW020830160426
43192CB00007B/587